all-new LIGHT COOKING

Publications International, Ltd.

Favorite Brand Name Recipes at www.fbnr.com

All recipes and photographs that contain specific brand names are copyrighted by those companies and/or associations, unless otherwise specified. All photographs *except* those on pages 22, 27, 35, 144 and 344 copyright © Publications International, Ltd.

DOLE® is a registered trademark of Dole Food Company, Inc.

Carnation and Nestlé are registered trademarks of Nestlé.

Fiber One® and Gold Medal® are registered trademarks of General Mills, Inc.

Some of the products listed in this publication may be in limited distribution.

Nutritional Analysis: Linda R. Yoakam, M.S., R.D., L.D.

Pictured on the front cover *(clockwise from top left):* Citrus Asparagus *(page 308),* Stuffed French Toast with Fresh Berry Topping *(page 8),* Pumpkin-Fig Cheesecake *(page 318)* and Crowd-Pleasing Burritos *(page 228).*

Pictured on the back cover: Chicken Noodle Roll-Up *(page 186).*

ISBN-13: 978-1-4127-2474-6
ISBN-10: 1-4127-2474-0

Manufactured in China.

8 7 6 5 4 3 2 1

Nutritional Analysis: The nutritional information that appears with each recipe was submitted in part by the participating companies and associations. Every effort has been made to check the accuracy of these numbers. However, because numerous variables account for a wide range of values for certain foods, nutritive analyses in this book should be considered approximate.

Microwave Cooking: Microwave ovens vary in wattage. Use the cooking times as guidelines and check for doneness before adding more time.

Preparation/Cooking Times: Preparation times are based on the approximate amount of time required to assemble the recipe before cooking, baking, chilling or serving. These times include preparation steps such as measuring, chopping and mixing. The fact that some preparations and cooking can be done simultaneously is taken into account. Preparation of optional ingredients and serving suggestions is not included.

CONTENTS

ENJOY FOOD FOR LIFE!

Think "Good"

Eating is one of life's greatest pleasures. What better feeling is there than the one you get when you sink your teeth into a bite of dark, rich, chocolate-fudge cake or into a thick and juicy grilled-to-perfection burger? Your taste buds tingle. Your whole body feels contentment. And yet all we do is try to keep ourselves from these "bad" foods—whether we're trying to lose weight or just wanting to stay healthy. It's hard to withstand the urge for these pleasures, though. We eat the cake. We feel guilty. We eat more cake. We feel even guiltier. We need to change the way we think about food. There are no "bad" foods. All edible foods can be included in a healthy meal plan. The key is moderation.

Out with Fads

Fad diets come and go. Somehow, though, we always tend to gravitate towards what best fuels our bodies' needs—an appropriate combination of carbohydrates, protein and fat. Excluding any one of these nutrients puts us at risk for not getting all the vitamins, minerals and other food components our bodies need to stay healthy. Researchers are still not entirely sure of the long-term ill effects some of these fad diets might have on our bodies. By including all nutrients in our meal plans and eating a wide variety of foods, we're more apt to stick to our goals and improve our chances of staying nutritionally healthy.

Choose Wisely

Fat tends to be the most talked-about nutrient when it comes to weight loss. Total calories consumed, though, should be our primary focus. The only way a person can lose weight is to take in fewer calories than he or she uses. Since fat is made up of more calories than the other nutrients, decreasing the amount of fat in our diets seems to be the easiest way to quickly cut calories. Some fat is necessary for good health, but we need to be aware of the types of fats we're consuming. Saturated fats, found most often in foods of animal origin, are the most unhealthy of the fats and should be eaten in limited amounts. Other fats, such as the ones found in fish and whole grains, have been shown to have health-protective benefits. Researchers suggest we consume these types of fats on a regular basis.

Bulk Up

Gone are the days when we equated fiber solely with the wrinkly, deep-purple natural laxative, prunes. Today we're realizing all the added cancer-preventive and heart-protective benefits of a diet filled with fiber. Healthy adults should consume between 21 and 38 grams of fiber each day. Fiber comes from a plethora of plant-based foods—fruits, vegetables and whole grains. An added benefit of fiber is its ability to give a feeling of fullness. And if you feel full, chances are better you won't eat too many extra calories. Just make sure you're drinking enough water if you start adding fiber to your diet. This will keep things moving in your system and prevent them from "binding you up."

Drink Up

Water, a necessity for life, plays an instrumental role in any healthy living plan. Healthy adults should consume between eight and ten 8-ounce cups of water a day. This amount should increase if you're taking part in any heavy physical activity and during extremely hot weather. Water is the quickest fix for a hungry belly, too. It's an easy and healthy way to fill up without a bunch of extra calories. And many times when you think you're hungry, you're actually just mildly dehydrated. So instead of going straight for that gooey chocolate brownie, first fill up on a tall glass of icy cold water and rehydrate!

Hold the Salt

The American Heart Association recommends healthy adults consume no greater than 2400 milligrams of sodium per day. While many people go through life unaffected by sodium, a great many of us have to think about it on a daily basis. Low-sodium versions of well-known foods are constantly being introduced into today's marketplace. The increased use of herbs and spices is largely a result of the heightened emphasis on lower sodium intakes for healthier living.

Plan It

Nutritional analyses are included with each recipe. Use the information as a guide in helping you plan a day full of healthy eating. While the vast majority of recipes have a lower fat content and are not extremely high in calories, you'll find a few recipes with higher amounts. Once again, moderation is the key. Any food can be part of a healthy meal plan. Just fit other foods around it.

See the Professionals

Regular checkups with your doctor are important for maintaining your current weight and health. Your blood pressure, cholesterol, blood glucose, weight and height will likely all be measured. Be especially sure to visit your doctor before embarking upon any weight-loss or exercise program. Your doctor will probably want to check your physical status before you begin. This is also a great way to get baseline numbers to measure your performance in later months. Your doctor will be able to refer you to a registered dietitian, too. This person will help design a meal plan that works best for you.

Moderation Is Key

Nutrition is a very young field. Researchers are making new discoveries nearly every day. More benefits of phytochemicals, or cancer-preventive substances in foods, are being discovered regularly. Keep an open mind and be flexible to new information. Until we know everything there is to know about nutrition, your best bet is to eat a variety of foods in moderation and not exclude any particular food group. Most importantly, remember no food is "bad food." So go ahead and enjoy a luscious piece of cheesecake…just plan your other foods around it.

BREAKFAST & BRUNCH

Easy Brunch Frittata

Nonstick cooking spray
1 cup small broccoli florets
2½ cups (12 ounces) frozen hash brown potatoes with onions and peppers (O'Brien style), thawed
1½ cups cholesterol-free egg substitute, thawed
2 tablespoons reduced-fat (2%) milk
¾ teaspoon salt
¼ teaspoon black pepper
½ cup (2 ounces) shredded reduced-fat Cheddar cheese
Sour cream (optional)

1. Preheat oven to 450°F. Coat medium nonstick ovenproof skillet with cooking spray. Heat skillet over medium heat until hot. Add broccoli; cook and stir 2 minutes. Add potatoes; cook and stir 5 minutes.

2. Beat together egg substitute, milk, salt and pepper in small bowl; pour over potato mixture. Cook 5 minutes or until edges are set (center will still be wet).

3. Transfer skillet to oven; bake 6 minutes or until center is set. Remove from oven. Sprinkle with cheese; let stand 2 to 3 minutes or until cheese is melted.

4. Cut into 6 wedges; serve with sour cream, if desired.

Makes 6 servings

Nutrients per Serving: 1 Frittata wedge (⅙ of total recipe) without sour cream

Calories: 102, Calories from Fat: 20%, Total Fat: 2g, Saturated Fat: 1g, Cholesterol: 7mg, Sodium: 627mg, Carbohydrate: 11g, Dietary Fiber: 1g, Protein: 9g

Dietary Exchanges: ½ Starch, 1 Lean Meat

Low-Cholesterol Omelet

3 thick style crispbreads, crushed
¼ cup skim milk
3 egg whites, slightly beaten
½ teaspoon dried basil leaves
½ cup snipped chives or green onions
½ cup (4 ounces) diced poached, skinless chicken breast
½ cup shredded JARLSBERG LITE™ Cheese

Combine crispbread crumbs, milk and egg whites; allow to stand 5 to 10 minutes or until softened. Stir in basil and chives.

Heat nonstick pan; pour in egg white mixture and cook over medium-low heat until omelet begins to set. Arrange chicken on top and sprinkle with cheese. Cover and cook over very low heat until cheese melts. With spatula, lift edge and fold omelet in half. Cut omelet in half crosswise.

Serving Suggestion: Serve with freshly ground pepper, sliced garden tomatoes and/or leftover cold ratatouille (eggplant salad).

Makes 2 servings

Nutrients per Serving: ½ Omelet (½ of total recipe)

Calories: 273, Calories from Fat: 27%, Total Fat: 8g, Saturated Fat: 5g, Cholesterol: 64mg, Sodium: 434mg, Carbohydrate: 17g, Dietary Fiber: 3g, Protein: 32g

Dietary Exchanges: 1 Starch, 4 Lean Meat

Stuffed French Toast with Fresh Berry Topping

2 cups mixed fresh berries (strawberries, raspberries, blueberries and/or blackberries)
2 tablespoons granulated sugar
⅔ cup lowfat ricotta cheese
¼ cup strawberry preserves
3 large eggs
⅔ cup NESTLÉ® CARNATION® Evaporated Fat Free Milk
2 tablespoons packed brown sugar
2 teaspoons vanilla extract
12 slices (about ¾-inch-thick) French bread
1 tablespoon vegetable oil, butter or margarine
Powdered sugar (optional)
Maple syrup, heated (optional)

COMBINE berries and granulated sugar in small bowl. Combine ricotta cheese and strawberry preserves in another small bowl; mix well. Combine eggs, evaporated milk, brown sugar and vanilla extract in pie plate or shallow bowl; mix well.

SPREAD ricotta-preserve mixture evenly over *6 slices* of bread. Top with *remaining* slices of bread to form sandwiches.

HEAT small amount of vegetable oil in large, nonstick skillet or griddle over medium heat. Dip sandwiches in egg mixture, coating both sides. Cook on each side for about 2 minutes or until golden brown.

SPRINKLE with powdered sugar, if desired. Serve with berries and maple syrup, if desired. *Makes 6 servings*

Nutrients per Serving: 1 sandwich (without powdered sugar and syrup)

Calories: 339, Calories from Fat: 14%, Total Fat: 7g, Saturated Fat: 2g, Cholesterol: 112mg, Sodium: 420mg, Carbohydrate: 54g, Dietary Fiber: 3g, Protein: 14g

Dietary Exchanges: 3 Starch, 1 Fruit, 1 Lean Meat, ½ Fat

Raisin-Streusel Coffee Cake

1½ cups all-purpose flour
2 teaspoons baking powder
¼ teaspoon baking soda
¼ teaspoon salt
¾ cup granulated sugar
2 tablespoons margarine, softened
¾ cup nonfat sour cream
1 egg
1 teaspoon vanilla extract
½ cup MOTT'S® Chunky Apple Sauce
⅓ cup firmly packed light brown sugar
¼ cup raisins
2 tablespoons crunchy nut-like cereal nuggets

1. Preheat oven to 350°F. Spray 9-inch round cake pan with nonstick cooking spray.

2. In small bowl, combine flour, baking powder, baking soda and salt.

3. In large bowl, beat granulated sugar and margarine with electric mixer at medium speed until blended. Whisk in sour cream, egg and vanilla. Gently mix in apple sauce.

4. Add flour mixture to apple sauce mixture; stir until well blended. Pour batter into prepared pan.

5. In small bowl, combine brown sugar, raisins and cereal. Sprinkle over batter.

6. Bake 50 minutes or until toothpick inserted into center comes out clean. Cool 15 minutes on wire rack. Serve warm or cool completely. Cut into 14 wedges. *Makes 14 servings*

Nutrients per Serving: 1 wedge Coffee Cake

Calories: 160, Calories from Fat: 12%, Total Fat: 2g, Saturated Fat: <1g, Cholesterol: 15mg, Sodium: 175mg, Carbohydrate: 32g, Dietary Fiber: 1g, Protein: 3g

Dietary Exchanges: 1 Starch, 1 Fruit, ½ Fat

T I P Choose a "lite" version of your favorite syrup, and you'll likely be cutting the number of calories in half!

Potato Pancakes with Apple-Cherry Chutney

Apple-Cherry Chutney (recipe follows)
1 pound baking potatoes (about 2 medium)
½ small onion
3 egg whites
2 tablespoons all-purpose flour
½ teaspoon salt
¼ teaspoon black pepper
4 teaspoons vegetable oil, divided

1. Prepare Apple-Cherry Chutney; set aside.

2. Wash and scrub potatoes; cut into chunks. Combine potatoes, onion, egg whites, flour, salt and pepper in food processor or blender; process until almost smooth (mixture will appear grainy).

3. Heat large nonstick skillet 1 minute over medium heat. Add 1 teaspoon oil. Spoon ⅓ cup batter per pancake into skillet. Cook 3 pancakes at a time, 3 minutes per side or until golden brown. Repeat with remaining batter, adding 1 teaspoon oil with each batch. Serve with Apple-Cherry Chutney. Garnish as desired.

Makes 6 servings (2 pancakes each)

Apple-Cherry Chutney

1 cup chunky applesauce
½ cup canned tart cherries, drained
2 tablespoons brown sugar
1 teaspoon lemon juice
½ teaspoon ground cinnamon
⅛ teaspoon ground nutmeg

Combine all ingredients in small saucepan; bring to a boil. Reduce heat; simmer 5 minutes. Serve warm.

Makes 1½ cups

Nutrients per Serving: 2 Pancakes with ¼ cup Chutney (without garnish)

Calories: 164, Calories from Fat: 17%, Total Fat: 3g, Saturated Fat: <1g, Cholesterol: <1mg, Sodium: 214mg, Carbohydrate: 31g, Dietary Fiber: 1g, Protein: 4g

Dietary Exchanges: 1½ Starch, ½ Fruit, ½ Fat

Power Breakfast

3 cups cooked brown rice
2 cups skim milk
¼ cup brown sugar
½ teaspoon cinnamon
½ cup whole milk
⅓ cup raisins
½ teaspoon vanilla extract
Sliced fresh fruit
¾ cup low-fat granola cereal (optional)
1 (6-ounce) container low-fat vanilla yogurt (optional)

Combine rice, skim milk, brown sugar and cinnamon in 2½- to 3-quart saucepan; heat over medium heat, stirring frequently, 10 to 12 minutes or until mixture thickens. Stir in whole milk, raisins and vanilla. Cook 5 minutes, stirring until mixture thickens slightly. Place rice mixture into serving bowls. Sprinkle with fruit. Top each serving with 2 tablespoons granola and yogurt, if desired.

Makes 6 servings

Favorite recipe from *USA Rice Federation*

Nutrients per Serving: 1 bowl Power Breakfast (⅙ of total recipe) without granola and yogurt

Calories: 213, Calories from Fat: 7%, Total Fat: 2g, Saturated Fat: 1g, Cholesterol: 4mg, Sodium: 62mg, Carbohydrate: 44g, Dietary Fiber: 2g, Protein: 6g

Dietary Exchanges: 3 Starch

Fruit Smoothies

1 cup orange juice
1 cup fat-free plain yogurt
1 peeled and frozen banana
1 cup frozen strawberries or raspberries
¼ cup EQUAL® SPOONFUL*

May substitute 6 packets Equal® sweetener.

• Peel and cut banana into large chunks. Place in plastic freezer bag; seal and freeze at least 5 to 6 hours or overnight.

• Place all ingredients in blender or food processor. Blend until smooth.

Makes 2 servings

Nutrients per Serving: 1 Smoothie (½ of total recipe)

Calories: 215, Calories from Fat: 5%, Total Fat: 1g, Saturated Fat: <1g, Cholesterol: 2mg, Sodium: 99mg, Carbohydrate: 45g, Dietary Fiber: 3g, Protein: 9g

Dietary Exchanges: 2 Fruit, 1 Milk

Potato Pancakes with Apple-Cherry Chutney 11

Banana-Walnut Bread

5 tablespoons margarine, softened
½ cup granulated sugar
½ cup packed light brown sugar
1 whole egg
2 egg whites
1 teaspoon vanilla
1½ cups mashed, very ripe bananas
1¾ cups all-purpose flour
1 teaspoon baking soda
½ teaspoon salt
¼ teaspoon baking powder
½ cup apple or orange juice
⅓ cup (2 ounces) coarsely chopped black or
    English walnuts

1. Preheat oven to 350°F. Spray bottom only of 9×5×3-inch loaf pan.

2. Beat margarine in large bowl with electric mixer at medium speed until fluffy. Beat in granulated and brown sugars. Beat in whole egg, egg whites and vanilla. Mix in bananas, beating at high speed 30 seconds.

3. Combine flour, baking soda, salt and baking powder in medium bowl. Add to margarine mixture alternately with apple juice, ending with flour mixture. Stir in walnuts.

4. Pour batter evenly into prepared loaf pan. Bake about 1 hour 15 minutes or until browned and toothpick inserted near center comes out clean.

5. Cool bread in pan on wire rack 10 minutes. Remove bread from pan; cool completely on wire rack. Garnish as desired. *Makes 18 servings*

Note: A crack will often form across the top of a quick bread loaf during baking; this is perfectly normal.

Prep Time: 15 minutes
Bake Time: 1 hour 15 minutes

Nutrients per Serving: 1 Bread slice (¹⁄₁₈ of total recipe) without garnish

Calories: 152, Calories from Fat: 29%, Total Fat: 5g, Saturated Fat: 1g, Cholesterol: 12mg, Sodium: 191mg, Carbohydrate: 25g, Dietary Fiber: 1g, Protein: 2g
Dietary Exchanges: 1½ Starch, 1 Fat

Baked Oatmeal

2¼ cups Quick QUAKER® Oats or 2¾ cups Old
    Fashioned QUAKER® Oats, uncooked
¾ cup firmly packed brown sugar
¾ cup raisins, dried cranberries or cherries
1 teaspoon ground cinnamon
½ teaspoon salt (optional)
3⅓ cups fat-free milk
4 egg whites, slightly beaten, or ½ cup egg
    substitute
1 tablespoon vegetable oil
1 tablespoon vanilla
    Optional toppings: nonfat yogurt and fruit

Heat oven to 350°F. Spray an 8-inch square glass baking dish with no-stick cooking spray. In large bowl, combine oats, brown sugar, raisins, cinnamon and salt, if desired; mix well. In medium bowl, combine milk, egg whites, oil and vanilla; mix well. Add to dry ingredients; mix until well blended. Pour into prepared baking dish. Bake, uncovered, 55 to 60 minutes or until center is set and firm to the touch. Cool slightly before serving. Top with yogurt and fruit, if desired. Store, covered, in refrigerator.
Makes 8 servings

Nutrients per Serving: ⅛ of total recipe (using 2¼ cups quick oats) without added salt and fruit and yogurt toppings

Calories: 272, Calories from Fat: 12%, Total Fat: 4g, Saturated Fat: 1g, Cholesterol: 2mg, Sodium: 91mg, Carbohydrate: 53g, Dietary Fiber: 3g, Protein: 9g
Dietary Exchanges: 2 Starch, 1½ Fruit, ½ Fat

Orange Banana Nog

1 cup orange juice
½ cup fat-free milk
½ cup no-cholesterol real egg product
1 small banana, sliced
2 to 3 tablespoons EQUAL® SPOONFUL*
    Ground nutmeg

*May substitute 3 to 4½ packets Equal® sweetener.

● Blend all ingredients except nutmeg in blender or food processor until smooth; pour into 4 glasses. Sprinkle lightly with nutmeg. *Makes 4 servings*

Nutrients per Serving: 1 Banana Nog (¼ of total recipe)

Calories: 83, Calories from Fat: 3%, Total Fat: <1g, Saturated Fat: <1g, Cholesterol: 1g, Sodium: 67mg, Carbohydrate: 16g, Dietary Fiber: 1g, Protein: 5g
Dietary Exchanges: 1 Fruit, ½ Lean Meat

Blueberry Kuchen

1½ cups all-purpose flour
2 teaspoons baking powder
½ cup EGG BEATERS® Healthy Real Egg
   Product
⅓ cup skim milk
1 teaspoon vanilla extract
½ cup granulated sugar
¼ cup FLEISCHMANN'S® Original Margarine,
   softened
1 (21-ounce) can blueberry pie filling and
   topping
   Streusel Topping (recipe follows)
   Powdered Sugar Glaze, optional (recipe
   follows)

In small bowl, combine flour and baking powder; set aside. In another small bowl, combine Egg Beaters®, milk and vanilla; set aside.

In medium bowl, with electric mixer at medium speed, beat granulated sugar and margarine until creamy. Alternately add flour mixture and egg mixture, blending well after each addition. Spread batter into greased 9-inch square baking pan.

Bake at 350°F for 20 minutes. Spoon blueberry pie filling over batter; sprinkle Streusel Topping over filling, if desired. Bake for 10 to 15 minutes more or until toothpick inserted into center comes out clean. Cool in pan on wire rack. Drizzle with Powdered Sugar Glaze, if desired. Cut into 12 (3×2-inch) pieces. *Makes 12 servings*

Streusel Topping: In small bowl, combine 3 tablespoons all-purpose flour, 3 tablespoons powdered sugar and ¼ teaspoon ground cinnamon. Cut in 1 tablespoon Fleischmann's® Original Margarine until crumbly.

Powdered Sugar Glaze: In small bowl, combine 1 cup powdered sugar and 5 to 6 teaspoons water until smooth.

Prep Time: 20 minutes
Cook Time: 35 minutes

Nutrients per Serving: 1 piece Kuchen (1/12 of total recipe) with Topping and without Glaze

Calories: 211, Calories from Fat: 21%, Total Fat: 5g, Saturated Fat: 1g, Cholesterol: <1mg, Sodium: 175mg, Carbohydrate: 38g, Dietary Fiber: 1g, Protein: 3g
Dietary Exchanges: 1½ Starch, 1 Fruit, 1 Fat

Blueberry Kuchen

Blueberry Muffins with a Twist of Lemon

1 cup all-purpose flour
1 cup uncooked old-fashioned oats
¼ cup packed brown sugar
1 teaspoon baking powder
1 teaspoon baking soda
¾ teaspoon ground cinnamon, divided
¼ teaspoon salt
8 ounces lemon-flavored low-fat yogurt
¼ cup cholesterol-free egg substitute *or* 2 egg
    whites
1 tablespoon vegetable oil
1 teaspoon grated lemon peel
1 teaspoon vanilla
1 cup fresh or frozen blueberries
1 tablespoon granulated sugar
1 tablespoon sliced almonds (optional)

1. Preheat oven to 400°F. Spray 12 (2½-inch) muffin cups with nonstick cooking spray.

2. Combine flour, oats, brown sugar, baking powder, baking soda, ½ teaspoon cinnamon and salt in large bowl.

3. Combine yogurt, egg substitute, oil, lemon peel and vanilla in small bowl; stir into flour mixture just until blended. Gently stir in blueberries. Spoon mixture into prepared muffin cups.

4. Mix granulated sugar, remaining ¼ teaspoon cinnamon and almonds, if desired, in small bowl. Sprinkle over muffin mixture.

5. Bake 18 to 20 minutes or until lightly browned and wooden pick inserted into centers comes out clean. Cool slightly before serving. *Makes 12 servings*

Nutrients per Serving: 1 Muffin (without almonds)

Calories: 125, Calories from Fat: 14%, Total Fat: 2g, Saturated Fat: 0g, Cholesterol: 1mg, Sodium: 198mg, Carbohydrate: 24g, Dietary Fiber: 1g, Protein: 3g
Dietary Exchanges: 1½ Starch, ½ Fat

Roasted Pepper and Sourdough Brunch Casserole

3 cups sourdough bread cubes
1 jar (12 ounces) roasted red peppers, drained
1 cup (4 ounces) shredded reduced-fat sharp Cheddar cheese
1 cup (4 ounces) shredded reduced-fat Monterey Jack cheese
1 cup fat-free cottage cheese
12 ounces cholesterol-free egg substitute
1 cup fat-free (skim) milk
¼ cup chopped fresh cilantro
¼ teaspoon black pepper

1. Spray 11×9-inch baking pan with nonstick cooking spray. Place bread cubes in pan. Arrange roasted peppers evenly over bread cubes. Sprinkle Cheddar and Monterey Jack cheeses over peppers.

2. Place cottage cheese in food processor or blender; process until smooth. Add egg substitute; process 10 seconds. Combine cottage cheese mixture and milk in small bowl; pour over ingredients in baking pan. Sprinkle with cilantro and black pepper. Cover with plastic wrap; refrigerate 4 to 12 hours.

3. Preheat oven to 375°F. Bake, uncovered, 40 minutes or until hot and bubbly and golden brown on top.

Makes 8 servings

Nutrients per Serving: ⅛ of total recipe

Calories: 179, Calories from Fat: 28%, Total Fat: 6g, Saturated Fat: 3g, Cholesterol: 22mg, Sodium: 704mg, Carbohydrate: 13g, Dietary Fiber: 1g, Protein: 19g
Dietary Exchanges: 1 Starch, 2 Lean Meat

T I P Easily cut fat and cholesterol by using egg substitutes in place of regular eggs in recipes. Substitute ¼ cup egg product for each whole egg.

Easy Danish Pastry

2 (1-pound) loaves frozen sweet dough*
9 tablespoons sugar, divided
4 tablespoons all-purpose flour, divided
¼ teaspoon salt
1 cup fat-free (skim) milk
1 egg, separated
1 teaspoon vanilla
2 tablespoons butter, softened, divided
½ teaspoon almond extract
2 tablespoons slivered almonds

Plain dough may be used.

Thaw dough loaves and shape into 2 balls. Let rise in warm place until warm and bubbly. While dough is rising, prepare pudding, almond filling, and topping.

For pudding, blend 4 tablespoons sugar, 2 tablespoons flour and salt in medium saucepan. Stir in milk. Cook over medium heat until boiling. Stir part of mixture into lightly beaten egg yolk and pour back into saucepan. Cook 1 minute. Add vanilla and cool.

For almond filling, mix 1 tablespoon butter with 3 tablespoons sugar and almond extract.

For topping, mix together remaining 1 tablespoon butter, 2 tablespoons flour, 2 tablespoons sugar and slivered almonds.

Roll each loaf into 15×8-inch rectangle. Spread ½ of filling mixture down center of each rectangle. Spread ½ of pudding down center of rectangle, leaving 2½ inches on sides without pudding. Make 10 to 12 cuts down long sides of each rectangle about 1½ to 2 inches into dough, making same number of cuts on each side. Fold one end in; lace bread, taking strip from each side and overlapping over previous strip.

Place on baking sheet coated with nonstick cooking spray. Beat egg white and brush over each loaf. Top each with ½ of topping. Let rise 10 minutes. Bake at 375°F for 15 to 20 minutes. Cool before cutting. *Makes 24 servings*

Favorite recipe from *North Dakota Wheat Commission*

Nutrients per Serving: 1 Pastry (¹⁄₁₂ of 1 loaf)

Calories: 361, Calories from Fat: 16%, Total Fat: 6g, Saturated Fat: 1g, Cholesterol: 12mg, Sodium: 680mg, Carbohydrate: 61g, Dietary Fiber: 5g, Protein: 12g
Dietary Exchanges: 4 Starch, 1½ Fat

Triple Berry Breakfast Parfait

2 cups vanilla sugar-free nonfat yogurt
¼ teaspoon ground cinnamon
1 cup sliced strawberries
½ cup blueberries
½ cup raspberries
1 cup low-fat granola without raisins

1. Combine yogurt and cinnamon in small bowl. Combine strawberries, blueberries and raspberries in medium bowl.

2. For each parfait, layer ¼ cup fruit mixture, 2 tablespoons granola and ¼ cup yogurt mixture in parfait glass. Repeat layers. Garnish with mint leaves, if desired.

Makes 4 servings

Nutrients per Serving: ½ Parfait (without garnish)

Calories: 236, Calories from Fat: 9%, Total Fat: 2g, Saturated Fat: <1g, Cholesterol: 0mg, Sodium: 101mg, Carbohydrate: 49g, Dietary Fiber: 2g, Protein: 9g

Dietary Exchanges: 2 Starch, 1 Fruit, ½ Milk

Triple Berry Breakfast Parfaits

Vegetable Omelet

Ratatouille (recipe follows)
Nonstick cooking spray
5 whole eggs
6 egg whites *or* ¾ cup cholesterol-free egg substitute
¼ cup fat-free (skim) milk
½ teaspoon salt
⅛ teaspoon black pepper
4 to 6 slices Italian bread
2 cloves garlic, halved

1. Prepare Ratatouille; keep warm. Spray 12-inch skillet with cooking spray; heat over medium heat. Beat whole eggs, egg whites, milk, salt and pepper in large bowl until foamy. Pour egg mixture into skillet; cook over medium-high heat 2 to 3 minutes or until bottom of omelet is set. Reduce heat to medium-low. Cover; cook 8 minutes or until top of omelet is set. Remove from heat.

2. Spoon half the Ratatouille down center of omelet. Carefully fold omelet in half; slide onto serving plate. Spoon remaining Ratatouille over omelet. Toast bread slices; rub both sides of warm toast with cut garlic cloves. Serve omelet with toast and fresh fruit, if desired.

Makes 4 to 6 servings

Ratatouille

1 cup chopped onion
½ cup chopped green bell pepper
2 cloves garlic, minced
4 cups cubed unpeeled eggplant
1 medium yellow summer squash, sliced
1 cup chopped fresh tomatoes
¼ cup finely chopped fresh basil *or* 1 tablespoon plus 1 teaspoon dried basil leaves
1 tablespoon finely chopped fresh oregano *or* 1 teaspoon dried oregano leaves
2 teaspoons finely chopped fresh thyme *or* ½ teaspoon dried thyme leaves

Spray large skillet with nonstick cooking spray; heat over medium heat. Add onion, bell pepper and garlic; cook and stir 5 minutes or until tender. Add eggplant, summer squash, tomatoes, and herbs. Cover; cook over medium heat 8 to 10 minutes or until vegetables are tender. Uncover; cook 2 to 3 minutes or until all liquid is absorbed.

Makes about 4 cups

Nutrients per Serving: ¼ of Omelet with about 1 cup Ratatouille and 1 toast slice (without fruit)

Calories: 274, Calories from Fat: 26%, Total Fat: 8g, Saturated Fat: 2g, Cholesterol: 266mg, Sodium: 620mg, Carbohydrate: 32g, Dietary Fiber: 2g, Protein: 19g

Dietary Exchanges: 1½ Starch, 1½ Vegetable, 2 Lean Meat, ½ Fat

Zucchini-Tomato Frittata

Olive oil-flavored nonstick cooking spray
1 cup sliced zucchini
1 cup broccoli florets
1 cup diced red or yellow bell pepper
3 whole eggs, lightly beaten*
5 egg whites, lightly beaten*
½ cup 1% low-fat cottage cheese
½ cup rehydrated sun-dried tomatoes (1 ounce dry), coarsely chopped
¼ cup chopped green onions with tops
¼ cup chopped fresh basil
⅛ teaspoon ground red pepper
2 tablespoons Parmesan cheese
Paprika (optional)

*Or, substitute cholesterol-free egg substitute to equal 6 large eggs.

1. Preheat broiler. Spray 10-inch nonstick ovenproof skillet with cooking spray. Place zucchini, broccoli and bell pepper in skillet; cook and stir over high heat 3 to 4 minutes or until crisp-tender.

2. Combine whole eggs, egg whites, cottage cheese, tomatoes, onions, basil and ground red pepper in medium bowl; mix well. Pour egg mixture over vegetables in skillet. Cook uncovered, gently lifting sides of frittata so uncooked egg flows underneath. Cook 7 to 8 minutes or until frittata is almost firm and golden brown on bottom. Remove from heat. Sprinkle with Parmesan.

3. Broil about 5 inches from heat 3 to 5 minutes or until golden brown on surface. Sprinkle with paprika, if desired. Cut into 4 wedges. Serve immediately.

Makes 4 servings

Nutrients per Serving: 1 Frittata wedge (¼ of total recipe)

Calories: 160, Calories from Fat: 29%, Total Fat: 5g, Saturated Fat: 2g, Cholesterol: 163mg, Sodium: 305mg, Carbohydrate: 13g, Dietary Fiber: 3g, Protein: 16g
Dietary Exchanges: 2½ Vegetable, 1½ Lean Meat

French Toast Sticks

1 cup EGG BEATERS® Healthy Real Egg Product
⅓ cup skim milk
1 teaspoon ground cinnamon
1 teaspoon vanilla extract
2 tablespoons FLEISCHMANN'S® Original Margarine, divided
16 (4×1×1-inch) sticks day-old white bread
Powdered sugar, optional
Maple-flavored syrup, optional

In shallow bowl, combine Egg Beaters®, milk, cinnamon and vanilla.

In large nonstick griddle or skillet, over medium-high heat, melt 2 teaspoons margarine. Dip bread sticks in egg mixture to coat; transfer to griddle. Cook sticks on each side until golden, adding remaining margarine as needed. Dust lightly with powdered sugar and serve with syrup, if desired.

Makes 4 servings

Prep Time: 15 minutes
Cook Time: 18 minutes

Nutrients per Serving: 4 French Toast Sticks (without powdered sugar and syrup)

Calories: 213, Calories from Fat: 32%, Total Fat: 7g, Saturated Fat: 1g, Cholesterol: 1mg, Sodium: 431mg, Carbohydrate: 25g, Dietary Fiber: 1g, Protein: 10g
Dietary Exchanges: 1½ Starch, 1 Lean Meat, 1 Fat

Banana Yogurt Shake

1½ cups 2% low-fat milk
2 ripe bananas, peeled
1 cup low-fat plain yogurt
¼ cup honey
1 teaspoon vanilla
½ teaspoon ground cinnamon
Dash ground nutmeg
5 ice cubes

Combine all ingredients except ice cubes in blender or food processor; process until thick and creamy. With motor running, add ice cubes; process until smooth. Pour into tall glasses to serve.

Makes 4 cups

Favorite recipe from *National Honey Board*

Nutrients per Serving: 1 cup Shake

Calories: 206, Calories from Fat: 12%, Total Fat: 3g, Saturated Fat: 2 g, Cholesterol: 11mg, Sodium: 90mg, Carbohydrate: 40g, Dietary Fiber: 2g, Protein: 7g
Dietary Exchanges: 2 Fruit, 1 Milk, ½ Fat

Zucchini-Tomato Frittata ～ 21

Blueberry-Bran Pancakes

1 cup FIBER ONE® cereal
2 egg whites *or* 1 egg, beaten slightly
1¼ cups buttermilk or milk
2 tablespoons vegetable oil
1 cup GOLD MEDAL® all-purpose flour
1 tablespoon sugar
1 teaspoon baking powder
½ teaspoon baking soda
½ teaspoon salt
½ cup fresh or frozen (thawed and well drained) blueberries

1. Spray unheated skillet or griddle with cooking spray, then heat over medium-high heat until hot (or electric griddle to 375°F).

2. Crush cereal.* Stir together egg whites, buttermilk, oil and cereal in medium bowl; let stand 7 minutes. Beat in flour, sugar, baking powder, baking soda and salt with wire whisk or fork until blended. Gently stir in blueberries.

3. Pour ¼ cup batter onto hot griddle for each pancake. (If batter is too thick, stir in additional milk, 1 tablespoon at a time, until desired consistency.)

4. Cook pancakes until puffed and full of bubbles, but before bubbles break. Turn and cook other sides until golden brown.   *Makes 10 (5-inch) pancakes*

*Place cereal in plastic bag or between sheets of waxed paper and crush with rolling pin. Or, crush in blender or food processor.

Prep Time: 15 minutes
Cook Time: 4 minutes per batch

Nutrients per Serving: 2 Pancakes (⅕ of total recipe) without butter and syrup

Calories: 212, Calories from Fat: 26%, Total Fat: 6g, Saturated Fat: 2g, Cholesterol: 2mg, Sodium: 596mg, Carbohydrate: 36g, Dietary Fiber: 6g, Protein: 6g

Dietary Exchanges: 2 Starch, 2 Fat

Blueberry-Bran Pancakes

Apricot Oatmeal Muffins

- 1 cup QUAKER® Oats (quick or old fashioned, uncooked)
- 1 cup low-fat buttermilk
- ¼ cup egg substitute *or* 2 egg whites
- 2 tablespoons margarine, melted
- 1 cup all-purpose flour
- ⅓ cup finely chopped dried apricots
- ¼ cup chopped nuts (optional)
- 3 tablespoons granulated sugar *or*
    - 1¾ teaspoons EQUAL® MEASURE™ (7 packets) *or* 2 tablespoons fructose
- 1 teaspoon baking powder
- ½ teaspoon baking soda
- ¼ teaspoon salt (optional)

Heat oven to 400°F. Lightly spray 12 medium muffin cups with vegetable oil cooking spray. Combine oats and buttermilk; let stand 10 minutes. Add egg substitute and margarine; mix well. In large bowl, combine remaining ingredients; mix well. Add wet ingredients to dry ingredients; mix just until moistened. Fill muffin cups almost full. Bake 20 to 25 minutes or until golden brown. Let muffins stand a few minutes; remove from pan.

Makes 1 dozen muffins

Nutrients per Serving: 1 Muffin made with granulated sugar (without nuts)

Calories: 110, Calories from Fat: 25%, Total Fat: 3g, Saturated Fat: 1g, Cholesterol: 0mg, Sodium: 125mg, Carbohydrate: 19g, Dietary Fiber: 1g, Protein: 4g

Dietary Exchanges: 1 Starch, ½ Fat

TIP Toast nuts for extra flavor. Spread them evenly in a small baking pan and bake them in a 400°F oven 5 to 7 minutes or until they are light golden brown. Or, spread the nuts on a plate and microwave them on HIGH 1 minute, then stir. Continue microwaving, checking every 30 seconds, until nuts are crunchy.

Cinnamon Fruit Crunch

- 1 cup low-fat granola cereal
- ¼ cup toasted sliced almonds
- 1 tablespoon margarine
- 2 tablespoons plus 1 teaspoon packed brown sugar, divided
- 2¼ teaspoons ground cinnamon, divided
- ½ cup vanilla low-fat yogurt
- ⅛ teaspoon ground nutmeg
- 2 cans (16 ounces each) mixed fruit chunks in juice, drained

Combine granola and almonds in small bowl. Melt margarine in small saucepan. Blend in 2 tablespoons brown sugar and 2 teaspoons cinnamon; simmer until sugar dissolves, about 2 minutes. Toss with granola and almonds; cool. Combine yogurt, 1 teaspoon brown sugar, ¼ teaspoon cinnamon and nutmeg in small bowl. To serve, spoon approximately ½ cup chunky mixed fruit onto each serving plate. Evenly top with yogurt mixture and sprinkle with granola mixture.

Makes 6 servings

Nutrients per Serving: ⅙ of total recipe

Calories: 259, Calories from Fat: 21%, Total Fat: 6g, Saturated Fat: 1g, Cholesterol: 1mg, Sodium: 109mg, Carbohydrate: 48g, Dietary Fiber: 6g, Protein: 4g

Dietary Exchanges: 2 Starch, 1 Fruit, 1 Fat

Cinnamon Fruit Crunch

Cornmeal Scones

½ cup currants
1 cup warm water
1⅓ cups all-purpose flour
⅔ cup cornmeal
½ cup plus 1 teaspoon sugar, divided
1½ teaspoons baking powder
½ teaspoon baking soda
¼ teaspoon salt
¼ cup margarine, cut into 4 pieces
¼ cup plain nonfat yogurt
3 tablespoons fat-free (skim) milk
1 egg, lightly beaten
1 egg white, lightly beaten

1. Preheat oven to 375°F. Lightly spray baking sheet with nonstick cooking spray.

2. Place currants in small mixing bowl. Add water; let stand 10 minutes. Drain and discard water.

3. Combine flour, cornmeal, ½ cup sugar, baking powder, baking soda and salt in large mixing bowl. Cut margarine into flour mixture with pastry blender or 2 knives until mixture resembles coarse crumbs. Stir in currants.

4. Combine yogurt, milk and whole egg in small bowl. Add to flour mixture, stirring just until dry ingredients are moistened.

5. Turn dough onto lightly floured surface; knead 5 or 6 times. Shape dough into 8-inch round. Place on baking sheet. Brush with egg white; sprinkle with remaining 1 teaspoon sugar. Cut into 8 wedges. Bake 20 minutes or until lightly browned. Place on wire rack to cool. Cut each wedge in half to make 16 servings.

Makes 16 servings

Nutrients per Serving: 1 Scone (1/16 of total recipe)

Calories: 132, Calories from Fat: 23%, Total Fat: 3g, Saturated Fat: 1g, Cholesterol: 13mg, Sodium: 170mg, Carbohydrate: 22g, Dietary Fiber: 1g, Protein: 3g
Dietary Exchanges: 1½ Starch, ½ Fat

Spinach Cheese Roulade

4 teaspoons FLEISCHMANN'S® Original Margarine, divided
2 tablespoons all-purpose flour
1 cup skim milk
2 cups EGG BEATERS® Healthy Real Egg Product
1 medium onion, chopped
1 (10-ounce) package fresh spinach, coarsely chopped
½ cup low fat cottage cheese (1% milkfat)
1 (8-ounce) can no-salt-added tomato sauce
½ teaspoon dried basil leaves
½ teaspoon garlic powder

In small saucepan, over medium heat, melt 3 teaspoons margarine; blend in flour. Cook, stirring until smooth and bubbly; remove from heat. Gradually blend in milk; return to heat. Heat to a boil, stirring constantly until thickened; cool slightly. Stir in Egg Beaters®. Spread mixture in bottom of 15½×10½×1-inch baking pan that has been greased, lined with foil and greased again. Bake at 350°F for 20 minutes or until set.

In medium skillet, sauté onion in remaining margarine until tender. Add spinach and cook until wilted, about 3 minutes; stir in cottage cheese. Keep warm.

Invert egg mixture onto large piece of foil. Spread with spinach mixture; roll up from short end. In small saucepan, combine tomato sauce, basil and garlic; heat until warm. To serve, slice roll into 8 pieces; top with warm sauce.

Makes 8 servings

Prep Time: 30 minutes
Cook Time: 25 minutes

Nutrients per Serving: 1/8 of total recipe

Calories: 92, Calories from Fat: 22%, Total Fat: 2g, Saturated Fat: 1g, Cholesterol: 1mg, Sodium: 233mg, Carbohydrate: 7g, Dietary Fiber: 3g, Protein: 10g
Dietary Exchanges: 1½ Vegetable, 1 Lean Meat

Brunch Rice

1 teaspoon margarine
¾ cup shredded carrots
¾ cup diced green bell pepper
¾ cup (about 3 ounces) sliced fresh mushrooms
6 egg whites, beaten
2 eggs, beaten
½ cup skim milk
½ teaspoon salt
¼ teaspoon ground black pepper
3 cups cooked brown rice
½ cup (2 ounces) shredded Cheddar cheese
6 corn tortillas, warmed (optional)

Heat margarine in large skillet over medium-high heat until hot. Add carrots, bell pepper and mushrooms; cook and stir 2 minutes. Combine egg whites, eggs, milk, salt and black pepper in small bowl. Reduce heat to medium and pour egg mixture over vegetables. Continue stirring 1½ to 2 minutes. Add rice and cheese; stir to gently separate grains. Heat 2 minutes. Serve immediately, or spoon mixture into warmed corn tortillas, if desired.

Makes 6 servings

Microwave Directions: Heat margarine in 2- to 3-quart microproof baking dish. Add carrots, bell pepper and mushrooms; cover and cook on HIGH (100% power) 4 minutes. Combine egg whites, eggs, milk, salt and black pepper in small bowl; pour over vegetables. Cook on HIGH 4 minutes, stirring with fork after each minute to cut cooked eggs into small pieces. Stir in rice and cheese; cook on HIGH about 1 minute or until thoroughly heated. Serve immediately, or spoon mixture into warmed corn tortillas.

Favorite recipe from *USA Rice Federation*

Nutrients per Serving: ⅙ of total recipe (without tortilla)

Calories: 214, Calories from Fat: 27%, Total Fat: 6g, Saturated Fat: 3g, Cholesterol: 81mg, Sodium: 356mg, Carbohydrate: 27g, Dietary Fiber: 3g, Protein: 12g

Dietary Exchanges: 2 Starch, 1 Lean Meat, ½ Fat

Strawberry Brunch Crêpes with Honey Suzette Sauce

½ cup honey
½ cup orange juice
1 tablespoon lemon juice
2 teaspoons grated orange peel
1½ teaspoons grated lemon peel
1½ teaspoons cornstarch
1 tablespoon butter or margarine
6 Low-Fat Honey Crêpes (recipe follows)
2 cups low-fat lemon yogurt
1½ cups sliced strawberries

To prepare sauce, whisk together honey, orange juice, lemon juice, orange peel, lemon peel and cornstarch in small saucepan until well blended and cornstarch is dissolved. Bring mixture to a boil over medium-high heat, whisking occasionally; cook until mixture thickens. Remove from heat. Whisk in butter. Cool to room temperature or refrigerate until ready to use. To assemble, press 1 crêpe into each of 6 ramekins or bowls to form a cup. Fill each with ⅓ cup yogurt. Top each with ¼ cup sliced strawberries and 2 to 3 tablespoons sauce.

Makes 6 servings

Favorite recipe from *National Honey Board*

Low-Fat Honey Crêpes

2 cups nonfat milk
1 cup all-purpose flour
2 egg whites
1 egg
1 tablespoon honey
1 tablespoon vegetable oil
⅛ teaspoon salt

Combine all ingredients in blender or food processor; blend until smooth. Spray 8-inch nonstick skillet lightly with nonstick cooking spray or rub with oiled paper towel; heat over medium-high heat. Spoon 3 to 4 tablespoons crêpe batter into skillet, tilting and rotating skillet to cover evenly with batter. Cook until edges begin to brown. Turn crêpe over and cook until lightly browned. Remove crêpe to plate to cool. Repeat process with remaining batter. Crêpes may be refrigerated 3 days or frozen up to 1 month in airtight container. *Makes 12 crêpes*

Favorite recipe from *National Honey Board*

Nutrients per Serving: 1 filled ramekin

Calories: 360, Calories from Fat: 17%, Total Fat: 7g, Saturated Fat: 3g, Cholesterol: 48mg, Sodium: 205mg, Carbohydrate: 65g, Dietary Fiber: 2g, Protein: 12g

Dietary Exchanges: 3 Starch, 1 Fruit, 1½ Fat

Scrambled Egg Burritos

Nonstick cooking spray
1 medium red bell pepper, chopped
5 green onions, sliced
½ teaspoon red pepper flakes
1 cup cholesterol-free egg substitute *or* 8 egg whites
1 tablespoon chopped fresh cilantro or parsley
4 (8-inch) flour tortillas
½ cup (2 ounces) shredded low-sodium reduced-fat Monterey Jack cheese
⅓ cup salsa

1. Spray medium nonstick skillet with cooking spray. Heat over medium heat until hot. Add bell pepper, green onions and red pepper flakes. Cook and stir 3 minutes or until vegetables are crisp-tender.

2. Add egg substitute to vegetables. Reduce heat to low. Cook and stir 3 minutes or until set. Sprinkle with cilantro.

3. Stack tortillas and wrap in paper towels. Microwave at HIGH 1 minute or until tortillas are hot.

4. Place one fourth of egg mixture on each tortilla. Sprinkle with cheese. Fold sides over to enclose filling. Serve with salsa. *Makes 4 servings*

Prep and Cook Time: 18 minutes

Nutrients per Serving: 1 Burrito (¼ of total recipe)

Calories: 186, Calories from Fat: 20%, Total Fat: 4g, Saturated Fat: 1g, Cholesterol: 6mg, Sodium: 425mg, Carbohydrate: 23g, Dietary Fiber: 1g, Protein: 14g

Dietary Exchanges: 1 Starch, 1 Vegetable, 1½ Lean Meat

Breakfast Blondies

2 cups (12 ounces) chopped dried fruits, such as mixture of cranberries or blueberries, cherries or strawberries, apricots, dates or raisins
2 cups (8 ounces) shredded JARLSBERG LITE™ cheese
1 (8½-ounce) package corn muffin mix
1 whole egg plus 1 egg white
½ cup fat-free (skim) milk
2 tablespoons cinnamon-sugar mixture

Preheat oven to 400°F.

Combine dried fruit, cheese and corn muffin mix; set aside.

Whisk together egg, egg white and milk in large bowl. Add fruit mixture; stir together and allow to stand 3 minutes. Spoon evenly into nonstick 10×6-inch baking pan or regular baking pan sprayed with nonstick cooking spray. Sprinkle top with cinnamon-sugar.

Bake 25 minutes or until toothpick inserted into center comes up clean. Cut into 12 squares. Serve warm or at room temperature. *Makes 12 blondies*

Nutrients per Serving: 1 Blondie (¹⁄₁₂ of total recipe)

Calories: 221, Calories from Fat: 27%, Total Fat: 7g, Saturated Fat: 3g, Cholesterol: 32mg, Sodium: 399mg, Carbohydrate: 34g, Dietary Fiber: 3g, Protein: 8g

Dietary Exchanges: 1½ Starch, 1 Fruit, 1 Lean Meat

French Toast

4 egg whites
1 egg
¼ cup skim milk
3 tablespoons packed brown sugar, divided
½ teaspoon almond extract
¼ teaspoon ground cinnamon
1 teaspoon vegetable oil
6 slices bread
1 ripe banana, sliced

Combine egg whites and egg in large bowl; beat with wire whisk until frothy. Add milk, 2 tablespoons sugar, almond extract and cinnamon. Heat oil over medium-high heat in nonstick skillet. Dip each bread slice in egg mixture. Place bread in skillet; cook each side 2 to 3 minutes until browned. If necessary, spray pan with nonstick cooking spray and continue to cook remaining bread slices. Top each piece with banana slices, sprinkle with remaining 1 tablespoon sugar and serve immediately. *Makes 6 servings*

Favorite recipe from *The Sugar Association, Inc.*

Nutrients per Serving: 1 French Toast slice with banana slices

Calories: 140, Calories from Fat: 17%, Total Fat: 3g, Saturated Fat: 1g, Cholesterol: 36mg, Sodium: 173mg, Carbohydrate: 24g, Dietary Fiber: 1g, Protein: 6g

Dietary Exchanges: 1 Starch, ½ Fruit, ½ Lean Meat

Vegetable Medley Quiche

Nonstick cooking spray

2 cups frozen diced potatoes with onions and peppers, thawed

1 (16-ounce) package frozen mixed vegetables (such as zucchini, carrots and beans), thawed and drained

1 can (10¾ ounces) reduced-fat condensed cream of mushroom soup, divided

1 cup cholesterol-free egg substitute *or* 4 eggs

½ cup grated Parmesan cheese, divided

¼ cup fat-free (skim) milk

¼ teaspoon dried dill weed

¼ teaspoon dried thyme leaves

¼ teaspoon dried oregano leaves

Dash salt and pepper (optional)

1. Preheat oven to 400°F. Spray 9-inch pie plate with cooking spray; press potatoes onto bottom and side of pan to form crust. Spray potatoes lightly with cooking spray. Bake 15 minutes.

2. Combine mixed vegetables, half of soup, egg substitute and ¼ cup cheese in small bowl; mix well. Pour egg mixture into potato shell; sprinkle with remaining ¼ cup cheese. *Reduce oven temperature to 375°F.* Bake 35 to 40 minutes or until set.

3. Combine remaining soup, milk and seasonings in small saucepan; mix. Simmer over low heat 5 minutes or until heated through. Serve with quiche.   *Makes 6 servings*

Nutrients per Serving: ⅙ of total recipe (without added salt and black pepper seasoning)

Calories: 129, Calories from Fat: 15%, Total Fat: 2g, Saturated Fat: 2g, Cholesterol: 5mg, Sodium: 436mg, Carbohydrate: 19g, Dietary Fiber: 4g, Protein: 9g

Dietary Exchanges: 1 Starch, 1 Vegetable, ½ Fat

Vegetable Medley Quiche

Cheddar Cheese Strata

1 pound French bread, cut into ½- to ¾-inch
    slices, crusts removed, divided
2 cups (8 ounces) shredded reduced-fat
    Cheddar cheese, divided
2 whole eggs
3 egg whites
1 quart fat-free (skim) milk
1 teaspoon dry mustard
1 teaspoon grated fresh onion
½ teaspoon salt
    Paprika to taste

1. Spray 13×9-inch glass baking dish with nonstick cooking spray. Place half the bread slices in bottom of prepared dish, overlapping slightly if necessary. Sprinkle with 1¼ cups cheese. Place remaining bread slices on top of cheese.

2. Whisk whole eggs and egg whites in large bowl. Add milk, mustard, onion and salt; whisk until well blended. Pour evenly over bread and cheese. Cover with remaining ¾ cup cheese and sprinkle with paprika. Cover and refrigerate 1 hour or overnight.

3. Preheat oven to 350°F. Bake about 45 minutes or until cheese is melted and bread is golden brown. Let stand 5 minutes before serving. Garnish with red bell pepper stars and fresh Italian parsley, if desired.

Makes 8 servings

Nutrients per Serving: ⅛ of total recipe (without red pepper stars and parsley)

Calories: 297, Calories from Fat: 23%, Total Fat: 7g, Saturated Fat: 3g, Cholesterol: 70mg, Sodium: 962mg, Carbohydrate: 38g, Dietary Fiber: <1g, Protein: 18g
Dietary Exchanges: 2 Starch, ½ Milk, 1 Lean Meat, 1 Fat

Eggs Primavera

4 small round loaves (4 inches) whole wheat bread
Nonstick cooking spray
1½ cups chopped onions
¾ cup chopped yellow summer squash
¾ cup chopped zucchini
½ cup chopped red bell pepper
2 ounces snow peas, trimmed and cut diagonally into thirds
¼ cup finely chopped fresh parsley
1½ teaspoons finely chopped fresh thyme *or* ¾ teaspoon dried thyme leaves
1 teaspoon finely chopped fresh rosemary *or* ½ teaspoon dried rosemary leaves, crushed
2 whole eggs
4 egg whites
¼ teaspoon black pepper
½ cup (2 ounces) shredded reduced-fat Swiss cheese

1. Preheat oven to 350°F. Slice top off each loaf of bread. Carefully hollow out each loaf, leaving sides and bottom ½ inch thick. Reserve centers for another use. Place loaves and tops, cut sides up, on baking sheet. Spray all surfaces with cooking spray; bake 15 minutes or until well toasted.

2. Spray large nonstick skillet with cooking spray and heat over medium heat until hot. Add onions; cook and stir 3 minutes or until soft. Add yellow squash, zucchini and bell pepper; cook and stir 3 minutes or until crisp-tender. Add snow peas and herbs; cook and stir 1 minute.

3. Whisk eggs, egg whites and black pepper in small bowl until blended. Add to vegetable mixture; gently stir until eggs begin to set. Sprinkle cheese over top; gently stir until cheese melts and eggs are set but not dry.

4. Fill each bread bowl with ¼ of egg mixture, about 1 cup. Place tops back on bread bowls before serving.

Makes 4 servings

Nutrients per Serving: 1 filled bread bowl (¼ of total recipe)

Calories: 201, Calories from Fat: 26%, Total Fat: 6g, Saturated Fat: 2g, Cholesterol: 114mg, Sodium: 336mg, Carbohydrate: 23g, Dietary Fiber: 4g, Protein: 14g
Dietary Exchanges: 1 Starch, 1 Vegetable, 1½ Lean Meat, ½ Fat

Eggs Primavera

Pineapple Crunch Coffee Cake

1¾ cups reduced-fat baking mix
½ cup plus 2 tablespoons fat-free (skim) milk
½ cup wheat germ
½ cup reduced-fat sour cream
¼ cup granulated sugar
1 egg
1 teaspoon vanilla
2 cans (8 ounces each) crushed pineapple in unsweetened pineapple juice, drained
⅓ cup packed dark brown sugar
⅓ cup uncooked old-fashioned or quick oats

1. Preheat oven to 350°F. Coat 8-inch square baking dish with nonstick cooking spray.

2. Combine baking mix, milk, wheat germ, sour cream, granulated sugar, egg and vanilla in medium bowl. Stir to blend thoroughly. (Batter will be lumpy.) Spread batter in prepared baking dish. Spoon pineapple evenly over batter. Sprinkle brown sugar and oats over pineapple.

3. Bake 30 minutes or until toothpick inserted into center comes out clean. Serve warm or at room temperature. Cut into 9 squares.

Makes 9 servings

Nutrients per Serving: 1 Coffee Cake square (⅑ of total recipe)

Calories: 237, Calories from Fat: 14%, Total Fat: 4g, Saturated Fat: 1g, Cholesterol: 28mg, Sodium: 267mg, Carbohydrate: 44g, Dietary Fiber: 2g, Protein: 6g
Dietary Exchanges: 2½ Starch, ½ Fruit, ½ Fat

Spicy Sausage Skillet Breakfast

2 bags SUCCESS® Rice
  Vegetable cooking spray
1 pound bulk turkey sausage
½ cup chopped onion
1 can (10 ounces) tomatoes with green chilies, undrained
1 tablespoon chili powder
1 cup (4 ounces) shredded reduced-fat Monterey Jack cheese

Prepare rice according to package directions.

Lightly spray large skillet with cooking spray. Crumble sausage into prepared skillet. Cook over medium heat until lightly browned, stirring occasionally.

Add onion; cook until tender. Stir in tomatoes, chili powder and rice; simmer 2 minutes. Reduce heat to low. Simmer until no liquid remains, about 8 minutes, stirring occasionally. Sprinkle with cheese.   *Makes 8 servings*

Nutrients per Serving: ⅛ of total recipe (without fruit)

Calories: 235, Calories from Fat: 38%, Total Fat: 10g, Saturated Fat: 4 g, Cholesterol: 54mg, Sodium: 619mg, Carbohydrate: 24g, Dietary Fiber: 1g, Protein: 15g
Dietary Exchanges: 1½ Starch, 1½ Lean Meat, 1 Fat

TIP The turkey sausage and the cheese contribute to this recipe's higher fat content. All foods can be enjoyed in moderation. Just be sure to balance this Spicy Sausage Skillet Breakfast with other lower fat foods throughout the day.

Triple-Decker Vegetable Omelet

1 cup finely chopped broccoli
½ cup diced red bell pepper
½ cup shredded carrot
⅓ cup sliced green onions
1 clove garlic, minced
2½ teaspoons FLEISCHMANN'S® Original Margarine, divided
¾ cup low fat cottage cheese (1% milkfat), divided
1 tablespoon plain dry bread crumbs
1 tablespoon grated Parmesan cheese
½ teaspoon Italian seasoning
1½ cups EGG BEATERS® Healthy Real Egg Product, divided
⅓ cup chopped tomato
  Chopped fresh parsley, for garnish

In 8-inch nonstick skillet, over medium-high heat, sauté broccoli, bell pepper, carrot, green onions and garlic in 1 teaspoon margarine until tender. Remove from skillet; stir in ½ cup cottage cheese. Keep warm. Combine bread crumbs, Parmesan cheese and Italian seasoning; set aside.

In same skillet, over medium heat, melt ½ teaspoon margarine. Pour ½ cup Egg Beaters® into skillet. Cook, lifting edges to allow uncooked portion to flow underneath. When almost set, slide unfolded omelet onto ovenproof serving platter. Top with half each of the vegetable mixture and bread crumb mixture; set aside.

Prepare 2 more omelets with remaining Egg Beaters® and margarine. Layer 1 omelet onto serving platter over vegetable and bread crumb mixture; top with remaining vegetable mixture and bread crumb mixture. Layer with remaining omelet. Top omelet with remaining cottage cheese and tomato. Bake at 425°F for 5 to 7 minutes or until heated through. Garnish with parsley. Cut into 4 wedges to serve.   *Makes 4 servings*

Nutrients per Serving: 1 wedge (¼ of total recipe)

Calories: 130, Calories from Fat: 22%, Total Fat: 3g, Saturated Fat: 1g, Cholesterol: 3mg, Sodium: 411mg, Carbohydrate: 9g, Dietary Fiber: 2g, Protein: 16g
Dietary Exchanges: 1 Vegetable, 2 Lean Meat

APPETIZERS & SNACKS

Far East Tabbouleh

¾ cup uncooked bulgur
1¾ cups boiling water
2 tablespoons reduced-sodium teriyaki sauce
2 tablespoons lemon juice
1 tablespoon olive oil
¾ cup diced seeded cucumber
¾ cup diced seeded tomato
½ cup thinly sliced green onions
½ cup minced fresh cilantro or parsley
1 tablespoon minced fresh ginger
1 clove garlic, minced

1. Combine bulgur and water in small bowl. Cover with plastic wrap; let stand 45 minutes or until bulgur is puffed, stirring occasionally. Drain in wire mesh sieve; discard liquid.

2. Combine bulgur, teriyaki sauce, lemon juice and oil in large bowl. Stir in cucumber, tomato, onions, cilantro, ginger and garlic until well blended. Cover; refrigerate 4 hours, stirring occasionally. Garnish as desired.

Makes 4 servings

Nutrients per Serving: ¼ of total recipe (without garnish)

Calories: 73, Calories from Fat: 23%, Total Fat: 2g, Saturated Fat: <1g, Cholesterol: 0mg, Sodium: 156mg, Carbohydrate: 13g, Dietary Fiber: 3g, Protein: 2g

Dietary Exchanges: ½ Starch, 1 Vegetable

Tortilla Pizza Wedges

Nonstick cooking spray
1 cup frozen corn, thawed
1 cup thinly sliced fresh mushrooms
4 (6-inch) corn tortillas
¼ cup reduced-sodium spaghetti sauce
1 to 2 teaspoons chopped jalapeño pepper*
¼ teaspoon dried oregano leaves
¼ teaspoon dried marjoram leaves
½ cup (2 ounces) shredded part-skim mozzarella cheese

Jalapeño peppers can sting and irritate the skin; wear rubber gloves when handling peppers and do not touch eyes. Wash hands after handling peppers.

1. Preheat oven to 450°F. Coat large nonstick skillet with cooking spray; heat over medium heat. Add corn and mushrooms. Cook and stir 4 to 5 minutes or until vegetables are tender.

2. Place tortillas on baking sheet. Bake about 4 minutes or until edges start to brown. Combine spaghetti sauce, jalapeño, oregano and marjoram in small bowl. Spread over tortillas. Arrange corn and mushrooms on top of tortillas. Sprinkle with cheese. Bake 4 to 5 minutes or until cheese melts and pizzas are heated through. Cut into 4 wedges.

Makes 4 servings

Nutrients per Serving: 1 Tortilla Pizza wedge (¼ of total recipe)

Calories: 155, Calories from Fat: 23%, Total Fat: 4g, Saturated Fat: 2g, Cholesterol: 8mg, Sodium: 136mg, Carbohydrate: 24g, Dietary Fiber: 3g, Protein: 7g

Dietary Exchanges: 1½ Starch, ½ Lean Meat, ½ Fat

Lox and Cheese Mini Pizzas

New York-Style Pizza Crust (recipe follows)
4 ounces reduced-fat cream cheese
2 tablespoons finely chopped red onion
1 tablespoon lemon juice
2 teaspoons grated fresh lemon peel
1½ teaspoons olive oil
4 ounces thinly sliced lox or smoked salmon
Black pepper
1 tablespoon small capers, 2 teaspoons snipped fresh chives *or* 20 tiny sprigs fresh dill, for garnish

1. Prepare New York-Style Pizza Crust.

2. Preheat oven to 500°F. Spray 2 large baking sheets with nonstick cooking spray.

3. Combine cream cheese, onion, lemon juice and lemon peel in small bowl; set aside.

4. Roll out dough into 10-inch log on lightly floured surface. Cut log into 20 (½-inch-thick) slices. Pat slices into 2¼- to 2½-inch discs.

5. Place dough slices slightly apart on prepared baking sheets. Pierce discs several times with fork; brush evenly with oil. Bake, 1 sheet at a time, 6 minutes or until light golden. Transfer to wire rack to cool slightly.

6. Spoon about 1 teaspoon cream cheese mixture onto center of each warm crust. Spread over surface, leaving ¼-inch border.

7. Cut lox into 2-inch pieces. Place over cream cheese. Sprinkle with pepper. Garnish each pizza as desired.
Makes 20 servings (20 mini pizzas)

TIP To prepare these mini pizzas in advance, let the baked crusts cool completely on wire racks after removing them from the oven. Store the crusts in an airtight container at room temperature for up to 1 day.

New York-Style Pizza Crust

⅔ cup warm water (110° to 115°F)
1 teaspoon sugar
½ (¼-ounce) package rapid-rise or active dry yeast
1¾ cups all-purpose or bread flour
½ teaspoon salt
1 tablespoon cornmeal (optional)

1. Combine water and sugar in small bowl; stir to dissolve sugar. Sprinkle yeast over top; stir to combine. Let stand 5 to 10 minutes or until foamy.

2. Combine flour and salt in medium bowl. Stir in yeast mixture. Mix until mixture forms soft dough.

3. Remove dough to lightly floured surface. Knead 5 minutes or until dough is smooth and elastic, adding additional flour (1 tablespoon at a time) as needed.

4. Place dough in medium bowl coated with nonstick cooking spray. Turn dough in bowl so top is coated with cooking spray; cover with towel or plastic wrap. Let rise in warm place 30 minutes or until doubled in bulk.
Makes 20 (2¼-inch) crusts

Nutrients per Serving: 1 Mini Pizza

Calories: 64, Calories from Fat: 23%, Total Fat: 2g, Saturated Fat: 1g, Cholesterol: 4mg, Sodium: 211mg, Carbohydrate: 9g, Dietary Fiber: <1g, Protein: 3g
Dietary Exchanges: ½ Starch, ½ Fat

Toasted Pesto Rounds

¼ cup thinly sliced fresh basil or chopped fresh
    dill
¼ cup (1 ounce) grated Parmesan cheese
3 tablespoons reduced-fat mayonnaise
1 medium clove garlic, minced
12 French bread slices, about ¼ inch thick
4 teaspoons chopped tomato
1 green onion with top, sliced
    Black pepper

1. Preheat broiler.

2. Combine basil, cheese, mayonnaise and garlic in small bowl; mix well.

3. Arrange bread slices in single layer on large nonstick baking sheet or broiler pan. Broil, 6 to 8 inches from heat, 30 to 45 seconds or until bread slices are lightly toasted.

4. Turn bread slices over; spread evenly with basil mixture. Broil 1 minute or until lightly browned. Top evenly with tomato and green onion. Season to taste with pepper. Transfer to serving plate. *Makes 12 servings*

Nutrients per Serving: 1 Pesto Round

Calories: 90, Calories from Fat: 25%, Total Fat: 2g,
Saturated Fat: 1g, Cholesterol: 3mg, Sodium: 195mg,
Carbohydrate: 14g, Dietary Fiber: <1g, Protein: 3g

Dietary Exchanges: 1 Starch, ½ Fat

Toasted Pesto Rounds

Tiny Seafood Tostadas with Black Bean Dip

Nonstick cooking spray
4 (8-inch) whole wheat or white flour tortillas,
    cut into 32 (2½-inch) rounds or shapes
1 cup Black Bean Dip (recipe follows)
1 cup shredded fresh spinach
¾ cup tiny cooked or canned shrimp
¾ cup salsa
½ cup (2 ounces) shredded reduced-fat
    Monterey Jack cheese
¼ cup reduced-fat sour cream

1. Preheat oven to 350°F. Spray nonstick baking sheet with cooking spray. Place tortilla rounds evenly on prepared baking sheet. Lightly spray rounds with cooking spray; bake 10 minutes. Turn over and spray again; bake 3 minutes more. Meanwhile, prepare Black Bean Dip.

2. To prepare tostadas, spread each toasted tortilla round with 1½ teaspoons Black Bean Dip. Layer each with 1½ teaspoons shredded spinach, 1 teaspoon shrimp, 1 teaspoon salsa, a sprinkle of cheese and a dab of sour cream. Garnish with thin green chili strips or fresh cilantro, if desired. Serve immediately with remaining Bean Dip.
Makes 8 servings

Black Bean Dip

1 can (15 ounces) black beans, undrained
1 teaspoon chili powder
¼ teaspoon salt
¼ teaspoon black pepper
¼ teaspoon ground cumin
2 drops hot pepper sauce
¾ cup minced white onion
2 cloves garlic, minced
1 can (4 ounces) chopped green chilies,
    drained

1. Drain beans, reserving 2 tablespoons liquid. Combine drained beans, reserved liquid, chili powder, salt, black pepper, cumin and hot pepper sauce in blender or food processor; process until smooth.

2. Combine onion and garlic in nonstick skillet or saucepan; cover and cook over low heat until onion is soft and translucent. Uncover and cook until slightly browned. Add chilies and cook 3 minutes more. Add bean mixture and mix well. *Makes about 1½ cups*

Nutrients per Serving: 4 Tostadas (without garnish)

Calories: 157, Calories from Fat: 20%, Total Fat: 4g,
Saturated Fat: 1g, Cholesterol: 31mg, Sodium: 747mg,
Carbohydrate: 23g, Dietary Fiber: 4g, Protein: 12g

Dietary Exchanges: 1 Starch, 1 Vegetable, 1 Lean Meat

Dreamy Orange Cheesecake Dip

1 package (8 ounces) reduced-fat cream
   cheese, softened
½ cup orange marmalade
½ teaspoon vanilla
   Grated orange peel (optional)
   Mint leaves (optional)
2 cups whole strawberries
2 cups cantaloupe chunks
2 cups apple slices

Combine cream cheese, marmalade and vanilla in small
bowl; mix well. Garnish with orange zest and mint leaves,
if desired. Serve with fruit dippers.   *Makes 12 servings*

Note: Dip may be prepared ahead of time. Store covered, in
refrigerator, for up to 2 days.

**Nutrients per Serving: 2 tablespoons Dip with
½ cup fruit (without garnish)**

Calories: 102, Calories from Fat: 29%, Total Fat: 4g,
Saturated Fat: 2g, Cholesterol: 7mg, Sodium: 111mg,
Carbohydrate: 18g, Dietary Fiber: 2g, Protein: 3g
Dietary Exchanges: 1 Fruit, ½ Lean Meat, ½ Fat

Cheesy Potato Skins

2 tablespoons grated Parmesan cheese
3 cloves garlic, finely chopped
2 teaspoons dried rosemary leaves, crushed
½ teaspoon salt
¼ teaspoon black pepper
4 baked potatoes
2 egg whites, lightly beaten
½ cup (2 ounces) shredded part-skim mozzarella
   cheese

Preheat oven to 400°F. Combine Parmesan cheese, garlic,
rosemary, salt and pepper. Cut potatoes lengthwise in half.
Remove pulp, leaving ¼-inch-thick shells. Cut each potato
half lengthwise into 2 wedges. Place on baking sheet. Brush
with egg whites; sprinkle with Parmesan cheese mixture.
Bake 20 minutes. Sprinkle with mozzarella cheese; bake
until melted. Serve with salsa, if desired.

Makes 8 servings

**Nutrients per Serving: 2 Potato Skin wedges
(without salsa)**

Calories: 90, Calories from Fat: 17%, Total Fat: 2g,
Saturated Fat: 1g, Cholesterol: 5mg, Sodium: 215mg,
Carbohydrate: 14g, Dietary Fiber: 2g, Protein: 5g
Dietary Exchanges: 1 Starch, ½ Lean Meat

California Rolls

1 cup reduced-fat ricotta cheese
2 (11-inch) flour tortillas
1 tomato, thinly sliced
2 cups washed and torn spinach leaves
1 cup chopped onion
½ teaspoon dried oregano leaves
½ teaspoon dried basil leaves
1 cup alfalfa sprouts
4 ounces sliced turkey breast

Spread cheese evenly over tortillas to within ¼ inch of
edges. Layer tomato, spinach, onion, oregano, basil, alfalfa
sprouts and turkey over ⅔ of each tortilla. Roll up tortillas.
Wrap in plastic wrap; refrigerate 1 hour. Cut crosswise into
10 slices before serving.   *Makes 4 servings*

Nutrients per Serving: 5 California Rolls

Calories: 209, Calories from Fat: 17%, Total Fat: 4g,
Saturated Fat: <1g, Cholesterol: 28mg, Sodium: 233mg,
Carbohydrate: 28g, Dietary Fiber: 2g, Protein: 16g
Dietary Exchanges: 1½ Starch, 1 Vegetable, 1½ Lean Meat

Fresh Garden Dip

1½ cups fat free or reduced fat mayonnaise
1½ cups shredded DOLE® Carrots
1 cup DOLE® Broccoli, finely chopped
⅓ cup finely chopped green onions
2 teaspoons dried dill weed
¼ teaspoon garlic powder
   DOLE® Cauliflower Florets or Peeled Mini
   Carrots

• Stir together mayonnaise, shredded carrots, broccoli,
green onions, dill and garlic powder in medium bowl until
blended.

• Spoon into serving bowl. Cover and chill 1 hour or
overnight. Serve with assorted fresh vegetables. Refrigerate
any leftovers in airtight container.   *Makes 3½ cups*

Prep Time: 15 minutes
Chill Time: 1 hour

**Nutrients per Serving: 1 tablespoon Dip (without
fresh vegetable dippers)**

Calories: 6, Calories from Fat: 2%, Total Fat: <1g,
Saturated Fat: <1g, Cholesterol: 0mg, Sodium: 47mg,
Carbohydrate: 1g, Dietary Fiber: <1g, Protein: <1g
Dietary Exchanges: Free

Stuffed Party Baguette

2 medium red bell peppers
1 French bread loaf, about 14 inches long
¼ cup plus 2 tablespoons prepared fat-free
    Italian dressing, divided
1 small red onion, very thinly sliced
8 large fresh basil leaves
3 ounces Swiss cheese, very thinly sliced

1. Preheat oven to 425°F. Cover large baking sheet with foil.

2. To roast bell peppers, cut peppers in half; remove stems, seeds and membranes. Place peppers, cut sides down, on prepared baking sheet. Bake 20 to 25 minutes or until skins are browned, turning occasionally.

3. Transfer peppers from baking sheet to paper bag; close bag tightly. Let stand 10 minutes or until peppers are cool enough to handle and skins are loosened. Peel off skins, using sharp knife; discard skins. Cut peppers into strips.

4. Trim ends from bread; discard. Cut loaf lengthwise in half. Remove soft insides of loaf; reserve removed bread for another use, if desired.

5. Brush ¼ cup Italian dressing evenly onto cut sides of bread. Arrange pepper strips in even layer in bottom half of loaf; top with even layer of onion. Brush onion with remaining 2 tablespoons Italian dressing; top with layer of basil and cheese. Replace bread top. Wrap loaf tightly in heavy-duty plastic wrap; refrigerate at least 2 hours or overnight.

6. When ready to serve, cut loaf crosswise into 12 (1-inch) slices. Secure with wooden picks and garnish, if desired.

Makes 12 servings

Nutrients per Serving: 1 Baguette slice (without garnish)

Calories: 98, Calories from Fat: 25%, Total Fat: 3g, Saturated Fat: 1g, Cholesterol: 7mg, Sodium: 239mg, Carbohydrate: 14g, Dietary Fiber: 1g, Protein: 4g

Dietary Exchanges: 1 Starch, ½ Fat

Stuffed Party Baguette

Egg Rolls

Sweet and Sour Sauce (recipe follows)
Nonstick cooking spray
3 green onions, finely chopped
3 cloves garlic, finely chopped
½ teaspoon ground ginger
½ pound boneless skinless chicken breasts, cooked and finely chopped
2 cups bean sprouts, rinsed and drained
½ cup shredded carrots
2 tablespoons reduced-sodium soy sauce
¼ teaspoon black pepper
8 egg roll wrappers
2 teaspoons vegetable oil

1. Prepare Sweet and Sour Sauce; set aside.

2. Spray large nonstick skillet with cooking spray. Heat over medium-high heat until hot. Add onions, garlic and ginger. Cook and stir 1 minute. Add chicken, bean sprouts and carrots. Cook and stir 2 minutes. Stir in soy sauce and pepper. Cook and stir 1 minute. Remove skillet from heat. Let mixture stand 10 minutes or until cool enough to handle.

3. Brush edges of egg roll wrappers with water. Spoon filling evenly down centers of wrappers. Fold ends over filling; roll up jelly-roll fashion.

4. Heat oil in another large nonstick skillet over medium heat until hot. Add rolls. Cook 3 to 5 minutes or until golden brown, turning occasionally. Serve hot with Sweet and Sour Sauce. *Makes 4 servings*

Sweet and Sour Sauce

1 tablespoon plus 1 teaspoon cornstarch
1 cup water
½ cup sugar
½ cup white vinegar
¼ cup tomato paste

Combine all ingredients in small saucepan. Bring to a boil over high heat, stirring constantly. Boil 1 minute, stirring constantly. Cool. *Makes 6 servings (about 1½ cups)*

Nutrients per Serving: 2 Egg Rolls with about ¼ cup Sauce

Calories: 351, Calories from Fat: 10%, Total Fat: 4g, Saturated Fat: 1g, Cholesterol: 38mg, Sodium: 543mg, Carbohydrate: 61g, Dietary Fiber: 3g, Protein: 20g
Dietary Exchanges: 4 Starch, 1 Lean Meat

Spicy Shrimp Cocktail

2 tablespoons olive or vegetable oil
¼ cup finely chopped onion
1 tablespoon chopped green bell pepper
1 clove garlic, minced
1 can (8 ounces) CONTADINA® Tomato Sauce
1 tablespoon chopped pitted green olives, drained
¼ teaspoon red pepper flakes
1 pound cooked shrimp, chilled

1. Heat oil in small skillet. Add onion, bell pepper and garlic; sauté until vegetables are tender. Stir in tomato sauce, olives and red pepper flakes. Bring to a boil; simmer, uncovered, for 5 minutes. Cover.

2. Chill thoroughly. Combine sauce with shrimp in small bowl. *Makes 6 servings*

Note: Serve over mixed greens, if desired.

Prep Time: 6 minutes
Cook Time: 10 minutes

Nutrients per Serving: ⅙ of total recipe (without mixed greens)

Calories: 129, Calories from Fat: 39%, Total Fat: 6g, Saturated Fat: 1g, Cholesterol: 147mg, Sodium: 402mg, Carbohydrate: 3g, Dietary Fiber: 1g, Protein: 17g
Dietary Exchanges: 2 Meat

Spicy Shrimp Cocktail

Fruit Antipasto Platter

2 cups DOLE® Fresh Pineapple, cut into wedges
2 medium, firm DOLE® Bananas, sliced
    diagonally
2 oranges, peeled and sliced
½ cup thinly sliced DOLE® Red Onion
½ pound low fat sharp Cheddar cheese, cut into
    1-inch cubes
2 jars (6 ounces each) marinated artichoke
    hearts, drained and halved
    DOLE® Green or Red Leaf Lettuce
½ cup fat free or light Italian salad dressing

• Arrange fruit, onion, cheese and artichoke hearts on lettuce-lined platter; serve with dressing. Garnish, if desired.

Makes 10 servings

Nutrients per Serving: ¹⁄₁₀ of total recipe (without garnish)

Calories: 185, Calories from Fat: 50%, Total Fat: 10g, Saturated Fat: 4g, Cholesterol: 16mg, Sodium: 482mg, Carbohydrate: 17g, Dietary Fiber: 2g, Protein: 6g

Dietary Exchanges: 1 Fruit, 1 Lean Meat, 1½ Fat

Fruit Antipasto Platter

Herbed Blue Cheese Spread with Garlic Toasts

1⅓ cups 1% low-fat cottage cheese
1¼ cups (5 ounces) crumbled blue, feta or goat
    cheese
1 large clove garlic
2 teaspoons lemon juice
2 green onions with tops, sliced (about ¼ cup)
¼ cup chopped fresh basil or oregano *or*
    1 teaspoon dried basil or oregano leaves
2 tablespoons toasted slivered almonds*
    Garlic Toasts (recipe follows)

To toast almonds, place almonds in shallow baking pan. Bake in preheated 350°F oven 8 to 10 minutes or until lightly toasted, stirring occasionally.

1. Combine cottage cheese, blue cheese, garlic and lemon juice in food processor; process until smooth. Add green onions, basil and almonds; pulse until well blended but still chunky.

2. Spoon cheese spread into small serving bowl; cover. Refrigerate until ready to serve.

3. When ready to serve, prepare Garlic Toasts. Spread 1 tablespoon cheese spread onto each toast slice. Garnish, if desired.

Makes 16 servings

Garlic Toasts

32 French bread slices, ½ inch thick
    Nonstick cooking spray
¼ teaspoon garlic powder
⅛ teaspoon salt

Place bread slices on nonstick baking sheet. Lightly coat both sides of bread slices with cooking spray. Combine garlic powder and salt in small bowl; sprinkle evenly onto bread slices. Broil, 6 to 8 inches from heat, 30 to 45 seconds on each side or until bread slices are lightly toasted on both sides.

Makes 32 pieces

Nutrients per Serving: 2 Garlic Toast pieces with 2 tablespoons Cheese Spread (1 tablespoon per Toast) without garnish

Calories: 189, Calories from Fat: 23%, Total Fat: 5g, Saturated Fat: 2g, Cholesterol: 7mg, Sodium: 521mg, Carbohydrate: 27g, Dietary Fiber: <1g, Protein: 9g

Dietary Exchanges: 2 Starch, 1 Fat

Herbed Blue Cheese Spread with Garlic Toasts ～ 47

Sesame Chicken Salad Wonton Cups

Nonstick cooking spray
20 (3-inch) wonton wrappers
1 tablespoon sesame seeds
2 small boneless skinless chicken breasts
  (about 8 ounces)
1 cup fresh green beans, cut diagonally into
  ½-inch pieces
¼ cup reduced-fat mayonnaise
1 tablespoon chopped fresh cilantro (optional)
2 teaspoons honey
1 teaspoon reduced-sodium soy sauce
⅛ teaspoon ground red pepper

1. Preheat oven to 350°F. Spray miniature muffin pan with cooking spray. Press 1 wonton wrapper into each muffin cup; spray with cooking spray. Bake 8 to 10 minutes or until golden brown. Cool in pan on wire rack before filling.

2. Place sesame seeds in shallow baking pan. Bake 5 minutes or until lightly toasted, stirring occasionally. Set aside to cool.

3. Meanwhile, bring 2 cups water to a boil in medium saucepan. Add chicken. Reduce heat to low; cover. Simmer 10 minutes or until chicken is no longer pink in center, adding green beans after 7 minutes. Drain.

4. Finely chop chicken. Place in medium bowl. Add green beans and remaining ingredients; mix lightly. Spoon lightly rounded tablespoonful of chicken mixture into each wonton cup. Garnish, if desired.   *Makes 10 servings*

Nutrients per Serving: 2 filled Wonton Cups (without garnish)

Calories: 103, Calories from Fat: 25%, Total Fat: 3g, Saturated Fat: 1g, Cholesterol: 18mg, Sodium: 128mg, Carbohydrate: 12g, Dietary Fiber: <1g, Protein: 7g
Dietary Exchanges: 1 Starch, ½ Lean Meat

TIP Wonton wrappers are thin, soft pieces of dough made from flour, eggs and water. They are sold as both squares and circles and can be found in the refrigerated and frozen foods sections of supermarkets.

Black Bean Cakes with Salsa Cruda

Salsa Cruda (recipe follows)
1 can (about 15 ounces) black beans, rinsed
  and drained
¼ cup all-purpose flour
¼ cup chopped fresh cilantro
2 tablespoons plain low-fat yogurt
1 tablespoon chili powder
2 cloves garlic, minced
Nonstick cooking spray

1. Prepare Salsa Cruda; set aside.

2. Place beans in medium bowl; mash with fork or potato masher until almost smooth, leaving some beans in larger pieces. Stir in flour, cilantro, yogurt, chili powder and garlic.

3. Spray large nonstick skillet with cooking spray; heat over medium-high heat until hot. For each cake, drop 2 heaping tablespoonfuls bean mixture onto bottom of skillet; flatten to form cake. Cook 6 to 8 minutes or until lightly browned, turning once. Serve with Salsa Cruda. Garnish as desired.   *Makes 4 servings*

Salsa Cruda

1 cup chopped seeded tomato
2 tablespoons minced onion
2 tablespoons minced fresh cilantro (optional)
2 tablespoons lime juice
½ jalapeño pepper,* seeded and minced
1 clove garlic, minced

*Jalapeño peppers can sting and irritate the skin. Wear rubber gloves when handling peppers and do not touch eyes. Wash hands after handling peppers.

Combine all ingredients in small bowl. Refrigerate 1 hour before serving.   *Makes 4 servings*

Nutrients per Serving: ¼ of total recipe (without garnish)

Calories: 145, Calories from Fat: 9%, Total Fat: 2g, Saturated Fat: <1g, Cholesterol: <1mg, Sodium: 415mg, Carbohydrate: 30g, Dietary Fiber: 8g, Protein: 11g
Dietary Exchanges: 2 Starch

Chili-Cheese Quesadillas with Salsa Cruda

2 tablespoons part-skim ricotta cheese
6 (6-inch) corn tortillas
½ cup (2 ounces) shredded reduced-fat
    Monterey Jack cheese
2 tablespoons diced mild green chilies
    Nonstick cooking spray
    Salsa Cruda (page 48)

1. To make 1 quesadilla, spread 2 teaspoons ricotta over tortilla. Sprinkle with heaping tablespoonful Monterey Jack cheese and 2 teaspoons diced chilies. Top with another tortilla. Repeat to make 2 more quesadillas.

2. Spray small nonstick skillet with cooking spray. Heat over medium-high heat. Add 1 quesadilla; cook 2 minutes or until bottom is golden. Turn quesadilla over; cook additional 2 minutes. Remove from heat. Cut into 4 wedges. Repeat with remaining quesadillas. Serve warm with Salsa Cruda.
Makes 4 servings

Nutrients per Serving: 3 Quesadilla wedges with about ¼ cup Salsa Cruda

Calories: 167, Calories from Fat: 21%, Total Fat: 4g, Saturated Fat: 1g, Cholesterol: 7mg, Sodium: 172mg, Carbohydrate: 25g, Dietary Fiber: 3g, Protein: 10g
Dietary Exchanges: 1½ Starch, ½ Vegetable, ½ Lean Meat, ½ Fat

Bell Pepper Nachos

    Nonstick cooking spray
1 medium green bell pepper
1 medium yellow or red bell pepper
2 Italian plum tomatoes, seeded and chopped
⅓ cup finely chopped onion
1 teaspoon chili powder
½ teaspoon ground cumin
1½ cups cooked white rice
½ cup (2 ounces) shredded reduced-fat
    Monterey Jack cheese
¼ cup chopped fresh cilantro
2 teaspoons jalapeño pepper sauce *or*
    ¼ teaspoon hot pepper sauce
½ cup (2 ounces) shredded reduced-fat sharp
    Cheddar cheese

1. Spray large nonstick baking sheets with cooking spray; set aside. Cut bell peppers into 2×1½-inch strips; cut strips into bite-sized triangles (each bell pepper strip should yield 2 or 3 triangles).

2. Spray large nonstick skillet with cooking spray. Add tomatoes, onion, chili powder and cumin. Cook over medium heat 3 minutes or until onion is tender, stirring occasionally. Remove from heat. Stir in rice, Monterey Jack cheese, cilantro and pepper sauce.

3. Top each pepper triangle with approximately 2 tablespoons rice mixture; sprinkle with Cheddar cheese. Place on prepared baking sheets; cover with plastic wrap. Refrigerate up to 8 hours before serving.

4. When ready to serve, preheat broiler. Remove plastic wrap. Broil nachos, 6 to 8 inches from heat, 3 to 4 minutes (or bake at 400°F 8 to 10 minutes) or until cheese is bubbly and rice is heated through. Transfer to serving plate; garnish, if desired.
Makes 8 servings

Nutrients per Serving: ⅛ of total recipe (without garnish)

Calories: 100, Calories from Fat: 24%, Total Fat: 3g, Saturated Fat: 1g, Cholesterol: 14mg, Sodium: 165mg, Carbohydrate: 14g, Dietary Fiber: 1g, Protein: 6g
Dietary Exchanges: 1 Starch, 1 Lean Meat

Pineapple-Scallop Bites

½ cup *French's®* Napa Valley Style Dijon Mustard
¼ cup orange marmalade
1 cup canned pineapple cubes (24 pieces)
12 sea scallops (8 ounces), cut in half crosswise
12 strips (6 ounces) uncooked turkey bacon, cut in half crosswise*

*Or substitute regular bacon for turkey bacon. Simmer 5 minutes in enough boiling water to cover; drain well before wrapping scallops.

1. Soak 12 (6-inch) bamboo skewers in hot water 20 minutes. Combine mustard and marmalade in small bowl. Reserve ½ cup mixture for dipping sauce.

2. Hold 1 pineapple cube and 1 scallop half together. Wrap with 1 bacon strip. Thread onto skewer. Repeat with remaining pineapple, scallops and bacon. Place skewers on oiled grid. Grill over medium heat 6 minutes, turning frequently and brushing with remaining mustard mixture. Serve hot with reserved dipping sauce.
Makes 6 servings

Nutrients per Serving: 2 skewers (using turkey bacon) with about 1 tablespoon plus 1 teaspoon dipping sauce

Calories: 179, Calories from Fat: 35%, Total Fat: 6g, Saturated Fat: 1g, Cholesterol: 32mg, Sodium: 1,015mg, Carbohydrate: 16g, Dietary Fiber: <1g, Protein: 10g
Dietary Exchanges: 1 Fruit, 1½ Meat, ½ Fat

Chile-Cheese Quesadillas with Salsa Cruda ～ 51

S'More Gorp

2 cups honey graham cereal
2 cups low-fat granola cereal
2 cups crispy multi-bran cereal squares
2 tablespoons reduced-fat margarine
1 tablespoon honey
¼ teaspoon ground cinnamon
¾ cup miniature marshmallows
½ cup dried fruit bits or raisins
¼ cup mini semisweet chocolate chips

1. Preheat oven to 275°F. Combine cereals in nonstick 15×10×1-inch jelly-roll pan.

2. Melt margarine in small saucepan; stir in honey and cinnamon. Pour margarine mixture evenly over cereal mixture; toss until cereal is well coated. Spread mixture evenly onto bottom of prepared pan.

3. Bake 35 to 40 minutes or until crisp, stirring after 20 minutes. Cool completely.

4. Add marshmallows, fruit bits and chocolate chips; toss to mix. *Makes 16 servings*

Nutrients per Serving: about ½ cup Gorp

Calories: 137, Calories from Fat: 17%, Total Fat: 3g, Saturated Fat: <1g, Cholesterol: <1mg, Sodium: 138mg, Carbohydrate: 28g, Dietary Fiber: 1g, Protein: 3g

Dietary Exchanges: 1½ Starch, ½ Fat

S'More Gorp

Bruschetta

Nonstick cooking spray
1 cup thinly sliced onion
½ cup chopped seeded tomato
2 tablespoons capers
¼ teaspoon black pepper
3 cloves garlic, finely chopped
1 teaspoon olive oil
4 slices French bread
½ cup (2 ounces) shredded reduced-fat Monterey Jack cheese

1. Spray large nonstick skillet with cooking spray. Heat over medium heat. Add onion. Cook and stir 5 minutes. Stir in tomato, capers and pepper. Cook 3 minutes.

2. Preheat broiler. Combine garlic and oil in small bowl; brush bread slices with mixture. Top with onion mixture; sprinkle with cheese. Place on baking sheet. Broil 3 minutes or until cheese melts. *Makes 4 servings*

Nutrients per Serving: 1 Bruschetta slice

Calories: 90, Calories from Fat: 20%, Total Fat: 2g, Saturated Fat: <1g, Cholesterol: 0mg, Sodium: 194mg, Carbohydrate: 17g, Dietary Fiber: <1g, Protein: 3g

Dietary Exchanges: 1 Starch

Bacon & Cheese Dip

2 packages (8 ounces each) reduced-fat cream cheese, softened, cut into cubes
4 cups (16 ounces) shredded reduced-fat sharp Cheddar cheese
1 cup evaporated skimmed milk
2 tablespoons prepared yellow mustard
1 tablespoon chopped onion
2 teaspoons Worcestershire sauce
½ teaspoon salt
¼ teaspoon hot pepper sauce
1 pound turkey bacon, crisp-cooked and crumbled

Slow Cooker Directions

Place all ingredients except bacon in slow cooker. Cover; cook, stirring occasionally, on LOW 1 hour or until cheese melts. Stir in bacon; adjust seasonings as desired. Serve with crusty bread or fruit and vegetable dippers.

Makes 16 servings (about 4 cups)

Nutrients per Serving: ¼ cup Dip (without bread and dippers)

Calories: 114, Calories from Fat: 64%, Total Fat: 8g, Saturated Fat: 4g, Cholesterol: 27mg, Sodium: 436mg, Carbohydrate: 2g, Dietary Fiber: <1g, Protein: 7g

Dietary Exchanges: 1 Lean Meat, 1 Fat

Thai Lamb & Couscous Rolls

16 large napa or Chinese cabbage leaves, stems trimmed
1 cup water
2 tablespoons minced fresh ginger
1 teaspoon red pepper flakes
⅔ cup uncooked quick-cooking couscous
Nonstick cooking spray
½ pound lean ground lamb
½ cup chopped green onions
3 cloves garlic, minced
¼ cup plus 2 tablespoons minced fresh cilantro or mint, divided
2 tablespoons reduced-sodium soy sauce
1 tablespoon lime juice
1 teaspoon dark sesame oil
1 cup plain nonfat yogurt

1. Place 4 cups water in medium saucepan; bring to a boil over high heat. Drop cabbage leaves into water; cook 30 seconds. Drain. Rinse under cold water until cool; pat dry with paper towels.

2. Place 1 cup water, ginger and red pepper in medium saucepan; bring to a boil over high heat. Stir in couscous; cover. Remove saucepan from heat; let stand 5 minutes.

3. Spray large saucepan with cooking spray; add lamb, onions and garlic. Cook and stir over medium-high heat 5 minutes or until lamb is no longer pink. Remove lamb from skillet; drain in colander.

4. Combine couscous, lamb, ¼ cup cilantro, soy sauce, lime juice and oil in medium bowl. Spoon evenly down centers of cabbage leaves. Fold ends of cabbage leaves over filling; roll up.

5. Combine yogurt and remaining 2 tablespoons cilantro in small bowl; spoon evenly over rolls. Serve warm. Garnish as desired. *Makes 16 appetizers*

Nutrients per Serving: 1 Roll with 1 tablespoon yogurt sauce (without garnish)

Calories: 53, Calories from Fat: 16%, Total Fat: 1g, Saturated Fat: <1g, Cholesterol: 7mg, Sodium: 75mg, Carbohydrate: 7g, Dietary Fiber: 1g, Protein: 4g
Dietary Exchanges: ½ Starch, ½ Lean Meat

South-of-the-Border Nachos

4 ounces low-fat tortilla chips
Nonstick cooking spray
¾ cup chopped onion
2 jalapeño peppers,* seeded and chopped
3 cloves garlic, finely chopped
2 teaspoons chili powder
½ teaspoon ground cumin
1 to 2 boneless skinless chicken breasts (about 6 ounces), cooked and chopped
1 can (14½ ounces) Mexican-style diced tomatoes, drained
1 cup (4 ounces) shredded reduced-fat Monterey Jack cheese
2 tablespoons black olives, chopped

Jalapeño peppers can sting and irritate the skin; wear rubber gloves when handling peppers and do not touch eyes. Wash hands after handling.

1. Preheat oven to 350°F. Place chips in 13×9-inch baking pan.

2. Spray large nonstick skillet with cooking spray. Heat over medium heat until hot. Add onion, peppers, garlic, chili powder and cumin. Cook 5 minutes or until vegetables are tender, stirring occasionally. Stir in chicken and tomatoes.

3. Spoon tomato mixture, cheese and olives over chips. Bake 5 minutes or until cheese melts. Serve immediately. *Makes 4 servings*

Nutrients per Serving: ¼ of total recipe

Calories: 226, Calories from Fat: 26%, Total Fat: 7g, Saturated Fat: 2g, Cholesterol: 34mg, Sodium: 273mg, Carbohydrate: 21g, Dietary Fiber: 2g, Protein: 22g
Dietary Exchanges: 1 Starch, 1 Vegetable, 2 Lean Meat, ½ Fat

TIP Asian sesame oil is amber-colored oil pressed from toasted sesame seeds. Its strong, nutty flavor contributes to its flavor-enhancing qualities. The pale-colored, cold-pressed sesame oil available in health food stores is best used for cooking and as a topping for salads. The two types of oil are not interchangeable.

Quick Pimiento Cheese Snacks

2 ounces reduced-fat cream cheese, softened
½ cup (2 ounces) shredded reduced-fat Cheddar cheese
1 jar (2 ounces) diced pimiento, drained
2 tablespoons finely chopped pecans
½ teaspoon hot pepper sauce
24 French bread slices, about ¼ inch thick, or party bread slices

1. Preheat broiler.

2. Combine cream cheese and Cheddar cheese in small bowl; mix well. Stir in pimiento, pecans and hot pepper sauce.

3. Place bread slices on broiler pan or nonstick baking sheet. Broil, 4 inches from heat, 1 to 2 minutes or until lightly toasted on both sides.

4. Spread cheese mixture evenly onto bread slices. Broil 1 to 2 minutes or until cheese mixture is hot and bubbly. Transfer to serving plate; garnish, if desired.

Makes 24 servings

Nutrients per Serving: 1 Snack (without garnish)

Calories: 86, Calories from Fat: 22%, Total Fat: 2g, Saturated Fat: 1g, Cholesterol: 3mg, Sodium: 195mg, Carbohydrate: 14g, Dietary Fiber: <1g, Protein: 3g

Dietary Exchanges: 1 Starch, ½ Fat

Quick Pimiento Cheese Snacks

Turkey Meatballs with Sweet & Sour Sauce

1 pound ground turkey
1 egg
½ cup seasoned bread crumbs
1 tablespoon dried onion flakes
1 tablespoon green bell pepper, chopped
2 tablespoons hoisin sauce
2 tablespoons cornstarch
½ cup lightly packed brown sugar
1 can (20 ounces) pineapple chunks, drained and juice reserved
⅓ cup water
3 tablespoons rice wine vinegar
1 tablespoon reduced sodium soy sauce
1 large red bell pepper, cut into ½-inch pieces

Preheat oven to 400°F. In medium bowl combine turkey, egg, bread crumbs, onion flakes, chopped green pepper and hoisin sauce. Mix well; cover and refrigerate for about 30 minutes or until mixture is well chilled. Shape 30 meatballs from turkey mixture (approximately 1 tablespoon for each meatball).

Coat 15×10×1-inch jelly-roll pan with nonstick cooking spray. Arrange meatballs on pan; bake 15 to 20 minutes or until meatballs are no longer pink in center.

Meanwhile, in 2-quart microwave-safe dish, combine cornstarch and brown sugar. Stir in reserved pineapple juice, water, vinegar and soy sauce. Microwave at HIGH (100% power) 2 minutes; stir in red pepper pieces. Microwave at HIGH 3 minutes, stirring halfway through cooking time. Fold in meatballs and pineapple chunks. Microwave at HIGH 2 minutes or until mixture is heated through. Transfer meatball mixture to chafing dish and serve with toothpicks. *Makes 15 servings*

Favorite recipe from *National Turkey Federation*

Nutrients per Serving: 2 Meatballs

Calories: 128, Calories from Fat: 22%, Total Fat: 3g, Saturated Fat: 1g, Cholesterol: 38mg, Sodium: 133mg, Carbohydrate: 19g, Dietary Fiber: 1g, Protein: 7g

Dietary Exchanges: 1 Starch, 1 Lean Meat

Apricot-Chicken Pot Stickers

2 cups plus 1 tablespoon water, divided
2 boneless skinless chicken breasts (about 8 ounces)
2 cups chopped finely shredded cabbage
½ cup all-fruit apricot preserves
2 green onions with tops, finely chopped
2 teaspoons reduced-sodium soy sauce
½ teaspoon grated fresh ginger
⅛ teaspoon black pepper
30 (3-inch) wonton wrappers
Prepared sweet and sour sauce (optional)

1. Bring 2 cups water to a boil in medium saucepan. Add chicken. Reduce heat to low; simmer, covered, 10 minutes or until chicken is no longer pink in center. Remove from saucepan; discard cooking water.

2. Add cabbage and remaining 1 tablespoon water to saucepan. Cook over high heat 1 to 2 minutes or until water evaporates, stirring occasionally. Remove from heat; cool slightly.

3. Finely chop chicken. Add to saucepan along with preserves, green onions, soy sauce, ginger and pepper; mix well.

4. To assemble pot stickers, remove 3 wonton wrappers at a time from package. Spoon slightly rounded tablespoonful chicken mixture onto center of each wrapper; brush edges of wrapper with water. Bring 4 corners together; press to seal. Repeat with remaining wrappers and filling.

5. Spray steamer with nonstick cooking spray. Assemble steamer so that water is ½ inch below steamer basket. Fill steamer basket with pot stickers, leaving enough space between them to prevent sticking. Cover; steam 5 minutes. Transfer pot stickers to serving plate. Serve with prepared sweet and sour sauce, if desired.

Makes 10 servings (3 pot stickers each)

Nutrients per Serving: 3 Pot Stickers (without sweet and sour sauce)

Calories: 145, Calories from Fat: 6%, Total Fat: 1g, Saturated Fat: <1g, Cholesterol: 17mg, Sodium: 223mg, Carbohydrate: 26g, Dietary Fiber: 1g, Protein: 8g

Dietary Exchanges: 1½ Starch, ½ Lean Meat

Southern Crab Cakes
with Rémoulade Dipping Sauce

keep warm in oven. Repeat with remaining 1 teaspoon oil and crab cakes.

3. To prepare dipping sauce, combine remaining ¼ cup mayonnaise, 1 tablespoon mustard and ¼ teaspoon hot pepper sauce in small bowl; mix well.

4. Serve crab cakes warm with lemon wedges and dipping sauce. *Makes 8 servings*

Nutrients per Serving: 1 Crab Cake with 1½ teaspoons Dipping Sauce

Calories: 81, Calories from Fat: 25%, Total Fat: 2g, Saturated Fat: <1g, Cholesterol: 30mg, Sodium: 376mg, Carbohydrate: 8g, Dietary Fiber: <1g, Protein: 7g
Dietary Exchanges: ½ Starch, 1 Lean Meat

Southern Crab Cakes with Rémoulade Dipping Sauce

10 ounces fresh lump crabmeat
1½ cups fresh white or sourdough bread crumbs, divided
¼ cup chopped green onions
½ cup fat-free or reduced-fat mayonnaise, divided
1 egg white, lightly beaten
2 tablespoons coarse grain or spicy brown mustard, divided
¾ teaspoon hot pepper sauce, divided
2 teaspoons olive oil, divided
Lemon wedges

1. Preheat oven to 200°F. Combine crabmeat, ¾ cup bread crumbs and green onions in medium bowl. Add ¼ cup mayonnaise, egg white, 1 tablespoon mustard and ½ teaspoon pepper sauce; mix well. Using ¼ cup mixture per cake, shape 8 (½-inch-thick) cakes. Roll crab cakes lightly in remaining ¾ cup bread crumbs.

2. Heat large nonstick skillet over medium heat until hot; add 1 teaspoon oil. Add 4 crab cakes; cook 4 to 5 minutes per side or until golden brown. Transfer to serving platter;

Roasted Garlic Spread with Three Cheeses

2 medium heads garlic
2 packages (8 ounces each) fat-free cream cheese, softened
1 package (3½ ounces) goat cheese
2 tablespoons (1 ounce) crumbled blue cheese
1 teaspoon dried thyme leaves

1. Preheat oven to 400°F.

2. Cut tops off garlic heads to expose tops of cloves. Place garlic in small baking pan; bake 45 minutes or until garlic is very tender. Remove from pan; cool completely. Squeeze garlic into small bowl; mash with fork.

3. Beat cream cheese and goat cheese in small bowl until smooth; stir in blue cheese, garlic and thyme. Cover; refrigerate 3 hours or overnight.

4. Spoon dip into serving bowl; serve with cucumbers, radishes, carrots, yellow bell peppers or crackers, if desired. Garnish with fresh thyme and red bell pepper strip, if desired. *Makes 21 servings*

Nutrients per Serving: 2 tablespoons Spread (without dippers and garnish)

Calories: 37, Calories from Fat: 29%, Total Fat: 1g, Saturated Fat: <1g, Cholesterol: 9mg, Sodium: 157mg, Carbohydrate: 2g, Dietary Fiber: <1g, Protein: 4g
Dietary Exchanges: ½ Lean Meat

Peppy Snack Mix

3 plain rice cakes, broken into bite-size pieces
1½ cups bite-size frosted shredded wheat biscuit
   cereal
¾ cup pretzel sticks, halved
3 tablespoons reduced-fat margarine, melted
2 teaspoons reduced-sodium Worcestershire
   sauce
¾ teaspoon chili powder
⅛ to ¼ teaspoon ground red pepper

1. Preheat oven to 300°F.

2. Combine rice cake pieces, cereal and pretzels in
13×9-inch baking pan. Combine margarine, Worcestershire,
chili powder and pepper in small bowl. Drizzle over cereal
mixture; toss to combine. Bake 20 minutes, stirring after
10 minutes.   *Makes 6 (⅔-cup) servings*

Nutrients per Serving: ⅔ cup Snack Mix

Calories: 118, Calories from Fat: 25%, Total Fat: 3g,
Saturated Fat: 1g, Cholesterol: 0mg, Sodium: 156mg,
Carbohydrate: 20g, Dietary Fiber: 1g, Protein: 2g

Dietary Exchanges: 1½ Starch, ½ Fat

Wild Wedges

2 (8-inch) fat-free flour tortillas
   Nonstick cooking spray
⅓ cup shredded reduced-fat Cheddar cheese
⅓ cup chopped cooked chicken or turkey
1 green onion, thinly sliced (about ¼ cup)
2 tablespoons mild, thick and chunky salsa

1. Heat large nonstick skillet over medium heat until hot.
Spray one side of one flour tortilla with nonstick cooking
spray; place sprayed side down in skillet. Top with cheese,
chicken, green onion and salsa. Place remaining tortilla
over mixture; spray with nonstick cooking spray.

2. Cook 2 to 3 minutes per side or until golden brown and
cheese is melted. Cut into 8 triangles.   *Makes 4 servings*

Variation: For bean quesadillas, omit the chicken and spread
⅓ cup canned fat-free refried beans over one of the tortillas.

Nutrients per Serving: 2 Wedges (made with chicken)

Calories: 76, Calories from Fat: 24%, Total Fat: 2g,
Saturated Fat: 1g, Cholesterol: 14mg, Sodium: 282mg,
Carbohydrate: 8g, Dietary Fiber: 4g, Protein: 7g

Dietary Exchanges: ½ Starch, 1 Lean Meat

Peppy Snack Mix

Grilled Red Bell Pepper Dip

1 medium red bell pepper, stemmed, seeded and halved
1 cup fat-free or reduced-fat ricotta cheese
4 ounces fat-free cream cheese
¼ cup grated Parmesan cheese
1 clove Grilled Garlic (recipe follows) *or* 1 clove garlic, minced
½ teaspoon Dijon mustard
¼ teaspoon salt
¼ teaspoon herbes de Provence*
    Mini pita pockets, Melba toast, pretzels or fresh vegetables (optional)

Substitute dash each rubbed sage, crushed dried rosemary, thyme, oregano, marjoram and basil leaves for herbes de Provence.

1. Grill bell pepper halves skin-side-down on covered grill over medium coals 15 to 25 minutes or until skin is charred, without turning. Remove from grill and place in plastic bag until cool enough to handle, about 10 minutes. Remove and discard skin with paring knife.

2. Place bell pepper in food processor. Add cheeses, garlic, mustard, salt and herbes de Provence; process until smooth. Serve with mini pita pockets or vegetables for dipping. *Makes about 2 cups*

Grilled Red Bell Pepper Dip

Grilled Garlic

2 cloves garlic
    Nonstick cooking spray

1. Soak wooden or bamboo skewer in water 20 minutes.

2. Thread garlic cloves onto skewer. Spray with cooking spray.* Grill on covered or uncovered grill over medium coals about 8 minutes or until browned and tender.

Or, place 2 garlic cloves on sheet of foil; lightly spray with cooking spray and carefully seal foil packet. Finish grilling as directed.

Nutrients per Serving: 2 tablespoons Dip made with fat-free ricotta cheese (without pita and vegetable dippers)

Calories: 26, Calories from Fat: 21%, Total Fat: 1g, Saturated Fat: <1g, Cholesterol: 3mg, Sodium: 130mg, Carbohydrate: 1g, Dietary Fiber: <1g, Protein: 4g
Dietary Exchanges: ½ Lean Meat

Crab Canapés

⅔ cup fat-free cream cheese, softened
2 teaspoons lemon juice
1 teaspoon hot pepper sauce
1 package (8 ounces) imitation crabmeat or lobster, flaked
⅓ cup chopped red bell pepper
2 green onions with tops, sliced (about ¼ cup)
64 cucumber slices (about 2½ medium cucumbers, cut ⅜ inch thick) or melba toast rounds

1. Combine cream cheese, lemon juice and hot pepper sauce in medium bowl; mix well. Stir in crabmeat, bell pepper and green onions; cover. Chill until ready to serve.

2. When ready to serve, spoon 1½ teaspoons crabmeat mixture onto each cucumber slice. Place on serving plate; garnish with parsley, if desired. *Makes 16 servings*

Note: To allow flavors to blend, chill crab mixture at least 1 hour before spreading onto cucumbers or melba toast rounds.

Nutrients per Serving: 4 Canapés made with cucumber slices (without garnish)

Calories: 31, Calories from Fat: 8%, Total Fat: <1g, Saturated Fat: <1g, Cholesterol: 5mg, Sodium: 178mg, Carbohydrate: 4g, Dietary Fiber: <1g, Protein: 4g
Dietary Exchanges: ½ Lean Meat

Caribbean Chutney Kabobs

Caribbean Chutney Kabobs

½ medium pineapple
1 medium red bell pepper, cut into 1-inch
     pieces
¾ pound boneless skinless chicken breasts, cut
     into 1-inch pieces
½ cup bottled mango chutney
2 tablespoons orange juice or pineapple juice
1 teaspoon vanilla
¼ teaspoon ground nutmeg

1. To prevent burning, soak 20 (4-inch) bamboo skewers in water at least 20 minutes before assembling kabobs.

2. Peel and core pineapple. Cut pineapple into 1-inch chunks. Alternately thread bell pepper, pineapple and chicken onto skewers. Place in shallow baking dish.

3. Combine chutney, orange juice, vanilla and nutmeg in small bowl; mix well. Pour over kabobs; cover. Refrigerate up to 4 hours.

4. Preheat broiler. Spray broiler pan with nonstick cooking spray. Place kabobs on prepared broiler pan; discard any leftover marinade. Broil kabobs, 6 to 8 inches from heat, 4 to 5 minutes on each side or until chicken is no longer pink in center. Transfer to serving plates.

Makes 10 servings

Nutrients per Serving: 2 Kabobs

Calories: 108, Calories from Fat: 10%, Total Fat: 1g, Saturated Fat: <1g, Cholesterol: 21mg, Sodium: 22mg, Carbohydrate: 16g, Dietary Fiber: 2g, Protein: 8g

Dietary Exchanges: 1 Fruit, 1 Lean Meat

Hot Black Bean Dip

1 can (about 15 ounces) black beans, rinsed
     and drained
1 can (about 16 ounces) whole tomatoes,
     drained and chopped
1 canned chipotle chili in adobo sauce, drained
     and finely chopped*
1 teaspoon dried oregano leaves
1 cup (4 ounces) shredded reduced-fat Cheddar
     cheese
   Baked tortilla chips (optional)

*Chipotle chilies can sting and irritate the skin; wear rubber gloves when handling chilies and do not touch eyes.

1. Place beans in medium bowl; mash with fork until smooth.

2. Place beans in small heavy saucepan. Stir in tomatoes, chipotle and oregano. Cook over medium heat 5 minutes or until heated through, stirring occasionally.

3. Remove saucepan from heat. Add cheese; stir constantly until cheese melts.

4. Transfer bean dip to serving bowl. Serve hot with tortilla chips, if desired. Garnish as desired.

Makes 8 servings

Nutrients per Serving: ⅛ of Dip (without tortilla chips and garnish)

Calories: 92, Calories from Fat: 22%, Total Fat: 3g, Saturated Fat: 1g, Cholesterol: 8mg, Sodium: 458mg, Carbohydrate: 13g, Dietary Fiber: 4g, Protein: 8g

Dietary Exchanges: ½ Starch, 1 Vegetable, ½ Fat

Shrimp Toast

12 large shrimp, shelled and deveined, tails intact
1 egg
2½ tablespoons cornstarch
¼ teaspoon salt
Dash black pepper
3 slices white sandwich bread, crusts removed, quartered
1 hard-cooked egg yolk, cut into ½-inch pieces
1 slice cooked ham, cut into ½-inch pieces
1 green onion with top, finely chopped
Vegetable oil for frying
Hard-cooked egg half and Green Onion Curls (recipe follows), for garnish (optional)

1. Cut deep slit down back of each shrimp; press gently with fingers to flatten.

2. Beat 1 egg, cornstarch, salt and pepper in large bowl until blended. Add shrimp; toss to coat well.

3. Place 1 shrimp, cut side down, on each bread piece; press shrimp gently into bread. Brush or rub small amount of leftover egg mixture onto each shrimp.

4. Place one piece each of egg yolk and ham and a scant ¼ teaspoon onion on top of each shrimp.

5. Heat oil in wok or large skillet over medium-high heat to 375°F. Add three or four bread pieces at a time; cook until golden, 1 to 2 minutes on each side. Drain on paper towels. Garnish, if desired.   *Makes 12 servings*

Green Onion Curls

6 to 8 medium green onions with tops
Cold water
10 to 12 ice cubes

1. Trim bulbs (white part) from onions; reserve for another use, if desired. Trim remaining stems (green part) to 4-inch lengths.

2. Using sharp scissors, cut each section of green stems lengthwise into very thin strips down to beginning of stems, cutting 6 to 8 strips from each stem section.

3. Fill large bowl about half full with cold water. Add green onions and ice cubes. Refrigerate until onions curl, about 1 hour; drain.   *Makes 6 to 8 curls*

Nutrients per Serving: 1 Shrimp Toast (without garnish)

Calories: 45, Calories from Fat: 20%, Total Fat: 1g, Saturated Fat: <1g, Cholesterol: 47mg, Sodium: 128mg, Carbohydrate: 4g, Dietary Fiber: <1g, Protein: 3g
Dietary Exchanges: ½ Starch

Grilled Turkey Ham Quesadillas

Nonstick cooking spray
¼ cup salsa
4 (7-inch) flour tortillas
½ cup shredded reduced-sodium reduced-fat Monterey Jack cheese
¼ cup finely chopped turkey ham
1 can (4 ounces) diced green chilies, drained

1. To prevent sticking, spray grid with cooking spray. Prepare coals for grilling.

2. Spread 1 tablespoon salsa onto each tortilla. Sprinkle cheese, turkey ham and chilies equally over half of each tortilla; fold over uncovered half to make "sandwich." Spray tops and bottoms of tortilla "sandwiches" with cooking spray.

3. Grill quesadillas on uncovered grill over medium coals 1½ minutes per side or until cheese is melted and tortillas are golden brown, turning once. Quarter each quesadilla and serve with additional salsa and nonfat sour cream, if desired.   *Makes 8 servings*

Nutrients per Serving: 2 Quesadilla "sandwich" quarters (without additional salsa and sour cream)

Calories: 66, Calories from Fat: 26%, Total Fat: 2g, Saturated Fat: 1g, Cholesterol: 5mg, Sodium: 195mg, Carbohydrate: 8g, Dietary Fiber: <1g, Protein: 4g
Dietary Exchanges: ½ Starch, ½ Lean Meat

Ginger Snap Sandwiches

¼ cup 1% low-fat cottage cheese
¼ cup vanilla nonfat yogurt
1 McIntosh apple, peeled, cored and grated
2 tablespoons sugar
30 ginger snaps

Add cottage cheese and yogurt to food processor or blender; process until smooth. Blend in apple and sugar. Using rubber spatula, spread apple filling onto flat side of ginger snap; top with another ginger snap to make sandwich. Repeat with remaining ingredients.

Makes 15 servings

Favorite recipe from *The Sugar Association, Inc.*

Nutrients per Serving: 1 Ginger Snap Sandwich

Calories: 76, Calories from Fat: 17%, Total Fat: 1g, Saturated Fat: <1g, Cholesterol: <1mg, Sodium: 110mg, Carbohydrate: 15g, Dietary Fiber: <1g, Protein: 1g
Dietary Exchanges: 1 Starch

SOUPS & SALADS

Cucumber Tomato Salad

½ cup rice vinegar*
3 tablespoons EQUAL® SPOONFUL**
3 cups unpeeled ¼-inch-thick sliced
    cucumbers, quartered (about 2 medium)
2 cups chopped tomato (about 1 large)
½ cup chopped red onion
    Salt and pepper to taste (optional)

Distilled white vinegar may be substituted for rice vinegar.

**May substitute 4½ packets Equal® sweetener.*

• Combine vinegar and Equal®. Add cucumbers, tomato and onion. Season to taste with salt and pepper, if desired; mix well. Refrigerate, covered, at least 30 minutes before serving. *Makes 6 servings*

Nutrients per Serving: ⅙ of total recipe (without added salt and pepper)

Calories: 26, Calories from Fat: 0%, Total Fat: 0g, Saturated Fat: 0g, Cholesterol: 0mg, Sodium: 7mg, Carbohydrate: 6g, Dietary Fiber: 1g, Protein: 1g
Dietary Exchanges: 1 Vegetable

Garden Potato Salad with Basil-Yogurt Dressing

6 new potatoes, quartered
8 ounces asparagus, cut into 1-inch slices
1¼ cups red, yellow or green bell pepper strips
⅔ cup plain low-fat yogurt
¼ cup sliced green onions
2 tablespoons chopped pitted ripe olives
1½ tablespoons chopped fresh basil *or*
    1½ teaspoons dried basil leaves, crushed
1 tablespoon chopped fresh thyme *or*
    1 teaspoon dried thyme leaves, crushed
1 tablespoon white vinegar
2 teaspoons sugar
    Dash ground red pepper

1. Bring 3 cups water to a boil in large saucepan over high heat. Add potatoes; return to a boil. Reduce heat to medium-low. Simmer, covered, 8 minutes. Add asparagus and bell peppers; return to a boil over high heat. Reduce heat to medium-low. Simmer, covered, about 3 minutes or until potatoes are just tender and asparagus and bell peppers are tender-crisp. Drain.

2. Meanwhile, combine yogurt, green onions, olives, basil, thyme, vinegar, sugar and ground red pepper in large bowl. Add vegetables; toss to combine. Refrigerate, covered, until well chilled. *Makes 4 servings*

Nutrients per Serving: ¼ of total recipe

Calories: 154, Calories from Fat: 14%, Total Fat: 3g, Saturated Fat: 1g, Cholesterol: 2mg, Sodium: 173mg, Carbohydrate: 30g, Dietary Fiber: 3g, Protein: 6g
Dietary Exchanges: 1½ Starch, 1 Vegetable, ½ Fat

New England Clam Chowder

Chicken Ravioli Soup

Chicken Ravioli (recipe follows)
8 cups fat-free reduced-sodium chicken broth
2 cups sliced fresh spinach leaves
1 cup sliced carrots
¼ teaspoon salt
⅛ teaspoon black pepper

1. Prepare Chicken Ravioli.

2. In large saucepan, heat chicken broth, spinach, carrots, salt and pepper to a boil. Reduce heat to low and simmer, covered, 10 minutes.

3. Return soup to a boil; add Chicken Ravioli. Reduce heat to low and simmer, uncovered, 2 to 3 minutes or until ravioli are tender and rise to surface of soup.

Makes 6 servings

Chicken Ravioli

⅓ cup ground chicken
1 tablespoon minced shallot or onion
1 clove garlic, minced
⅛ teaspoon salt
⅛ teaspoon ground nutmeg
⅛ teaspoon black pepper
24 wonton wrappers
Water

1. Combine chicken, shallot, garlic, salt, nutmeg and pepper in small bowl. Place rounded teaspoonful of chicken mixture in center of each of 12 wonton wrappers. Moisten edges of wonton wrappers with water. Top with remaining wonton wrappers; press to seal edges.

2. Refrigerate, covered, until ready to cook.

Makes 12 ravioli

Nutrients per Serving: 1 bowl Soup (⅙ of total recipe) with 2 Ravioli

Calories: 130, Calories from Fat: 14%, Total Fat: 2g, Saturated Fat: <1g, Cholesterol: 26mg, Sodium: 205mg, Carbohydrate: 21g, Dietary Fiber: 2g, Protein: 7g

Dietary Exchanges: 1 Starch, 1 Vegetable, ½ Lean Meat

New England Clam Chowder

1 can (5 ounces) whole baby clams, undrained
1 baking potato, peeled and coarsely chopped
¼ cup finely chopped onion
⅔ cup evaporated skimmed milk
¼ teaspoon white pepper
¼ teaspoon dried thyme leaves
1 tablespoon reduced-fat margarine

Drain clams, reserving juice. Add enough water to reserved juice to measure ⅔ cup. Combine clam juice mixture, potato and onion in large saucepan. Bring to a boil over high heat; reduce heat and simmer 8 minutes or until potato is tender. Add milk, pepper and thyme to saucepan. Increase heat to medium-high. Cook and stir 2 minutes. Add margarine. Cook 5 minutes or until soup thickens, stirring occasionally. Add clams; cook and stir 5 minutes or until clams are firm. *Makes 2 servings*

Nutrients per Serving: 1 bowl Chowder (½ of total recipe)

Calories: 204, Calories from Fat: 17%, Total Fat: 4g, Saturated Fat: 1g, Cholesterol: 47mg, Sodium: 205mg, Carbohydrate: 30g, Dietary Fiber: 1g, Protein: 14g

Dietary Exchanges: 1 Starch, 1 Milk, 1 Lean Meat

Chicken Ravioli Soup ⌒ 71

Oriental Garden Toss

⅓ cup thinly sliced green onions
3 tablespoons reduced-sodium soy sauce
3 tablespoons water
1½ teaspoons roasted sesame oil
1 teaspoon EQUAL® FOR RECIPES *or* 3 packets
   EQUAL® sweetener *or* 2 tablespoons
   EQUAL® SPOONFUL™
¼ teaspoon garlic powder
⅛ teaspoon crushed red pepper flakes
1 package (3 ounces) low-fat ramen noodle
   soup
2 cups fresh pea pods, halved crosswise
1 cup fresh bean sprouts
1 cup sliced fresh mushrooms
1 can (8¾ ounces) baby corn, drained and
   halved crosswise
1 red bell pepper, cut into bite-size strips
3 cups shredded Chinese cabbage
⅓ cup chopped lightly salted cashews (optional)

• Combine green onions, soy sauce, water, sesame oil, Equal®, garlic powder and red pepper flakes in screw-top jar; set aside.

• Break up ramen noodles (discard seasoning packet); combine with pea pods in large bowl. Pour boiling water over mixture to cover. Let stand 1 minute; drain.

• Combine noodles, pea pods, bean sprouts, mushrooms, baby corn and bell pepper in large bowl. Shake dressing and add to noodle mixture; toss to coat. Cover and chill 2 to 24 hours. Just before serving, add shredded cabbage; toss to combine. Sprinkle with cashews, if desired.

Makes 6 (1-cup) servings

Nutrients per Serving: 1 cup salad (without cashews)

Calories: 124, Calories from Fat: 11%, Total Fat: 2g, Saturated Fat: <1g, Cholesterol: 0mg, Sodium: 605mg, Carbohydrate: 21g, Dietary Fiber: 3g, Protein: 6g

Dietary Exchanges: 1 Starch, 1 Vegetable, ½ Fat

Garden Gazpacho

6 large ripe tomatoes, peeled and seeded
½ cup chopped, seeded, peeled cucumber
½ cup coarsely chopped green bell pepper
½ cup coarsely chopped onion
1 clove garlic, minced
1 cup reduced-sodium tomato juice
1 teaspoon lemon juice
⅛ teaspoon hot pepper sauce
⅛ teaspoon black pepper

Combine tomatoes, cucumber, bell pepper, onion and garlic in food processor or blender; process, using on/off pulsing action, just until mixture is thick and chunky. Pour into medium bowl. Stir in remaining ingredients. Cover and chill until ready to serve. Garnish with nonfat yogurt, if desired. *Makes 4 (1¼-cup) servings*

Nutrients per Serving: 1¼ cups Gazpacho (without yogurt garnish)

Calories: 68, Calories from Fat: 9%, Total Fat: 1g, Saturated Fat: <1g, Cholesterol: 0mg, Sodium: 25mg, Carbohydrate: 15g, Dietary Fiber: 4g, Protein: 3g

Dietary Exchanges: 3 Vegetable

Turkey Fruited Bow Tie Salad

½ pound turkey breast, cut into ½-inch cubes
2 cups bow tie pasta, cooked according to
   package directions and drained
1 can (10½ ounces) mandarin oranges, drained
1 medium red apple, chopped
1 cup seedless grapes, cut in half
½ cup celery, sliced
½ cup low-fat lemon yogurt
2 tablespoons frozen orange juice concentrate,
   thawed
¼ teaspoon ground ginger

1. In large bowl, combine turkey, pasta, oranges, apple, grapes and celery.

2. In small bowl, combine yogurt, juice and ginger. Fold dressing into turkey mixture and toss to coat. Cover and refrigerate until ready to serve. *Makes 4 servings*

Favorite recipe from *National Turkey Federation*

Nutrients per Serving: ¼ of total recipe

Calories: 269, Calories from Fat: 6%, Total Fat: 2g, Saturated Fat: 1g, Cholesterol: 49mg, Sodium: 71mg, Carbohydrate: 43g, Dietary Fiber: 3g, Protein: 22g

Dietary Exchanges: 2 Starch, ½ Fruit, 2 Lean Meat

Japanese Noodle Soup

1 package (8½ ounces) Japanese udon noodles
1 teaspoon vegetable oil
1 medium red bell pepper, cut into thin strips
1 medium carrot, diagonally sliced
2 green onions, thinly sliced
2 cans (14½ ounces each) fat-free reduced-sodium beef broth
1 cup water
1 teaspoon reduced-sodium soy sauce
½ teaspoon grated fresh ginger
½ teaspoon black pepper
2 cups thinly sliced fresh shiitake mushrooms, stems removed
4 ounces daikon (Japanese radish), peeled and cut into thin strips
4 ounces firm tofu, drained and cut into ½-inch cubes

1. Cook noodles according to package directions, omitting salt; drain. Rinse; set aside.

2. Heat oil in large nonstick saucepan until hot. Add red bell pepper, carrot and green onions; cook until slightly softened, about 3 minutes. Stir in beef broth, water, soy sauce, ginger and black pepper; bring to a boil. Add mushrooms, daikon and tofu. Reduce heat; simmer 5 minutes. Place noodles in soup tureen; ladle soup over top. *Makes 6 servings*

Nutrients per Serving: 1 bowl Soup (⅙ of total recipe)

Calories: 144, Calories from Fat: 16%, Total Fat: 3g, Saturated Fat: <1g, Cholesterol: 0mg, Sodium: 107mg, Carbohydrate: 24g, Dietary Fiber: 3g, Protein: 9g

Dietary Exchanges: 1½ Starch, ½ Vegetable, ½ Fat

Cold Cucumber Soup

1 cucumber, peeled
1 cup low-fat buttermilk
2 tablespoons red onion, finely chopped
1 teaspoon dried mint leaves, crushed
1 teaspoon sugar
   Dash hot sauce

Blend all ingredients thoroughly in food processor. Serve immediately or chill before serving. *Makes 2 servings*

Favorite recipe from *The Sugar Association, Inc.*

Nutrients per Serving: 1 bowl Soup (½ of recipe)

Calories: 79, Calories from Fat: 14%, Total Fat: 1g, Saturated Fat: 1g, Cholesterol: 5mg, Sodium: 132mg, Carbohydrate: 13g, Dietary Fiber: 1g, Protein: 5g

Dietary Exchanges: ½ Milk, 1 Vegetable, ½ Fat

Green Pea and Potato Soup

1 can (14½ ounces) fat-free reduced-sodium chicken broth*
1 cup diced peeled potato
1 cup fresh or frozen green peas
½ cup sliced green onion tops
2 leaves green lettuce, chopped
1 teaspoon dried dill weed
⅛ teaspoon white pepper
1½ cups low-fat buttermilk
   Dash paprika

To defat chicken broth, skim fat from surface of broth with spoon. Or, place can of broth in refrigerator at least 2 hours ahead of time. Before using, remove fat that has hardened on surface of broth.

1. Combine chicken broth, potato, peas, green onions, lettuce, dill and pepper in medium saucepan. Bring to a boil over high heat. Reduce heat to medium. Cook, covered, 10 minutes or until potatoes are just tender. Let cool, uncovered, to room temperature.

2. Place vegetables and cooking liquid in food processor. Process 45 seconds or until almost smooth. Return mixture to saucepan; stir in buttermilk. Cook and stir over low heat 5 minutes or until heated through. Sprinkle with paprika. *Makes 6 servings*

Note: Soup may be served cold. Chill at least 8 hours before serving.

Nutrients per Serving: 1 bowl Soup (⅙ of total recipe)

Calories: 90, Calories from Fat: 8%, Total Fat: 1g, Saturated Fat: <1g, Cholesterol: 2mg, Sodium: 77mg, Carbohydrate: 16g, Dietary Fiber: 3g, Protein: 5g

Dietary Exchanges: 1 Starch, ½ Vegetable

Mediterranean Fish Soup

4 ounces uncooked pastina or other small pasta
Nonstick cooking spray
¾ cup chopped onion
2 cloves garlic, minced
1 teaspoon fennel seeds
1 can (14½ ounces) no-salt-added stewed tomatoes
1 can (14½ ounces) fat-free reduced-sodium chicken broth
1 tablespoon minced fresh parsley
½ teaspoon black pepper
¼ teaspoon ground turmeric
8 ounces firm white-fleshed fish (such as cod or orange roughy), cut into 1-inch pieces
3 ounces small shrimp, peeled and deveined

1. Cook pasta according to package directions, omitting salt. Drain and set aside.

2. Spray large nonstick saucepan with cooking spray. Add onion, garlic and fennel seeds; cook over medium heat 3 minutes or until onion is tender.

3. Stir in tomatoes, chicken broth, parsley, pepper and turmeric. Bring to a boil; reduce heat and simmer 10 minutes. Add fish and cook 1 minute. Add shrimp and cook until shrimp just begins to turn pink and opaque.

4. Divide pasta evenly among bowls; ladle soup over pasta.
Makes 4 (1½-cup) servings

Nutrients per Serving: 1½ cups Soup with ½ cup pasta

Calories: 209, Calories from Fat: 10%, Total Fat: 2g, Saturated Fat: <1g, Cholesterol: 59mg, Sodium: 111mg, Carbohydrate: 28g, Dietary Fiber: 3g, Protein: 19g

Dietary Exchanges: 1½ Starch, 1½ Vegetable, 1½ Lean Meat

Mediterranean Fish Soup

Blackened Chicken Salad

2 cups cubed sourdough or French bread
  Nonstick cooking spray
1 tablespoon paprika
1 teaspoon onion powder
1 teaspoon garlic powder
½ teaspoon dried oregano leaves
½ teaspoon dried thyme leaves
½ teaspoon white pepper
½ teaspoon ground red pepper
½ teaspoon black pepper
1 pound boneless skinless chicken breasts
4 cups bite-size pieces fresh spinach leaves
2 cups bite-size pieces romaine lettuce
2 cups cubed zucchini
2 cups cubed seeded cucumber
½ cup sliced green onions with tops
1 medium tomato, cut into 8 wedges
  Ranch Salad Dressing (recipe follows)

1. Preheat oven to 375°F. To make croutons, spray bread cubes lightly with cooking spray; place in 15×10-inch jelly-roll pan. Bake 10 to 15 minutes or until browned, stirring occasionally.

2. Combine paprika, onion powder, garlic powder, oregano, thyme, white pepper, red pepper and black pepper in small bowl; rub on all surfaces of chicken. Broil chicken, 6 inches from heat source, 7 to 8 minutes on each side or until chicken is no longer pink in center. Or, grill chicken on covered grill over medium-hot coals 10 minutes on each side or until chicken is no longer pink in center. Cool slightly. Cut chicken into thin strips.

3. Combine warm chicken with greens, zucchini, cucumber, green onions, tomato and croutons in large bowl. Drizzle with Ranch Salad Dressing; toss to coat. Serve immediately. *Makes 4 servings*

Ranch Salad Dressing

¼ cup water
3 tablespoons reduced-fat cucumber-ranch
  salad dressing
1 tablespoon prepared reduced-fat mayonnaise
  or salad dressing
1 tablespoon lemon juice
2 teaspoons minced fresh parsley
⅛ teaspoon salt
⅛ teaspoon black pepper

Combine all ingredients in small jar with tight-fitting lid; shake well. Refrigerate until ready to use; shake before using. *Makes about ½ cup*

Nutrients per Serving: ¼ of total recipe (with 2 tablespoons Salad Dressing)

Calories: 222, Calories from Fat: 16%, Total Fat: 4g, Saturated Fat: 1g, Cholesterol: 69mg, Sodium: 191mg, Carbohydrate: 17g, Dietary Fiber: 5g, Protein: 30g

Dietary Exchanges: ½ Starch, 2 Vegetable, 3 Lean Meat

Blackened Chicken Salad

Wild Rice and Mixed Greens Salad

4 cups mixed baby greens
3 ounces baked or poached chicken or fish
⅓ cup cooked brown and wild rice mixture*
2 tablespoons prepared reduced-fat salad
  dressing

Cook rice in fat-free reduced-sodium chicken broth for extra flavor.

Arrange greens on serving plate. Top with chicken. Sprinkle rice mixture over chicken and greens. Drizzle with dressing. *Makes 1 serving*

Nutrients per Serving: 1 Salad

Calories: 279, Calories from Fat: 16%, Total Fat: 5g, Saturated Fat: 1g, Cholesterol: 72mg, Sodium: 361mg, Carbohydrate: 27g, Dietary Fiber: 6g, Protein: 31g

Dietary Exchanges: 1 Starch, 2 Vegetable, 3 Lean Meat

Southwest Bean Chili

1 cup uncooked dried garbanzo beans
¾ cup uncooked dried red kidney beans
¾ cup uncooked dried black beans
5½ cups canned fat-free reduced-sodium chicken broth
4 cloves garlic, minced
3 ears fresh corn, shucked and kernels cut from cobs
2 medium green bell peppers, seeded and chopped
1 can (16 ounces) tomato sauce
1 can (14½ ounces) Mexican-style stewed tomatoes, undrained
3 tablespoons chili powder
1 tablespoon cocoa powder
1 teaspoon ground cumin
½ teaspoon salt
2½ cups hot cooked rice
   Shredded cheese and ripe olive, avocado and green onion slices (optional)

1. Rinse beans thoroughly in colander under cold running water, removing debris and any blemished beans.

2. Place beans in large bowl; cover with 4 inches of water. Let stand at room temperature overnight.

3. Drain beans. Combine beans, chicken broth and garlic in large heavy saucepan. Bring to a boil over high heat. Reduce heat to low; simmer, covered, 1 hour.

4. Add corn, bell peppers, tomato sauce, tomatoes with juice, chili powder, cocoa powder, cumin and salt to bean mixture. Cover partially; simmer 45 minutes or until beans are tender and mixture is thick.

5. Spoon rice into bowls; top with chili. Serve with cheese, olives, avocado and onions, if desired.

Makes 10 servings

Quick-Soak Method: Place sorted dried beans in large saucepan; cover with 4 inches of water. Bring to a boil over high heat. Uncover pan; boil 2 minutes. Remove pan from heat; cover. Let stand 1 hour; then rinse and drain beans. Cook beans as directed.

Nutrients per Serving: 1 bowl Chili with ¼ cup cooked rice (¹⁄₁₀ of total recipe) without cheese, olives, avocado and onions

Calories: 325, Calories from Fat: 10%, Total Fat: 4g, Saturated Fat: 1g, Cholesterol: 14mg, Sodium: 631mg, Carbohydrate: 59g, Dietary Fiber: 13g, Protein: 18g
Dietary Exchanges: 3 Starch, 1½ Vegetable, 1 Lean Meat

Turkey and Black Bean Soup

1 can (14.5 ounces) HUNT'S® Diced Tomatoes with Roasted Garlic
2 cans (14½ ounces each) low fat and low sodium chicken broth
1 can (15 ounces) black beans, rinsed and drained
1 cup frozen whole kernel corn
1 teaspoon oregano leaves, crushed
¼ teaspoon ground cumin
6 ounces fully cooked reduced fat smoked turkey sausage, halved lengthwise and thinly sliced.

In medium saucepan combine Hunt's® Tomatoes and *remaining* ingredients *except* sausage. Bring to a boil. Reduce heat; simmer, uncovered, for 3 minutes. Stir in sausage; heat through.   *Makes 6 (1-cup) servings*

Nutrients per Serving: 1 cup Soup

Calories: 159, Calories from Fat: 19%, Total Fat: 4g, Saturated Fat: 1g, Cholesterol: 32mg, Sodium: 867mg, Carbohydrate: 20g, Dietary Fiber: 4g, Protein: 13g
Dietary Exchanges: 1 Starch, 1 Vegetable, 1 Lean Meat

Chunky Chicken Stew

1 teaspoon olive oil
1 small onion, chopped
1 cup thinly sliced carrots
1 cup fat-free reduced-sodium chicken broth
1 can (14½ ounces) no-salt-added diced tomatoes, undrained
1 cup diced cooked chicken breast
3 cups sliced kale or baby spinach leaves

1. Heat oil in large saucepan over medium-high heat. Add onion; cook and stir about 5 minutes or until golden brown, stirring occasionally. Stir in carrots, then broth; bring to a boil.

2. Reduce heat and simmer, uncovered, 5 minutes. Add tomatoes; simmer 5 minutes or until carrots are tender. Add chicken; heat through. Add kale, stirring until kale is wilted. Simmer 1 minute. Ladle into soup bowls.

Makes 2 servings

Nutrients per Serving: 1 bowl Soup (½ of total recipe)

Calories: 274, Calories from Fat: 21%, Total Fat: 6g, Saturated Fat: 1g, Cholesterol: 0mg, Sodium: 209mg, Carbohydrate: 25g, Dietary Fiber: 7g, Protein: 30g
Dietary Exchanges: 4½ Vegetable, 3 Lean Meat

Hearty Tortilla Chip Soup

Stove Top Directions: Bring 2 tablespoons broth to a boil in 3-quart saucepan over medium-high heat. Add onion, carrots and garlic; cook and stir about 5 minutes until vegetables are tender. Finely crush half the tortilla chips. Add crushed chips, remaining broth, water, salsa and tomato paste; stir well. Cook over medium heat until soup comes to a boil. Reduce heat to low; simmer 5 minutes. Serve as directed.

Nutrients per Serving: 1 bowl Soup (⅛ of total recipe)

Calories: 183, Calories from Fat: 20%, Total Fat: 4g, Saturated Fat: 2g, Cholesterol: 10mg, Sodium: 337mg, Carbohydrate: 25g, Dietary Fiber: 3g, Protein: 11g

Dietary Exchanges: 1 Starch, 2 Vegetable, ½ Lean Meat, ½ Fat

Spinach Salad with Hot Apple Dressing

6 strips turkey bacon
¾ cup apple cider
2 tablespoons brown sugar
1 tablespoon plus 1 teaspoon rice wine vinegar
¼ teaspoon black pepper
6 cups washed and torn spinach
2 cups sliced mushrooms
1 medium tomato, cut into wedges
½ cup thinly sliced red onion

1. Heat medium nonstick skillet over medium heat until hot. Add bacon and cook 2 to 3 minutes per side or until crisp; remove from pan. Coarsely chop 3 pieces; set aside. Finely chop remaining 3 pieces; return to skillet. Add apple cider, sugar, vinegar and pepper. Heat just to a simmer; remove from heat.

2. Combine spinach, mushrooms, tomato and onion in large bowl. Add dressing; toss to coat. Top with reserved bacon.   *Makes 6 servings*

Nutrients per Serving: ⅙ of total recipe

Calories: 95, Calories from Fat: 28%, Total Fat: 3g, Saturated Fat: 1g, Cholesterol: 9mg, Sodium: 256mg, Carbohydrate: 14g, Dietary Fiber: 2g, Protein: 5g

Dietary Exchanges: ½ Fruit, 1½ Vegetable, ½ Fat

Hearty Tortilla Chip Soup

1 cup chopped onion
¾ cup finely chopped carrots
1 clove garlic, minced
6 ounces GUILTLESS GOURMET® Unsalted Baked Tortilla Chips
3 cans (14½ ounces each) low sodium chicken broth, defatted
2 cups water
1 cup GUILTLESS GOURMET® Roasted Red Pepper Salsa
1 can (6 ounces) low sodium tomato paste
1 cup (4 ounces) shredded low fat Monterey Jack cheese

Microwave Directions

Combine onion, carrots and garlic in 3-quart microwave-safe casserole. Cover with vented plastic wrap or lid; microwave on HIGH (100% power) 7 minutes or until vegetables are tender. Finely crush half the tortilla chips. Add crushed chips, broth, water, salsa and tomato paste; stir well. Cover; microwave on HIGH 6 minutes or until soup bubbles. Microwave on MEDIUM (50% power) 5 minutes. To serve, divide remaining tortilla chips and half the cheese among 8 individual soup bowls. Ladle soup over cheese and chips, dividing evenly. Sprinkle with remaining cheese.   *Makes 8 servings*

Grilled Vegetable Pasta Salad

3. Stir dressing into pasta in large bowl. Dice peppers and add to pasta. Slice zucchini crosswise into ½-inch pieces and add to pasta along with tomatoes. Sprinkle with Parmesan and gently stir to combine. Garnish as desired.

Makes 6 servings

Grilled Bell Pepper

1 bell pepper (any color), stemmed, seeded and halved

Grill bell pepper halves skin-side-down on covered grill over medium to hot coals 15 to 25 minutes or until skin is charred, without turning. Remove from grill and place in plastic bag until cool enough to handle, about 10 minutes. Remove skin with paring knife and discard.

Nutrients per Serving: ⅙ of total recipe (without garnish)

Calories: 118, Calories from Fat: 24%, Total Fat: 5g, Saturated Fat: 1g, Cholesterol: 1mg, Sodium: 56mg, Carbohydrate: 16g, Dietary Fiber: 2g, Protein: 5g

Dietary Exchanges: 1 Starch, 1 Vegetable, 1 Fat

Grilled Vegetable Pasta Salad

1 tablespoon plus 1 teaspoon olive oil, divided
1 tablespoon plus 2 teaspoons fresh lemon juice, divided
1 tablespoon plus 1 teaspoon Dijon mustard
1 tablespoon capers, drained and rinsed (optional)
2 teaspoons minced fresh tarragon *or* ½ teaspoon dried tarragon leaves
2 yellow Grilled Bell Peppers (recipe follows)
2 small (8 ounces) green zucchini, halved lengthwise
½ pint (6 ounces) cherry tomatoes
6 ounces uncooked rotini, cooked and drained
2 tablespoons grated Parmesan cheese

1. Prepare wooden skewers by soaking in water 20 to 30 minutes to keep from burning. To make dressing, whisk together 1 tablespoon oil, 1 tablespoon lemon juice and mustard. Stir in capers, if desired, and tarragon; set aside.

2. Prepare Grilled Bell Peppers. Combine remaining 1 teaspoon oil and 2 teaspoons lemon juice in small bowl. Brush onto zucchini and tomatoes. Grill zucchini on covered grill over medium coals 10 to 13 minutes or until grillmarked and tender, basting and turning once. To grill cherry tomatoes, thread tomatoes onto prepared skewers. Grill on covered grill over medium coals 5 minutes or until blistered and browned, basting and turning once.

Onion Soup with Pasta

Nonstick cooking spray
3 cups sliced onions (about 4 medium)
3 cloves garlic, minced
½ teaspoon sugar
2 cans (14½ ounces each) reduced-sodium beef broth
½ cup uncooked small pasta stars
2 tablespoons dry sherry
¼ teaspoon salt
⅛ teaspoon black pepper
Grated Parmesan cheese (optional)

1. Spray large saucepan with cooking spray; heat over medium heat until hot. Add onions and garlic. Cook, covered, 5 to 8 minutes or until onions are wilted. Stir in sugar; cook about 15 minutes or until onion mixture is very soft and browned.

2. Add broth to saucepan; bring to a boil. Add pasta and simmer, uncovered, 6 to 8 minutes or until tender. Stir in sherry, salt and pepper. Ladle soup into 4 bowls; sprinkle lightly with Parmesan cheese, if desired.

Makes 4 servings

Nutrients per Serving: 1 bowl Soup (¼ of total recipe) without Parmesan cheese

Calories: 141, Calories from Fat: 3%, Total Fat: 1g, Saturated Fat: <1g, Cholesterol: 0mg, Sodium: 201mg, Carbohydrate: 25g, Dietary Fiber: 2g, Protein: 8g

Dietary Exchanges: 1 Starch, 3 Vegetable

Jerk Turkey Salad

6 ounces turkey breast tenderloin
1½ teaspoons Caribbean jerk seasoning
4 cups packaged mixed salad greens
¾ cup sliced peeled cucumber
⅔ cup chopped fresh pineapple
⅔ cup quartered strawberries or raspberries
½ cup slivered peeled jicama or sliced celery
1 green onion, sliced
¼ cup lime juice
3 tablespoons honey

1. Prepare grill for direct grilling. Rub turkey with jerk seasoning.

2. Grill turkey over medium coals 15 to 20 minutes or until turkey is no longer pink in center and juices run clear, turning once. Remove from grill and cool.

3. Cut turkey into bite-size pieces. Toss together greens, turkey, cucumber, pineapple, strawberries, jicama and green onion.

4. Combine lime juice and honey. Toss with greens mixture. Serve immediately.   *Makes 2 servings*

Nutrients per Serving: ½ of total recipe

Calories: 265, Calories from Fat: 6%, Total Fat: 2g,
Saturated Fat: 1g, Cholesterol: 34mg, Sodium: 356mg,
Carbohydrate: 48g, Dietary Fiber: 6g, Protein: 17g
Dietary Exchanges: 2 Fruit, 2 Vegetable, 2 Lean Meat

Sensational Spinach Salad with Orange Poppy Seed Vinaigrette

¼ cup orange juice
3 tablespoons red wine vinegar
2 tablespoons sugar
1 tablespoon olive oil
1 teaspoon grated orange peel
1 teaspoon poppy seeds
¼ teaspoon salt
9 cups packed torn stemmed spinach
1½ cups sliced mushrooms
1 can (15 ounces) chilled mandarin orange segments, drained
1 small red onion, sliced and separated into rings
3 hard-cooked egg whites, coarsely chopped

1. To prepare vinaigrette, whisk orange juice, red wine vinegar, sugar, olive oil, orange peel, poppy seeds and salt in small bowl until well blended; set aside.

2. To prepare salad, combine spinach, mushrooms, orange segments, onion and egg whites in large serving bowl. Pour vinaigrette over spinach mixture just before serving; toss to coat. Serve immediately.   *Makes 4 servings*

Nutrients per Serving: ¼ of total recipe

Calories: 168, Calories from Fat: 23%, Total Fat: 5g,
Saturated Fat: 1g, Cholesterol: 0mg, Sodium: 279mg,
Carbohydrate: 20g, Dietary Fiber: 5g, Protein: 8g
Dietary Exchanges: 1 Fruit, 2 Vegetable, ½ Lean Meat, ½ Fat

Mushroom, Chicken and Spinach Salad

1 tablespoon fat-free margarine
2 cups small mushrooms, cleaned
1 tablespoon white wine (optional)
¼ cup white vinegar or apple cider vinegar
1 red onion, thinly sliced and separated into rings
1 bag (5 ounces) fresh baby spinach
4 small boneless skinless chicken breasts (about 12 ounces), cooked and cut into slices
1 cup sliced water chestnuts, drained and rinsed
2 tablespoons reduced-sodium soy sauce
1 tablespoon peanut oil
1 tablespoon brown sugar substitute

1. Heat margarine in small skillet over medium-low heat until melted. Add mushrooms and wine, if desired, and cook and stir 3 to 4 minutes or until liquid evaporates and mushrooms are tender. Remove skillet from heat; set aside.

2. Pour vinegar over onion rings in shallow bowl; set aside.

3. Arrange spinach on serving platter. Arrange mushrooms over spinach. Drain vinegar from onions; discard vinegar. Arrange onions, chicken and water chestnuts over mushrooms.

4. Whisk together soy sauce, peanut oil and brown sugar substitute in small microwavable bowl. Microwave at MEDIUM (50% power) until warm, about 30 seconds. Drizzle warm dressing over salad; serve immediately.
          Makes 4 servings

Nutrients per Serving: ¼ of total recipe

Calories: 221, Calories from Fat: 28%, Total Fat: 7g,
Saturated Fat: 1g, Cholesterol: 72mg, Sodium: 418mg,
Carbohydrate: 9g, Dietary Fiber: 5g, Protein: 30g
Dietary Exchanges: 2 Vegetable, 3 Lean Meat

Quick Vegetable & Pesto Salad

¼ cup reduced-fat mayonnaise
¼ cup refrigerated pesto sauce
1 tablespoon balsamic vinegar
6 cups assorted fresh vegetables from salad bar, such as sliced mushrooms, shredded carrots, red onion strips, sliced radishes, peas, broccoli florets and bell pepper strips (about 1½ pounds)
   Lettuce leaves

1. Combine mayonnaise, pesto and vinegar in large bowl; stir until well blended.

2. Add vegetables; toss well to coat. Cover and refrigerate 10 minutes. Arrange lettuce leaves on salad plates. Top with vegetable mixture. Chill in refrigerator 30 minutes before serving, if desired.   *Makes 6 (1-cup) servings*

Prep Time: 15 minutes

Nutrients per Serving: 1 cup Salad

Calories: 130 Calories from Fat: 56%, Total Fat: 8g, Saturated Fat: 1g, Cholesterol: 5mg, Sodium: 186mg, Carbohydrate: 11g, Dietary Fiber: 3g, Protein: 4g
Dietary Exchanges: 2 Vegetable, 1½ Fat

Marinated Bean and Vegetable Salad

¼ cup orange juice
3 tablespoons white wine vinegar
1 tablespoon canola or vegetable oil
2 cloves garlic, minced
1 can (15 ounces) Great Northern beans, rinsed and drained
1 can (15 ounces) kidney beans, rinsed and drained
¼ cup coarsely chopped red cabbage
¼ cup chopped red onion
¼ cup chopped green bell pepper
¼ cup chopped red bell pepper
¼ cup sliced celery

1. For dressing, combine orange juice, vinegar, oil and garlic in small jar with tight-fitting lid; shake well.

2. Combine Great Northern beans, kidney beans, cabbage, onion, bell peppers and celery in large bowl. Pour dressing over bean mixture; toss to coat.

3. Refrigerate, covered, 1 to 2 hours to allow flavors to blend. Toss before serving.   *Makes 8 servings*

Nutrients per Serving: ⅛ of total recipe

Calories: 136, Calories from Fat: 14%, Total Fat: 2g, Saturated Fat: <1g, Cholesterol: 0mg, Sodium: 180mg, Carbohydrate: 23g, Dietary Fiber: 3g, Protein: 7g
Dietary Exchanges: 1 Starch, 1½ Vegetable, ½ Fat

Moroccan Lentil & Vegetable Soup

1 tablespoon olive oil
1 cup chopped onion
4 medium cloves garlic, minced
½ cup dried lentils, sorted, rinsed and drained
1½ teaspoons ground coriander
1½ teaspoons ground cumin
½ teaspoon black pepper
½ teaspoon ground cinnamon
3¾ cups fat-free reduced-sodium chicken broth
½ cup chopped celery
½ cup chopped sun-dried tomatoes (not packed in oil)
1 medium yellow summer squash, chopped
½ cup chopped green bell pepper
½ cup chopped fresh parsley
1 cup chopped plum tomatoes
¼ cup chopped fresh cilantro or basil

1. Heat oil in medium saucepan over medium heat. Add onion and garlic; cook 4 to 5 minutes or until onion is tender, stirring occasionally. Stir in lentils, coriander, cumin, black pepper and cinnamon; cook 2 minutes. Add chicken broth, celery and sun-dried tomatoes; bring to a boil over high heat. Reduce heat to low; simmer, covered, 25 minutes.

2. Stir in squash, bell pepper and parsley. Continue cooking, covered, 10 minutes or until lentils are tender.

3. Top with plum tomatoes and cilantro just before serving. *Makes 6 servings*

Nutrients per Serving: 1 bowl Soup (⅙ of total recipe)

Calories: 131, Calories from Fat: 20%, Total Fat: 3g, Saturated Fat: <1g, Cholesterol: 0mg, Sodium: 264mg, Carbohydrate: 20g, Dietary Fiber: 2g, Protein: 8g

Dietary Exchanges: 1 Starch, 1 Vegetable, ½ Fat

Moroccan Lentil & Vegetable Soup

Cioppino

1 quart plus 2 tablespoons water, divided
1 cup dry white wine
2 onions, thinly sliced
1 rib celery, chopped
3 sprigs parsley
1 bay leaf
¾ pound ocean perch or snapper fillets
1 can (14½ ounces) whole peeled tomatoes, undrained
1 tablespoon tomato paste
1 clove garlic, minced
1 teaspoon dried oregano leaves
1 teaspoon salt
½ teaspoon sugar
⅛ teaspoon black pepper
6 to 8 hard-shell clams, scrubbed and soaked
1 pound fresh halibut or haddock fillets, skinned and cut into 1-inch pieces
2 large potatoes, peeled and chopped
2 large ripe tomatoes, seeded and chopped
½ pound fresh medium shrimp, peeled and deveined
2 tablespoons chopped fresh parsley

1. To make fish stock, combine 1 quart water, wine, onions, celery, parsley sprigs and bay leaf in 6-quart stockpot or Dutch oven. Bring to a boil over high heat; reduce heat to low. Add perch; uncover and gently simmer 20 minutes.

2. Strain fish stock through sieve into large bowl. Remove perch to plate with slotted spatula; set aside. Discard onions, celery, parsley sprigs and bay leaf.

3. Return stock to stockpot; press canned tomatoes with juice through sieve into stockpot. Discard seeds. Stir in tomato paste, garlic, oregano, salt, sugar and pepper. Simmer, uncovered, over medium-low heat 20 minutes.

4. Combine clams and remaining 2 tablespoons water in large saucepan or stockpot. Cover and cook over medium heat 5 to 10 minutes or until clams open; remove clams immediately as they open. Discard any clams with unopened shells. Rinse clams; set aside.

5. Add halibut, potatoes and fresh tomatoes to soup mixture in stockpot. Bring to a boil over high heat; reduce heat to medium-low. Cover and cook 12 to 15 minutes or until potatoes are fork-tender. Add shrimp to soup mixture in stockpot.

6. Cook over medium heat 1 to 2 minutes or just until shrimp turn opaque and are cooked through. Flake reserved perch with fork; stir perch, reserved clams and chopped parsley into soup. Garnish, if desired. Serve immediately.   *Makes 6 to 8 servings (about 10 cups)*

Nutrients per Serving: 1 bowl Cioppino (⅙ of total recipe) without garnish

Calories: 295, Calories from Fat: 12%, Total Fat: 4g, Saturated Fat: 1g, Cholesterol: 110mg, Sodium: 674mg, Carbohydrate: 20g, Dietary Fiber: 3g, Protein: 38g

Dietary Exchanges: 1 Starch, 1 Vegetable, 4 Lean Meat

Hearty White Bean Soup

2⅔ cups water, divided
1 can (15 ounces) Great Northern beans or navy beans, rinsed and drained
1 cup chopped carrots
1 cup chopped green bell pepper
1 cup fat-free reduced-sodium chicken broth
½ cup chopped celery
2 tablespoons chopped fresh thyme *or* 2 teaspoons dried thyme leaves, crushed
2 tablespoons chopped fresh marjoram *or* 2 teaspoons dried marjoram leaves, crushed
½ teaspoon ground cumin
¼ teaspoon black pepper
3 tablespoons all-purpose flour
⅔ cup (about 3 ounces) shredded reduced-fat Swiss or Cheddar cheese

1. Combine 2⅓ cups water, beans, carrots, bell pepper, broth, celery, thyme, marjoram, cumin and black pepper in 3-quart saucepan. Bring to a boil over high heat. Reduce heat to medium-low. Cover; simmer 20 to 25 minutes or until vegetables are tender, stirring occasionally.

2. Combine remaining ⅓ cup water and flour in small bowl. Stir into mixture in saucepan. Cook and stir over medium heat until mixture boils and thickens. Cook and stir 1 minute more.

3. Ladle soup into 4 bowls. Sprinkle with cheese.
Makes 4 servings

Nutrients per Serving: 1 bowl Soup (¼ of total recipe)

Calories: 207, Calories from Fat: 14%, Total Fat: 3g, Saturated Fat: <1g, Cholesterol: 0mg, Sodium: 721mg, Carbohydrate: 35g, Dietary Fiber: 9g, Protein: 8g
Dietary Exchanges: 2 Starch, 1 Vegetable, ½ Fat

Chicken, Tortellini & Roasted Vegetable Salad

Sun-Dried Tomato & Basil Vinaigrette (recipe follows)
3 cups whole medium mushrooms
2 cups cubed zucchini
2 cups cubed eggplant
¾ cup red onion wedges (about 1 medium)
Olive oil-flavored nonstick cooking spray
1½ packages (9-ounce-size) reduced-fat cheese tortellini
6 cups bite-size pieces leaf lettuce and arugula
1 pound boneless skinless chicken breasts, cooked and cut into 1½-inch pieces

1. Prepare Sun-Dried Tomato & Basil Vinaigrette. Preheat oven to 425°F.

2. Place mushrooms, zucchini, eggplant and onion in 15×10-inch jelly-roll pan. Spray generously with cooking spray; toss to coat. Bake 20 to 25 minutes or until vegetables are browned. Cool to room temperature.

3. Meanwhile, cook tortellini according to package directions; drain. Cool to room temperature.

4. Combine vegetables, tortellini, lettuce and chicken in large bowl. Drizzle with vinaigrette; toss to coat.

Makes 8 servings

Sun-Dried Tomato & Basil Vinaigrette

4 sun-dried tomato halves, not packed in oil
Boiling water
½ cup fat-free reduced-sodium chicken broth
2 tablespoons finely chopped fresh basil *or* 2 teaspoons dried basil leaves
2 tablespoons olive oil
2 tablespoons lemon juice
2 tablespoons water
1 clove garlic, minced
¼ teaspoon salt
¼ teaspoon black pepper

1. Place tomatoes in small bowl. Cover with boiling water. Let stand 5 to 10 minutes or until soft. Drain well; chop.

2. In small jar with tight-fitting lid, combine tomatoes and remaining ingredients; shake well. Chill until ready to use; shake before using.

Makes about 1 cup

Nutrients per Serving: ⅛ of total recipe (with 2 tablespoons Vinaigrette)

Calories: 210, Calories from Fat: 27%, Total Fat: 7g, Saturated Fat: 1g, Cholesterol: 31mg, Sodium: 219mg, Carbohydrate: 24g, Dietary Fiber: 3g, Protein: 16g

Dietary Exchanges: 1 Starch, 2 Vegetable, 1½ Lean Meat, ½ Fat

Italian Bread Salad

3 slices (½-inch-thick) day-old whole wheat bread
½ cup low-fat buttermilk
1 small clove garlic, minced
1 tablespoon minced fresh dill *or* 1 teaspoon dried dill weed
1½ teaspoons onion powder
¼ teaspoon black pepper
2 large tomatoes, cored and cut into 1-inch cubes
1 small cucumber, peeled, cut into halves, seeded and thinly sliced
1 small rib celery, thinly sliced
2 tablespoons minced fresh parsley
⅛ teaspoon salt

1. Preheat oven to 400°F. Cut bread into 1-inch pieces. Place on baking sheet; bake 5 to 7 minutes or until lightly toasted and dry, stirring occasionally. Remove from pan; let cool.

2. For dressing, combine buttermilk, garlic, dill, onion powder and pepper in small jar with tight-fitting lid; shake well. Let stand 15 minutes to allow flavors to blend.

3. Combine tomatoes, cucumber, celery and parsley in large bowl. Sprinkle with salt; toss well. Just before serving, toss toasted bread with vegetables. Shake dressing; pour over salad and toss to coat. Serve immediately.

Makes 4 servings

Nutrients per Serving: ¼ of total recipe

Calories: 92, Calories from Fat: 14%, Total Fat: 2g, Saturated Fat: <1g, Cholesterol: 1mg, Sodium: 220mg, Carbohydrate: 17g, Dietary Fiber: 1g, Protein: 4g

Dietary Exchanges: 1 Starch, ½ Vegetable

Chicken & Orzo Soup

Olive oil-flavored nonstick cooking spray
3 ounces boneless skinless chicken breast, cut into bite-size pieces
1 can (14½ ounces) fat-free reduced-sodium chicken broth
1 cup water
⅔ cup shredded carrot
⅓ cup sliced green onion
¼ cup uncooked orzo pasta
1 teaspoon grated fresh ginger
⅛ teaspoon ground turmeric
2 teaspoons lemon juice
Dash black pepper
Sliced green onions (optional)

1. Spray medium saucepan with cooking spray. Heat over medium-high heat. Add chicken. Cook and stir 2 to 3 minutes or until no longer pink. Remove from saucepan and set aside.

2. In same saucepan, combine broth, water, carrot, onion, orzo, ginger and turmeric. Bring to a boil. Reduce heat and simmer, covered, 8 to 10 minutes or until orzo is tender. Stir in chicken and lemon juice; cook until hot. Season to taste with pepper.

3. Ladle into 2 serving bowls. Sprinkle with green onions, if desired. *Makes 2 servings*

Nutrients per Serving: 1 bowl Soup (½ of total recipe) without green onions

Calories: 176, Calories from Fat: 8%, Total Fat: 2g, Saturated Fat: <1g, Cholesterol: 26mg, Sodium: 182mg, Carbohydrate: 21g, Dietary Fiber: 2g, Protein: 18g

Dietary Exchanges: 1 Starch, 1 Vegetable, 1½ Lean Meat

Chicken & Orzo Soup

Garlic Lovers' Chicken Caesar Salad

Dressing
1 can (10¾ ounces) reduced-fat condensed cream of chicken soup, undiluted
½ cup fat-free reduced-sodium chicken broth
¼ cup balsamic vinegar
¼ cup fat-free shredded Parmesan cheese, divided
3 cloves garlic, minced
1 tablespoon reduced-sodium Worcestershire sauce
¼ teaspoon black pepper

Salad
2 heads romaine lettuce, torn into 2-inch pieces
4 grilled boneless skinless chicken breasts (about 1 pound), cut into 2-inch strips
½ cup fat-free herb-seasoned croutons

1. Combine soup, chicken broth, vinegar, 2 tablespoons Parmesan cheese, garlic, Worcestershire sauce and pepper in food processor or blender; process until smooth.

2. Combine lettuce and 1 cup dressing in large salad bowl; toss well to coat. Top with chicken and croutons; sprinkle with remaining 2 tablespoons cheese.

Makes 8 servings

Nutrients per Serving: ⅛ of total recipe

Calories: 132, Calories from Fat: 15%, Total Fat: 2g, Saturated Fat: 1g, Cholesterol: 40mg, Sodium: 185mg, Carbohydrate: 10g, Dietary Fiber: 1g, Protein: 17g

Dietary Exchanges: ½ Starch, 2 Lean Meat

Golden Tomato Soup

4 teaspoons reduced-calorie margarine
1 cup chopped onion
2 cloves garlic, coarsely chopped
½ cup chopped carrot
¼ cup chopped celery
8 medium Florida tomatoes, blanched, peeled, seeded and chopped
6 cups chicken broth
¼ cup uncooked rice
2 tablespoons tomato paste
1 tablespoon Worcestershire sauce
½ teaspoon dried thyme leaves, crushed
¼ to ½ teaspoon ground black pepper
5 drops hot pepper sauce

Melt margarine in large Dutch oven over medium-high heat. Add onion and garlic; cook and stir 1 to 2 minutes or until onion is tender. Add carrot and celery; cook and stir 7 to 9 minutes or until tender, stirring frequently. Stir in tomatoes, broth, rice, tomato paste, Worcestershire sauce, thyme, black pepper and hot pepper sauce. Reduce heat to low; cook about 30 minutes, stirring frequently.

Remove from heat. Let cool about 10 minutes. In food processor or blender, process soup in small batches until smooth. Return soup to Dutch oven; simmer 3 to 5 minutes or until heated through. Garnish as desired.

Makes 8 servings

Favorite recipe from *Florida Tomato Committee*

Nutrients per Serving: 1 bowl Soup (⅛ of total recipe) without garnish

Calories: 96, Calories from Fat: 26%, Total Fat: 3g, Saturated Fat: 1g, Cholesterol: 0mg, Sodium: 830mg, Carbohydrate: 15g, Dietary Fiber: 2g, Protein: 4g

Dietary Exchanges: 1 Starch, ½ Fat

Sweet Potato Bisque

1 pound sweet potatoes, peeled
2 teaspoons margarine
½ cup minced onion
1 teaspoon curry powder
½ teaspoon ground coriander
¼ teaspoon salt
⅔ cup unsweetened apple juice
1 cup low-fat buttermilk
¼ cup water
    Plain low-fat yogurt, for garnish (optional)

1. Bring 2 quarts water and potatoes to a boil in large saucepan over high heat. Cook, uncovered, 40 minutes or until potatoes are fork-tender. Drain; run under cold water until cool enough to handle.

2. Meanwhile, melt margarine in small saucepan over medium heat. Add onion; cook and stir 2 minutes. Stir in curry, coriander and salt; cook and stir about 45 seconds. Remove saucepan from heat; stir in apple juice. Set aside until potatoes have cooled.

3. Cut potatoes into pieces. Combine potatoes, buttermilk and onion mixture in food processor or blender; process until smooth. Pour soup back into large saucepan; stir in ¼ cup water to thin to desired consistency. (If soup is too thick, add 1 to 2 more tablespoons water.) Cook and stir over medium heat until heated through. Do not boil. Garnish each serving with dollop of yogurt, if desired.

Makes 4 servings

Nutrients per Serving: 1 bowl Bisque (¼ of total recipe) without yogurt

Calories: 160, Calories from Fat: 15%, Total Fat: 3g, Saturated Fat: 1g, Cholesterol: 2mg, Sodium: 231mg, Carbohydrate: 31g, Dietary Fiber: 4g, Protein: 4g

Dietary Exchanges: 1½ Starch, ½ Fruit, ½ Fat

Egg Drop Soup

2 cans (14½ ounces each) fat-free reduced-sodium chicken broth
1 tablespoon reduced-sodium soy sauce
2 teaspoons cornstarch
½ cup cholesterol-free egg substitute
¼ cup thinly sliced green onions

1. Bring broth to a boil over high heat in large saucepan; reduce heat to a simmer.

2. Blend soy sauce and cornstarch in cup until smooth; stir into broth. Cook and stir 2 minutes or until soup boils and thickens slightly.

3. Stirring constantly in one direction, slowly pour egg substitute in thin stream into soup.

4. Ladle into 4 soup bowls. Sprinkle with onions.

Makes 4 servings

Nutrients per Serving: about ¾ cup Soup

Calories: 45, Calories from Fat: 7%, Total Fat: <1g, Saturated Fat: <1g, Cholesterol: 0mg, Sodium: 243mg, Carbohydrate: 3g, Dietary Fiber: <1g, Protein: 7g

Dietary Exchanges: 1 Lean Meat

Vietnamese Beef Soup

discard. Meanwhile, place rice noodles in large bowl and cover with warm water; let stand until pliable, about 20 minutes.

2. Slice beef across grain into very thin strips. Drain noodles. Place noodles and carrots in simmering broth; cook 2 to 3 minutes or until noodles are tender. Add beef and bean sprouts; cook 1 minute or until beef is no longer pink.

3. Remove from heat; stir in red onion, cilantro, basil and jalapeño peppers. To serve, lift noodles from soup with fork and evenly place in bowls. Ladle remaining ingredients and broth evenly over noodles. *Makes 6 servings*

Nutrients per Serving: 1 bowl Soup (⅙ of total recipe)

Calories: 180, Calories from Fat: 15%, Total Fat: 3g, Saturated Fat: 1g, Cholesterol: 32mg, Sodium: 800mg, Carbohydrate: 23g, Dietary Fiber: 1g, Protein: 16g

Dietary Exchanges: 1 Starch, 1 Vegetable, 1½ Lean Meat

Vietnamese Beef Soup

¾ pound boneless lean beef, such as sirloin or round steak
3 cups water
1 can (14½ ounces) beef broth
1 can (10½ ounces) condensed consommé
2 tablespoons reduced-sodium soy sauce
2 tablespoons minced fresh ginger
1 cinnamon stick (3 inches long)
4 ounces rice noodles (rice sticks), about ⅛ inch wide
½ cup thinly sliced or julienned carrots
2 cups fresh mung bean sprouts
1 small red onion, halved and thinly sliced
½ cup chopped fresh cilantro
½ cup chopped fresh basil
2 jalapeño peppers,* stemmed, seeded and minced, *or* 1 to 3 teaspoons Chinese chili sauce or paste

Jalapeño peppers can sting and irritate the skin; wear rubber gloves when handling peppers and do not touch eyes. Wash hands after handling peppers.

1. Place beef in freezer 45 minutes or until firm. Meanwhile, combine water, beef broth, consommé, soy sauce, ginger and cinnamon stick in large saucepan; bring to a boil over high heat. Reduce heat to low; simmer, covered, 20 to 30 minutes. Remove cinnamon stick;

Pineapple Boats with Citrus Creme

1 large DOLE® Fresh Pineapple
1 DOLE® Banana, peeled, sliced
1 orange, peeled, sliced
1 apple, cored, sliced
1 DOLE® Pear, cored, sliced
1 cup seedless DOLE® Grapes (red and green)
Citrus Creme
1 cup plain nonfat yogurt
2 tablespoons brown sugar
1 tablespoon minced crystallized ginger, optional
1 teaspoon grated orange peel
1 teaspoon grated lime peel

• Cut pineapple in half lengthwise through the crown. Cut fruit from shells, leaving shells intact. Core and chunk fruit.

• Combine pineapple chunks with remaining fruit. Spoon into pineapple boats.

• Combine all ingredients for Citrus Creme. Serve with pineapple boats. *Makes 8 servings*

Prep Time: 20 minutes

Nutrients per Serving: ⅛ of total recipe

Calories: 117, Calories from Fat: 5%, Total Fat: 1g, Saturated Fat: <1g, Cholesterol: 1mg, Sodium: 26mg, Carbohydrate: 28g, Dietary Fiber: 3g, Protein: 3g

Dietary Exchanges: 2 Fruit

Thai Beef Salad

8 ounces beef flank steak
¼ cup reduced-sodium soy sauce
2 jalapeño peppers,* finely chopped
2 tablespoons packed brown sugar
1 clove garlic, minced
½ cup lime juice
6 green onions, thinly sliced
4 carrots, diagonally cut into thin slices
½ cup finely chopped fresh cilantro
4 romaine lettuce leaves

*Jalapeño peppers can sting and irritate the skin; wear rubber gloves when handling peppers and do not touch eyes. Wash hands after handling peppers.

1. Place flank steak in resealable plastic food storage bag. Combine soy sauce, jalapeños, brown sugar and garlic in small bowl; mix well. Pour mixture over flank steak.

2. Close bag securely; turn to coat steak. Marinate in refrigerator 2 hours.

3. Preheat broiler. Drain steak; discard marinade. Place steak on rack of broiler pan. Broil 4 inches from heat about 4 minutes per side or until desired doneness. Remove from heat; let stand 15 minutes.

4. Thinly slice steak across grain. Toss with lime juice, green onions, carrots and cilantro in large bowl. Serve salad immediately over lettuce leaves. Garnish with chives and radish flowers, if desired.   *Makes 4 servings*

Thai Beef Salad

Nutrients per Serving: ¼ of total recipe (without garnish)

Calories: 141, Calories from Fat: 26%, Total Fat: 4g, Saturated Fat: 2g, Cholesterol: 27mg, Sodium: 238mg, Carbohydrate: 14g, Dietary Fiber: 3g, Protein: 13g

Dietary Exchanges: 2 Vegetable, 1½ Lean Meat

Quick Tuscan Bean, Tomato and Spinach Soup

2 cans (14½ ounces each) diced tomatoes with onions, undrained
1 can (14½ ounces) fat-free reduced-sodium chicken broth
2 teaspoons sugar
2 teaspoons dried basil leaves
¾ teaspoon reduced-sodium Worcestershire sauce
1 can (15 ounces) small white beans, rinsed and drained
3 ounces fresh baby spinach leaves or chopped spinach leaves, stems removed
2 teaspoons extra-virgin olive oil

1. Combine tomatoes with juice, chicken broth, sugar, basil and Worcestershire sauce in Dutch oven or large saucepan; bring to a boil over high heat. Reduce heat and simmer, uncovered, 10 minutes.

2. Stir in beans and spinach and cook 5 minutes longer or until spinach is tender.

3. Remove from heat; stir in oil just before serving.
Makes 6 (1-cup) servings

Nutrients per Serving: 1 cup Soup

Calories: 148, Calories from Fat: 20%, Total Fat: 4g, Saturated Fat: 1g, Cholesterol: 0mg, Sodium: 1,218mg, Carbohydrate: 26g, Dietary Fiber: 7g, Protein: 9g

Dietary Exchanges: 1½ Starch, 1 Lean Meat

Shrimp and Fish Gumbo

8 ounces fresh or frozen orange roughy or other fish fillets
3¾ cups water, divided
6 ounces deveined shelled raw shrimp
1 cup chopped onion
½ cup chopped green bell pepper
2 cloves garlic, minced
½ teaspoon chicken or fish bouillon granules
2 cans (14½ ounces each) no-salt-added stewed tomatoes, undrained
1½ cups frozen okra, thawed
1 teaspoon dried thyme leaves
1 teaspoon dried savory leaves
¼ teaspoon ground red pepper
⅛ teaspoon black pepper
2 tablespoons cornstarch
2 tablespoons finely chopped reduced-sodium ham
2 cups hot cooked brown rice

1. Remove and discard skin from fish; cut fish into 1-inch pieces.

2. Bring 3 cups water to a boil in medium saucepan over high heat. Add fish and shrimp; cook 3 to 4 minutes or until fish flakes easily when tested with fork and shrimp are opaque. Drain; set aside.

3. Combine onion, bell pepper, additional ½ cup water, garlic and bouillon granules in large saucepan. Bring to a boil over medium-high heat; reduce to medium-low. Cover and simmer 2 to 3 minutes or until vegetables are crisp-tender.

4. Stir in stewed tomatoes with juice, okra, thyme, savory, red pepper and black pepper. Return to a boil; reduce heat. Simmer, uncovered, 3 to 5 minutes or until okra is tender.

5. Combine remaining ¼ cup water and cornstarch in small bowl. Stir into mixture in saucepan. Cook and stir over medium heat until mixture boils and thickens. Cook and stir 2 minutes more. Add fish, shrimp and ham; heat through. Serve over rice. *Makes 4 servings*

Nutrients per Serving: ¼ of Gumbo with ½ cup cooked rice

Calories: 338, Calories from Fat: 17%, Total Fat: 7g,
Saturated Fat: 1g, Cholesterol: 77mg, Sodium: 274mg,
Carbohydrate: 49g, Dietary Fiber: 7g, Protein: 22g
Dietary Exchanges: 2 Starch, 3 Vegetable, 2 Lean Meat

Summer Minestrone

Olive oil-flavored nonstick cooking spray
2 carrots, sliced
1 cup halved green beans
½ cup sliced celery
½ cup thinly sliced leek
2 cloves garlic, minced
1 tablespoon fresh sage *or* 1 teaspoon dried sage leaves
1 tablespoon fresh oregano *or* 1 teaspoon dried oregano leaves
3 cans (14½ ounces each) fat-free reduced-sodium chicken broth
1 zucchini, halved lengthwise and cut into ½-inch-thick slices
1 cup quartered mushrooms
8 ounces cherry tomatoes, halved
¼ cup minced fresh parsley
3 ounces uncooked small rotini
Salt (optional)
Black pepper (optional)
8 teaspoons grated Parmesan cheese

1. Spray large saucepan with cooking spray. Heat over medium heat until hot. Add carrots, green beans, celery, leek, garlic, sage and oregano. Cook and stir 3 to 5 minutes.

2. Add chicken broth to saucepan; bring to a boil. Reduce heat and simmer about 5 minutes or until vegetables are just crisp-tender.

3. Add zucchini, mushrooms, tomatoes and parsley; bring to a boil. Stir in pasta. Reduce heat and simmer, uncovered, about 8 minutes or until pasta and vegetables are tender. Season to taste with salt and pepper, if desired.

4. Ladle soup into 8 bowls; sprinkle each with 1 teaspoon Parmesan cheese. *Makes 8 servings (about 1 cup each)*

Nutrients per Serving: 1 cup Minestrone (without added salt and pepper)

Calories: 93, Calories from Fat: 9%, Total Fat: 1g,
Saturated Fat: <1g, Cholesterol: 1mg, Sodium: 96mg,
Carbohydrate: 15g, Dietary Fiber: 2g, Protein: 7g
Dietary Exchanges: ½ Starch, 2 Vegetable

SANDWICHES & WRAPS

Turkey Sandwiches with Roasted Bell Peppers

2 large red bell peppers
8 slices whole-grain or millet bread
¼ cup reduced-fat mayonnaise
4 romaine lettuce leaves *or* 8 spinach leaves
8 thin slices red onion
8 ounces thinly sliced skinless roast turkey breast
8 large basil leaves (optional)

1. Preheat broiler. Cut bell peppers into quarters; discard stems and seeds. Place peppers skin-side-up on foil-lined baking sheet. Broil 3 inches from heat 10 minutes or until skin is blackened. Wrap peppers in foil from baking sheet; let stand 10 minutes. Peel and discard skin.

2. Spread 4 bread slices with mayonnaise. Top with lettuce, onion, turkey, peppers and basil, if desired. Top with remaining bread slices. *Makes 4 servings*

Nutrients per Serving: 1 Sandwich

Calories: 282, Calories from Fat: 19%, Total Fat: 7g, Saturated Fat: 1g, Cholesterol: 47mg, Sodium: 282mg, Carbohydrate: 37g, Dietary Fiber: 7g, Protein: 27g
Dietary Exchanges: 2 Starch, 3 Lean Meat

Chicken and Grape Pita Sandwiches

1 pound boneless skinless chicken breasts
½ cup plain nonfat yogurt
¼ cup reduced-fat mayonnaise
2 tablespoons fresh tarragon leaves, minced, *or* 2 teaspoons dried tarragon leaves
2 teaspoons Dijon mustard
2 teaspoons honey
½ teaspoon black pepper
1 cup thinly sliced celery
1 cup red seedless grapes, cut into halves
1 medium head red leaf lettuce, washed
3 (6-inch) rounds pita bread

1. Cut chicken breasts into ½-inch cubes. Bring 1 quart water to a boil in large saucepan. Stir in chicken. Cover; remove from heat. Let stand 6 minutes or until chicken is no longer pink in center. Rinse under cold water until cool; drain well.

2. Meanwhile, stir yogurt, mayonnaise, tarragon, mustard, honey and pepper in large bowl until blended. Add chicken, celery and grapes; stir to coat with dressing. Separate lettuce leaves. Select 6 large leaves and discard stems. Tear or shred remaining leaves.

3. Cut each pita in half crosswise; gently open. Line each half with 1 large lettuce leaf. Add handful of torn leaves and spoon about ⅔ cup chicken mixture into each pita. *Makes 6 servings*

Nutrients per Serving: 1 Sandwich (1 filled half)

Calories: 249, Calories from Fat: 21%, Total Fat: 6g, Saturated Fat: 1g, Cholesterol: 50mg, Sodium: 278mg, Carbohydrate: 28g, Dietary Fiber: 1g, Protein: 22g
Dietary Exchanges: 1 Starch, 2½ Vegetable, 2 Lean Meat

Tangy Italian Chicken Sandwiches

2 cups (8 ounces) chopped cooked chicken or turkey breast
⅓ cup drained bottled hot or mild pickled vegetables (jardinière)
2 ounces reduced-fat provolone cheese slices, diced
¼ cup chopped fresh parsley
3 tablespoons prepared reduced-fat Italian salad dressing
¼ teaspoon dried oregano leaves
4 rounds pita bread
8 leaves romaine or red leaf lettuce

1. Combine chicken, pickled vegetables, cheese, parsley, dressing and oregano in medium bowl; mix well.

2. Cut pitas in half crosswise. Line each half with lettuce leaf; fill with ⅛ of chicken mixture.   *Makes 4 servings*

Nutrients per Serving: 2 Sandwiches (2 filled pita halves)

Calories: 330, Calories from Fat: 20%, Total Fat: 7g, Saturated Fat: 3g, Cholesterol: 53mg, Sodium: 610mg, Carbohydrate: 39g, Dietary Fiber: 6g, Protein: 28g
Dietary Exchanges: 2½ Starch, 2 Lean Meat, ½ Fat

Apple Burgers

1 pound ground turkey breast
1 (16-ounce) jar MOTT'S® Apple Sauce, divided
2 tablespoons finely chopped onion
2 tablespoons finely chopped red or green bell pepper
¾ teaspoon salt
⅛ teaspoon ground white pepper
6 toasted buns

1. Spray broiler pan with nonstick cooking spray.

2. In large bowl, combine turkey, ½ cup apple sauce, onion, bell pepper, salt and white pepper; mix lightly. Shape mixture into 6 uniform patties. Arrange on prepared broiler pan.

3. Broil, 4 inches from heat, 5 minutes on each side or until lightly browned and no longer pink in center. Top each burger with remaining apple sauce; serve on buns. Refrigerate leftovers.   *Makes 6 servings*

Nutrients per Serving: 1 Apple Burger with bun

Calories: 238, Calories from Fat: 12%, Total Fat: 3g, Saturated Fat: 1g, Cholesterol: 30mg, Sodium: 586mg, Carbohydrate: 31g, Dietary Fiber: 2g, Protein: 21g
Dietary Exchanges: 2 Starch, 2 Lean Meat

Italian Meatball Subs

Nonstick cooking spray
½ cup chopped onion
3 teaspoons finely chopped garlic, divided
1 can (14½ ounces) Italian-style crushed tomatoes, undrained
2 bay leaves
2½ teaspoons dried basil leaves, divided
2 teaspoons dried oregano leaves, divided
¾ teaspoon black pepper, divided
¼ teaspoon red pepper flakes
½ pound 95% lean ground beef
⅓ cup chopped green onions
⅓ cup dry bread crumbs
¼ cup chopped fresh parsley
1 egg white
2 tablespoons water
½ teaspoon dried marjoram leaves
½ teaspoon ground mustard
4 French bread rolls, warmed and cut in half lengthwise

1. Spray large nonstick saucepan with cooking spray. Heat over medium heat until hot. Add onion and 2 teaspoons garlic. Cook and stir 5 minutes or until onion is tender.

2. Add tomatoes with juice, bay leaves, 2 teaspoons basil, 1 teaspoon oregano, ½ teaspoon black pepper and red pepper flakes; cover. Simmer 30 minutes, stirring occasionally. Remove and discard bay leaves.

3. Combine beef, green onions, bread crumbs, parsley, egg white, water, remaining 1 teaspoon garlic, ½ teaspoon basil, 1 teaspoon oregano, ¼ teaspoon black pepper, marjoram and mustard in medium bowl until well blended. Shape into 16 small meatballs.

4. Spray large nonstick skillet with cooking spray. Heat over medium heat until hot. Add meatballs. Cook 5 minutes or until meatballs are no longer pink in centers, turning occasionally.

5. Add meatballs to tomato sauce. Cook 5 minutes, stirring occasionally.

6. Place 4 meatballs in each roll. Spoon additional sauce over meatballs. Serve immediately.   *Makes 4 servings*

Nutrients per Serving: 1 Sub (with 4 Meatballs)

Calories: 282, Calories from Fat: 30%, Total Fat: 9g, Saturated Fat: 3g, Cholesterol: 35mg, Sodium: 497mg, Carbohydrate: 32g, Dietary Fiber: 1g, Protein: 18g
Dietary Exchanges: 2 Starch, 1 Vegetable, 2 Lean Meat

Meatball Grinders

¼ cup chopped onion
1 can (15 ounces) diced tomatoes, drained and juices reserved
1 can (8 ounces) no-salt-added tomato sauce
2 tablespoons tomato paste
1 teaspoon dried Italian seasoning
1 pound ground chicken
½ cup fresh whole wheat or white bread crumbs (1 slice bread)
1 egg white, lightly beaten
3 tablespoons finely chopped fresh parsley
2 cloves garlic, minced
¼ teaspoon salt
⅛ teaspoon black pepper
  Nonstick cooking spray
4 small hard rolls, split
2 tablespoons grated Parmesan cheese

Slow Cooker Directions

1. Combine onion, diced tomatoes, ½ cup reserved juice, tomato sauce, tomato paste and Italian seasoning in slow cooker. Cover and cook on LOW 3 to 4 hours or until onions are soft.

2. Halfway through cooking time, prepare meatballs. Combine chicken, bread crumbs, egg white, parsley, garlic, salt and pepper in medium bowl. With wet hands, form mixture into 12 to 16 meatballs. Spray medium nonstick skillet with cooking spray; heat over medium heat until hot. Add meatballs; cook about 8 to 10 minutes or until well browned on all sides. Remove meatballs to slow cooker; cook on LOW 1 to 2 hours or until meatballs are no longer pink in centers and are heated through.

3. Place 3 to 4 meatballs in each roll. Divide sauce evenly; spoon over meatballs. Sprinkle with cheese.

Makes 4 servings

Nutrients per Serving: 1 Grinder sandwich

Calories: 322, Calories from Fat: 16%, Total Fat: 6g, Saturated Fat: 1g, Cholesterol: 41mg, Sodium: 1,076mg, Carbohydrate: 43g, Dietary Fiber: 4g, Protein: 25g

Dietary Exchanges: 2 Starch, 2 Vegetable, 2 Lean Meat

Meatball Grinder

Asian Wraps

  Nonstick cooking spray
8 ounces boneless skinless chicken thighs or breasts, cut into ½-inch pieces
1 teaspoon minced fresh or bottled ginger
1 teaspoon minced fresh or bottled garlic
¼ teaspoon red pepper flakes
¼ cup reduced-sodium teriyaki sauce
4 cups (about 8 ounces) packaged cole slaw mix
½ cup sliced green onions
4 (10-inch) flour tortillas
8 teaspoons no-sugar-added plum fruit spread

1. Spray nonstick wok or large skillet with cooking spray; heat over medium-high heat. Stir-fry chicken 2 minutes. Add ginger, garlic and pepper flakes; stir-fry 2 minutes. Add teriyaki sauce; mix well.* Add cole slaw mix and green onions; stir-fry 4 minutes or until chicken is no longer pink and cabbage is crisp-tender.

2. Spread each tortilla with 2 teaspoons fruit spread; spoon chicken mixture down center of tortillas. Roll up to form wrap.

Makes 4 servings

If sauce is too thick, add up to 2 tablespoons water to reach desired consistency.

Prep Time: 10 minutes
Cook Time: 10 minutes

Nutrients per Serving: 1 Wrap

Calories: 241, Calories from Fat: 24%, Total Fat: 6g, Saturated Fat: 1g, Cholesterol: 34mg, Sodium: 665mg, Carbohydrate: 31g, Dietary Fiber: 3g, Protein: 14g

Dietary Exchanges: 1½ Starch, 2½ Vegetable, 1 Lean Meat, ½ Fat

Broiled Turkey Burger

Egg Salad Sandwiches

1 cup EGG BEATERS® Healthy Real Egg
   Product, hard-cooked and chopped
¼ cup chopped celery
¼ cup chopped onion
2 tablespoons fat-free mayonnaise
12 slices whole wheat bread, divided
6 lettuce leaves
1 large tomato, cut into 6 thin slices

In small bowl, combine hard-cooked Egg Beaters®, celery, onion and mayonnaise. On each of 6 bread slices, place lettuce leaf and tomato slice; top each with about ¼ cup egg salad and remaining bread slice.   *Makes 6 servings*

Prep Time: 20 minutes

Nutrients per Serving: 1 Sandwich

Calories: 270, Calories from Fat: 18%, Total Fat: 6g, Saturated Fat: 1g, Cholesterol: 1mg, Sodium: 704mg, Carbohydrate: 46g, Dietary Fiber: 7g, Protein: 12g

Dietary Exchanges: 3 Starch, 1 Lean Meat

Broiled Turkey Burgers

1 pound ground turkey breast
¼ cup finely chopped green onions
¼ cup finely chopped fresh parsley
2 tablespoons dry red wine
1 teaspoon dried Italian seasoning
¼ teaspoon salt
¼ teaspoon black pepper
4 whole wheat hamburger buns
   Lettuce, grilled pineapple slices and bell
   pepper strips (optional)

1. Preheat broiler. Combine turkey, onions, parsley, wine, Italian seasoning, salt and black pepper in large bowl; mix well. Shape turkey mixture into 4 (¾-inch-thick) burgers.

2. Spray rack of broiler pan with nonstick cooking spray; place burgers on rack. Broil burgers, 4 inches from heat source, 5 to 6 minutes per side or until burgers are no longer pink in centers. Serve on whole wheat buns with lettuce, grilled pineapple slice and bell pepper strips, if desired.   *Makes 4 servings*

Nutrients per Serving: 1 Burger with bun (without toppings)

Calories: 243, Calories from Fat: 12%, Total Fat: 3g, Saturated Fat: 1g, Cholesterol: 74mg, Sodium: 384mg, Carbohydrate: 20g, Dietary Fiber: 0g, Protein: 31g

Dietary Exchanges: 1½ Starch, 4 Lean Meat

Mediterranean Vegetable Sandwiches

1 small eggplant, peeled, halved and cut into
   ¼-inch-thick slices
  Salt
1 small zucchini, halved and cut lengthwise
   into ¼-inch-thick slices
1 green or red bell pepper, sliced
3 tablespoons balsamic vinegar
½ teaspoon garlic powder
2 French bread rolls, halved

1. Place eggplant in non-aluminum colander; lightly sprinkle eggplant with salt. Let stand 30 minutes to drain. Rinse eggplant; pat dry with paper towels.

2. Preheat broiler. Spray rack of broiler pan with nonstick cooking spray. Place vegetables on rack. Broil 4 inches from heat 8 to 10 minutes or until vegetables are browned, turning once.

3. Combine vinegar, ½ teaspoon salt and garlic powder in medium bowl until well blended. Add vegetables; toss to coat. Divide vegetable mixture evenly between rolls. Serve immediately. Garnish as desired.   *Makes 2 servings*

Nutrients per Serving: 1 Sandwich

Calories: 178, Calories from Fat: 10%, Total Fat: 2g, Saturated Fat: <1g, Cholesterol: 0mg, Sodium: 775mg, Carbohydrate: 36g, Dietary Fiber: 1g, Protein: 5g

Dietary Exchanges: 1½ Starch, 3 Vegetable

Grilled Mozzarella & Roasted Red Pepper Sandwich

1 tablespoon reduced-fat olive oil vinaigrette or Italian salad dressing
2 slices (2 ounces) Italian-style sandwich bread
Basil leaves (optional)
⅓ cup roasted red peppers, rinsed, drained and patted dry
2 slices (1 ounce each) part-skim mozzarella or reduced-fat Swiss cheese
Olive oil-flavored nonstick cooking spray

1. Brush dressing on one side of one slice of bread; top with basil, if desired, peppers, cheese and second bread slice. Lightly spray both sides of sandwich with cooking spray.

2. Heat skillet over medium heat until hot. Place sandwich in skillet and grill 4 to 5 minutes on each side or until brown and cheese is melted. Cut in half, if desired.

Makes 1 sandwich

Nutrients per Serving: 1 Sandwich (2 halves)

Calories: 303, Calories from Fat: 29%, Total Fat: 9g, Saturated Fat: 5g, Cholesterol: 25mg, Sodium: 727mg, Carbohydrate: 35g, Dietary Fiber: 2g, Protein: 16g
Dietary Exchanges: 2 Starch, 1 Vegetable, 1 Lean Meat, 1½ Fat

Grilled Veggie Burger

4 frozen veggie burgers
4 slices sweet onion, such as Vidalia
4 slices reduced-fat Swiss cheese

1. Preheat grill for direct cooking. Spray lightly with nonstick cooking spray.

2. Place burgers and onion slices on grill. Grill 5 minutes or until burgers are heated through and onion is soft, turning once.

3. Place cheese slices on burgers; top with onion slices. Serve immediately.

Makes 4 servings

Nutrients per Serving: 1 Cheeseburger with onion slice

Calories: 215, Calories from Fat: 24%, Total Fat: 5g, Saturated Fat: 2g, Cholesterol: 15mg, Sodium: 410mg, Carbohydrate: 8g, Dietary Fiber: 3g, Protein: 32g
Dietary Exchanges: 4 Lean Meat

Black Bean & Rice Burritos

½ cup nonfat cottage cheese
2 tablespoons soft fresh goat cheese
1½ cups cooked brown rice or long-grain rice, kept warm
3 tablespoons minced red onion
3 tablespoons chopped fresh cilantro
¼ teaspoon ground cumin
¼ cup low sodium chicken broth, defatted
8 whole wheat tortillas (6 inches each)
¾ cup GUILTLESS GOURMET® Spicy Black Bean Dip
½ cup (2 ounces) shredded low fat Monterey Jack cheese
3 cups finely shredded lettuce
½ cup GUILTLESS GOURMET® Southwestern Grill Salsa
Fresh cilantro sprigs (optional)

Preheat oven to 350°F. Place cottage and goat cheeses in medium bowl; blend with fork until smooth. Add rice, onion, chopped cilantro and cumin. Mix well; set aside.

Place broth in shallow bowl. Working with 1 tortilla at a time, dip tortilla in broth to moisten each side. Spread 1 heaping tablespoonful bean dip on tortilla, then top with 1 heaping tablespoonful rice mixture. Roll up tortilla and place in 12×8-inch baking dish, seam side down. Repeat with remaining tortillas, bean dip and rice mixture. Cover with foil.

Bake about 25 to 30 minutes or until heated through. Remove foil; top with shredded cheese. Return to oven until cheese melts. To serve, arrange burritos on plate. Top with lettuce and salsa. Garnish with cilantro sprigs, if desired.

Makes 8 burritos

Nutrients per Serving: 1 Burrito (without garnish)

Calories: 224, Calories from Fat: 20%, Total Fat: 5g, Saturated Fat: 2g, Cholesterol: 7mg, Sodium: 425mg, Carbohydrate: 34g, Dietary Fiber: 1g, Protein: 11g
Dietary Exchanges: 2 Starch, 1 Lean Meat, ½ Fat

Garden Tuna Salad

1 can (6 ounces) tuna packed in water, drained
1 medium carrot, chopped
1 rib celery, chopped
½ cup (¼-inch) reduced-fat Monterey Jack
    cheese cubes
¼ cup frozen green peas, thawed and drained
¼ teaspoon dried parsley flakes
⅓ cup prepared reduced-fat Italian salad
    dressing
2 rounds pita bread
    Lettuce
    Tomato slices

1. Place tuna in large bowl; break into chunks. Add carrot, celery, cheese, peas and parsley; toss to blend.

2. Pour dressing over tuna mixture; toss lightly to coat.

3. Cut pitas in half crosswise. Place one piece lettuce and one tomato slice in each pita half. Divide tuna salad evenly among pita halves. *Makes 4 servings*

Nutrients per Serving: 1 sandwich (1 filled pita half)

Calories: 213, Calories from Fat: 23%, Total Fat: 6g,
Saturated Fat: 2g, Cholesterol: 24mg, Sodium: 605mg,
Carbohydrate: 22g, Dietary Fiber: 4g, Protein: 19g
Dietary Exchanges: 1½ Starch, 2 Lean Meat

Lentil Burgers

1 can (14½ ounces) fat-free reduced-sodium
    chicken broth
1 cup dried lentils
1 small carrot, grated
¼ cup coarsely chopped mushrooms
1 egg
¼ cup dry unseasoned bread crumbs
3 tablespoons finely chopped onion
2 to 4 cloves garlic, minced
1 teaspoon dried thyme leaves, crushed
    Nonstick cooking spray
¼ cup plain nonfat yogurt
¼ cup chopped seeded cucumber
¼ teaspoon dried dill weed, crushed
½ teaspoon dried mint leaves, crushed
¼ teaspoon black pepper
⅛ teaspoon salt
    Dash hot pepper sauce

1. Bring chicken broth to a boil in medium saucepan over high heat. Stir in lentils; reduce heat to low. Simmer, covered, about 30 minutes or until lentils are tender and liquid is absorbed. Let cool to room temperature.

2. Place lentils, carrot and mushrooms in food processor or blender; process until finely chopped but not smooth. (Some whole lentils should still be visible.) Remove mixture to large bowl. Stir in egg, bread crumbs, onion, garlic and thyme. Refrigerate, covered, 2 to 3 hours.

3. Shape lentil mixture into 4 (½-inch-thick) patties. Coat large skillet with cooking spray; heat over medium heat. Cook patties over medium-low heat about 10 minutes or until browned on each side.

4. For sauce, combine yogurt, cucumber, dill, mint, black pepper, salt and hot pepper sauce in small bowl. Serve sauce over burgers. *Makes 4 servings*

Nutrients per Serving: 1 Lentil Burger with about 1 tablespoon sauce

Calories: 124, Calories from Fat: 14%, Total Fat: 2g,
Saturated Fat: 1g, Cholesterol: 54mg, Sodium: 166mg,
Carbohydrate: 21g, Dietary Fiber: 1g, Protein: 9g
Dietary Exchanges: ½ Starch, 2½ Vegetable, ½ Lean Meat

Meatless Sloppy Joes

2 cups thinly sliced onions
2 cups chopped green bell peppers
1 can (about 15 ounces) kidney beans, drained
    and mashed
1 can (8 ounces) tomato sauce
2 tablespoons ketchup
2 cloves garlic, finely chopped
1 tablespoon mustard
1 teaspoon chili powder
    Cider vinegar (optional)
2 sandwich rolls, halved

Slow Cooker Directions
Combine all ingredients except rolls in slow cooker. Cover and cook on LOW 5 to 5½ hours or until vegetables are tender. Serve on rolls. *Makes 4 servings*

Nutrients per Serving: 1 sandwich (¼ Sloppy Joe mixture with 1 roll half)

Calories: 241, Calories from Fat: 8%, Total Fat: 2g,
Saturated Fat: <1g, Cholesterol: 0mg, Sodium: 980mg,
Carbohydrate: 48g, Dietary Fiber: 11g, Protein: 10g
Dietary Exchanges: 3 Starch, 1 Vegetable

Smoked Turkey Wraps

Turkey Wraps

- 1 can (14½ ounces) fat-free reduced-sodium chicken broth
- ¾ teaspoon chopped fresh tarragon
- ½ teaspoon minced garlic
  Dash black pepper
- 2 medium carrots, cut into 3×¼-inch strips
- 1 large red bell pepper, cut into ¼-inch strips
- 1 medium onion, halved and thinly sliced
- 5 to 6 green onions or scallions, green part only, sliced in half lengthwise
  Ice water
- ¾ cup water
- 1 package (10 ounces) frozen broccoli spears, thawed
- 10 slices (about 12 ounces) smoked turkey breast

Sauce

- 6 tablespoons no-sugar-added raspberry fruit spread
- 1 tablespoon plus 1 teaspoon water
- 1 teaspoon frozen orange juice concentrate, thawed

1. Combine broth, tarragon, garlic and black pepper in medium saucepan; bring to a boil. Reduce heat and simmer 3 minutes. Add carrots, bell pepper and onion; cook about 7 minutes or until crisp-tender. Remove vegetables with slotted spoon to small bowl; set aside. Add green onions to broth and cook 1 minute or just until soft; remove and drop into ice water. Pat dry with paper towels.

2. Add ¾ cup water to remaining broth and return to a boil. Add broccoli and cook 5 minutes; drain.

3. Take 2 green onion strips and knot ends together so total length is at least 12 inches. Repeat steps with remaining green onions until there are 5 (12-inch) strips.

4. Preheat oven to 350°F. Place 2 turkey slices side by side, with long sides overlapping 1 inch, on top of 1 green onion strip. Arrange ⅕ of broccoli in middle of 2 turkey slices; place ⅕ of vegetable mixture on top of broccoli. Fold turkey edges together over vegetables; tie green onion into double knot. Repeat steps with remaining turkey, green onion strips and vegetables. Place turkey wraps in 13×9-inch baking dish. Bake, covered, 25 to 28 minutes.

5. Meanwhile, heat fruit spread, water and orange juice concentrate in small saucepan, stirring, until smooth. Spoon over wraps.
Makes 5 servings

Nutrients per Serving: 1 Wrap with about 1 tablespoon plus 1 teaspoon Sauce

Calories: 154, Calories from Fat: 8%, Total Fat: 1g, Saturated Fat: <1g, Cholesterol: 24mg, Sodium: 738mg, Carbohydrate: 19g, Dietary Fiber: 3g, Protein: 17g
Dietary Exchanges: 3 Vegetable, 2 Lean Meat

Jamaican Chicken Sandwich

- 1 teaspoon Jerk Seasoning (recipe follows)
- 4 boneless skinless chicken breasts (about 1 pound)
- 2 tablespoons reduced-fat mayonnaise
- 2 tablespoons plain nonfat yogurt
- 1 tablespoon mango chutney
- 4 onion rolls, split and toasted
- 4 lettuce leaves
- 8 slices peeled mango or papaya

1. Prepare Jerk Seasoning. Sprinkle chicken with jerk seasoning and set aside. Spray grid with nonstick cooking spray. Prepare grill for direct cooking.

2. Place chicken on grid, 3 to 4 inches from medium-hot coals. Grill 5 to 7 minutes on each side or until no longer pink in center.

3. Combine mayonnaise, yogurt and chutney in small bowl; spread 1 tablespoonful onto each onion roll.

4. Place chicken on onion roll bottoms; top each with lettuce leaf, 2 slices of fruit and roll top.
Makes 4 servings

Jerk Seasoning

- 1½ teaspoons salt
- 1½ teaspoons ground allspice
- 1 teaspoon sugar
- 1 teaspoon ground thyme leaves
- 1 teaspoon black pepper
- ½ teaspoon garlic powder
- ½ teaspoon ground red pepper
- ¼ teaspoon ground cinnamon
- ¼ teaspoon ground nutmeg

Combine all ingredients in small bowl.

Nutrients per Serving: 1 Sandwich

Calories: 302, Calories from Fat: 23%, Total Fat: 8g, Saturated Fat: 2g, Cholesterol: 72mg, Sodium: 373mg, Carbohydrate: 28g, Dietary Fiber: 1g, Protein: 30g
Dietary Exchanges: 1½ Starch, ½ Fruit, 3 Lean Meat

Shrimp and Black Bean Wraps

4 large flour tortillas
1 tablespoon olive oil
8 ounces small shrimp, peeled and deveined
1 (15-ounce) can black beans, drained
1 large tomato, chopped
2 green onions, sliced
1½ teaspoons TABASCO® brand Pepper Sauce
½ teaspoon salt

Preheat oven to 375°F. Wrap tortillas in foil; place in oven 10 minutes to warm. Heat oil in 10-inch skillet over medium-high heat. Add shrimp; cook and stir until pink. Mash ½ cup beans in medium bowl; stir in remaining beans, shrimp, tomato, green onions, TABASCO® Sauce and salt. To assemble, place ¼ of mixture on each tortilla; roll up tortillas, tucking in sides.   *Makes 4 servings*

Nutrients per Serving: 1 Wrap

Calories: 413, Calories from Fat: 21%, Total Fat: 9g, Saturated Fat: 2g, Cholesterol: 111mg, Sodium: 1,112mg, Carbohydrate: 57g, Dietary Fiber: 7g, Protein: 24g

Dietary Exchanges: 3½ Starch, 1 Vegetable, 2 Lean Meat, ½ Fat

Sub on the Run

2 (2 ounces each) hard rolls, split into halves
4 tomato slices
14 turkey pepperoni slices
2 ounces fat-free oven-roasted turkey breast
¼ cup (1 ounce) shredded part-skim mozzarella or reduced-fat sharp Cheddar cheese
1 cup packaged coleslaw mix or shredded lettuce
¼ medium green bell pepper, thinly sliced (optional)
2 tablespoons prepared fat-free Italian salad dressing

Top each of two bottom halves of rolls with 2 tomato slices, 7 pepperoni slices, half of turkey, 2 tablespoons cheese, ½ cup coleslaw mix and half of bell pepper slices, if desired. Drizzle with salad dressing. Top with roll tops. Cut into halves, if desired.   *Makes 2 servings*

Nutrients per Serving: (1 Sub sandwich)

Calories: 275, Calories from Fat: 21%, Total Fat: 7g, Saturated Fat: 2g, Cholesterol: 47mg, Sodium: 1,050mg, Carbohydrate: 34g, Dietary Fiber: 2g, Protein: 19g

Dietary Exchanges: 1½ Starch, 2 Vegetable, 2 Lean Meat

Shrimp and Black Bean Wrap

Blackened Chicken Salad in Pitas

1 tablespoon paprika
1 teaspoon onion powder
½ teaspoon garlic powder
½ teaspoon dried oregano leaves
½ teaspoon dried thyme leaves
¼ teaspoon salt
¼ teaspoon white pepper
¼ teaspoon ground red pepper
¼ teaspoon black pepper
2 boneless skinless chicken breasts (about 12 ounces)
4 rounds pita bread
1 cup bite-size pieces spinach leaves
2 small tomatoes, cut into 8 slices
8 thin slices cucumber
½ cup prepared reduced-fat ranch dressing

1. Combine paprika, onion powder, garlic powder, oregano, thyme, salt and peppers in small bowl; rub on all surfaces of chicken. Grill chicken on covered grill over medium-hot coals 10 minutes per side or until chicken is no longer pink in center. Cool slightly. Cut into thin strips.

2. Wrap 2 pita bread rounds in paper towels. Microwave at HIGH 20 to 30 seconds or just until warm. Repeat with remaining pita breads.

3. Divide spinach, chicken strips, tomato slices, cucumber slices and ranch dressing among pita breads. Fold edges over and secure with wooden picks. Serve warm.

Makes 4 servings

Nutrients per Serving: 1 Wrap

Calories: 347, Calories from Fat: 22%, Total Fat: 8g, Saturated Fat: 2g, Cholesterol: 50mg, Sodium: 938mg, Carbohydrate: 41g, Dietary Fiber: 3g, Protein: 27g
Dietary Exchanges: 2 Starch, 2 Vegetable, 2½ Lean Meat

Blackened Chicken Salad in Pita

Chicken Phyllo Wraps

Vegetable cooking spray
1 pound ground chicken
1 cup chopped fresh mushrooms
1 medium onion, chopped
3 cups cooked rice (cooked without salt and fat)
1 package (10 ounces) chopped spinach, thawed and well drained
1 cup nonfat low-salt ricotta cheese
1 can (2¼ ounces) sliced black olives, drained
¼ cup pine nuts, toasted*
2 cloves garlic, minced
1 teaspoon ground oregano
1 teaspoon lemon pepper
12 phyllo dough sheets

To toast nuts, place on baking sheet. Bake at 350°F 5 to 7 minutes or until lightly browned.

Coat large skillet with cooking spray; heat over medium-high heat until hot. Add chicken, mushrooms, and onion; cook and stir 2 to 4 minutes or until chicken is no longer pink and vegetables are tender. Reduce heat to medium. Add rice, spinach, ricotta cheese, olives, nuts, garlic, oregano, and lemon pepper; cook and stir 3 to 4 minutes until well blended and thoroughly heated. Working with 1 phyllo sheet at a time, spray 1 sheet with cooking spray; fold sheet in half lengthwise. Place ¾ to 1 cup rice mixture on one end of phyllo strip. Fold left bottom corner over mixture, forming a triangle. Continue folding back and forth into triangle at end of strip. Repeat with remaining phyllo sheets and rice mixture. Place triangles, seam sides down, on baking sheets coated with cooking spray. Coat top of each triangle with cooking spray. Bake at 400°F 15 to 20 minutes or until golden brown. Serve immediately.

Makes 12 servings

Favorite recipe from *USA Rice Federation*

Nutrients per Serving: 1 Wrap

Calories: 214, Calories from Fat: 28%, Total Fat: 7g, Saturated Fat: 1g, Cholesterol: 2mg, Sodium: 246mg, Carbohydrate: 25g, Dietary Fiber: 2g, Protein: 14g
Dietary Exchanges: 2 Starch, 1 Lean Meat, ½ Fat

Moroccan Grilled Turkey with Cucumber Yogurt Sauce

Cucumber Yogurt Sauce

1 cup fat free yogurt
½ cup shredded cucumber
1 teaspoon grated lime peel
1 teaspoon salt
½ teaspoon ground cumin

Combine yogurt, cucumber, lime peel, salt and cumin in medium bowl. Chill.

Nutrients per Serving: 1 sandwich (made with about 2 ounces grilled turkey breast) with about ¼ cup Sauce

Calories: 195, Calories from Fat: 9%, Total Fat: 2g, Saturated Fat: <1g, Cholesterol: 46mg, Sodium: 647mg, Carbohydrate: 20g, Dietary Fiber: 1g, Protein: 23g

Dietary Exchanges: 1 Starch, 2 Lean Meat

Moroccan Grilled Turkey with Cucumber Yogurt Sauce

1 package BUTTERBALL® Fresh Boneless
    Turkey Breast Cutlets
⅓ cup fresh lime juice
2 cloves garlic, minced
½ teaspoon curry powder
½ teaspoon salt
¼ teaspoon ground cumin
¼ teaspoon cayenne pepper
3 large pitas, cut in half*

Pitas may be filled and folded in half.

Prepare grill for medium-direct-heat cooking. Lightly spray unheated grill rack with nonstick cooking spray. Combine lime juice, garlic, curry powder, salt, cumin and cayenne pepper in medium bowl. Dip cutlets in lime juice mixture. Place cutlets on rack over medium-hot grill. Grill 5 to 7 minutes on each side or until meat is no longer pink in center. Place turkey and Cucumber Yogurt Sauce in pitas.
Makes 6 servings

Preparation Time: 20 Minutes

Mediterranean Pita Sandwiches

1 cup plain nonfat yogurt
1 tablespoon chopped fresh cilantro
2 cloves garlic, minced
1 teaspoon lemon juice
1 can (15 ounces) chick-peas, drained and
    rinsed
1 can (14 ounces) cooked artichoke hearts,
    drained, rinsed and coarsely chopped
1½ cups thinly sliced cucumbers, cut into halves
½ cup shredded carrot
½ cup chopped green onions
4 rounds whole wheat pita bread
    Chopped fresh tomatoes (optional)

1. Combine yogurt, cilantro, garlic and lemon juice in small bowl.

2. Combine chick-peas, artichoke hearts, cucumbers, carrot and green onions in medium bowl. Stir in yogurt mixture until well blended.

3. Cut pitas in half crosswise. Divide cucumber mixture among pita halves. Garnish with chopped tomatoes, if desired.
Makes 4 servings

Nutrients per Serving: 2 Sandwiches (2 filled pita halves) without garnish

Calories: 297, Calories from Fat: 9%, Total Fat: 3g, Saturated Fat: 1g, Cholesterol: 1mg, Sodium: 726mg, Carbohydrate: 57g, Dietary Fiber: 9g, Protein: 15g

Dietary Exchanges: 3 Starch, 2½ Vegetable, ½ Fat

Sassy Southwestern Veggie Wraps

½ cup diced zucchini
½ cup diced red or yellow bell pepper
½ cup frozen corn, thawed
1 jalapeño pepper,* seeded and chopped
¾ cup shredded reduced-fat Mexican cheese blend
3 tablespoons prepared salsa or picante sauce
2 (8-inch) fat-free flour tortillas

*Jalapeño peppers can sting and irritate the skin; wear rubber gloves when handling peppers and do not touch eyes. Wash hands after handling peppers.

1. Combine zucchini, bell pepper, corn and jalapeño pepper in small bowl. Stir in cheese and salsa; mix well.

2. Soften tortillas according to package directions. Spoon vegetable mixture down center of tortillas; roll up burrito-style. Serve wraps cold or warm.* Garnish as desired.

Makes 2 servings

*To warm each wrap, cover loosely with plastic wrap and microwave at HIGH 40 to 45 seconds or until cheese is melted.

Nutrients per Serving: 1 Wrap (without garnish)

Calories: 221, Calories from Fat: 27%, Total Fat: 7g, Saturated Fat: 5g, Cholesterol: 19mg, Sodium: 664mg, Carbohydrate: 26g, Dietary Fiber: 8g, Protein: 16g

Dietary Exchanges: 1½ Starch, 1 Vegetable, 1 Lean Meat, ½ Fat

Grilled Vegetable Pitas

1 eggplant (about 1 pound), cut into ½-inch-thick slices
1 large portobello mushroom (5 to 6 ounces)
1 small red bell pepper, quartered
1 small yellow or green bell pepper, quartered
2 (¼-inch-thick) slices large red onion
½ cup prepared low-fat Italian or honey-dijon salad dressing, divided
4 (8-inch) rounds whole wheat or white pita bread
4 ounces reduced-fat shredded Italian cheese blend

1. Brush both sides of eggplant slices, mushroom, bell pepper quarters and onion slices with ⅓ cup dressing. Grill over medium coals, or broil 4 to 5 inches from heat source 4 to 5 minutes per side or until vegetables are crisp-tender. Cut into bite-size pieces. Toss with remaining dressing.

2. Cut pitas in half crosswise; open pockets and fill with vegetable mixture. Evenly sprinkle cheese over top.

Makes 8 servings

Nutrients per Serving: 1 Sandwich (1 filled pita half)

Calories: 202, Calories from Fat: 26%, Total Fat: 6g, Saturated Fat: 2g, Cholesterol: 9mg, Sodium: 412mg, Carbohydrate: 29g, Dietary Fiber: 5g, Protein: 9g

Dietary Exchanges: 1½ Starch, 1 Vegetable, ½ Lean Meat, 1 Fat

Mediterranean Sandwiches

Nonstick cooking spray
1¼ pounds chicken tenders, cut crosswise in half
1 large tomato, cut into bite-size pieces
½ small cucumber, seeded and sliced
½ cup sweet onion slices (about 1 small)
2 tablespoons cider vinegar
1 tablespoon olive oil or vegetable oil
3 teaspoons minced fresh oregano or
   ½ teaspoon dried oregano leaves
2 teaspoons minced fresh mint or ¼ teaspoon dried mint leaves
¼ teaspoon salt
6 rounds whole wheat pita bread
12 lettuce leaves (optional)

1. Spray large nonstick skillet with cooking spray; heat over medium heat until hot. Add chicken; cook and stir 7 to 10 minutes or until browned and no longer pink in center. Cool slightly.

2. Combine chicken, tomato, cucumber and onion in medium bowl. Drizzle with vinegar and oil; toss to coat. Sprinkle with oregano, mint and salt; toss to combine.

3. Cut pitas in half crosswise. Place 1 lettuce leaf in each pita bread half, if desired. Divide chicken mixture evenly; spoon into pita bread halves.

Makes 6 servings

Nutrients per Serving: 2 Sandwiches (2 filled pita halves)

Calories: 242, Calories from Fat: 21%, Total Fat: 6g, Saturated Fat: 1g, Cholesterol: 50mg, Sodium: 353mg, Carbohydrate: 24g, Dietary Fiber: 2g, Protein: 23g

Dietary Exchanges: 1½ Starch, 2½ Lean Meat

Grilled Chicken Breast and Peperonata Sandwiches

1 tablespoon olive oil or vegetable oil
1 medium red bell pepper, cut into strips
1 medium green bell pepper, cut into strips
¾ cup onion slices (about 1 medium onion)
2 cloves garlic, minced
¼ teaspoon salt
¼ teaspoon black pepper
4 boneless skinless chicken breasts (about 1 pound)
4 small French rolls, split and toasted

1. Heat oil in large nonstick skillet over medium heat until hot. Add bell peppers, onion and garlic; cook and stir 5 minutes. Reduce heat to low; cook and stir about 20 minutes or until vegetables are very soft. Sprinkle with salt and black pepper.

2. Grill chicken on covered grill over medium-hot coals 10 minutes on each side or until chicken is no longer pink in center. Or, broil chicken, 6 inches from heat source, 7 to 8 minutes on each side or until chicken is no longer pink in center.

3. Place chicken in rolls. Divide bell pepper mixture evenly; spoon over chicken.   *Makes 4 servings*

Nutrients per Serving: 1 Sandwich

Calories: 321, Calories from Fat: 22%, Total Fat: 8g, Saturated Fat: 2g, Cholesterol: 58mg, Sodium: 497mg, Carbohydrate: 36g, Dietary Fiber: 3g, Protein: 27g

Dietary Exchanges: 2 Starch, 1½ Vegetable, 2½ Lean Meat

TIP Chicken breasts are available in both whole and halved pieces. Recipe references to chicken breasts usually imply breast halves.

Chunky Joes

Nonstick cooking spray
1 pound 95% lean ground beef
1½ cups finely chopped green bell pepper
1 can (14½ ounces) stewed tomatoes
¼ cup water
2 tablespoons tomato paste
1 tablespoon chili powder
1 tablespoon Worcestershire sauce
1 packet sugar substitute
1 teaspoon ground cumin, divided
6 hamburger buns, warmed

1. Lightly coat 12-inch skillet with cooking spray. Heat over high heat until hot. Add beef; cook and stir 3 minutes or until no longer pink. Drain on paper towels; set aside. Wipe out skillet with paper towel.

2. Coat skillet with cooking spray; heat over medium-high heat until hot. Add bell pepper; cook and stir 4 minutes or until just tender. Add tomatoes, water, tomato paste, chili powder, Worcestershire sauce, sugar substitute and ½ teaspoon cumin. Bring to a boil. Reduce heat and simmer, covered, 20 minutes or until thickened.

3. Remove from heat and stir in remaining ½ teaspoon cumin. If thicker consistency is desired, cook 5 minutes longer, uncovered, stirring frequently.

4. Spoon ½ cup mixture onto each bun.

Makes 6 servings

Nutrients per Serving: 1 Chunky Joe sandwich

Calories: 251, Calories from Fat: 18%, Total Fat: 5g, Saturated Fat: 1g, Cholesterol: 39mg, Sodium: 505mg, Carbohydrate: 32g, Dietary Fiber: 4g, Protein: 19g

Dietary Exchanges: 2 Starch, 1 Vegetable, 2 Lean Meat

Grilled Chicken Breast and Peperonata Sandwich ~ 123

Veggie Club Sandwiches

¼ cup reduced-fat mayonnaise
1 clove garlic, minced
⅛ teaspoon dried marjoram leaves
⅛ teaspoon dried tarragon leaves
8 slices Savory Summertime Oat Bread (recipe follows) or whole-grain bread
8 washed leaf lettuce leaves
1 large tomato, thinly sliced
1 small cucumber, thinly sliced
4 slices (1 ounce each) reduced-fat Cheddar cheese
1 medium red onion, thinly sliced and separated into rings
½ cup alfalfa sprouts

1. To prepare mayonnaise spread, combine mayonnaise, garlic, marjoram and tarragon in small bowl. Refrigerate until ready to use.

2. To assemble sandwiches, spread each of 4 bread slices with 1 tablespoon mayonnaise spread. Divide lettuce, tomato, cucumber, cheese, onion and sprouts evenly among bread slices. Top each with bread slice. Cut sandwiches into halves and serve immediately.

Makes 4 sandwiches

Savory Summertime Oat Bread

Nonstick cooking spray
½ cup finely chopped onion
2 cups whole wheat flour
4¼ to 4½ cups all-purpose flour, divided
2 cups uncooked old-fashioned oats
¼ cup sugar
2 packages quick-rising active dry yeast
1½ teaspoons salt
1½ cups water
1¼ cups fat-free (skim) milk
¼ cup margarine
1 cup finely shredded carrots
3 tablespoons dried parsley leaves
1 tablespoon margarine, melted

1. Spray small nonstick skillet with cooking spray; heat over medium heat until hot. Cook and stir onion 3 minutes or until tender. Set aside.

2. Stir together whole wheat flour, 1 cup all-purpose flour, oats, sugar, yeast and salt in large mixer bowl. Heat water, milk and ¼ cup margarine in medium saucepan over low heat until mixture reaches 120° to 130°F. Add to flour mixture. Blend at low speed just until dry ingredients are

moistened; beat 3 minutes at medium speed. Stir in carrots, onion, parsley and remaining 3¼ to 3½ cups all-purpose flour until dough is no longer sticky.

3. Knead dough on lightly floured surface 5 to 8 minutes or until smooth and elastic. Place in large bowl lightly sprayed with cooking spray; turn dough over to coat. Cover and let rise in warm place about 30 minutes or until doubled in bulk. Punch dough down. Cover and let rest 10 minutes.

4. Spray 2 (8×4-inch) loaf pans with cooking spray. Shape dough into 2 loaves; place in pans. Brush with melted margarine. Cover; let rise in warm place 30 minutes or until doubled in bulk. Meanwhile, preheat oven to 350°F.

5. Bake 40 to 45 minutes or until bread sounds hollow when tapped. Remove from pans; cool on wire racks.

Makes 2 loaves (24 slices)

Nutrients per Serving: 2 Veggie Club Sandwich halves

Calories: 289, Calories from Fat: 28%, Total Fat: 10g, Saturated Fat: 4g, Cholesterol: 10mg, Sodium: 430mg, Carbohydrate: 43g, Dietary Fiber: 8g, Protein: 18g
Dietary Exchanges: 2½ Starch, 1 Lean Meat, 1 Fat

Garden Style Pita

1 tablespoon CRISCO® Oil*
2 cups diagonally sliced zucchini (about ½ pound)
2 cups diagonally sliced yellow squash (about ½ pound)
⅛ teaspoon dried basil leaves
⅛ teaspoon salt
⅛ teaspoon pepper
2 tablespoons grated Parmesan cheese
2 (6-inch) whole wheat pita breads, halved
Boston lettuce leaves

*Use your favorite Crisco Oil product.

1. Heat oil in large skillet on medium-high heat. Add zucchini and yellow squash. Cook and stir 7 to 8 minutes or until tender. Add basil, salt and pepper. Toss to mix. Remove from heat. Sprinkle with Parmesan cheese.

2. Line pita pocket with lettuce. Spoon about ½ cup vegetable mixture into each pocket. *Makes 4 servings*

Nutrients per Serving: 1 Sandwich (1 filled pita half)

Calories: 147, Calories from Fat: 30%, Total Fat: 5g, Saturated Fat: 1g, Cholesterol: 2mg, Sodium: 303mg, Carbohydrate: 21g, Dietary Fiber: 4g, Protein: 6g
Dietary Exchanges: 1 Starch, 1 Vegetable, 1 Fat

Tandoori Chicken Breast Sandwiches with Yogurt Sauce

4 boneless skinless chicken breasts (about 12 ounces)
1 tablespoon lemon juice
¼ cup plain nonfat yogurt
2 large cloves garlic, minced
1½ teaspoons finely chopped fresh ginger
¼ teaspoon ground cardamom
¼ teaspoon ground red pepper
   Yogurt Sauce (recipe follows)
2 rounds whole wheat pita bread
½ cup grated carrot
½ cup finely shredded red cabbage
½ cup finely chopped red bell pepper

1. Lightly score chicken breasts 3 or 4 times with sharp knife. Place in medium bowl; sprinkle with lemon juice and toss to coat.

2. Combine yogurt, garlic, ginger, cardamom and ground red pepper in small bowl; add to chicken. Coat all pieces well with marinade; cover and refrigerate at least 1 hour or overnight.

3. Remove chicken from refrigerator 15 minutes before cooking. Preheat broiler. Prepare Yogurt Sauce; set aside.

4. Line broiler pan with foil. Arrange chicken on foil (do not let pieces touch) and brush with any remaining marinade. Broil 3 inches from heat about 5 to 6 minutes per side or until chicken is no longer pink in center.

5. Cut pitas in half crosswise. Place one chicken breast in each pita half with 2 tablespoons each of carrot, cabbage and bell pepper. Evenly drizzle sandwiches with Yogurt Sauce. Garnish, if desired.   *Makes 4 servings*

Yogurt Sauce

½ cup plain nonfat yogurt
2 teaspoons minced red onion
1 teaspoon minced cilantro
¼ teaspoon ground cumin
¼ teaspoon salt
   Dash ground red pepper

Blend all ingredients well in small bowl. Cover and refrigerate until ready to use.   *Makes about ½ cup*

Nutrients per Serving: 1 Sandwich (1 filled pita half) with 2 tablespoons Yogurt Sauce (without garnish)

Calories: 211, Calories from Fat: 12%, Total Fat: 3g, Saturated Fat: 1g, Cholesterol: 44mg, Sodium: 380mg, Carbohydrate: 25g, Dietary Fiber: 1g, Protein: 22g
Dietary Exchanges: 1½ Starch, 2 Lean Meat

Tandoori Chicken Breast Sandwich with Yogurt Sauce

Veggie Pita Wraps

½ cup fat-free mayonnaise
1 clove garlic, minced
¼ teaspoon dried marjoram leaves
¼ teaspoon dried tarragon leaves
4 rounds whole wheat pita bread
4 slices (1 ounce each) fat-free Cheddar cheese
½ cup rinsed and drained alfalfa sprouts
½ cucumber, thinly sliced
8 tomato slices
1 medium red onion, thinly sliced
2 cups chopped romaine lettuce

1. Combine mayonnaise, garlic, marjoram and tarragon in small bowl.

2. Wrap 2 pita breads in paper towels. Microwave at HIGH 20 to 30 seconds or just until soft and slightly warm. Repeat with remaining pita breads.

3. Spread 2 tablespoons mayonnaise mixture over half of each pita bread. Fold pitas in half; divide remaining ingredients evenly among pitas.   *Makes 4 servings*

Nutrients per Serving: 1 Wrap

Calories: 249, Calories from Fat: 7%, Total Fat: 2g, Saturated Fat: <1g, Cholesterol: 0mg, Sodium: 898mg, Carbohydrate: 47g, Dietary Fiber: 6g, Protein: 13g
Dietary Exchanges: 2 Starch, 2 Vegetable, 1 Lean Meat

Grilled Vegetable Muffuletta

10 cloves garlic, peeled
    Nonstick cooking spray
 1 tablespoon balsamic vinegar
 1 tablespoon fresh lemon juice
 1 tablespoon olive oil
¼ teaspoon black pepper
 1 loaf round whole wheat sourdough bread
    (1 pound)
 1 medium eggplant, cut crosswise into
    8 (¼-inch-thick) slices
 2 small yellow squash, cut lengthwise into thin
    slices
 1 small red onion, thinly sliced
 1 large red bell pepper, seeded and quartered
 2 slices (1 ounce each) reduced-fat Swiss
    cheese
 8 washed spinach leaves

1. Preheat oven to 350°F. Place garlic in ovenproof dish. Spray garlic with cooking spray. Cover with foil; bake 30 to 35 minutes or until garlic is very soft and golden brown.

2. Place garlic, vinegar, lemon juice, olive oil and black pepper in food processor; process, using on-off pulsing action, until smooth. Set aside.

3. Slice top from bread loaf. Hollow out loaf, leaving ½-inch-thick shell. Reserve bread for another use, if desired.

4. Prepare grill for direct grilling. Brush eggplant, squash, onion and bell pepper with garlic mixture. Arrange vegetables on grid over medium coals. Grill 10 to 12 minutes or until vegetables are crisp-tender, turning once. Separate onion slices into rings.

5. Layer half of eggplant, squash, onion, bell pepper, cheese and spinach in hollowed bread, pressing gently after each layer. Repeat layers with remaining vegetables, cheese and spinach. Replace bread top and serve immediately, or cover with plastic wrap and refrigerate up to 4 hours. Cut into 6 wedges before serving. *Makes 6 servings*

Nutrients per Serving: 1 sandwich wedge

Calories: 214, Calories from Fat: 23%, Total Fat: 6g, Saturated Fat: 2g, Cholesterol: 7mg, Sodium: 262mg, Carbohydrate: 34g, Dietary Fiber: 1g, Protein: 9g

Dietary Exchanges: 1½ Starch, 2 Vegetable, 1 Fat

Huevos Ranchwich

¼ cup EGG BEATERS® Healthy Real Egg
    Product
 1 teaspoon diced green chiles
 1 whole wheat hamburger roll, split and toasted
 1 tablespoon thick and chunky salsa, heated
 1 tablespoon shredded reduced-fat Cheddar and
    Monterey Jack cheese blend

On lightly greased griddle or skillet, pour Egg Beaters® into lightly greased 4-inch egg ring or biscuit cutter. Sprinkle with chiles. Cook 2 to 3 minutes or until bottom of egg patty is set. Remove egg ring and turn egg patty over. Cook 1 to 2 minutes longer or until done.

To serve, place egg patty on bottom of roll. Top with salsa, cheese and roll top. *Makes 1 sandwich*

Prep Time: 10 minutes
Cook Time: 5 minutes

Nutrients per Serving: 1 sandwich

Calories: 168, Calories from Fat: 20%, Total Fat: 4g, Saturated Fat: 1g, Cholesterol: 5mg, Sodium: 495mg, Carbohydrate: 21g, Dietary Fiber: 2g, Protein: 13g

Dietary Exchanges: 1½ Starch, 1 Lean Meat

Quick Pork Fajitas

 1 pork tenderloin, about 1 pound, thinly sliced*
 2 to 3 tablespoons fajita seasoning or marinade
½ onion, sliced
½ green pepper, sliced
 4 to 6 flour tortillas, warmed

Placing pork tenderloin in freezer for about 20 minutes makes slicing easier.

In a shallow bowl, toss pork pieces with fajita seasoning. In large non-stick skillet over medium-high heat, stir-fry pork pieces with onion and green pepper until all is just tender. Wrap portions in flour tortillas with salsa, if desired.

Makes 4 servings

Favorite recipe from *National Pork Board*

Nutrients per Serving: 1 Fajita (without salsa)

Calories: 259, Calories from Fat: 22%, Total Fat: 6g, Saturated Fat: 2g, Cholesterol: 73mg, Sodium: 510mg, Carbohydrate: 22g, Dietary Fiber: 2g, Protein: 27g

Dietary Exchanges: 1½ Starch, 3 Lean Meat

Chicken and Mozzarella Melts

2 cloves garlic, crushed
4 boneless skinless chicken breasts (about 12 ounces)
　Nonstick cooking spray
⅛ teaspoon salt
⅛ teaspoon black pepper
1 tablespoon prepared pesto sauce
4 small hard rolls, split
12 fresh spinach leaves
8 fresh basil leaves* (optional)
3 plum tomatoes, sliced
½ cup (2 ounces) shredded part-skim mozzarella cheese

*Omit basil leaves if fresh are unavailable. Do not substitute dried basil leaves.

1. Preheat oven to 350°F. Rub garlic on all surfaces of chicken. Spray medium nonstick skillet with cooking spray; heat over medium heat until hot. Add chicken; cook 5 to 6 minutes on each side or until no longer pink in center. Sprinkle with salt and pepper.

2. Brush pesto sauce onto bottom halves of rolls; layer with spinach, basil, if desired, and tomatoes. Place chicken in rolls; sprinkle cheese evenly over chicken. (If desired, sandwiches may be prepared up to this point and wrapped in aluminum foil. Refrigerate until ready to serve. Bake in preheated 350°F oven until chicken is warm, about 20 minutes.)

3. Wrap sandwiches in aluminum foil; bake about 10 minutes or until cheese is melted.　　*Makes 4 servings*

Nutrients per Serving: 1 Melt sandwich

Calories: 299, Calories from Fat: 16%, Total Fat: 5g, Saturated Fat: 3g, Cholesterol: 47mg, Sodium: 498mg, Carbohydrate: 37g, Dietary Fiber: 3g, Protein: 27g

Dietary Exchanges: 2 Starch, 1 Vegetable, 2½ Lean Meat

Chicken and Mozzarella Melt

Chicken Fajita Wraps

1 pound chicken tenders
¼ cup lime juice
4 cloves garlic, minced, divided
  Nonstick cooking spray
1 medium red bell pepper, sliced
1 medium green bell pepper, sliced
1 medium yellow bell pepper, sliced
1 large red onion, cut into ¼-inch-thick slices
½ teaspoon ground cumin
¼ teaspoon salt
¼ teaspoon ground red pepper
8 (8-inch) flour tortillas, warmed
  Salsa (optional)

1. Combine chicken, lime juice and 2 cloves garlic in medium bowl; toss to coat. Cover and marinate 30 minutes in refrigerator, stirring occasionally.

2. Spray large nonstick skillet with cooking spray; heat over medium heat until hot. Add chicken mixture, cook and stir 5 to 7 minutes or until chicken is browned and no longer pink in center. Remove chicken from skillet. Drain excess liquid from skillet, if necessary; discard.

3. Add bell peppers, onion and remaining 2 cloves garlic to skillet; cook and stir about 5 minutes or until vegetables are tender. Sprinkle with cumin, salt and red pepper. Return chicken to skillet; cook and stir 1 to 2 minutes.

4. Fill tortillas with chicken mixture. Serve with salsa and garnish, if desired.   *Makes 4 servings*

Nutrients per Serving: 2 Wraps (2 filled tortillas) without salsa and garnish

Calories: 385, Calories from Fat: 16, Total Fat: 7g,
Saturated Fat: 2g, Cholesterol: 66mg, Sodium: 517mg,
Carbohydrate: 47g, Dietary Fiber: 4g, Protein: 34g
Dietary Exchanges: 2½ Starch, 2 Vegetable, 3 Lean Meat

MEAT ENTRÉES

Hoppin' John Supper

1 cup uncooked converted white rice
1 can (14½ ounces) fat-free reduced-sodium chicken broth
¼ cup water
1 package (16 ounces) frozen black-eyed peas, thawed
1 tablespoon vegetable oil
1 cup chopped onions
1 cup diced carrots (¼-inch pieces)
¾ cup thinly sliced celery with leaves
3 cloves garlic, minced
12 ounces reduced-sodium lean fully cooked ham, cut into ¾-inch pieces
¾ teaspoon hot pepper sauce
½ teaspoon salt

1. Combine rice, chicken broth and water in large saucepan; bring to a boil over high heat. Reduce heat; cover and simmer 10 minutes. Stir in black-eyed peas; cover and simmer 10 minutes or until rice and peas are tender and liquid is absorbed.

2. Meanwhile, heat oil in large skillet over medium heat. Add onions, carrots, celery and garlic; cook and stir 15 minutes or until vegetables are tender. Add ham; heat through. Add hot rice mixture, pepper sauce and salt; mix well. Cover; cook over low heat 10 minutes. Sprinkle with parsley, if desired.   *Makes 6 servings*

Nutrients per Serving: ⅙ of total recipe (without parsley)

Calories: 327, Calories from Fat: 13%, Total Fat: 5g, Saturated Fat: 1g, Cholesterol: 26mg, Sodium: 833mg, Carbohydrate: 51g, Dietary Fiber: 6g, Protein: 21g
Dietary Exchanges: 3 Starch, 1 Vegetable, 1½ Lean Meat

Fruited Beef Kabobs

1 package (1.27 ounces) LAWRY'S® Spices & Seasonings for Fajitas
½ cup undiluted orange juice concentrate
1 can (8 ounces) pineapple chunks, juice reserved
½ teaspoon freshly grated orange peel
¾ pound sirloin steak, cut into 1-inch cubes
1 can (10½ ounces) mandarin oranges, drained
1 small green bell pepper, cut into 1-inch pieces
1 onion, cut into wedges
Skewers

In large resealable plastic food storage bag, combine Spices & Seasonings for Fajitas, orange juice concentrate, reserved pineapple juice and orange peel; mix well. Add beef cubes, orange segments, pineapple, bell pepper and onion; seal bag. Marinate in refrigerator 2 hours or overnight. Remove steak and vegetables from marinade; discard used marinade. Alternately thread bell pepper, beef cubes, orange segments, pineapple and onion onto 6 wooden skewers. Bake, covered, in 350°F oven 15 to 20 minutes or until beef is to desired doneness. Uncover and broil 1 to 2 minutes to brown.   *Makes 6 servings*

Serving Suggestion: Serve with crisp green salad and a rice side dish.

Hint: If using wooden skewers, soak in water overnight before using, to prevent scorching.

Nutrients per Serving: 1 Kabob

Calories: 181, Calories from Fat: 11%, Total Fat: 2g, Saturated Fat: 1g, Cholesterol: 27mg, Sodium: 573mg, Carbohydrate: 27g, Dietary Fiber: 2g, Protein: 14g
Dietary Exchanges: 1½ Fruit, 2 Lean Meat

Grilled Pork Tenderloin with Tomato Mango Salsa

2 pork tenderloins (¾ pound each)
⅓ cup reduced-sodium teriyaki sauce
2 medium tomatoes, seeded and diced
1 cup diced mango
½ cup minced yellow or green bell pepper
¼ cup hot jalapeño jelly, melted
2 tablespoons white wine vinegar

1. Rub pork tenderloins all over with teriyaki sauce; let stand 5 minutes.

2. Combine tomatoes, mango, bell pepper, jelly and vinegar in medium bowl; mix well. Set aside.

3. Grill pork, covered, over medium-hot coals 20 to 25 minutes or until meat thermometer inserted into thickest part registers 160°F, turning once. Slice and serve with prepared salsa. *Makes 6 servings*

Prep and Cook Time: 30 minutes

Nutrients per Serving: ⅙ of total recipe

Calories: 222, Calories from Fat: 17%, Total Fat: 4g, Saturated Fat: 1g, Cholesterol: 66mg, Sodium: 444mg, Carbohydrate: 20g, Dietary Fiber: 1g, Protein: 25g
Dietary Exchanges: ½ Fruit, 1 Vegetable, 3 Lean Meat

Beef Picante and Sour Cream Casserole

6 ounces uncooked wagon wheel pasta
8 ounces 95% lean ground beef
1½ cups reduced-sodium mild picante sauce
1 cup canned red kidney beans, rinsed and drained
¾ cup water
1 tablespoon chili powder
1 teaspoon ground cumin
½ cup fat-free cottage cheese
½ cup fat-free sour cream
½ cup chopped green onions, with tops
1 can (2¼ ounces) sliced black olives
¼ cup chopped fresh cilantro or fresh parsley

1. Preheat oven to 325°F. Spray 9-inch square baking pan with nonstick cooking spray; set aside. Cook pasta according to package directions, omitting salt; drain. Place in bottom of prepared pan; set aside.

2. Brown beef in large nonstick skillet over medium-high heat 4 to 5 minutes or until no longer pink, stirring to separate beef; drain fat. Add picante sauce, beans, water, chili powder and cumin; blend well. Bring to a boil over high heat. Reduce heat to low; simmer, covered, 20 minutes.

3. Combine cottage cheese, sour cream and green onions in food processor or blender; process until smooth. Spread cottage cheese mixture evenly over pasta in prepared pan. Spoon meat mixture evenly over cottage cheese mixture; cover with foil. Bake 20 minutes or until heated through. Remove from oven; let stand 10 minutes to allow flavors to blend. Top evenly with olives and cilantro.
Makes 4 servings

Nutrients per Serving: ¼ of total recipe

Calories: 344, Calories from Fat: 13%, Total Fat: 5g, Saturated Fat: 1g, Cholesterol: 27mg, Sodium: 755mg, Carbohydrate: 51g, Dietary Fiber: 4g, Protein: 26g
Dietary Exchanges: 3 Starch, 2½ Lean Meat

Orange Teriyaki Pork

Nonstick cooking spray
1 pound lean pork stew meat, cut into 1-inch cubes
1 package (16 ounces) frozen pepper blend for stir-fry
4 ounces sliced water chestnuts, drained
½ cup orange juice
2 tablespoons quick-cooking tapioca
2 tablespoons packed light brown sugar
2 tablespoons teriyaki sauce
½ teaspoon ground ginger
½ teaspoon dry mustard
1⅓ cups hot cooked white rice

Slow Cooker Directions

1. Spray large nonstick skillet with cooking spray; heat skillet over medium heat until hot. Add pork; brown on all sides. Remove from heat; set aside.

2. Place peppers and water chestnuts in slow cooker. Top with browned pork. Mix orange juice, tapioca, brown sugar, teriyaki sauce, ginger and mustard in large bowl. Pour over pork mixture in slow cooker. Cover; cook on LOW 3 to 4 hours. Serve with rice. *Makes 4 servings*

Nutrients per Serving: ¼ of Pork mixture with ⅓ cup cooked rice

Calories: 313, Calories from Fat: 18%, Total Fat: 6g, Saturated Fat: 2g, Cholesterol: 49mg, Sodium: 406mg, Carbohydrate: 42g, Dietary Fiber: 4g, Protein: 21g
Dietary Exchanges: 2 Starch, 2 Vegetable, 2 Lean Meat

Grilled Pork Tenderloin with Tomato Mango Salsa ～ 135

Southwestern Beef and Bean Lasagna

½ pound 95% lean ground beef
1 can (16 ounces) pinto beans, drained
1 teaspoon cumin seeds *or* ½ teaspoon ground cumin
1 teaspoon olive oil
1½ cups chopped onions
1 tablespoon seeded and minced jalapeño pepper*
1 clove garlic, minced
4 cups no-salt-added tomato sauce
1 can (4 ounces) diced green chilies, undrained
2 teaspoons chili powder
1 teaspoon dried oregano leaves
1 container (8 ounces) fat-free cottage cheese
1½ cups (6 ounces) shredded reduced-fat Cheddar cheese, divided
1 egg white
¼ cup chopped fresh cilantro
½ teaspoon salt
¼ teaspoon black pepper
8 ounces uncooked lasagna noodles (about 10 noodles)
1 cup water

Jalapeño peppers can sting and irritate the skin; wear rubber gloves when handling peppers and do not touch eyes. Wash hands after handling peppers.

1. Brown beef in large skillet. Drain off fat. Stir in beans; set aside.

2. Place cumin seeds in large nonstick skillet. Cook and stir over medium heat 2 minutes or until fragrant. Remove from skillet.

3. In same skillet, heat oil. Add onions, jalapeño pepper and garlic; cook until onions are soft. Add tomato sauce, green chilies, chili powder, oregano and cumin seeds. Bring to a boil; reduce heat. Simmer, uncovered, 20 minutes.

4. Preheat oven to 350°F. Combine cottage cheese, ½ cup Cheddar cheese, egg white, cilantro, salt and black pepper in medium bowl. Spray 13×9-inch baking pan with cooking spray. Cover bottom with ¾ cup tomato sauce mixture. Place layer of noodles on sauce. Spread half the beef mixture over noodles, then place another layer of noodles on top. Spread cheese mixture over noodles. Spread with remaining beef mixture. Layer with noodles. Pour remaining sauce mixture over all; sprinkle with remaining 1 cup Cheddar cheese. Pour water around edges. Cover tightly with foil. Bake 1 hour and 15 minutes or until pasta is tender. Cool 10 minutes. Cut into 8 wedges before serving. *Makes 8 servings*

Nutrients per Serving: 1 Lasagna wedge (⅛ of total recipe)

Calories: 344, Calories from Fat: 26%, Total Fat: 10g, Saturated Fat: 4g, Cholesterol: 27mg, Sodium: 661mg, Carbohydrate: 41g, Dietary Fiber: 6g, Protein: 24g
Dietary Exchanges: 2 Starch, 2 Vegetable, 2 Lean Meat, 1 Fat

Glazed Pork and Pepper Kabobs

1 pound lean boneless pork loin, cut into 1½-inch pieces
1 large red bell pepper, cut into 1-inch pieces
1 large yellow bell pepper, cut into 1-inch pieces
1 large green bell pepper, cut into 1-inch pieces
¼ cup reduced-sodium soy sauce
3 cloves garlic, minced
¼ cup sweet and sour sauce
1 tablespoon Chinese hot mustard

1. Place pork and peppers in large resealable plastic food storage bag. Combine soy sauce and garlic in cup; pour over meat and peppers. Seal bag; turn to coat. Marinate in refrigerator at least 30 minutes or up to 2 hours, turning once.

2. Drain meat and peppers; discard marinade. Alternately thread meat and peppers onto 4 metal skewers.

3. Combine sweet and sour sauce and hot mustard in small bowl; reserve half of sauce for dipping. Grill or broil kabobs 5 to 6 inches from heat 14 to 16 minutes or until pork is no longer pink, turning occasionally and brushing with remaining sauce mixture during last 5 minutes of cooking. Serve with reserved dipping sauce. *Makes 4 servings*

Nutrients per Serving: 1 Kabob with 1½ teaspoons dipping sauce

Calories: 230, Calories from Fat: 26%, Total Fat: 7g, Saturated Fat: 2g, Cholesterol: 68mg, Sodium: 656mg, Carbohydrate: 15g, Dietary Fiber: 2g, Protein: 27g
Dietary Exchanges: 3 Vegetable, 3 Lean Meat

TIP Green bell peppers contain twice as much vitamin C as citrus fruits. And red bell peppers (fully matured green bell peppers) contain three times as much vitamin C as the green variety! Plus, red bell peppers are loaded with beta carotene. Both vitamin C and beta carotene are well known for their health benefits.

Pork with Sweet Hungarian Paprika

1 teaspoon olive oil, divided
1 onion, sliced
2 cloves garlic, minced
1 medium tomato, chopped
1 medium red bell pepper, chopped
1 large Anaheim pepper *or* 1 medium green bell
    pepper, chopped
1½ cups fat-free reduced-sodium chicken broth,
    divided
2 tablespoons sweet Hungarian paprika
1 pork tenderloin (about ¾ pound)
3 tablespoons all-purpose flour
⅓ cup reduced-fat sour cream
6 ounces uncooked egg noodles, cooked
¼ cup minced parsley (optional)

1. Heat ½ teaspoon oil in medium saucepan over medium heat. Add onion and garlic. Cook and stir 2 minutes. Add tomato, peppers, ½ cup broth and paprika. Reduce heat to low; cover and simmer 5 minutes.

2. Cut pork crosswise into 8 slices. Using flat side of meat mallet or rolling pin, pound pork between two pieces of plastic wrap to ¼-inch thickness Heat remaining ½ teaspoon oil in large nonstick skillet over medium heat until hot. Cook pork 1 minute on each side or until browned. Add onion mixture. Reduce heat to low and simmer 5 minutes. Whisk together remaining chicken broth and flour in small bowl.

3. Remove pork from skillet; keep warm. Stir flour mixture into liquid in skillet. Bring liquid to a boil. Remove skillet from heat. Stir in sour cream. Serve sauce over pork and noodles. Garnish with additional sweet Hungarian paprika and parsley, if desired. *Makes 4 servings*

Nutrients per Serving: ¼ of total recipe (with 2 slices Pork and about ½ cup cooked noodles) without garnish

Calories: 380, Calories from Fat: 22%, Total Fat: 9g, Saturated Fat: 2g, Cholesterol: 110mg, Sodium: 96mg, Carbohydrate: 45g, Dietary Fiber: 2g, Protein: 28g

Dietary Exchanges: 2½ Starch, 1½ Vegetable, 3 Lean Meat

Pork with Sweet Hungarian Paprika

Chili Beef & Red Pepper Fajitas with Chipotle Salsa

  6 ounces top sirloin steak, thinly sliced
  ½ lime
1½ teaspoons chili powder
  ½ teaspoon ground cumin
  ½ cup diced plum tomatoes
  ¼ cup mild picante sauce
  ½ canned chipotle chili pepper in adobo sauce
    Nonstick cooking spray
  ½ cup sliced onion
  ½ medium red bell pepper, cut into thin strips
  2 (10-inch) fat-free flour tortillas, warmed
  ¼ cup fat-free sour cream
  2 tablespoons chopped cilantro leaves (optional)

1. Place steak on plate. Squeeze lime juice over steak; sprinkle with chili powder and cumin. Toss to coat well; let stand 10 minutes.

2. Meanwhile, to prepare salsa, combine tomatoes and picante sauce in small bowl. Place chipotle on small plate. Using fork, mash completely. Stir mashed chipotle into tomato mixture.

3. Coat 12-inch nonstick skillet with cooking spray. Heat over high heat until hot. Add onion and pepper; cook and stir 3 minutes or until beginning to blacken on edges. Remove from skillet. Lightly spray skillet with cooking spray. Add beef; cook and stir 1 minute. Return onion and pepper to skillet; cook 1 minute longer.

4. Place ½ the beef mixture in center of each tortilla; top with ¼ cup salsa, 2 tablespoons sour cream and cilantro, if desired. Fold or serve open-faced. *Makes 2 servings*

Nutrients per Serving: 1 Fajita (with ¼ cup Salsa and 2 tablespoons fat-free sour cream) without garnish

Calories: 245, Calories from Fat: 16%, Total Fat: 4g, Saturated Fat: 2g, Cholesterol: 45mg, Sodium: 530mg, Carbohydrate: 31g, Dietary Fiber: 9g, Protein: 21g

Dietary Exchanges: 1½ Starch, 1 Vegetable, 2 Lean Meat

Fajita-Stuffed Shells

¼ cup fresh lime juice
1 clove garlic, minced
½ teaspoon dried oregano leaves
¼ teaspoon ground cumin
1 boneless lean round or flank steak (about
    6 ounces)
1 medium green bell pepper, halved and seeded
1 medium onion, cut in half
12 uncooked jumbo pasta shells (about 6 ounces)
½ cup reduced-fat sour cream
2 tablespoons shredded reduced-fat Cheddar
    cheese
1 tablespoon minced fresh cilantro
⅔ cup chunky salsa
2 cups shredded leaf lettuce

1. Combine lime juice, garlic, oregano and cumin in shallow nonmetallic dish. Add steak, bell pepper and onion. Cover and refrigerate 8 hours or overnight.

2. Preheat oven to 350°F. Cook pasta shells according to package directions, omitting salt. Drain and rinse well under cold water; set aside.

3. Grill steak and vegetables over medium-hot coals 3 to 4 minutes per side or until desired doneness; cool slightly. Cut steak into thin slices. Chop vegetables. Place steak slices and vegetables in medium bowl. Stir in sour cream, Cheddar cheese and cilantro. Stuff shells evenly with meat mixture, mounding slightly.

4. Arrange shells in 8-inch baking dish. Pour salsa over filled shells. Cover with foil and bake 15 minutes or until heated through. Divide lettuce evenly among 4 plates; arrange 3 shells on each plate. *Makes 4 servings*

Nutrients per Serving: 3 Stuffed Shells

Calories: 265, Calories from Fat: 16%, Total Fat: 5g,
Saturated Fat: 2g, Cholesterol: 33mg, Sodium: 341mg,
Carbohydrate: 36g, Dietary Fiber: 3g, Protein: 19g

Dietary Exchanges: 2 Starch, 1 Vegetable, 1½ Lean Meat

Lamb & Stuffing Dinner Casserole

2 tablespoons margarine
1 cup chopped onion
1 clove garlic, minced
1 can (14½ ounces) reduced-sodium chicken
    broth, divided
1 cup coarsely shredded carrots
¼ cup fresh parsley, minced *or* 1 tablespoon
    dried parsley flakes
12 ounces cooked fresh American lamb, cut into
    cubes *or* 1 pound ground American lamb,
    cooked and drained
1 (6-ounce) box herb-flavored stuffing mix
1 (8-ounce) can whole tomatoes, drained and
    chopped

Melt margarine over medium heat; sauté onion and garlic 1 minute. Add ¼ cup of broth, carrots and parsley. Cover and cook until carrots are crisp-tender, about 5 minutes. In large bowl, lightly combine lamb and stuffing mix. Add vegetable mixture, remaining broth and tomatoes. Toss lightly until well mixed.

Spoon lamb mixture into greased 8×8×2-inch baking dish. Cover and bake at 375°F for 20 minutes or until heated through. *Makes 6 servings*

Favorite recipe from *American Lamb Council*

Nutrients per Serving: ⅙ of total recipe (made with fat-free reduced-sodium chicken broth)

Calories: 255, Calories from Fat: 27%, Total Fat: 8g,
Saturated Fat: 2g, Cholesterol: 43mg, Sodium: 603mg,
Carbohydrate: 28g, Dietary Fiber: 3g, Protein: 18g

Dietary Exchanges: 2 Starch, 2 Lean Meat

Mafalda and Meatballs

1 teaspoon olive oil
2 cloves garlic, minced, divided
2 cans (14½ ounces each) no-salt-added
   stewed tomatoes, undrained
½ teaspoon dried basil leaves
12 ounces 93% lean ground turkey
4 ounces 95% lean ground beef
⅓ cup dry French bread crumbs
3 tablespoons fat-free reduced-sodium chicken
   broth
3 tablespoons cholesterol-free egg substitute
1 teaspoon fennel seeds
¼ teaspoon salt
⅛ teaspoon black pepper
8 ounces uncooked mafalda or spaghetti
   noodles
Shredded Parmesan cheese (optional)

1. Heat oil in large nonstick saucepan over medium-high heat. Add half of garlic; cook 1 minute. Add tomatoes and basil; bring to a boil. Reduce heat. Simmer, uncovered, 20 to 25 minutes or until sauce thickens, stirring occasionally.

2. Meanwhile, combine beef, turkey, bread crumbs, chicken broth, egg substitute, fennel seeds, remaining half of garlic, salt and pepper in large bowl; mix well. With wet hands, shape meat mixture into 12 (1-inch) balls.

3. Preheat broiler. Spray broiler pan with nonstick cooking spray. Arrange meatballs on broiler pan. Broil, 4 inches from heat, 10 minutes or until no longer pink in center. Remove and add to tomato mixture. Cover; cook 5 to 10 minutes or until heated through.

4. Cook noodles according to package directions, omitting salt. Drain. Arrange noodles on serving platter. Pour meatballs and sauce over pasta. Serve with shredded Parmesan cheese, if desired. *Makes 6 servings*

Nutrients per Serving: 2 meatballs with ⅔ cup noodles and about ¼ cup sauce (without shredded Parmesan cheese)

Calories: 342, Calories from Fat: 25%, Total Fat: 9g,
Saturated Fat: 2g, Cholesterol: 58mg, Sodium: 244mg,
Carbohydrate: 41g, Dietary Fiber: 3g, Protein: 21g
Dietary Exchanges: 2 Starch, 2 Vegetable, 2 Lean Meat, 1 Fat

Beef- and Bean-Stuffed Peppers

1½ cups FIBER ONE® cereal
1 can (15 ounces) tomato purée
4 medium bell peppers
½ pound lean ground beef
1 medium onion, finely chopped (½ cup)
2 teaspoons chili powder
½ teaspoon ground cumin, if desired
1 can (8 ounces) kidney beans, rinsed and
   drained
1 can (4 ounces) chopped green chilies,
   undrained
¼ cup shredded Cheddar cheese (1 ounce),
   if desired

1. Heat oven to 350°F. Crush cereal.* Stir together cereal and tomato purée; let stand 5 minutes. Cut bell peppers lengthwise in half. Remove seeds and membranes. Place peppers, cut sides up, in ungreased rectangular baking dish, 13×9×2 inches.

2. Cook beef and onion in 10-inch skillet over medium heat, stirring frequently, until beef is brown; drain. Stir in tomato mixture and remaining ingredients except cheese. Divide beef mixture evenly among peppers.

3. Cover and bake 40 to 45 minutes or until peppers are tender. Sprinkle each pepper with ½ tablespoon cheese; let stand 5 minutes. *Makes 8 servings*

Place cereal in plastic bag or between sheets of waxed paper and crush with rolling pin.

Prep Time: 18 minutes
Bake Time: 45 minutes

Nutrients per Serving: 1 filled Pepper half (with shredded Cheddar cheese)

Calories: 180, Calories from Fat: 40%, Total Fat: 8g,
Saturated Fat: 3g, Cholesterol: 25mg, Sodium: 331mg,
Carbohydrate: 23g, Dietary Fiber: 10g, Protein: 10g
Dietary Exchanges: 1 Starch, 1 Vegetable, 1 Lean Meat, ½ Fat

Vegetable Pork Stir-Fry

¾ pound pork tenderloin
1 tablespoon vegetable oil
1½ cups (about 6 ounces) sliced fresh mushrooms
1 large green bell pepper, cut into strips
1 medium zucchini, thinly sliced
2 ribs celery, cut into diagonal slices
1 cup thinly sliced carrots
1 clove garlic, minced
1 cup chicken broth
2 tablespoons reduced-sodium soy sauce
1½ tablespoons cornstarch
3 cups hot cooked rice

Slice pork across the grain into ⅛-inch strips. Brown pork strips in oil in large skillet over medium-high heat. Push meat to side of skillet. Add mushrooms, pepper, zucchini, celery, carrots and garlic; stir-fry about 3 minutes. Combine broth, soy sauce and cornstarch. Add to skillet and cook, stirring, until thickened; cook 1 minute longer. Serve over rice.   *Makes 6 servings*

Favorite recipe from *USA Rice Federation*

Nutrients per Serving: ⅙ of Stir-Fry mixture with ½ cup cooked rice

Calories: 232, Calories from Fat: 18%, Total Fat: 5g, Saturated Fat: 1g, Cholesterol: 37mg, Sodium: 379mg, Carbohydrate: 31g, Dietary Fiber: 2g, Protein: 16g

Dietary Exchanges: 1½ Starch, 1 Vegetable, 1½ Lean Meat

Vegetable Pork Stir-Fry

Italian-Style Brisket

¾ cup fat-free reduced-sodium beef broth or water, divided
½ cup chopped onion
1 clove garlic, minced
1 can (14½ ounces) no-salted-added diced tomatoes, undrained
¼ cup dry red wine
¾ teaspoon dried oregano leaves
¼ teaspoon dried thyme leaves
¼ teaspoon black pepper
1¼ pounds well-trimmed beef brisket
3 cups sliced mushrooms
3 cups halved and thinly sliced zucchini (about 1 pound)
3 cups cooked egg noodles

1. Heat ¼ cup beef broth in Dutch oven. Add onion and garlic; cover and simmer 5 minutes.

2. Stir in tomatoes with juice, remaining ½ cup beef broth, red wine, oregano, thyme and pepper. Bring to a boil. Reduce heat to low; add beef brisket. Cover and simmer 1½ hours, basting occasionally with tomato mixture.

3. Add mushrooms and zucchini; simmer, covered, 30 to 45 minutes or until beef is tender.

4. Remove beef. Simmer vegetable mixture 5 to 10 minutes to thicken slightly. Cut beef across the grain into 12 thin slices. Serve 2 slices beef with ½ cup vegetable sauce and ½ cup noodles.   *Makes 6 servings*

Nutrients per Serving: 2 slices beef with ½ cup vegetable sauce and ½ cup cooked noodles

Calories: 282, Calories from Fat: 20%, Total Fat: 6g, Saturated Fat: 2g, Cholesterol: 81mg, Sodium: 107mg, Carbohydrate: 28g, Dietary Fiber: 3g, Protein: 27g

Dietary Exchanges: 1 Starch, 2 Vegetable, 3 Lean Meat

TIP Don't cut out the pork! Flavorful pork can easily fit into a healthful eating plan. In fact, pork contains more protein and less sodium per ounce than chicken. Just be sure to choose leaner cuts, such as pork loin roasts, loin chops and tenderloin.

Beef and Parsnip Stroganoff

Cook, covered, on LOW 4½ to 5 hours or until beef and parsnips are tender.

4. Turn off slow cooker. Remove beef and vegetables with slotted spoon to large bowl; reserve cooking liquid from beef. Blend sour cream, mustard and cornstarch in medium bowl. Gradually add reserved liquid to sour cream mixture; stir well to blend. Stir sour cream mixture into beef and vegetable mixture. Sprinkle with parsley; serve over hot noodles. Garnish, if desired.   *Makes 4 servings*

Nutrients per Serving: ¼ of Beef mixture with ¼ cup cooked noodles (without garnish)

Calories: 347, Calories from Fat: 15%, Total Fat: 6g, Saturated Fat: 2g, Cholesterol: 46mg, Sodium: 242mg, Carbohydrate: 46g, Dietary Fiber: 5g, Protein: 28g

Dietary Exchanges: 3 Starch, 2 Lean Meat

Beef and Parsnip Stroganoff

1 beef bouillon cube
¾ cup boiling water
¾ pound well-trimmed boneless top round beef steak, 1 inch thick
    Olive oil-flavored nonstick cooking spray
2 cups cubed peeled parsnips or potatoes*
1 medium onion, halved and thinly sliced
¾ pound mushrooms, sliced
2 teaspoons minced garlic
¼ teaspoon black pepper
¼ cup water
1 tablespoon plus 1½ teaspoons all-purpose flour
3 tablespoons reduced-fat sour cream
1½ teaspoons Dijon mustard
¼ teaspoon cornstarch
1 tablespoon chopped fresh parsley
4 ounces uncooked yolk-free wide noodles, cooked without salt, drained and kept hot

If using potatoes, cut into 1-inch chunks and do not sauté.

Slow Cooker Directions

1. Dissolve bouillon cube in ¾ cup boiling water; cool. Meanwhile, cut steak into 2×½-inch strips. Spray large nonstick skillet with cooking spray; heat over high heat. Add beef; cook and stir 4 minutes or until meat begins to brown and is barely pink. Transfer beef and juices to slow cooker.

2. Spray same skillet with cooking spray; heat over high heat. Add parsnips and onion; cook and stir about 4 minutes or until browned. Add mushrooms, garlic and pepper; cook and stir about 5 minutes or until mushrooms are tender. Transfer mixture to slow cooker; mix with beef.

3. Stir ¼ cup water into flour in small bowl until smooth. Stir flour mixture into cooled bouillon. Add to slow cooker.

Pork Tenderloin with Sherry-Mushroom Sauce

1 lean pork tenderloin (1 to 1½ pounds)
1½ cups chopped button mushrooms or shiitake mushroom caps
2 tablespoons sliced green onion
1 clove garlic, minced
1 tablespoon reduced-fat margarine
1 tablespoon cornstarch
1 tablespoon chopped fresh parsley
½ teaspoon dried thyme leaves
    Dash black pepper
⅓ cup water
1 tablespoon dry sherry
½ teaspoon beef bouillon granules

1. Preheat oven to 375°F. Place pork on rack in shallow baking pan. Insert meat thermometer into thickest part of tenderloin. Roast, uncovered, 25 to 35 minutes or until thermometer registers 165°F. Let stand covered, 5 to 10 minutes, while preparing sauce.

2. Cook and stir mushrooms, green onion and garlic in margarine in small saucepan over medium heat until vegetables are tender. Stir in cornstarch, parsley, thyme and pepper. Stir in water, sherry and bouillon granules. Cook and stir until sauce boils and thickens. Cook and stir 2 minutes more. Slice pork; serve with sauce.   *Makes 4 servings*

Nutrients per Serving: ¼ of total recipe

Calories: 179, Calories from Fat: 30%, Total Fat: 6g, Saturated Fat: 2g, Cholesterol: 81mg, Sodium: 205mg, Carbohydrate: 4g, Dietary Fiber: <1g, Protein: 26g

Dietary Exchanges: 1 Vegetable, 3 Lean Meat

Beef Burgundy and Mushrooms

8 ounces uncooked yolk-free egg noodles
¼ cup water
2 tablespoons all-purpose flour
1⅓ cups fat-free reduced-sodium beef broth
2 tablespoons dry red wine
½ teaspoon Worcestershire sauce
¾ teaspoon granulated sugar
1 bay leaf
   Nonstick cooking spray
1½ teaspoons extra-virgin olive oil
1 package (16 ounces) sliced fresh mushrooms
4 cloves garlic, minced
1 pound beef top sirloin, cut into thin strips
½ cup chopped green onions with tops
¼ cup chopped fresh parsley
   Black pepper

1. Cook noodles according to package directions, omitting salt. Drain; set aside.

2. Meanwhile, combine water and flour in small bowl; whisk until smooth. Slowly whisk in beef broth, wine, Worcestershire sauce, sugar and bay leaf; set aside.

3. Spray large nonstick skillet with cooking spray; add oil. Heat over high heat until hot. Add mushrooms and garlic; cook 2 minutes. Reduce heat to medium-high; cook 3 to 4 minutes or until tender. Remove to separate bowl; set aside.

4. Recoat skillet with cooking spray. Brown sirloin strips over high heat 2 to 3 minutes. Add green onions, mushrooms and broth mixture. Bring to a boil. Reduce heat to medium-low; simmer, uncovered, 30 minutes or until meat is tender. Remove from heat; add parsley. Sprinkle with pepper to taste. Let stand 10 minutes before serving. Serve over hot cooked egg noodles.

Makes 6 servings

Nutrients per Serving: ⅙ of Beef mixture with about ½ cup cooked noodles

Calories: 308, Calories from Fat: 19%, Total Fat: 6g,
Saturated Fat: 2g, Cholesterol: 36mg, Sodium: 99mg,
Carbohydrate: 35g, Dietary Fiber: 3g, Protein: 26g
Dietary Exchanges: 2 Starch, 1½ Vegetable, 2 Lean Meat

Beef & Vegetable Stir-Fry

½ cup fat-free reduced-sodium beef broth
3 tablespoons reduced-sodium soy sauce
2 teaspoons cornstarch
1 teaspoon sugar
½ teaspoon ground ginger
½ teaspoon garlic powder
½ teaspoon dark sesame oil
¼ teaspoon salt
¼ teaspoon black pepper
1 teaspoon vegetable oil
½ pound beef flank steak, cut diagonally into 1-inch slices
2 medium green bell peppers, thinly sliced
1 medium tomato, cut into wedges
8 green onions, cut into 1-inch pieces
2 cups hot cooked white rice

1. Combine beef broth, soy sauce, cornstarch, sugar, ginger, garlic powder, sesame oil, salt and black pepper in medium bowl.

2. Heat vegetable oil in wok or large nonstick skillet over medium-high heat until hot. Add beef; stir-fry 3 minutes or until beef is browned. Add bell peppers, tomato and onions; stir-fry 2 minutes or until vegetables are crisp-tender.

3. Stir beef broth mixture; add to wok. Cook and stir 3 minutes or until sauce boils and thickens.

4. Serve beef mixture over hot cooked white rice.

Makes 4 servings

Nutrients per Serving: ¼ of Stir-Fry mixture with ½ cup cooked rice

Calories: 263, Calories from Fat: 21%, Total Fat: 6g,
Saturated Fat: 2g, Cholesterol: 23mg, Sodium: 584mg,
Carbohydrate: 34g, Dietary Fiber: 3g, Protein: 18g
Dietary Exchanges: 2 Starch, 1 Vegetable, 2 Lean Meat

Beef Tenderloin with Roasted Vegetables

1 beef tenderloin (3 pounds), well trimmed
½ cup chardonnay or other dry white wine
½ cup reduced-sodium soy sauce
2 cloves garlic, sliced
1 tablespoon fresh rosemary
1 tablespoon Dijon mustard
1 teaspoon dry mustard
1 pound small red or white potatoes, cut into 1-inch pieces
1 pound Brussels sprouts
1 package (12 ounces) baby carrots
Fresh rosemary, for garnish (optional)

1. Place tenderloin in large resealable plastic food storage bag. Combine wine, soy sauce, garlic, rosemary, Dijon mustard and dry mustard in small bowl. Pour over tenderloin. Seal bag; turn to coat. Marinate in refrigerator 4 to 12 hours, turning several times.

2. Preheat oven to 425°F. Spray 13×9-inch baking pan with nonstick cooking spray. Place potatoes, Brussels sprouts and carrots in pan. Remove tenderloin from marinade. Pour marinade over vegetables; toss to coat well. Cover vegetables with foil. Bake 30 minutes; stir.

3. Place tenderloin on vegetables. Bake 45 minutes for medium or until internal temperature reaches 145°F when tested with meat thermometer inserted into thickest part of roast.

4. Transfer roast to cutting board; cover with foil. Let stand 10 to 15 minutes before carving. (Internal temperature will continue to rise 5° to 10°F during stand time.)

5. Stir vegetables; test for doneness and continue to bake if not tender. Slice tenderloin; arrange on serving platter with roasted vegetables. Garnish with fresh rosemary, if desired.

Makes 12 servings

Nutrients per Serving: ¹⁄₁₂ of total recipe (without garnish)

Calories: 326, Calories from Fat: 26%, Total Fat: 10g,
Saturated Fat: 3g, Cholesterol: 71mg, Sodium: 546mg,
Carbohydrate: 24g, Dietary Fiber: <1g, Protein: 34g

Dietary Exchanges: 1 Starch, 1½ Vegetable, 4 Lean Meat

Hungarian Lamb Goulash

1 package (16 ounces) frozen cut green beans
1 cup chopped onion
1¼ pounds lean lamb stew meat, cut into 1-inch pieces
1 can (15 ounces) chunky tomato sauce
1¾ cups fat-free reduced-sodium chicken broth
1 can (6 ounces) tomato paste
4 teaspoons paprika
3 cups hot cooked egg noodles

Slow Cooker Directions

Place green beans and onion in slow cooker. Top with lamb. Combine remaining ingredients, except noodles, in large bowl. Pour over lamb. Cover; cook on LOW 6 to 8 hours. Stir. Serve over noodles..   *Makes 6 servings*

Nutrients per Serving: ⅙ of Lamb mixture with ½ cup cooked noodles

Calories: 289, Calories from Fat: 16%, Total Fat: 5g,
Saturated Fat: 2g, Cholesterol: 67mg, Sodium: 772mg,
Carbohydrate: 39g, Dietary Fiber: 6g, Protein: 22g

Dietary Exchanges: 2 Starch, 2 Vegetable, 2 Lean Meat

TIP • 8 ounces uncooked macaroni-type pasta yields about 4½ cups cooked.

• 8 ounces uncooked spaghetti or linguine yields about 3½ cups cooked.

• 8 ounces uncooked egg noodles yields about 2½ cups cooked.

Pasta Picadillo

12 ounces uncooked medium shell pasta
   Nonstick cooking spray
 1 pound 95% lean ground beef
⅔ cup finely chopped green bell pepper
½ cup finely chopped onion
 2 cloves garlic, minced
 1 (8-ounce) can tomato sauce
½ cup water
⅓ cup raisins
 3 tablespoons chopped pimiento-stuffed
   green olives
 2 tablespoons drained capers
 2 tablespoons vinegar
½ teaspoon black pepper
¼ teaspoon salt

1. Cook pasta according to package directions, omitting salt. Drain; set aside.

2. Spray large nonstick skillet with cooking spray. Add beef, bell pepper, onion and garlic. Brown beef over medium-high heat 5 minutes or until no longer pink, stirring to separate beef; drain fat. Stir in tomato sauce, water, raisins, olives, capers, vinegar, black pepper and salt. Reduce heat to medium-low; cook, covered, 15 minutes, stirring occasionally.

Pasta Picadillo

3. Add cooked pasta to skillet; toss to coat. Cover and heat through, about 2 minutes.   *Makes 6 (1-cup) servings*

Prep Time: 10 minutes
Cook Time: 20 minutes

Nutrients per Serving: 1 cup

Calories: 366, Calories from Fat: 13%, Total Fat: 5g, Saturated Fat: 2g, Cholesterol: 43mg, Sodium: 568mg, Carbohydrate: 56g, Dietary Fiber: 2g, Protein: 23g

Dietary Exchanges: 3 Starch, 1½ Vegetable, 2 Lean Meat

Italian Pork Cutlets

 1 teaspoon CRISCO® Oil*
 6 (4 ounces each) lean, boneless center-cut
   pork loin slices, ¾ inch thick
 1 can (8 ounces) tomato sauce
1½ cups sliced fresh mushrooms
 1 small green bell pepper, cut into strips
½ cup sliced green onions with tops
 1 teaspoon Italian seasoning
½ teaspoon salt
⅛ teaspoon black pepper
¼ cup water
 1 teaspoon cornstarch
½ cup (2 ounces) shredded low moisture part-
   skim mozzarella cheese
 3 cups hot cooked rice (cooked without salt
   or fat)

*Use your favorite Crisco Oil product.

1. Heat oil in large skillet on medium heat. Add meat. Cook until browned on both sides.

2. Add tomato sauce, mushrooms, green bell pepper, onions, Italian seasoning, salt and black pepper. Reduce heat to low. Cover. Simmer 30 minutes or until meat is tender.

3. Combine water and cornstarch in small bowl. Stir until well blended. Add to juices in skillet. Cook and stir until thickened.

4. Sprinkle cheese over meat mixture. Cover. Heat until cheese melts. Serve with rice.   *Makes 6 servings*

Nutrients per Serving: 1 pork slice with ½ cup sauce and ½ cup rice

Calories: 314, Calories from Fat: 23%, Total Fat: 8g, Saturated Fat: 3g, Cholesterol: 77mg, Sodium: 544mg, Carbohydrate: 28g, Dietary Fiber: 1g, Protein: 30g

Dietary Exchanges: 1 Starch, 2½ Vegetable, 3 Lean Meat

Hearty Hungarian Goulash

1 pound beef round steak
1 teaspoon canola oil
1 medium onion, chopped
3 cloves garlic, minced
2 teaspoons paprika
2 teaspoons caraway seeds
¾ cup water
2 carrots, cut crosswise into ¼-inch-thick slices
1 large red potato, peeled and cut into ½-inch cubes
1 teaspoon hot pepper sauce
  Nonstick cooking spray
1 cup fat-free sour cream
1 teaspoon salt
16 ounces uncooked yolk-free egg noodles, cooked according to package directions, without added salt or fat
  Fresh parsley sprig (optional)

1. Trim fat from round steak. Cut steak into ³/₄-inch pieces; set aside.

2. Heat oil in large nonstick skillet over medium heat. Add onion, garlic, paprika and caraway seeds; cook 5 to 7 minutes, stirring occasionally. Stir in water, carrots, potato and hot pepper sauce; cover and cook 15 minutes or until vegetables are tender.

3. Meanwhile, spray medium nonstick skillet with cooking spray; heat over medium heat. Add steak; cook and stir about 4 minutes or until just beginning to brown. Add to vegetable mixture; cook 5 minutes, stirring occasionally.

4. Stir in sour cream and salt; cook until heated through. Serve over hot cooked noodles. Garnish with fresh parsley, if desired. *Makes 6 servings*

Nutrients per Serving: ⅙ of beef mixture with ¾ cup cooked noodles (without garnish)

Calories: 447, Calories from Fat: 14%, Total Fat: 7g, Saturated Fat: 2g, Cholesterol: 48mg, Sodium: 442mg, Carbohydrate: 64g, Dietary Fiber: 4g, Protein: 32g

Dietary Exchanges: 4 Starch, 1 Vegetable, 2½ Lean Meat

Meatballs in Creamy Mustard Sauce

6 ounces 95% lean ground beef
⅓ cup fresh bread crumbs
2 tablespoons chopped green onion with top
1 tablespoon plus 1 teaspoon Dijon mustard, divided
½ teaspoon lemon pepper
¼ teaspoon salt
3 ounces uncooked fettuccine *or* 1¼ cups tri-color rotini pasta
½ cup fat-free reduced-sodium beef broth
2 teaspoons cornstarch
3 tablespoons reduced-fat sour cream
  Minced fresh parsley (optional)

1. Preheat oven to 400°F. Spray broiler pan with nonstick cooking spray.

2. Combine beef, bread crumbs, green onion, 1 tablespoon mustard, lemon pepper and salt in small bowl. Shape into 8 meatballs. Place in single layer on prepared broiler pan. Bake, uncovered, 15 minutes or until no longer pink in centers.

3. Meanwhile, cook fettuccine in medium saucepan according to package directions, omitting salt. Drain and keep warm.

4. Whisk together beef broth, remaining 1 teaspoon mustard and cornstarch in same saucepan until smooth. Cook over low heat, stirring constantly, until mixture comes to a boil. Remove from heat. Stir about 1 tablespoon broth mixture into sour cream. Stir sour cream mixture into broth mixture in saucepan. Heat over low heat 1 minute. *Do not boil.* Remove from heat; stir in meatballs. Serve immediately.

5. Divide fettuccine between 2 serving plates and top evenly with meatballs and sauce. Sprinkle with parsley, if desired. *Makes 2 servings*

Nutrients per Serving: ½ of total recipe (without garnish)

Calories: 318, Calories from Fat: 23%, Total Fat: 8g, Saturated Fat: 3g, Cholesterol: 52mg, Sodium: 657mg, Carbohydrate: 37g, Dietary Fiber: 2g, Protein: 24g

Dietary Exchanges: 2½ Starch, 2½ Lean Meat

Hearty Hungarian Goulash ❧ 155

Lemon-Capered Pork Tenderloin

1 boneless pork tenderloin (about 1½ pounds)
1 tablespoon crushed capers
1 teaspoon dried rosemary leaves, crushed
⅛ teaspoon black pepper
1 cup water
¼ cup lemon juice

1. Preheat oven to 350°F. Trim fat from tenderloin; discard. Set tenderloin aside.

2. Combine capers, rosemary and black pepper in small bowl. Rub mixture over tenderloin. Place tenderloin in shallow roasting pan. Pour water and lemon juice over tenderloin.

3. Bake, uncovered, 1 hour or until thermometer inserted into thickest part of tenderloin registers 160°F. Remove from oven; cover with foil. Allow to stand 10 minutes. Cut evenly into 8 slices before serving. Garnish as desired.

Makes 8 servings

Nutrients per Serving: 1 Pork slice (without garnish)

Calories: 114, Calories from Fat: 28%, Total Fat: 3g, Saturated Fat: 1g, Cholesterol: 45mg, Sodium: 59mg, Carbohydrate: <1g, Dietary Fiber: <1g, Protein: 19g

Dietary Exchanges: 2 Lean Meat

Pasta Bourguignonne

1 pound boneless beef eye of round steak, visible fat trimmed, beef cut into 1½-inch cubes
3 to 4 tablespoons all-purpose flour
1 tablespoon olive or vegetable oil
1 teaspoon *each* dried oregano leaves, dried marjoram leaves and dried thyme leaves
2 bay leaves
1 can (14½ ounces) beef broth
2 medium onions, quartered
3 cups sliced mushrooms
2 cups sliced carrots
 Salt and black pepper (optional)
8 ounces uncooked fettuccine, cooked

1. Coat beef with flour. Heat oil in large saucepan over medium heat until hot. Add beef; cook until browned. Add oregano, marjoram, thyme and bay leaves; cook 1 minute.

2. Add beef broth; bring to a boil. Reduce heat; simmer, covered, 20 minutes or until beef is tender. Add vegetables; simmer, covered, 10 to 15 minutes or until vegetables are tender. Remove bay leaves. Season to taste with salt and pepper, if desired. Serve over pasta. *Makes 6 servings*

Nutrients per Serving: ⅙ of beef mixture with ⅔ cup cooked pasta (without added salt and pepper seasoning)

Calories: 309, Calories from Fat: 17%, Total Fat: 6g, Saturated Fat: 1g, Cholesterol: 37mg, Sodium: 67mg, Carbohydrate: 42g, Dietary Fiber: 3g, Protein: 22g

Dietary Exchanges: 2 Starch, 2 Vegetable, 2 Lean Meat

Pasta Paprikash

Nonstick cooking spray
12 ounces boneless beef eye of round steak, visible fat trimmed and beef cut into 1-inch cubes
4 tablespoons all-purpose flour, divided
2 cans (14½ ounces each) beef broth, divided
2 medium green bell peppers, sliced
1 medium onion, sliced
2 cloves garlic, minced
2 tablespoons sweet Hungarian paprika
¼ teaspoon black pepper
⅛ teaspoon ground red pepper
1 can (6 ounces) no-salt-added tomato paste
1 cup reduced-fat sour cream
Salt (optional)
8 ounces uncooked fettuccine, cooked

1. Spray large skillet with cooking spray. Heat over medium heat until hot. Coat beef with 2 tablespoons flour; cook 5 to 8 minutes or until browned. Add 1 cup beef broth and bring to a boil. Reduce heat and simmer, covered, 15 to 20 minutes or until beef is tender. Remove meat from skillet.

2. Add bell peppers, onion and garlic to skillet; cook and stir about 5 minutes or until tender. Stir in remaining 2 tablespoons flour, paprika, black pepper and red pepper; cook, stirring constantly, 1 minute. Stir in tomato paste and ½ cup remaining broth. Add beef and remaining broth and bring to a boil. Reduce heat and simmer, uncovered, 5 to 7 minutes or until sauce is thickened.

3. Stir in sour cream; cook over low heat 1 to 2 minutes, stirring frequently. Season to taste with salt, if desired. Serve over cooked fettuccine. *Makes 6 servings*

Nutrients per Serving: ⅙ of beef mixture with ⅔ cup cooked pasta (without added salt)

Calories: 327, Calories from Fat: 15%, Total Fat: 5g, Saturated Fat: 1g, Cholesterol: 40mg, Sodium: 109mg, Carbohydrate: 45g, Dietary Fiber: 2g, Protein: 22g
Dietary Exchanges: 2½ Starch, 2 Vegetable, 1½ Lean Meat

Pasta Paprikash

Pork Chops in Creamy Garlic Sauce

1 cup fat-free reduced-sodium chicken broth
¼ cup garlic cloves, peeled and crushed (about 12 to 15 cloves)
½ teaspoon olive oil
4 boneless pork loin chops, about ¼ inch thick each (about 12 ounces)
1 tablespoon minced fresh parsley
½ teaspoon dried tarragon leaves
¼ teaspoon salt
¼ teaspoon black pepper
1 tablespoon all-purpose flour
2 tablespoons water
1 tablespoon dry sherry
2 cups hot cooked white rice

1. Place chicken broth and garlic in small saucepan. Bring to a boil over high heat. Cover; reduce heat to low. Simmer 25 to 30 minutes or until garlic mashes easily. Set aside to cool. Purée in blender or food processor until smooth.

2. Heat oil in large nonstick skillet over medium-high heat. Add pork; cook 1 to 1½ minutes per side or until browned. Pour garlic purée into skillet. Sprinkle with parsley, tarragon, salt and pepper. Bring to a boil; cover. Reduce heat to low; simmer 10 to 15 minutes or until pork is juicy and barely pink in center. Remove pork; keep warm.

3. Combine flour and water in small cup. Slowly pour flour mixture into skillet; bring to a boil. Cook and stir until mixture thickens. Stir in sherry. Serve sauce over pork and rice. Garnish as desired. *Makes 4 servings*

Nutrients per Serving: 1 Pork Chop with ¼ of Sauce and ½ cup cooked rice (without garnish)

Calories: 293, Calories from Fat: 28%, Total Fat: 9g, Saturated Fat: 3g, Cholesterol: 40mg, Sodium: 231mg, Carbohydrate: 27g, Dietary Fiber: 1g, Protein: 23g
Dietary Exchanges: 2 Starch, 2 Lean Meat, ½ Fat

Grilled Caribbean Steak with Tropical Fruit Rice

1 (1½-pound) flank steak
¼ cup soy sauce
1¼ cups orange juice, divided
1 teaspoon ground ginger
1 can (8 ounces) pineapple chunks in juice
¼ teaspoon ground allspice
1 cup UNCLE BEN'S® ORIGINAL CONVERTED® Brand Rice
1 can (11 ounces) mandarin orange segments, drained

1. Place steak in large resealable plastic food storage bag. In small bowl, combine soy sauce, ¼ cup orange juice and ginger; pour over steak. Seal bag, turning to coat steak with marinade. Refrigerate steak, turning bag occasionally, at least 8 or up to 24 hours.

2. Drain pineapple, reserving juice. Combine remaining 1 cup orange juice and pineapple juice in 1-quart glass measure; add enough water to make 2¼ cups liquid.

3. In medium saucepan, combine juice mixture, allspice and salt to taste, if desired. Bring to a boil; stir in rice. Cover; reduce heat to low and simmer 20 minutes. Remove from heat and let stand, covered, 5 minutes.

4. Meanwhile, remove steak from marinade; discard marinade. Grill steak 7 minutes on each side for medium or until desired doneness. Cut steak diagonally across the grain into thin slices.

5. Place rice in serving bowl. Stir in pineapple and oranges. Serve with steak. *Makes 6 servings*

Serving Suggestion: For an authentic Caribbean touch, add 1 cup diced peeled mango to rice with pineapple chunks and oranges.

Nutrients per Serving: ⅙ of total recipe (without added salt and mango)

Calories: 381, Calories from Fat: 21%, Total Fat: 9g, Saturated Fat: 4g, Cholesterol: 50mg, Sodium: 284mg, Carbohydrate: 41g, Dietary Fiber: 1g, Protein: 33g

Dietary Exchanges: 1½ Starch, 1 Fruit, 4 Lean Meat

Chinese Noodles and Soy Beef

12 ounces top beef sirloin, cut into thin strips
¼ cup reduced-sodium soy sauce, divided
1 cup water
1 teaspoon beef bouillon granules
⅛ teaspoon red pepper flakes
1 tablespoon packed brown sugar
1 tablespoon cornstarch
½ teaspoon five-spice powder (optional)
4 ounces uncooked vermicelli
   Nonstick cooking spray
2 cloves garlic, minced
1 teaspoon grated fresh ginger
1 cup thinly sliced onions
½ medium red bell pepper, thinly sliced
3 ounces frozen snow peas, thawed
1 can (8 ounces) bamboo shoots, well drained

1. Combine sirloin strips and 2 tablespoons soy sauce in large resealable plastic food storage bag. Seal bag; turn to coat. Marinate 15 minutes, turning occasionally.

2. Combine water, bouillon granules, red pepper flakes, sugar, cornstarch and five-spice powder, if desired, in small bowl. Stir until completely dissolved; set aside.

3. Cook noodles according to package directions, omitting salt. Drain; set aside.

4. Spray large nonstick skillet with cooking spray. Heat over high heat until hot. Remove beef from resealable plastic food storage bag; discard marinade. Add beef, garlic and ginger to skillet; cook, stirring constantly, 3 minutes or until liquid has evaporated and glaze appears. Remove from skillet; set aside. Reduce heat to medium-high. Add onions and bell pepper slices; cook, stirring constantly, 3 to 4 minutes or until crisp-tender.

5. Stir reserved cornstarch mixture. Add snow peas, bamboo shoots, reserved cornstarch mixture and beef to skillet; cook 1 to 2 minutes or until slightly thickened. Gently stir in cooked noodles. Sprinkle with remaining 2 tablespoons soy sauce. *Makes 4 servings*

Nutrients per Serving: ¼ of total recipe

Calories: 282, Calories from Fat: 14%, Total Fat: 4g, Saturated Fat: 2g, Cholesterol: 49mg, Sodium: 805mg, Carbohydrate: 38g, Dietary Fiber: 3g, Protein: 23g

Dietary Exchanges: 2 Starch, 1½ Vegetable, 2 Lean Meat

Tandoori Pork Sauté

Nutty Rice (recipe follows)
8 ounces lean pork, cut into 2×½-inch strips
½ cup sliced onion
1 clove garlic, minced
4 fresh California plums, halved, pitted and cut
   into thick wedges
1 cup plain low-fat yogurt
1 tablespoon all-purpose flour
1½ teaspoons grated fresh ginger
½ teaspoon ground turmeric
⅛ teaspoon ground black pepper
   Additional plum wedges, orange sections and
   sliced green onions (optional)

Prepare Nutty Rice. Cook pork in nonstick skillet
2 minutes or until browned, turning occasionally. Transfer
to platter. Add onion and garlic to skillet; cook 1 minute.
Add plums; cook and stir 1 minute. Remove from heat and
return pork to pan. Combine yogurt and flour; add to
skillet. Stir in ginger, turmeric and pepper. Bring to a boil;
reduce heat and simmer 10 minutes, stirring occasionally.
Serve over Nutty Rice and surround with plum wedges,
orange sections and green onions.   *Makes 4 servings*

Nutty Rice: Bring 2 cups water to a boil in medium
saucepan. Add ¾ cup brown rice and ¼ cup wheat berries. (Or,
omit wheat berries and use 1 cup brown rice.) Return to a boil.
Reduce heat to low; cover and simmer 40 to 45 minutes or until
rice is tender and liquid is absorbed.

Favorite recipe from *California Tree Fruit Agreement*

Nutrients per Serving: ¼ of total recipe (without additional plum wedges, orange sections and green onions)

Calories: 331, Calories from Fat: 15%, Total Fat: 6g,
Saturated Fat: 2g, Cholesterol: 37mg, Sodium: 78mg,
Carbohydrate: 50g, Dietary Fiber: 4g, Protein: 20g
Dietary Exchanges: 2 Starch, 1 Fruit, 2 Lean Meat

Baked Pasta Casserole

1½ cups (3 ounces) uncooked wagon wheel or
   rotelle pasta
3 ounces 95% lean ground beef
2 tablespoons chopped onion
2 tablespoons chopped green bell pepper
1 clove garlic, minced
½ cup fat-free spaghetti sauce
   Dash black pepper
2 tablespoons shredded Italian-style mozzarella
   and Parmesan cheese blend
   Peperoncini (optional)

1. Preheat oven to 350°F. Cook pasta according to package
directions, omitting salt; drain. Return pasta to saucepan.

2. Meanwhile, heat medium nonstick skillet over
medium-high heat. Add beef, onion, bell pepper and garlic;
cook and stir 3 to 4 minutes or until beef is browned and
vegetables are crisp-tender. Drain.

3. Add beef mixture, spaghetti sauce and black pepper to
pasta in saucepan; mix well. Spoon mixture into 1-quart
baking dish. Sprinkle with cheese.

4. Bake 15 minutes or until heated through. Serve with
peperoncini, if desired.   *Makes 2 servings*

Note: To make ahead, assemble casserole as directed above
through step 3. Cover and refrigerate several hours or overnight.
Bake, uncovered, in preheated 350°F oven 30 minutes or until
heated through.

Nutrients per Serving: ½ of total recipe (without peperoncini)

Calories: 282, Calories from Fat: 23%, Total Fat: 7g,
Saturated Fat: 3g, Cholesterol: 31mg, Sodium: 368mg,
Carbohydrate: 37g, Dietary Fiber: 3g, Protein: 16g
Dietary Exchanges: 2 Starch, 2 Vegetable, 1 Lean Meat, 1 Fat

Bolognese Sauce & Penne Pasta

8 ounces 95% lean ground beef
⅓ cup chopped onion
1 clove garlic, minced
1 can (8 ounces) tomato sauce
⅓ cup chopped carrot
¼ cup water
2 tablespoons red wine
1 teaspoon dried Italian seasoning
1½ cups hot cooked penne pasta
   Chopped fresh parsley

1. Heat medium saucepan over medium heat until hot.
Add beef, onion and garlic; cook and stir 5 to 7 minutes,
breaking up meat with spoon, until beef is browned.

2. Add tomato sauce, carrot, water, wine and Italian
seasoning. Bring to a boil. Reduce heat and simmer
15 minutes. Serve sauce over pasta. Sprinkle with parsley.
          Makes 2 servings

Nutrients per Serving: ¾ cup cooked Pasta with ½ of Sauce

Calories: 292, Calories from Fat: 14%, Total Fat: 5g,
Saturated Fat: 2g, Cholesterol: 45mg, Sodium: 734mg,
Carbohydrate: 40g, Dietary Fiber: 4g, Protein: 21g
Dietary Exchanges: 2 Starch, 1 Vegetable, 2 Lean Meat

POULTRY ENTRÉES

Turkey Sausage & Pasta Toss

8 ounces uncooked penne or gemelli pasta
1 can (14½ ounces) no-salt-added stewed tomatoes, undrained
6 ounces turkey kielbasa or smoked turkey sausage
2 cups fresh (1-inch) asparagus pieces or broccoli florets
2 tablespoons prepared reduced-fat pesto sauce
2 tablespoons grated Parmesan cheese

1. Cook pasta according to package directions, omitting salt.

2. Meanwhile, heat tomatoes in medium saucepan. Cut sausage crosswise into ¼-inch slices; add to tomatoes. Stir in asparagus and pesto; cover and simmer about 6 minutes or until asparagus is crisp-tender.

3. Drain pasta; toss with tomato mixture and sprinkle with cheese. *Makes 4 servings*

Prep and Cook Time: 25 minutes

Nutrients per Serving: ¼ of total recipe

Calories: 342, Calories from Fat: 18%, Total Fat: 7g, Saturated Fat: 2g, Cholesterol: 30mg, Sodium: 483mg, Carbohydrate: 53g, Dietary Fiber: 5g, Protein: 18g
Dietary Exchanges: 3 Starch, 1 Vegetable, 2 Lean Meat

Angel Hair Noodles with Peanut Sauce

¼ cup Texas peanuts, puréed
2 tablespoons low-fat chicken broth or water
1 tablespoon soy sauce
1 tablespoon rice vinegar
10 ounces dried bean thread noodles
½ tablespoon vegetable oil
1 pound chicken breast, boned, skinned and thinly sliced
½ cucumber, peeled, seeded and cut into matchstick pieces
2 medium carrots, shredded

To make sauce, combine peanut purée, chicken broth, soy sauce and vinegar in small bowl; set aside.

Bring 4 cups water to a boil in medium saucepan. Add noodles, stirring to separate strands. Cook, stirring, 30 seconds or until noodles are slightly soft. Drain in colander and rinse under cold running water. Drain well; cut noodles into halves and set aside.

Heat wok or skillet over high heat. Add oil; swirl to coat sides. Add chicken; stir-fry 1 minute or until opaque. Add cucumber, carrots and sauce; cook, stirring to mix well. Remove from heat. Add noodles; toss to coat. Sprinkle with extra peanuts, if desired. *Makes 6 servings*

Favorite recipe from *Texas Peanut Producers Board*

Nutrients per Serving: ⅙ of total recipe (without extra peanuts)

Calories: 306, Calories from Fat: 16%, Total Fat: 5g, Saturated Fat: 1g, Cholesterol: 44mg, Sodium: 214mg, Carbohydrate: 44g, Dietary Fiber: 2g, Protein: 20g
Dietary Exchanges: 3 Starch, 2 Lean Meat

Chicken Pot Pie

2 teaspoons margarine
½ cup plus 2 tablespoons fat-free reduced-
   sodium chicken broth, divided
2 cups sliced mushrooms
1 cup diced red bell pepper
½ cup chopped onion
½ cup chopped celery
2 tablespoons all-purpose flour
½ cup fat-free half-and-half
2 cups cubed cooked chicken breasts
1 teaspoon minced fresh dill
½ teaspoon salt
¼ teaspoon black pepper
2 reduced-fat refrigerated crescent rolls

1. Heat margarine and 2 tablespoons chicken broth in medium saucepan until margarine is melted. Add mushrooms, bell pepper, onion and celery. Cook 7 to 10 minutes or until vegetables are tender, stirring frequently.

2. Stir in flour; cook 1 minute. Stir in remaining ½ cup chicken broth; cook and stir until liquid thickens. Reduce heat and stir in half-and-half. Add chicken, dill, salt and black pepper.

3. Preheat oven to 375°F. Spray 1-quart casserole with nonstick cooking spray. Spoon chicken mixture into prepared dish. Roll out crescent rolls and place on top of chicken mixture.

4. Bake pot pie 20 minutes or until topping is golden and filling is bubbly.   *Makes 4 (1-cup) servings*

Nutrients per Serving: 1 cup

Calories: 286, Calories from Fat: 27%, Total Fat: 8g, Saturated Fat: 2g, Cholesterol: 54mg, Sodium: 740mg, Carbohydrate: 25g, Dietary Fiber: 2g, Protein: 26g
Dietary Exchanges: 1 Starch, 2 Vegetable, 3 Lean Meat

TIP For 2 cups cubed cooked chicken breast, gently simmer 4 small chicken breasts in 2 cups fat-free reduced-sodium chicken broth about 20 minutes or until meat is no longer pink in center. Cool and cut into cubes. Reserve chicken broth for pot pie, if desired.

Turkey Yakitori

½ teaspoon low sodium chicken bouillon
   granules
2 tablespoons boiling water
2 tablespoons reduced sodium soy sauce
2 tablespoons dry sherry
1 teaspoon ground ginger
1 garlic clove, minced
2 pounds turkey breast cutlets, cut into
   1-inch-wide strips
8 metal skewers (9 inches long)
½ pound fresh whole mushrooms
½ large red bell pepper, cut into 1-inch pieces
½ large green bell pepper, cut into 1-inch pieces

1. Dissolve bouillon in boiling water in small bowl.

2. Combine bouillon mixture, soy sauce, sherry, ginger, garlic and turkey in large resealable plastic bag. Seal bag and turn mixture to coat. Refrigerate 4 hours or overnight. Drain marinade and discard.*

3. Weave turkey strips around mushrooms and pepper pieces on skewers.

4. Remove grill rack from charcoal grill and lightly coat with cooking spray; set aside. Preheat charcoal grill for direct-heat cooking. Grill turkey skewers 4 to 5 minutes or until turkey is no longer pink.   *Makes 4 servings*

*If desired, prepare another recipe of marinade (by combining first six ingredients) to use for brushing on grilled skewers or to be served as a dipping sauce. DO NOT use any of original marinade for dipping.

Favorite recipe from *National Turkey Federation*

Nutrients per Serving: 2 skewers (without additional dipping sauce)

Calories: 288, Calories from Fat: 4%, Total Fat: 1g, Saturated Fat: <1g, Cholesterol: 150mg, Sodium: 344mg, Carbohydrate: 7g, Dietary Fiber: 1g, Protein: 58g
Dietary Exchanges: 5 Lean Meat

Tuscan Pasta

1 pound boneless skinless chicken breasts, cut into 1-inch pieces
1 can (15½ ounces) red kidney beans, rinsed and drained
1 can (15 ounces) tomato sauce
2 cans (14½ ounces each) Italian-style stewed tomatoes
1 medium green bell pepper, chopped
1 jar (4½ ounces) sliced mushrooms, drained
½ cup chopped onion
½ cup chopped celery
4 cloves garlic, minced
1 cup water
1 teaspoon dried Italian seasoning
6 ounces uncooked thin spaghetti, broken in half

Slow Cooker Directions

Place all ingredients except spaghetti in slow cooker. Cover and cook on LOW 4 hours or until vegetables are tender. Turn to HIGH. Stir in spaghetti; cover. Stir again after 10 minutes. Cover and cook 45 minutes or until pasta is tender. Garnish with basil and bell pepper strips, if desired.

Makes 8 servings

Nutrients per Serving: ⅛ of total recipe (without garnish)

Calories: 266, Calories from Fat: 6%, Total Fat: 2g, Saturated Fat: 1g, Cholesterol: 34mg, Sodium: 814mg, Carbohydrate: 40g, Dietary Fiber: 6g, Protein: 21g

Dietary Exchanges: 2 Starch, 2 Vegetable, 1½ Lean Meat

Lighter Stuffed Peppers

1 can (10¾ ounces) reduced-fat condensed tomato soup, undiluted, divided
¼ cup water
8 ounces ground turkey breast
1 cup cooked rice
¾ cup frozen corn, thawed
¼ cup sliced celery
¼ cup chopped red bell pepper
1 teaspoon dried Italian seasoning
½ teaspoon hot pepper sauce
2 green, yellow or red bell peppers, cut in half lengthwise and seeds removed

1. Blend ¼ cup soup and water in small bowl. Pour into 8×8-inch baking dish; set aside. Brown turkey in large nonstick skillet over medium-high heat; drain well. Combine remaining soup with cooked turkey, rice, corn, celery, chopped pepper, Italian seasoning and hot pepper sauce in large bowl; mix well.

2. Fill pepper halves equally with turkey mixture. Place stuffed peppers on top of soup mixture in baking dish. Cover and bake at 350°F 35 to 40 minutes. To serve, place peppers on serving dish; evenly spoon remaining sauce from dish over tops of peppers. *Makes 4 servings*

Nutrients per Serving: 1 Stuffed Pepper half

Calories: 204, Calories from Fat: 13%, Total Fat: 3g, Saturated Fat: 1g, Cholesterol: 22mg, Sodium: 326mg, Carbohydrate: 33g, Dietary Fiber: 3g, Protein: 13g

Dietary Exchanges: 1½ Starch, 1½ Vegetable, 1 Lean Meat

Tuscan Pasta

Turkey Tostados

2 cups cubed cooked turkey
1 package (1½ ounces) taco seasoning mix
    Water
4 corn tortillas
¼ cup canned refried beans
¼ cup (1 ounce) shredded reduced-fat Cheddar
    cheese
½ cup chopped tomatoes
½ cup shredded lettuce
2 tablespoons chopped onions
½ cup taco sauce
    Plain low-fat yogurt (optional)
    Guacamole (optional)

Preheat oven to 375°F. In large skillet, over medium heat, combine turkey and taco seasoning mix. Add water according to package directions. Bring mixture to a boil; reduce heat to low and simmer 5 minutes, stirring occasionally.

Place tortillas on large cookie sheet. Bake 5 to 7 minutes or until tortillas are crispy and lightly browned. Spread each tortilla with 1 tablespoon beans. Top evenly with turkey mixture and cheese. Return to oven 2 to 3 minutes or until cheese is melted.

To serve, top with tomatoes, lettuce, onions and taco sauce. Garnish with yogurt and guacamole, if desired.

Makes 4 servings

Favorite recipe from *National Turkey Federation*

Nutrients per Serving: 1 Tostado (without yogurt and guacamole)

Calories: 260, Calories from Fat: 19%, Total Fat: 5g,
Saturated Fat: 2g, Cholesterol: 56mg, Sodium: 1,329mg,
Carbohydrate: 27g, Dietary Fiber: 3g, Protein: 25g
Dietary Exchanges: 1 Starch, 1 Vegetable, 3 Lean Meat

Tuscan Chicken with White Beans

1 large fresh fennel bulb (about ¾ pound)
1 teaspoon olive oil
8 ounces boneless skinless chicken thighs, cut
    into ¾-inch pieces
1 teaspoon dried rosemary leaves, crushed
½ teaspoon black pepper
1 can (14½ ounces) no-salt-added stewed
    tomatoes, undrained
1 can (14½ ounces) fat-free reduced-sodium
    chicken broth
1 can (15 ounces) cannellini beans, rinsed and
    drained
    Hot pepper sauce (optional)

1. Cut off and reserve ¼ cup chopped feathery fennel tops. Chop bulb into ½-inch pieces. Heat oil in large saucepan over medium heat. Add chopped fennel bulb; cook 5 minutes, stirring occasionally.

2. Sprinkle chicken with rosemary and pepper. Add to saucepan; cook and stir 2 minutes. Add tomatoes and chicken broth; bring to a boil. Cover and simmer 10 minutes. Stir in beans; simmer, uncovered, 15 minutes or until chicken is cooked through and sauce thickens. Season to taste with hot sauce, if desired. Ladle into 4 shallow bowls; top with reserved fennel tops.

Makes 4 servings

Prep Time: 15 minutes
Cook Time: 35 minutes

Nutrients per Serving: 1½ cups soup

Calories: 215, Calories from Fat: 25%, Total Fat: 6g,
Saturated Fat: 2g, Cholesterol: 34mg, Sodium: 321mg,
Carbohydrate: 24g, Dietary Fiber: 7g, Protein: 17g
Dietary Exchanges: 1½ Starch, 2 Lean Meat

Lemon-Garlic Chicken

2 tablespoons olive oil
2 cloves garlic, pressed
1 teaspoon grated lemon peel
1 teaspoon lemon juice
¼ teaspoon salt
¼ teaspoon black pepper
4 skinless boneless chicken breast halves
    (about 1 pound)

Combine oil, garlic, lemon peel, lemon juice, salt and pepper in small bowl. Brush oil mixture over both sides of chicken to coat. Lightly oil grid to prevent sticking. Grill chicken over medium KINGSFORD® Briquets 8 to 10 minutes or until chicken is no longer pink in center, turning once.

Makes 4 servings

Nutrients per Serving: 1 Chicken breast

Calories: 187, Calories from Fat: 40%, Total Fat: 8g,
Saturated Fat: 1g, Cholesterol: 66mg, Sodium: 205mg,
Carbohydrate: 1g, Dietary Fiber: <1g, Protein: 26g
Dietary Exchanges: 3 Lean Meat

Cheese Ravioli with Spinach Pesto and Chicken

Spinach Pesto (recipe follows)
2 (9-ounce) packages refrigerated low-fat cheese ravioli
Nonstick cooking spray
¾ cup matchstick-size carrot strips
¾ cup thinly sliced celery
½ cup chopped onion (about 1 small)
2 cloves garlic, minced
1½ pounds chicken tenders, cut crosswise into halves
1 can (14½ ounces) no-salt-added stewed tomatoes
¼ cup dry white wine
2 teaspoons dried rosemary leaves, crushed
¼ teaspoon salt
⅛ teaspoon black pepper

1. Prepare Spinach Pesto; set aside. Prepare ravioli according to package directions, omitting salt; drain and keep warm.

2. Spray large nonstick skillet with cooking spray; heat over medium heat. Add carrots, celery, onion and garlic; cook and stir about 5 minutes or until crisp-tender.

3. Add chicken, tomatoes, wine, rosemary, salt and pepper; heat to a boil. Reduce heat to low and simmer, uncovered, about 10 minutes or until chicken is no longer pink in center.

4. Arrange ravioli on serving plates; spoon chicken and vegetable mixture over ravioli. Top with Spinach Pesto.
Makes 8 servings

Spinach Pesto

2 cups loosely packed fresh spinach leaves
2 tablespoons grated Romano cheese
2 tablespoons olive oil or vegetable oil
1 to 2 tablespoons lemon juice
1 tablespoon dried basil leaves
3 cloves garlic

Process all ingredients in food processor or blender until smooth.
Makes about 1 cup

Nutrients per Serving: ⅛ of total recipe

Calories: 284, Calories from Fat: 26%, Total Fat: 8g,
Saturated Fat: 1g, Cholesterol: 74mg, Sodium: 173mg,
Carbohydrate: 28g, Dietary Fiber: 3g, Protein: 23g
Dietary Exchanges: 1½ Starch, 1½ Vegetable, 2½ Lean Meat

Cheese Ravioli with Spinach Pesto and Chicken

Spinach & Turkey Skillet

6 ounces turkey breast tenderloin
⅛ teaspoon salt
2 teaspoons olive oil
¼ cup chopped onion
2 cloves garlic, minced
⅓ cup uncooked rice
¾ teaspoon dried Italian seasoning
¼ teaspoon black pepper
1 cup fat-free reduced-sodium chicken broth, divided
2 cups torn fresh spinach leaves
⅔ cup diced plum tomatoes
3 tablespoons freshly grated Parmesan cheese

1. Cut turkey tenderloins into bite-size pieces; sprinkle with salt.

2. Heat oil in medium skillet over medium-high heat. Add turkey pieces; cook and stir until lightly browned. Remove from skillet. Reduce heat to low. Add onion and garlic; cook and stir until tender. Return turkey to skillet. Stir in rice, Italian seasoning and pepper.

3. Reserve 2 tablespoons chicken broth. Stir remaining broth into mixture in skillet. Bring to a boil. Reduce heat; simmer, covered, 14 minutes. Stir in spinach and reserved broth. Cover; cook 2 to 5 minutes or until liquid is absorbed and spinach is wilted. Stir in tomatoes; heat through. Serve with Parmesan cheese.
Makes 2 servings

Nutrients per Serving: ½ of total recipe

Calories: 316, Calories from Fat: 26%, Total Fat: 9g,
Saturated Fat: 3g, Cholesterol: 39mg, Sodium: 309mg,
Carbohydrate: 33g, Dietary Fiber: 3g, Protein: 25g
Dietary Exchanges: 2 Starch, 3 Lean Meat

Oven-Fried Chicken

2 boneless skinless chicken breasts (about 8 ounces), cut into halves
4 small skinless chicken drumsticks (about 10 ounces)
3 tablespoons all-purpose flour
½ teaspoon poultry seasoning
¼ teaspoon garlic salt
¼ teaspoon black pepper
1½ cups cornflakes, crushed
1 tablespoon dried parsley flakes
1 egg white
1 tablespoon water
Nonstick cooking spray

1. Preheat oven to 375°F. Rinse chicken. Trim off any fat. Pat dry with paper towels.

2. Combine flour, poultry seasoning, garlic salt and pepper in resealable plastic food storage bag. Mix together cornflake crumbs and parsley in shallow bowl. Whisk together egg white and water in small bowl.

3. Add chicken to flour mixture, one or two pieces at a time. Seal bag; shake until chicken is well coated. Remove chicken from bag, shaking off excess flour. Dip into egg white mixture, coating all sides. Roll in crumb mixture. Place in shallow baking pan. Repeat with remaining chicken, flour mixture, egg white and crumb mixture.

4. Lightly spray chicken pieces with cooking spray. Bake breast pieces 18 to 20 minutes or until no longer pink in center. Bake drumsticks about 25 minutes or until juices run clear. *Makes 4 servings*

Nutrients per Serving: (1 Chicken breast half plus 1 drumstick)

Calories: 208, Calories from Fat: 18%, Total Fat: 4g, Saturated Fat: 1g, Cholesterol: 75mg, Sodium: 348mg, Carbohydrate: 14g, Dietary Fiber: 1g, Protein: 27g
Dietary Exchanges: 1 Starch, 3 Lean Meat

Caribbean Grilled Turkey

1 package BUTTERBALL® Fresh Boneless Turkey Breast Tenderloins
4 green onions
4 cloves garlic
2 tablespoons peach preserves
2 tablespoons fresh lime juice
1 teaspoon salt
1 teaspoon shredded lime peel
1 teaspoon bottled hot sauce
1 teaspoon soy sauce
¼ teaspoon black pepper

Lightly spray unheated grill rack with nonstick cooking spray. Prepare grill for medium-direct-heat cooking. In food processor or blender, process onions, garlic, preserves, lime juice, salt, lime peel, hot sauce, soy sauce and pepper until smooth. Spread over tenderloins. Place tenderloins on rack over medium-hot grill. Grill 20 minutes or until meat is no longer pink, turning frequently for even browning.
Makes 6 servings

Preparation Time: 25 minutes

Nutrients per Serving: ⅙ of total recipe

Calories: 88, Calories from Fat: 3%, Total Fat: <1g, Saturated Fat: <1g, Cholesterol: 37mg, Sodium: 488mg, Carbohydrate: 7g, Dietary Fiber: <1g, Protein: 14g
Dietary Exchanges: 2 Lean Meat

90's-Style Slow Cooker Coq au Vin

2 packages BUTTERBALL® Boneless Skinless Chicken Breast Fillets
1 pound fresh mushrooms, sliced thick
1 jar (15 ounces) pearl onions, drained
½ cup dry white wine
1 teaspoon thyme leaves
1 bay leaf
1 cup chicken broth
⅓ cup flour
½ cup chopped fresh parsley

Slow Cooker Directions
Place chicken, mushrooms, onions, wine, thyme and bay leaf in slow cooker. Combine chicken broth and flour; pour into slow cooker. Cover and cook 5 hours on low setting. Add parsley. Serve over wild rice pilaf, if desired.
Makes 8 servings

Note: Remove and discard bay leaf before serving.

Prep Time: 30 minutes plus cooking time

Nutrients per Serving: ⅛ of total recipe (using 3 ounces uncooked chicken, cooked, per serving) without rice pilaf

Calories: 175, Calories from Fat: 8%, Total Fat: 2g, Saturated Fat: <1g, Cholesterol: 49mg, Sodium: 181mg, Carbohydrate: 15g, Dietary Fiber: 1g, Protein: 23g
Dietary Exchanges: 2 Vegetable, 2½ Lean Meat

Spicy Turkey Casserole

- 1 tablespoon olive oil
- 1 pound turkey breast cutlets, cut into ½-inch pieces
- 2 spicy chicken or turkey sausages (about 3 ounces each), sliced ½ inch thick
- 1 cup diced green bell pepper
- ½ cup sliced mushrooms
- ½ cup diced onion
- 1 jalapeño pepper,* seeded and minced (optional)
- ½ cup fat-free reduced-sodium chicken broth or water
- 1 can (14½ ounces) no-salt-added diced tomatoes, undrained
- 1 teaspoon Italian seasoning
- ¼ teaspoon black pepper
- ½ teaspoon paprika
- 1 cup cooked yolk-free egg noodles
- 6 tablespoons grated Parmesan cheese
- 2 tablespoons coarse bread crumbs

Jalapeño peppers can sting and irritate the skin; wear rubber gloves when handling peppers and do not touch eyes. Wash hands after handling peppers.

1. Preheat oven to 350°F. Heat oil in large nonstick skillet. Add turkey and sausages; cook and stir over medium heat 2 minutes. Add bell pepper, mushrooms, onion and jalapeño pepper, if desired. Cook and stir 5 minutes. Add chicken broth; cook 1 minute, scraping any browned bits off bottom of skillet. Add tomatoes with juice, seasonings and noodles.

2. Spoon mixture into shallow 10-inch round casserole. Sprinkle evenly with cheese and bread crumbs. Bake 15 to 20 minutes or until mixture is hot and bread crumbs are brown. Garnish as desired.   *Makes 6 servings*

Nutrients per Serving: 1 cup (without garnish)

Calories: 268, Calories from Fat: 23%, Total Fat: 6g, Saturated Fat: 2g, Cholesterol: 52mg, Sodium: 347mg, Carbohydrate: 23g, Dietary Fiber: 3g, Protein: 25g

Dietary Exchanges: 1 Starch, 1 Vegetable, 3 Lean Meat

Fire Eaters' Chicken

- 1 package (about 1¼ pounds) PERDUE® FIT 'N EASY® Skinless & Boneless Chicken Breasts
- 3 tablespoons lemon juice
- 1 tablespoon olive oil
- 2 garlic cloves, minced
- 2 teaspoons paprika
- 1 teaspoon ground red pepper or to taste
- ¾ teaspoon salt
- Lemon wedges (optional)

Place chicken in shallow dish. In small bowl, combine remaining ingredients except lemon wedges. Pour marinade over chicken, turning to coat both sides. Cover and refrigerate 1 hour or longer.

Prepare lightly greased grill for cooking. Drain chicken; discard marinade. Grill chicken breasts, uncovered, 5 to 6 inches over white-hot coals 6 to 8 minutes on each side until cooked through. To serve, garnish with lemon wedges.

Makes 4 servings

Nutrients per Serving: ¼ of total recipe (without garnish)

Calories: 195, Calories from Fat: 25%, Total Fat: 5g, Saturated Fat: 1g, Cholesterol: 82mg, Sodium: 511mg, Carbohydrate: 2g, Dietary Fiber: <1g, Protein: 33g

Dietary Exchanges: 4 Lean Meat

Grilled Chicken Adobo

- ½ cup chopped onion
- ⅓ cup lime juice
- 6 cloves garlic, coarsely chopped
- 1 teaspoon dried oregano leaves, crushed
- 1 teaspoon ground cumin
- ½ teaspoon dried thyme leaves
- ¼ teaspoon ground red pepper
- 6 boneless skinless chicken breasts (about 1½ pounds)
- 3 tablespoons chopped fresh cilantro

1. Combine onion, lime juice and garlic in food processor. Process until onion is finely minced. Transfer to resealable plastic food storage bag. Add oregano, cumin, thyme and red pepper; knead bag until blended. Place chicken in bag; press out air and seal. Turn to coat chicken with marinade. Refrigerate 30 minutes or up to 4 hours.

2. Spray grid with nonstick cooking spray. Prepare grill for direct cooking. Remove chicken from marinade; discard marinade. Place chicken on grid 3 to 4 inches from medium-hot coals. Grill 5 to 7 minutes on each side or until chicken is no longer pink in center.

3. Transfer to clean serving platter and sprinkle with cilantro.   *Makes 6 servings*

Nutrients per Serving: 1 grilled Chicken breast

Calories: 139, Calories from Fat: 19%, Total Fat: 3g, Saturated Fat: <1g, Cholesterol: 69mg, Sodium: 61mg, Carbohydrate: 1g, Dietary Fiber: <1g, Protein: 25g

Dietary Exchanges: 3 Lean Meat

Southern Style Mustard BBQ Chicken Kabobs

1½ cups catsup
1 cup prepared mustard
½ to ⅔ cup cider vinegar
½ cup EQUAL® SPOONFUL*
1 tablespoon Worcestershire sauce
½ teaspoon maple flavoring
½ teaspoon coarsely ground black pepper
2 tablespoons butter or margarine
1½ pounds skinless, boneless chicken breasts, cut into ¾-inch cubes
2 small yellow summer squash, cut crosswise into 1-inch slices
12 medium mushroom caps
1 large red or green bell pepper, cut into 1-inch pieces

*May substitute 12 packets Equal® sweetener.

• Mix all ingredients, except chicken and vegetables, in medium saucepan. Cook over medium heat 3 to 4 minutes or until sauce is hot and butter is melted.

• Assemble chicken cubes and vegetables on 6 skewers; grill over medium heat 10 to 15 minutes until chicken is no longer pink in center, turning occasionally and basting generously with sauce. Bring remaining sauce to a boil in small saucepan. Serve with kabobs. *Makes 6 servings*

Note: Kabobs can also be baked. Arrange kabobs in greased baking pan; spray with nonstick cooking spray. Bake, uncovered, in preheated 375°F oven until chicken is no longer pink and vegetables are tender, about 20 minutes. Turn kabobs and baste generously with sauce during last 10 minutes of baking time.

Note: Kabobs can also be broiled. Broil 6 inches from heat source until chicken is no longer pink and vegetables are tender, 10 to 12 minutes, turning occasionally and basting generously with sauce. Do not baste during last 5 minutes of broiling.

Nutrients per Serving: 1 Kabob with sauce

Calories: 286, Calories from Fat: 23%, Total Fat: 8g,
Saturated Fat: 3g, Cholesterol: 77mg, Sodium: 1,273mg,
Carbohydrate: 27g, Dietary Fiber: 4g, Protein: 31g
Dietary Exchanges: 1 Starch, 2 Vegetable, 3 Lean Meat

Turkey Paprikash

1 cup uncooked yolk-free extra-broad noodles
   Nonstick cooking spray
6 ounces turkey tenderloin, cut into ½-inch pieces
8 ounces mushrooms, sliced
1 cup diced green bell pepper
1 cup thinly sliced carrots
1 cup slivered onion
2 cloves garlic, minced
2 teaspoons paprika
¾ cup water
1 tablespoon plus 1½ teaspoons tomato paste
⅛ teaspoon salt
⅛ teaspoon black pepper
3 tablespoons reduced-fat sour cream
2 teaspoons minced fresh parsley

1. Cook noodles according to package directions, omitting salt. Drain and keep warm.

2. Meanwhile, spray medium skillet with cooking spray. Heat over medium heat until hot. Add turkey; cook and stir 1 minute or until browned on all sides. Add mushrooms, bell pepper, carrots and onion; cook and stir 3 minutes or until crisp-tender. Add garlic and paprika. Cook and stir 30 seconds or until garlic is fragrant.

3. Stir in water, tomato paste, salt and black pepper. Simmer, uncovered, 10 minutes. Remove from heat; stir in cooked noodles. Stir several tablespoons of liquid into sour cream, then stir sour cream mixture into turkey mixture. Top each serving with parsley. *Makes 2 servings*

Nutrients per Serving: ½ of total recipe

Calories: 330, Calories from Fat: 19%, Total Fat: 7g,
Saturated Fat: 3g, Cholesterol: 47mg, Sodium: 484mg,
Carbohydrate: 43g, Dietary Fiber: 8g, Protein: 26g
Dietary Exchanges: 2 Starch, 3 Vegetable, 2 Lean Meat

TIP The catsup, mustard and Worcestershire sauce in the Southern Style Mustard BBQ Chicken Kabobs are contributing to its higher sodium content. Certain brands contain less sodium than others. You can find this information simply by checking the products' food labels.

Crispy Baked Chicken

Crispy Baked Chicken

    8 ounces (1 cup) fat-free French onion dip
½ cup fat-free (skim) milk
    1 cup cornflake crumbs
½ cup wheat germ
    6 skinless chicken breasts or thighs (about
        1½ pounds)

1. Preheat oven to 350°F. Spray shallow baking pan with nonstick cooking spray.

2. Place dip in shallow bowl; stir until smooth. Add milk, 1 tablespoon at a time, until pourable consistency is reached.

3. Combine cornflake crumbs and wheat germ on plate.

4. Dip chicken pieces in milk mixture, then roll in cornflake mixture. Place chicken in single layer in prepared pan. Bake 45 to 50 minutes or until juices run clear when chicken is pierced with fork and chicken is no longer pink near bone.   *Makes 6 servings*

Nutrients per Serving: 1 Baked Chicken breast

Calories: 253, Calories from Fat: 8%, Total Fat: 2g,
Saturated Fat: <1g, Cholesterol: 66mg, Sodium: 437mg,
Carbohydrate: 22g, Dietary Fiber: 1g, Protein: 35g
Dietary Exchanges: 1½ Starch, 3 Lean Meat

Roast Turkey Breast with Apple-Corn Bread Stuffing

    Nonstick cooking spray
    1 medium onion, chopped
1¼ cups fat-free reduced-sodium chicken broth
    1 package (8 ounces) corn bread stuffing mix
    1 Granny Smith apple, diced
¾ teaspoon dried sage, divided
¾ teaspoon dried thyme leaves, divided
    1 boneless turkey breast (1½ pounds)
    1 teaspoon paprika
¼ teaspoon black pepper
    1 cup whole-berry cranberry sauce (optional)

1. Preheat oven to 450°F. Coat 1½-quart casserole with cooking spray; set aside.

2. Coat large saucepan with cooking spray; heat over medium heat. Add onion; cook and stir 5 minutes. Add broth; bring to a simmer. Stir in stuffing mix, apple, ¼ teaspoon sage and ¼ teaspoon thyme. Transfer mixture to prepared casserole; set aside.

3. Coat shallow roasting pan with cooking spray. Place turkey breast in pan, skin side up; coat turkey with cooking spray. Mix paprika, remaining ½ teaspoon sage, ½ teaspoon thyme and pepper in small bowl; sprinkle over turkey. Spray lightly with cooking spray.

4. Place turkey in preheated oven; roast 15 minutes. *Reduce oven temperature to 350°F.* Place stuffing in oven alongside turkey; continue to roast 35 minutes or until internal temperature of turkey reaches 170°F when tested with meat thermometer inserted into thickest part of breast.

5. Transfer turkey to cutting board; cover with foil and let stand 10 to 15 minutes before carving. (Internal temperature will rise 5° to 10°F during stand time). Remove stuffing from oven; cover to keep warm. Carve turkey into thin slices; serve with stuffing and cranberry sauce, if desired.   *Makes 6 servings*

Nutrients per Serving: ⅙ of total recipe (without cranberry sauce)

Calories: 304, Calories from Fat: 8%, Total Fat: 3g,
Saturated Fat: 1g, Cholesterol: 75mg, Sodium: 580mg,
Carbohydrate: 34g, Dietary Fiber: 7g, Protein: 33g
Dietary Exchanges: 2 Starch, 4 Lean Meat

Chicken & Vegetable Tortilla Roll-Ups

1 pound boneless skinless chicken breasts, cooked
1 cup chopped broccoli
1 cup diced carrots
1 can (10¾ ounces) reduced-fat condensed cream of celery soup, undiluted
¼ cup reduced-fat (2%) milk
1 tablespoon dry sherry
½ cup grated Parmesan cheese
6 (10-inch) fat-free flour tortillas

1. Preheat oven to 350°F. Spray 13×9-inch baking dish with nonstick cooking spray; set aside. Cut chicken into 1-inch pieces; set aside.

2. Combine broccoli and carrots in 1-quart microwavable dish. Cover and microwave at HIGH 2 to 3 minutes or until vegetables are crisp-tender; set aside.

3. Combine soup, milk and sherry in small saucepan over medium heat; cook and stir 5 minutes. Stir in Parmesan cheese, chicken, broccoli and carrots. Cook 2 minutes or until cheese is melted. Remove from heat.

4. Spoon ¼ cup chicken mixture onto each tortilla. Roll up and place seam-side-down in prepared baking dish. Bake, covered, 20 minutes or until heated through.

Makes 6 servings

Nutrients per Serving: 1 Roll-Up

Calories: 284, Calories from Fat: 27%, Total Fat: 8g, Saturated Fat: 3g, Cholesterol: 51mg, Sodium: 714mg, Carbohydrate: 25g, Dietary Fiber: 3g, Protein: 25g
Dietary Exchanges: 1½ Starch, ½ Vegetable, 3 Lean Meat

Turkey Breast with Barley-Cranberry Stuffing

2 cups fat-free reduced-sodium chicken broth
1 cup uncooked quick-cooking barley
½ cup chopped onion
½ cup dried cranberries
2 tablespoons slivered almonds, toasted
½ teaspoon rubbed sage
½ teaspoon garlic-pepper seasoning
   Nonstick cooking spray
1 fresh or frozen bone-in turkey breast half (about 2 pounds), thawed and skinned
⅓ cup finely chopped fresh parsley

Slow Cooker Directions

1. Combine broth, barley, onion, cranberries, almonds, sage and garlic-pepper seasoning in slow cooker.

2. Spray large nonstick skillet with cooking spray. Heat over medium heat until hot. Brown turkey breast on all sides; add to slow cooker. Cover and cook on LOW 3 to 4 hours or until internal temperature of turkey reaches 170°F when tested with meat thermometer inserted into thickest part of breast, not touching bone.

3. Transfer turkey to cutting board; cover with foil and let stand 10 to 15 minutes before carving. (Internal temperature will rise 5° to 10°F during stand time.) Stir parsley into sauce mixture in slow cooker. Serve sliced turkey with sauce and stuffing.

Makes 6 servings

Nutrients per Serving: ⅙ of total recipe

Calories: 298, Calories from Fat: 13%, Total Fat: 5g, Saturated Fat: 1g, Cholesterol: 55mg, Sodium: 114mg, Carbohydrate: 33g, Dietary Fiber: 6g, Protein: 31g
Dietary Exchanges: 2 Starch, 3 Lean Meat

Grilled Honey Mustard Chicken with Toasted Almonds

¼ cup GREY POUPON® Dijon Mustard
3 tablespoons honey
1 tablespoon lemon juice
1 clove garlic, crushed
8 boneless skinless chicken breasts (about 2 pounds)
¼ cup PLANTERS® Sliced Almonds, toasted

1. Blend mustard, honey, lemon juice and garlic in small bowl.

2. Grill or broil chicken 6 inches from heat source for 10 to 15 minutes, turning occasionally and brushing with mustard mixture frequently. Do not brush during last 5 minutes of grilling or broiling. Sprinkle with almonds before serving.

Makes 8 servings

Nutrients per Serving: 1 Chicken breast

Calories: 182, Calories from Fat: 20%, Total Fat: 4g, Saturated Fat: 1g, Cholesterol: 66mg, Sodium: 102mg, Carbohydrate: 8g, Dietary Fiber: 1g, Protein: 28g
Dietary Exchanges: ½ Starch, 3 Lean Meat

Chicken Breasts with Crabmeat Stuffing

4 boneless skinless chicken breasts (about 1 pound)
¾ cup whole wheat cracker crumbs, divided
3 ounces canned crabmeat, rinsed twice and drained
¼ cup fat-free mayonnaise
2 tablespoons grated Parmesan cheese
2 tablespoons finely chopped green onions
2 tablespoons fresh lemon juice
¼ teaspoon hot pepper sauce
1 tablespoon dried parsley flakes
1 teaspoon paprika
1 teaspoon black pepper
½ cup low-fat (1%) milk

1. Pound chicken breasts between two pieces of plastic wrap to ¼-inch thickness using flat side of meat mallet or rolling pin.

2. Combine ¼ cup cracker crumbs, crabmeat, mayonnaise, cheese, green onions, lemon juice and pepper sauce in medium bowl. Divide filling evenly among chicken breasts. Roll up each chicken breast from short side, tucking in ends; secure with toothpick.

Chicken Breast with Crabmeat Stuffing

3. Combine remaining ½ cup cracker crumbs, parsley flakes, paprika and black pepper in medium bowl. Dip chicken in milk; roll in cracker crumb mixture. Reserve remaining milk.

4. Place chicken in microwavable round or square baking dish. Cover with waxed paper. Microwave at HIGH 10 minutes or until chicken is no longer pink in center. Remove chicken from dish.

5. Add reserved milk to pan juices; microwave at HIGH until sauce boils at least 1 minute. Cut chicken into slices before serving, if desired. Serve sauce over chicken.

Makes 4 servings

Nutrients per Serving: 1 Stuffed Breast with ¼ of sauce

Calories: 246, Calories from Fat: 17%, Total Fat: 5g, Saturated Fat: 2g, Cholesterol: 83mg, Sodium: 424mg, Carbohydrate: 21g, Dietary Fiber: <1g, Protein: 30g

Dietary Exchanges: 1½ Starch, 3 Lean Meat

Turkey Shanghai

Nonstick cooking spray
12 ounces turkey breast tenderloin, thinly sliced
1 cup thinly sliced carrots
½ cup sliced green onions
3 cloves garlic, minced
4 cups fat-free reduced-sodium chicken broth
6 ounces uncooked angel hair pasta
2 cups frozen French-style green beans
¼ cup plus 2 tablespoons stir-fry sauce
1 teaspoon dark sesame oil

1. Spray large nonstick skillet with cooking spray; heat over medium heat until hot. Add turkey and carrots; cook and stir 5 minutes or until turkey is no longer pink. Stir in onions and garlic; cook and stir 2 minutes.

2. Add chicken broth to skillet; bring to a boil over high heat. Stir in pasta. Return to a boil. Reduce heat to low. Simmer, uncovered, 5 minutes, stirring frequently.

3. Stir green beans into skillet. Simmer 2 to 3 minutes or until pasta is just tender, stirring occasionally. Remove from heat. Stir in stir-fry sauce and sesame oil. Let stand 5 minutes. Garnish as desired. *Makes 6 servings*

Nutrients per Serving: ⅙ of total recipe (without garnish)

Calories: 209, Calories from Fat: 12%, Total Fat: 3g, Saturated Fat: 1g, Cholesterol: 25mg, Sodium: 712mg, Carbohydrate: 28g, Dietary Fiber: 3g, Protein: 20g

Dietary Exchanges: 1½ Starch, 1 Vegetable, 1½ Lean Meat

Caponata Stir-Fry

Nonstick cooking spray
1 can (14½ ounces) fat-free reduced-sodium chicken broth plus 1 can water
1 cup polenta or whole grain cornmeal
2 tablespoons minced garlic (10 to 12 cloves), divided
½ teaspoon black pepper
¼ cup shredded Parmesan cheese
1 medium eggplant, cut into 1½-inch cubes (about ¾ pound)
8 ounces boneless skinless chicken breasts
1 medium onion, chopped
1 tablespoon olive oil
1 can (14½ ounces) no-salt-added stewed tomatoes
1 small green bell pepper, diced
1 small red bell pepper, diced
2 tablespoons drained capers *or* ⅓ cup drained green olives, coarsely chopped
1½ teaspoons dried Italian herbs
2 tablespoons balsamic vinegar or red wine vinegar

1. Spray 8×8×2-inch baking pan with cooking spray; set aside. Place chicken broth, water, polenta, 1 tablespoon garlic and black pepper in large saucepan. Bring to a boil over high heat. Reduce heat to a simmer; cook and stir 5 minutes or until polenta thickens and pulls away from side of saucepan. Fold in Parmesan cheese. Spread evenly into prepared pan. Place on wire rack to cool.

2. Place eggplant in large microwavable bowl; cover. Microwave at HIGH 10 to 12 minutes, stirring every 3 minutes, or until tender when pierced (eggplant will feel springy when pressed). Set aside.

3. Preheat broiler. Cut chicken breasts into thin strips. Spray large nonstick skillet with cooking spray; heat over high heat. Add chicken; stir-fry 3 minutes or until no longer pink. Remove chicken; set aside. Add onion to same skillet; stir-fry 4 minutes or until golden. Remove onion; set aside.

4. Heat oil in same skillet. Add eggplant and remaining 1 tablespoon garlic; stir-fry 2 to 3 minutes or until golden. Add chicken, onion, tomatoes, bell peppers, capers and Italian herbs. Reduce heat to medium; simmer 4 to 6 minutes or until liquid evaporates. Remove from heat. Stir in vinegar.

5. Meanwhile, spray top of polenta with cooking spray. Broil 2 to 3 inches from heat 3 to 4 minutes or until top is golden. Cut into 4 pieces. Transfer pieces to 4 plates. Spoon caponata mixture evenly over top.   *Makes 4 servings*

Nutrients per Serving: ¼ of total recipe

Calories: 301, Calories from Fat: 25%, Total Fat: 8g, Saturated Fat: 3g, Cholesterol: 42mg, Sodium: 506mg, Carbohydrate: 34g, Dietary Fiber: 6g, Protein: 22g
Dietary Exchanges: 1 Starch, 3 Vegetable, 2 Lean Meat, ½ Fat

Chicken Noodle Roll-Ups

9 uncooked lasagna noodles (about 9 ounces)
8 ounces boneless skinless chicken breasts, cut into chunks
Nonstick cooking spray
2 cups finely chopped broccoli
2 cups low-fat (1%) cottage cheese
1 egg
2 teaspoons minced fresh chives
¼ teaspoon ground nutmeg
¼ teaspoon black pepper
1 tablespoon reduced-fat margarine
2 tablespoons all-purpose flour
1 cup reduced-sodium chicken broth
½ cup fat-free (skim) milk
½ teaspoon dry mustard
1 medium tomato, seeded and chopped

1. Cook lasagna noodles according to package directions, omitting salt. Drain and rinse well under cold water. Place in single layer on aluminum foil.

2. Preheat oven to 375°F. Place chicken in food processor or blender; process until finely chopped. Spray large nonstick skillet with cooking spray; heat over medium heat. Add chicken; cook 4 minutes or until chicken is no longer pink. Stir in broccoli; cook about 3 minutes or until broccoli is crisp-tender. Cool.

3. Combine cottage cheese, egg, chives, nutmeg and black pepper in medium bowl. Stir in chicken mixture. Spread a generous ⅓ cup filling over each lasagna noodle. Roll up noodle, starting at short end. Place filled rolls seam-side-down in 10×8-inch baking dish; set aside.

4. Melt margarine in small saucepan. Stir in flour; cook 1 minute. Whisk in chicken broth, milk and mustard. Cook, stirring constantly, until thickened. Pour sauce evenly over filled rolls; sprinkle with tomato. Cover dish with foil. Bake 30 to 35 minutes or until filling is set. Garnish as desired.   *Makes 9 servings*

Nutrients per Serving: 1 Roll-Up (without garnish)

Calories: 179, Calories from Fat: 22%, Total Fat: 4g, Saturated Fat: 1g, Cholesterol: 46mg, Sodium: 291mg, Carbohydrate: 17g, Dietary Fiber: 2g, Protein: 18g
Dietary Exchanges: 1 Starch, 2 Lean Meat

Spinach-Stuffed Chicken Breast

4. Place stuffed chicken breasts seam-side-down in 9-inch square baking pan. Lightly spray chicken with cooking spray. Pour white grape juice over top. Bake 30 minutes or until chicken is no longer pink.

5. Remove string; cut chicken rolls into ½-inch diagonal slices. Arrange on plate. Pour pan juices over chicken. Garnish as desired. *Makes 4 servings*

Nutrients per Serving: 1 Stuffed Chicken Breast (without garnish)

Calories: 187, Calories from Fat: 21%, Total Fat: 4g, Saturated Fat: 2g, Cholesterol: 71mg, Sodium: 302mg, Carbohydrate: 10g, Dietary Fiber: 2g, Protein: 26g

Dietary Exchanges: 1 Vegetable, 3 Lean Meat

Low Fat Turkey Bacon Frittata

1 package (12 ounces) BUTTERBALL® Turkey Bacon, heated and chopped
6 ounces uncooked angel hair pasta, broken
2 teaspoons olive oil
1 small onion, sliced
1 red bell pepper, cut into thin strips
4 containers (4 ounces each) egg substitute
1 container (5 ounces) fat free ricotta cheese
1 cup (4 ounces) shredded fat free mozzarella cheese
1 cup (4 ounces) shredded reduced fat Swiss cheese
½ teaspoon salt
½ teaspoon black pepper
1 package (10 ounces) frozen spinach, thawed and squeezed dry

Cook and drain pasta. Heat oil in large skillet over medium heat until hot. Cook and stir onion and bell pepper until tender. Combine egg substitute, cheeses, salt, black pepper and cooked pasta in large bowl. Add vegetables, spinach and turkey bacon. Spray 10-inch quiche dish with nonstick cooking spray; pour mixture into dish. Bake in preheated 350°F oven 30 minutes. Cut into 8 wedges. Serve with spicy salsa, if desired.

Makes 8 servings

Preparation Time: 15 minutes plus baking time

Nutrients per Serving: 1 Frittata wedge (⅛ of total recipe) without spicy salsa

Calories: 267, Calories from Fat: 35%, Total Fat: 10g, Saturated Fat: 2g, Cholesterol: 61mg, Sodium: 1,030mg, Carbohydrate: 18g, Dietary Fiber: 2g, Protein: 25g

Dietary Exchanges: 1 Starch, 3 Lean Meat

Spinach-Stuffed Chicken Breasts

4 boneless skinless chicken breasts (about 1 pound)
5 ounces frozen chopped spinach, thawed and well drained
2 tablespoons freshly grated Parmesan cheese
1 teaspoon grated lemon peel
¼ teaspoon black pepper
Olive oil-flavored nonstick cooking spray
1 cup thinly sliced mushrooms
6 slices (2 ounces) thinly sliced low-fat turkey-ham
1 cup white grape juice

1. Trim fat from chicken; discard. Place each chicken breast between 2 sheets of plastic wrap. Pound with meat mallet until chicken is about ¼ inch thick.

2. Preheat oven to 350°F. Pat spinach dry with paper towels. Combine spinach, Parmesan, lemon peel and black pepper in large bowl. Spray small nonstick skillet with cooking spray; add mushrooms. Cook and stir over medium heat 3 to 4 minutes or until tender.

3. Arrange 1½ slices turkey-ham over each chicken breast. Spread each with one-fourth of spinach mixture. Top each with mushrooms. Beginning with longer side, roll chicken tightly. Tie with kitchen string.

Polynesian Chicken and Rice

1 can (20 ounces) DOLE® Pineapple Tidbits or Pineapple Chunks
½ cup DOLE® Seedless or Golden Raisins
½ cup sliced green onions
2 teaspoons finely chopped fresh ginger or
    ½ teaspoon ground ginger
1 clove garlic, finely chopped
3 cups cooked white or brown rice
2 cups chopped cooked chicken breast or turkey breast
2 tablespoons low-sodium soy sauce

• Drain pineapple tidbits; reserve 4 tablespoons juice.

• Heat 2 tablespoons reserved juice over medium heat in large, nonstick skillet. Add raisins, green onions, ginger and garlic; cook and stir 3 minutes.

• Stir in pineapple tidbits, rice, chicken, soy sauce and remaining 2 tablespoons juice. Cover; reduce heat to low and cook 5 minutes more or until heated through. Garnish with cherry tomatoes and green onions, if desired.

Makes 4 servings

Prep Time: 20 minutes
Cook Time: 10 minutes

Nutrients per Serving: ¼ of total recipe (without garnish)

Calories: 420, Calories from Fat: 6%, Total Fat: 3g, Saturated Fat: 1g, Cholesterol: 54mg, Sodium: 304mg, Carbohydrate: 74g, Dietary Fiber: 3g, Protein: 26g
Dietary Exchanges: 3 Starch, 2 Fruit, 2 Lean Meat

Slow Cooker Turkey Breast

1 bone-in turkey breast half (about 2 pounds)
    Garlic powder
    Paprika
    Dried parsley flakes

Slow Cooker Directions

Place turkey in slow cooker. Sprinkle with garlic powder, paprika and parsley to taste. Cover and cook on LOW 3 to 4 hours or until internal temperature reaches 170°F when tested with meat thermometer inserted into thickest part of breast, not touching bone. Transfer turkey to cutting board; cover with foil and let stand 10 to 15 minutes before carving. (Internal temperature will rise 5° to 10°F during stand time.)

Makes 8 servings

Nutrients per Serving: ⅛ of total recipe

Calories: 140, Calories from Fat: 19%, Total Fat: 3g, Saturated Fat: 1g, Cholesterol: 79mg, Sodium: 41mg, Carbohydrate: 0g, Dietary Fiber: 0g, Protein: 27g
Dietary Exchanges: 3 Lean Meat

Curried Chicken & Vegetables with Rice

1 pound chicken tenders or boneless skinless chicken breasts, cut crosswise into ½-inch slices
2 teaspoons curry powder
¼ teaspoon salt
¼ teaspoon ground red pepper
1 tablespoon vegetable oil
1 medium onion, chopped
3 cloves garlic, minced
1¼ cups fat-free reduced-sodium chicken broth, divided
1 package (16 ounces) frozen mixed vegetable medley, such as broccoli, red bell peppers, cauliflower and sugar snap peas, thawed
2 tablespoons tomato paste
2 teaspoons cornstarch
3 cups hot cooked white rice
½ cup plain nonfat yogurt
⅓ cup chopped fresh cilantro

1. Toss chicken with curry powder, salt and ground red pepper in medium bowl; set aside.

2. Heat oil in large nonstick skillet over medium heat. Add onion; cook 5 minutes, stirring occasionally. Add chicken and garlic; cook 4 minutes or until chicken is no longer pink in center, stirring occasionally. Add 1 cup chicken broth, vegetables and tomato paste; bring to a boil over high heat. Reduce heat to medium; simmer, uncovered, 3 to 4 minutes or until vegetables are crisp-tender.

3. Combine remaining ¼ cup chicken broth and cornstarch, mixing until smooth. Stir into chicken mixture; simmer 2 minutes or until sauce thickens, stirring occasionally. Serve over rice; top evenly with yogurt and cilantro.

Makes 6 servings

Nutrients per Serving: ⅙ of total recipe

Calories: 269, Calories from Fat: 16%, Total Fat: 5g, Saturated Fat: 1g, Cholesterol: 46mg, Sodium: 199mg, Carbohydrate: 33g, Dietary Fiber: 3g, Protein: 23g
Dietary Exchanges: 1½ Starch, 1½ Vegetable, 2 Lean Meat

Matchstick Stir Fry

1 package BUTTERBALL® Fresh Boneless
    Turkey Breast Strips
1 tablespoon cornstarch
1 cup orange juice
1 tablespoon reduced sodium soy sauce
1 clove garlic, minced
2 teaspoons grated orange peel
2 teaspoons minced fresh ginger
1 teaspoon sugar
½ teaspoon salt
¼ teaspoon red pepper flakes
1 tablespoon vegetable oil
¼ pound snow peas, trimmed
2 small carrots, cut into thin strips
1 small onion, cut into strips
1 small red bell pepper, cut into thin strips
2 oranges, peeled and sectioned

Combine cornstarch, orange juice, soy sauce, garlic, orange peel, ginger, sugar, salt and red pepper flakes in small bowl. Stir until mixture is smooth; set aside. Heat oil in large skillet or wok over high heat until hot; add turkey. Cook and stir 4 to 5 minutes or until turkey is no longer pink; remove from skillet. Add snow peas, carrots, onion and bell pepper. Cook and stir 1 minute; remove from skillet. Add cornstarch mixture to skillet. Cook and stir until mixture thickens; add turkey and vegetables. Reduce heat to low; simmer, covered, 1 minute. Add orange sections. Serve with almond rice, if desired.   *Makes 6 servings*

Note: If short on time, substitute packaged frozen stir-fry blend vegetables for fresh vegetables.

Prep Time: 20 minutes

Nutrients per Serving: ⅙ of total recipe (using 2 ounces uncooked turkey, cooked, per serving) without rice

Calories: 161, Calories from Fat: 16%, Total Fat: 3g, Saturated Fat: <1g, Cholesterol: 37mg, Sodium: 310mg, Carbohydrate: 18g, Dietary Fiber: 3g, Protein: 16g
Dietary Exchanges: ½ Fruit, 1 Vegetable, 2 Lean Meat

TIP To cut a bell pepper into thin strips, stand the pepper on its end on a cutting board. Cut off 3 to 4 lengthwise slices from the sides with a utility knife, cutting close to, but not through, the stem. Discard the stem and seeds. Scrape out any remaining seeds, and rinse the inside of the pepper under cold running water. Slice each piece lengthwise into long, thin strips.

Chicken Tetrazzini

8 ounces uncooked vermicelli or other thin
    noodle
2 teaspoons margarine
8 ounces fresh mushrooms, sliced
¼ cup chopped green onions
1 can (14½ ounces) fat-free reduced-sodium
    chicken broth
1 cup low-fat (1%) milk, divided
2 tablespoons dry sherry
¼ cup all-purpose flour
¼ teaspoon salt
¼ teaspoon ground nutmeg
⅛ teaspoon white pepper
2 ounces chopped pimiento, drained
4 tablespoons (1 ounce) grated Parmesan
    cheese, divided
½ cup reduced-fat sour cream
2 cups cooked boneless skinless chicken
    breasts, cut into bite-sized pieces

1. Preheat oven to 350°F. Lightly coat 1½-quart casserole with nonstick cooking spray. Cook noodles according to package directions, omitting salt. Drain; set aside.

2. Melt margarine in large nonstick skillet over medium-high heat. Add mushrooms and onions; cook and stir until onions are tender. Add chicken broth, ½ cup milk and sherry to onion mixture.

3. Pour remaining ½ cup milk into small jar with tight-fitting lid; add flour, salt, nutmeg and pepper. Shake well. Slowly stir flour mixture into skillet. Bring to a boil; cook 1 minute. Reduce heat; stir in pimiento and 2 tablespoons Parmesan cheese. Stir in sour cream; blend well. Add chicken and noodles; mix well.

4. Spread mixture evenly into prepared casserole. Sprinkle with remaining 2 tablespoons Parmesan cheese. Bake 30 to 35 minutes or until hot. Let cool slightly before serving.
Makes 6 servings

Nutrients per Serving: ⅙ of total recipe

Calories: 338, Calories from Fat: 16%, Total Fat: 6g, Saturated Fat: 2g, Cholesterol: 40mg, Sodium: 343mg, Carbohydrate: 44g, Dietary Fiber: 1g, Protein: 23g
Dietary Exchanges: 2½ Starch, 1 Vegetable, 2 Lean Meat

SEAFOOD ENTRÉES

Shrimp Java

¼ cup reduced-sodium soy sauce
2 tablespoons lime juice
1 tablespoon brown sugar
2 cloves garlic, minced
1 teaspoon ground cumin
½ teaspoon chili powder
1 pound raw large shrimp, peeled and deveined
½ small bunch fresh cilantro, coarsely chopped
3 tablespoons vegetable oil
3 cups hot cooked rice

1. Combine soy sauce, lime juice, brown sugar, garlic, cumin and chili powder in large bowl; stir until well mixed. Add shrimp and toss to coat. Marinate 15 minutes.

2. Meanwhile, remove and discard large stems from cilantro. Rinse cilantro; drain and dry in salad spinner, or pat dry with paper towels.

3. Heat wok over high heat about 1 minute or until hot. Drizzle oil into wok and heat 30 seconds. Add shrimp mixture; stir-fry about 4 minutes or until shrimp turn pink and opaque. Add half the cilantro; toss to combine. Transfer to serving dish. Garnish with remaining cilantro. Serve with rice. *Makes 6 servings*

Nutrients per Serving: ⅙ of Shrimp mixture with ½ cup cooked rice

Calories: 269, Calories from Fat: 29%, Total Fat: 9g, Saturated Fat: 1g, Cholesterol: 115mg, Sodium: 455mg, Carbohydrate: 28g, Dietary Fiber: 1g, Protein: 19g
Dietary Exchanges: 2 Starch, 2 Lean Meat, ½ Fat

Fish Burritos

PAM® No-Stick Cooking Spray
1 cup diced onion
1 pound orange roughy fillets or any white fish fillets
3 limes
1 (16-ounce) can ROSARITA® No Fat Traditional Refried Beans
8 burrito-size fat-free flour tortillas
2 cups cooked white rice
1½ cups shredded cabbage
¾ cup reduced-fat shredded sharp Cheddar cheese
¾ cup diced tomatoes
ROSARITA® Traditional Mild Salsa

1. Spray large no-stick skillet with PAM® Cooking Spray. Sauté onion until tender.

2. Add fish and juice from 1 lime. Cook until fish becomes flaky; shred with fork. Remove from heat. Set aside.

3. Evenly divide Rosarita Beans among *each* tortilla; spread beans down center of tortillas. Top beans with even amounts of fish, rice, cabbage, cheese and tomatoes.

4. Roll burrito-style, folding in edges. Serve with Rosarita Salsa and lime wedges. *Makes 8 burritos*

Nutrients per Serving: 1 Burrito (without Salsa)

Calories: 291, Calories from Fat: 8%, Total Fat: 3g, Saturated Fat: 1g, Cholesterol: 15mg, Sodium: 718mg, Carbohydrate: 52g, Dietary Fiber: 14g, Protein: 19g
Dietary Exchanges: 3 Starch, 2 Lean Meat

Shrimp in Mock Lobster Sauce

½ cup fat-free reduced-sodium beef or chicken broth
¼ cup oyster sauce
1 tablespoon cornstarch
1 egg
1 egg white
1 tablespoon peanut or vegetable oil
¾ pound raw medium or large shrimp, peeled and deveined
2 cloves garlic, minced
3 green onions with tops, cut into ½-inch pieces
2 cups hot cooked Chinese egg noodles

1. Stir broth and oyster sauce into cornstarch in small bowl until smooth. Beat egg with egg white in separate small bowl. Set aside.

2. Heat wok over medium-high heat 1 minute or until hot. Drizzle oil into wok and heat 30 seconds. Add shrimp and garlic; stir-fry 3 to 5 minutes or until shrimp turn opaque.

3. Stir broth mixture; add to wok. Add onions; stir-fry 1 minute or until sauce boils and thickens.

4. Stir eggs into wok; stir-fry 1 minute or just until eggs are set. Serve over noodles.   *Makes 4 servings*

Shrimp in Mock Lobster Sauce

Note: Oyster sauce is a thick, brown, concentrated sauce made of ground oysters, soy sauce and brine. It imparts a slight fish flavor and is used as a seasoning. It is readily available in the Asian section of large supermarkets.

Nutrients per Serving: ½ cup cooked noodles with ¼ of Sauce

Calories: 276, Calories from Fat: 21, Total Fat: 6g, Saturated Fat: 1g, Cholesterol: 182mg, Sodium: 628mg, Carbohydrate: 33g, Dietary Fiber: <1g, Protein: 21g
Dietary Exchanges: 2 Starch, 2 Lean Meat

Tuna Noodle Casserole

6 ounces uncooked noodles
1 tablespoon margarine
8 ounces fresh mushrooms, sliced
1 small onion, chopped
1 cup fat-free reduced-sodium chicken broth
1 cup fat-free (skim) milk
¼ cup all-purpose flour
1 can (12 ounces) tuna packed in water, drained
1 cup frozen peas, thawed
1 jar (2 ounces) chopped pimiento, drained
½ teaspoon dried thyme leaves
¼ teaspoon salt
⅛ teaspoon black pepper

1. Cook noodles according to package directions, omitting salt. Drain; cover. Set aside.

2. Melt margarine in large nonstick skillet over medium-high heat. Add mushrooms and onion; cook and stir 5 minutes or until onion is tender.

3. Using wire whisk, blend chicken broth, milk and flour in small bowl. Stir into mushroom mixture; bring to a boil. Cook and stir about 2 minutes or until thickened.

4. Reduce heat to medium; stir in tuna, peas, pimiento, thyme and salt. Add noodles and pepper; mix thoroughly. (Casserole can be served at this point.)

5. Preheat oven to 350°F. Spray 2-quart casserole with nonstick cooking spray. Spread noodle mixture evenly into prepared casserole. Bake 30 minutes or until bubbly and heated through. Let stand 5 minutes before serving.
           Makes 6 servings

Nutrients per Serving: ⅙ of total recipe

Calories: 254, Calories from Fat: 11%, Total Fat: 3g, Saturated Fat: 1g, Cholesterol: 18mg, Sodium: 585mg, Carbohydrate: 33g, Dietary Fiber: 2g, Protein: 23g
Dietary Exchanges: 2 Starch, 2 Lean Meat

Tuna Noodle Casserole ～ 197

Oriental Baked Cod

2 tablespoons reduced-sodium soy sauce
2 tablespoons apple juice
1 tablespoon finely chopped fresh ginger
2 cloves garlic, minced
1 teaspoon crushed Szechwan peppercorns
4 cod fillets (about 1 pound)
4 green onions, white parts only, thinly sliced

1. Preheat oven to 375°F. Spray roasting pan with nonstick cooking spray; set aside.

2. Combine soy sauce, apple juice, ginger, garlic and peppercorns in small bowl; mix well.

3. Place cod fillets in prepared pan; pour soy sauce mixture over fish. Bake about 10 minutes or until fish is opaque and flakes easily when tested with fork.

4. Transfer fish to serving dish; pour pan juices over fish and sprinkle with green onions. Garnish, if desired.

Makes 4 servings

Nutrients per Serving: 1 fillet (without garnish)

Calories: 100, Calories from Fat: 7%, Total Fat: 1g, Saturated Fat: <1g, Cholesterol: 45mg, Sodium: 329mg, Carbohydrate: 3g, Dietary Fiber: <1g, Protein: 20g

Dietary Exchanges: 2½ Lean Meat

Maryland Crab Cakes

1 pound fresh backfin crabmeat, cartilage removed
10 reduced-sodium crackers (2 inches each), crushed to equal ½ cup crumbs
1 rib celery, finely chopped
1 green onion, finely chopped
¼ cup cholesterol-free egg substitute
3 tablespoons fat-free tartar sauce
1 teaspoon seafood seasoning
Nonstick cooking spray
2 teaspoons vegetable oil

1. Combine crabmeat, cracker crumbs, celery and onion in medium bowl; set aside. Mix egg substitute, tartar sauce and seafood seasoning in small bowl; pour over crabmeat mixture. Gently mix. Shape into 6 (³/₄-inch-thick) patties. Cover; refrigerate 30 minutes.

2. Spray skillet with cooking spray. Add oil; heat over medium-high heat. Place crab cakes in skillet; cook 3 to 4 minutes on each side or until cakes are lightly browned. Garnish, if desired.

Makes 6 servings

Nutrients per Serving: 1 Crab Cake (without garnish)

Calories: 127, Calories from Fat: 27%, Total Fat: 4g, Saturated Fat: 0g, Cholesterol: 44mg, Sodium: 382mg, Carbohydrate: 8g, Dietary Fiber: 0g, Protein: 14g

Dietary Exchanges: ½ Starch, 1½ Lean Meat

Chilled Poached Salmon with Cucumber Sauce

1 cup water
½ teaspoon chicken or fish bouillon granules
⅛ teaspoon black pepper
4 fresh or thawed frozen pink salmon fillets
    (about 3 to 4 ounces each)
½ cup chopped seeded peeled cucumber
⅓ cup plain low-fat yogurt
2 tablespoons sliced green onion
2 tablespoons fat-free salad dressing or
    mayonnaise
1 tablespoon chopped fresh cilantro
1 teaspoon Dijon mustard
2 cups shredded lettuce

1. Combine water, bouillon granules and pepper in large skillet. Bring to a boil over high heat. Carefully place salmon in skillet; return just to a boil. Reduce heat to medium-low. Cover and simmer 8 to 10 minutes or until salmon flakes easily when tested with fork. Remove salmon. Cover and refrigerate.

2. Meanwhile, combine cucumber, yogurt, onion, salad dressing, cilantro and mustard in small bowl. Cover and refrigerate. To serve, place chilled salmon fillets on 4 lettuce-lined plates. Spoon cucumber sauce evenly over salmon. *Makes 4 servings*

Nutrients per Serving: 1 (3-ounce) Salmon fillet, cooked, with about 3 tablespoons Sauce

Calories: 150, Calories from Fat: 37%, Total Fat: 6g, Saturated Fat: 2g, Cholesterol: 46mg, Sodium: 277mg, Carbohydrate: 4g, Dietary Fiber: 1g, Protein: 19g
Dietary Exchanges: 1 Vegetable, 2½ Lean Meat

Caribbean Shrimp with Rice

1 package (12 ounces) frozen shrimp, thawed
½ cup fat-free reduced-sodium chicken broth
1 clove garlic, minced
1 teaspoon chili powder
½ teaspoon salt
½ teaspoon dried oregano leaves
1 cup frozen peas
½ cup diced tomatoes
2 cups cooked rice

Slow Cooker Directions

Combine shrimp, broth, garlic, chili powder, salt and oregano in slow cooker. Cover and cook on LOW 2 hours. Add peas and tomatoes. Cover and cook on LOW

5 minutes. Stir in rice. Cover and cook on LOW an additional 5 minutes. *Makes 4 servings*

Nutrients per Serving: ¼ of total recipe

Calories: 238, Calories from Fat: 9, Total Fat: 2g, Saturated Fat: <1g, Cholesterol: 132mg, Sodium: 492mg, Carbohydrate: 31g, Dietary Fiber: 3g, Protein: 23g
Dietary Exchanges: 2 Starch, 2 Lean Meat

Spicy Snapper & Black Beans

1½ pounds fresh red snapper fillets, cut into
    4 portions (6 ounces each)
    Juice of 1 lime
½ teaspoon coarsely ground black pepper
    Nonstick cooking spray
1 cup GUILTLESS GOURMET® Spicy Black
    Bean Dip
½ cup water
½ cup (about 35) crushed GUILTLESS
    GOURMET® Baked Tortilla Chips (yellow or
    white corn)
1 cup GUILTLESS GOURMET® Roasted Red
    Pepper Salsa

Wash fish thoroughly; pat dry with paper towels. Place fish in 13×9-inch glass baking dish. Pour juice over top; sprinkle with pepper. Cover and refrigerate 1 hour.

Preheat oven to 350°F. Coat 11×7-inch glass baking dish with cooking spray. Combine bean dip and water in small bowl; spread 1 cup bean mixture in bottom of prepared baking dish. Place fish over bean mixture, discarding juice. Spread remaining bean mixture over top of fish; sprinkle with crushed chips.

Bake about 20 minutes or until chips are lightly browned and fish turns opaque and flakes easily when tested with fork. To serve, divide fish among 4 serving plates; spoon ¼ cup salsa over top of each serving. *Makes 4 servings*

Note: This recipe can be made with 4 boneless skinless chicken breast halves in place of red snapper fillets. Prepare as directed and bake about 40 minutes or until chicken is no longer pink in center. Serve as directed.

Nutrients per Serving: 1 Snapper fillet with ¼ cup salsa

Calories: 300, Calories from Fat: 8%, Total Fat: 3g, Saturated Fat: <1g, Cholesterol: 62mg, Sodium: 550mg, Carbohydrate: 24g, Dietary Fiber: 2g, Protein: 40g
Dietary Exchanges: 1 Starch, 5 Lean Meat

Halibut with Cilantro and Lime

1 pound halibut, tuna or swordfish steaks
2 tablespoons fresh lime juice
¼ cup reduced-sodium soy sauce
1 teaspoon cornstarch
½ teaspoon minced fresh ginger
½ teaspoon vegetable oil
½ cup slivered red or yellow onion
2 cloves garlic, minced
¼ cup coarsely chopped fresh cilantro
   Lime wedges (optional)

1. Cut halibut into 1-inch pieces; sprinkle with lime juice.

2. Place soy sauce and cornstarch in cup; blend until smooth. Stir in ginger; set aside.

3. Heat oil in wok or large nonstick skillet over medium heat until hot. Add onion and garlic; stir-fry 2 minutes. Add halibut; stir-fry 2 minutes or until fish flakes easily when tested with fork.

4. Stir soy sauce mixture; add to wok. Stir-fry 30 seconds or until sauce boils and thickens. Sprinkle with cilantro. Garnish with lime wedges, if desired. *Makes 4 servings*

Nutrients per Serving: ¼ of total recipe (made with halibut) without garnish

Calories: 154, Calories from Fat: 19%, Total Fat: 3g,
Saturated Fat: <1g, Cholesterol: 36mg, Sodium: 592mg,
Carbohydrate: 5g, Dietary Fiber: <1g, Protein: 25g
Dietary Exchanges: 1 Vegetable, 2½ Lean Meat

Halibut with Cilantro and Lime

Grilled Oriental Shrimp Kabobs

3 tablespoons reduced-sodium soy sauce
1 tablespoon regular or seasoned rice vinegar
1 tablespoon dark sesame oil
2 cloves garlic, minced
¼ teaspoon red pepper flakes
1 pound raw large shrimp, peeled and deveined

1. For marinade, combine soy sauce, vinegar, oil, garlic and red pepper flakes in small bowl; mix well. Cover; refrigerate up to 3 days.

2. To complete recipe, combine marinade and shrimp in large resealable plastic food storage bag. Seal bag securely. Refrigerate at least 30 minutes or up to 2 hours, turning bag once.

3. Spray barbecue grid with nonstick cooking spray. Prepare barbecue grill for direct cooking.

4. Drain shrimp, reserving marinade. Thread shrimp onto 4 (12-inch-long) metal skewers. Place skewers on prepared grid; brush with half of reserved marinade.

5. Grill skewers, on covered grill, over medium coals 5 minutes. Turn skewers over; brush with remaining half of marinade. Grill 3 to 5 minutes or until shrimp are opaque. *Makes 4 servings*

Serving Suggestion: Serve with fried rice and fresh pineapple spears, if desired.

Make-Ahead Time: up to 3 days in refrigerator
Final Prep and Cook Time: 20 minutes

Nutrients per Serving: 1 Kabob (without fried rice and pineapple spears)

Calories: 129, Calories from Fat: 32%, Total Fat: 4g,
Saturated Fat: <1g, Cholesterol: 173mg, Sodium: 596mg,
Carbohydrate: 1g, Dietary Fiber: <1g, Protein: 20g
Dietary Exchanges: 2½ Lean Meat

Shrimp with Spicy Black Bean Sauce

3. Combine cornstarch, soy sauce and vinegar in small bowl until well blended; stir into wok. Cook and stir 3 minutes or until sauce boils and thickens. Stir in green onions; cook and stir 1 minute. Serve over hot cooked rice.

Makes 4 servings

Nutrients per Serving: ½ cup cooked rice with ¼ of Shrimp Sauce mixture

Calories: 296, Calories from Fat: 15%, Total Fat: 5g, Saturated Fat: 1g, Cholesterol: 174mg, Sodium: 493mg, Carbohydrate: 36g, Dietary Fiber: 2g, Protein: 26g

Dietary Exchanges: 2½ Starch, 2 Lean Meat

Shrimp with Spicy Black Bean Sauce

1 can (15 ounces) black beans, rinsed and drained
1 tablespoon peanut oil
1 tablespoon minced fresh ginger
2 cloves garlic, minced
¼ teaspoon red pepper flakes
1 pound raw medium shrimp, peeled, with tails left on, and deveined
½ cup fat-free reduced-sodium chicken broth
2 teaspoons cornstarch
2 tablespoons reduced-sodium soy sauce
1 tablespoon rice wine vinegar
4 green onions, finely chopped
2 cups hot cooked white rice

1. Place beans in medium bowl; mash with fork until smooth.

2. Heat oil in large wok or nonstick skillet over medium-high heat until hot. Add ginger, garlic and red pepper; stir-fry 1 minute. Stir beans, shrimp and chicken broth into wok. Cook and stir 5 minutes or until shrimp are opaque.

Impossibly Easy Salmon Pie

1 can (7½ ounces) salmon packed in water, drained and deboned
½ cup grated Parmesan cheese
¼ cup sliced green onions
1 jar (2 ounces) chopped pimiento, drained
½ cup low-fat (1%) cottage cheese
1 tablespoon lemon juice
1½ cups low-fat (1%) milk
¾ cup reduced-fat baking and pancake mix
2 whole eggs
2 egg whites *or* ¼ cup egg substitute
¼ teaspoon dried dill weed
¼ teaspoon salt
¼ teaspoon paprika (optional)

1. Preheat oven to 375°F. Spray 9-inch pie plate with nonstick cooking spray. Combine salmon, Parmesan cheese, onions and pimiento in prepared pie plate; set aside.

2. Combine cottage cheese and lemon juice in blender or food processor; blend until smooth. Add milk, baking mix, whole eggs, egg whites, dill and salt. Blend 15 seconds. Pour over salmon mixture in pie plate. Sprinkle with paprika, if desired.

3. Bake 35 to 40 minutes or until lightly golden and knife inserted halfway between center and edge comes out clean. Cool 5 minutes. Cut into 8 wedges before serving. Garnish as desired.

Makes 8 servings

Nutrients per Serving: 1 Pie wedge (⅛ of total recipe) without garnish

Calories: 155, Calories from Fat: 34%, Total Fat: 6g, Saturated Fat: 2g, Cholesterol: 74mg, Sodium: 565mg, Carbohydrate: 11g, Dietary Fiber: <1g, Protein: 14g

Dietary Exchanges: 1 Starch, 2 Lean Meat

Penne Pasta with Shrimp & Roasted Red Pepper Sauce

12 ounces uncooked penne pasta
1 cup low-sodium chicken or vegetable broth, defatted
1 cup GUILTLESS GOURMET® Roasted Red Pepper Salsa
1 cup chopped fresh or low-sodium canned and drained tomatoes
12 ounces medium raw shrimp, peeled and deveined
Fresh Italian parsley sprigs (optional)

Cook pasta according to package directions, omitting salt; drain and keep warm.

Meanwhile, combine broth, salsa and tomatoes in 1-quart saucepan. Bring to a boil over medium-high heat. Reduce heat to medium; simmer about 5 minutes or until hot. Allow to cool slightly.

Pour broth mixture into food processor or blender; process until smooth. Return to saucepan; bring back to a simmer. Add shrimp; simmer 2 minutes or just until shrimp turn pink and opaque. Do not overcook. To serve, divide pasta among 4 warm serving plates. Cover each serving with sauce, dividing shrimp equally among each serving. Garnish with parsley, if desired. _Makes 4 servings_

Nutrients per Serving: 1½ cups cooked Pasta with ¼ of Sauce (without garnish)

Calories: 442, Calories from Fat: 5%, Total Fat: 3g, Saturated Fat: <1g, Cholesterol: 166mg, Sodium: 478mg, Carbohydrate: 70g, Dietary Fiber: 4g, Protein: 30g
Dietary Exchanges: 4 Starch, 1 Vegetable, 2 Lean Meat

Skillet Fish with Lemon Tarragon "Butter"

2 teaspoons reduced-fat margarine
4 teaspoons lemon juice, divided
½ teaspoon grated lemon peel
¼ teaspoon prepared mustard
¼ teaspoon dried tarragon leaves
⅛ teaspoon salt
Nonstick cooking spray
2 (4-ounce) lean white fish fillets,* rinsed and patted dry with paper towels
¼ teaspoon paprika

*Cod, orange roughy, flounder, haddock, halibut and sole may be used.

1. Combine margarine, 2 teaspoons lemon juice, lemon peel, mustard, tarragon and salt in small bowl. Blend well with fork; set aside.

2. Coat 12-inch nonstick skillet with cooking spray. Heat over medium heat until hot.

3. Drizzle fillets with remaining 2 teaspoons lemon juice. Sprinkle one side of each fillet with paprika. Place fillets in skillet, paprika side down; cook 3 minutes. Gently turn and cook 3 minutes longer or until opaque in center. Place fillets on serving plates; top evenly with margarine mixture. _Makes 2 servings_

Nutrients per Serving: ½ of total recipe

Calories: 125, Calories from Fat: 24%, Total Fat: 3g, Saturated Fat: 1g, Cholesterol: 60mg, Sodium: 291mg, Carbohydrate: 1g, Dietary Fiber: <1g, Protein: 22g
Dietary Exchanges: 3 Lean Meat

Lemony Vegetable Salmon Pasta

½ pound salmon fillet
Juice of 1 SUNKIST® lemon, divided
2 cups broccoli florets
2 medium carrots, thinly sliced diagonally
1 cup reduced-sodium chicken broth
1 teaspoon sesame oil
1 tablespoon cornstarch
1½ cups (4 ounces) uncooked spiral-shaped pasta, cooked and drained

In large non-stick skillet, cover salmon with water. Add juice of ½ lemon. Bring to a boil; reduce heat and simmer 10 to 12 minutes or until fish flakes easily with fork. Remove salmon; cool enough to remove skin and flake fish. Discard liquid and, in clean skillet, combine broccoli, carrots, chicken broth and sesame oil. Bring to a boil. Reduce heat; cover and briskly simmer 5 minutes or until vegetables are just tender. Combine cornstarch with remaining juice of ½ lemon; stir into vegetable mixture. Cook, stirring, until mixture thickens. Add cooked pasta and reserved salmon; heat. Serve with lemon wedges, if desired. _Makes 4 servings_

Nutrients per Serving: ¼ of total recipe

Calories: 281, Calories from Fat: 19%, Total Fat: 6g, Saturated Fat: 1g, Cholesterol: 31mg, Sodium: 105mg, Carbohydrate: 40g, Dietary Fiber: 3g, Protein: 17g
Dietary Exchanges: 2 Starch, 2 Vegetable, 2 Lean Meat

Southern Breaded Catfish

⅓ cup pecan halves, finely chopped
¼ cup cornmeal
2 tablespoons all-purpose flour
1 teaspoon paprika
¼ teaspoon ground red pepper
2 egg whites
4 catfish fillets (about 1 pound)
  Nonstick cooking spray
2 cups cooked rice

1. Combine pecans, cornmeal, flour, paprika and ground red pepper in shallow bowl.

2. Beat egg whites in small bowl with wire whisk until foamy. Dip catfish fillets in pecan mixture, then in egg whites and again in any remaining pecan mixture. Place fillets on plate; cover and refrigerate at least 15 minutes.

3. Spray large nonstick skillet with cooking spray; heat over medium-high heat. Place catfish fillets in single layer in skillet. Cook fillets 2 minutes per side or until golden brown and fillets flake easily when tested with fork. Serve over rice. Serve with vegetables and garnish, if desired.

Makes 4 servings

Nutrients per Serving: 1 fillet with ½ cup cooked white rice (without vegetables and garnish)

Calories: 297, Calories from Fat: 25%, Total Fat: 8g, Saturated Fat: 1g, Cholesterol: 65mg, Sodium: 76mg, Carbohydrate: 33g, Dietary Fiber: 2g, Protein: 22g

Dietary Exchanges: 2 Starch, 2½ Lean Meat

Caribbean Sea Bass with Mango Salsa

4 (4 ounces each) skinless sea bass fillets, about 1 inch thick
1 teaspoon Caribbean jerk seasoning
  Nonstick cooking spray
1 ripe mango, peeled, pitted and diced, *or* 1 cup diced drained bottled mango
2 tablespoons chopped fresh cilantro
2 teaspoons fresh lime juice
1 teaspoon minced fresh or bottled jalapeño pepper*

Jalapeño peppers can sting and irritate the skin; wear rubber gloves when handling peppers and do not touch eyes. Wash hands after handling peppers.

1. Prepare grill or preheat broiler. Sprinkle fish with seasoning; coat lightly with cooking spray. Grill fish over medium coals, or broil 5 inches from heat, 4 to 5 minutes per side or until fish flakes easily when tested with fork.

2. Meanwhile, combine mango, cilantro, lime juice and jalapeño pepper; mix well. Serve salsa over fish.

Makes 4 servings

Nutrients per Serving: 1 fillet with about ¼ cup Mango Salsa

Calories: 146, Calories from Fat: 15%, Total Fat: 3g, Saturated Fat: 1g, Cholesterol: 47mg, Sodium: 189mg, Carbohydrate: 9g, Dietary Fiber: 1g, Protein: 21g

Dietary Exchanges: ½ Fruit, 2 Lean Meat

Southern Breaded Catfish

Baked Fish with Fresh Mediterranean Salsa

Baked Fish with Fresh Mediterranean Salsa

4 (6 ounces each) lean, mild fish fillets, such as flounder, tilapia or snapper
2 tablespoons water
½ teaspoon chili powder
1 large tomato, seeded and chopped
1 can (2½ ounces) sliced ripe olives or kalamata olives, drained
2 tablespoons chopped fresh parsley
2 tablespoons lemon juice
1 tablespoon capers, drained
2 teaspoons extra-virgin olive oil
1 teaspoon dried oregano leaves

1. Preheat oven to 350°F. Coat 12×8-inch glass baking dish with nonstick cooking spray; arrange fillets in single layer. Pour water over fillets and sprinkle with chili powder. Cover tightly with aluminum foil and bake 15 minutes or until fish is opaque in center.

2. Meanwhile, combine tomato, olives, parsley, lemon juice, capers, oil and oregano in small bowl; mix well. Remove fish from dish with slotted spatula and place on 4 individual plates; spoon ⅓ cup salsa over each serving.

Makes 4 servings

Nutrients per Serving: 1 fillet with ⅓ cup Salsa

Calories: 212, Calories from Fat: 28%, Total Fat: 6g, Saturated Fat: 1g, Cholesterol: 90mg, Sodium: 382mg, Carbohydrate: 5g, Dietary Fiber: 2g, Protein: 33g
Dietary Exchanges: 4 Lean Meat

Thai Seafood Stir-Fry

1 tablespoon cornstarch
2 tablespoons lemon juice
1 tablespoon reduced-sodium soy sauce
2 teaspoons sugar
½ teaspoon ground ginger
¼ teaspoon red pepper flakes
8 ounces broccoli
2 ribs celery
1 large onion
3 tablespoons vegetable oil
¼ cup water
1 pound surimi seafood chunks or imitation crabmeat, thawed if frozen
½ cup sliced water chestnuts
3 cups hot cooked rice

1. Combine cornstarch, lemon juice, soy sauce, sugar, ginger and red pepper in small bowl; stir until smooth. Set aside.

2. Remove woody stems from broccoli; discard. Cut tops into small florets; rinse. Cut celery diagonally into ½-inch slices. Cut onion lengthwise in half; cut crosswise into slices.

3. Heat wok over high heat about 1 minute or until hot. Drizzle oil into wok and heat 30 seconds. Add onion; stir-fry 1 minute. Add broccoli and celery; stir-fry 2 minutes. Reduce heat to medium-high. Add water; cover and cook until vegetables are crisp-tender. Add surimi and water chestnuts; stir-fry gently 1 minute to combine.

4. Stir cornstarch mixture until smooth and add to wok. Stir-fry until sauce boils and thickens. Spoon into serving dish or place wok on table over wok ring stand or trivet. Serve with rice.

Makes 6 servings

Note: Surimi seafood is processed fish, typically pollack, that is flavored and restructured to make seafood products. It comes in flakes, chunks, sticks or nuggets. This convenient seafood product is wonderful for creating quick, delicious meals such as this one.

Nutrients per Serving: ½ cup cooked white rice with ⅙ of Stir-Fry mixture

Calories: 278, Calories from Fat: 27%, Total Fat: 8g, Saturated Fat: 1g, Cholesterol: 15mg, Sodium: 744mg, Carbohydrate: 38g, Dietary Fiber: 2g, Protein: 13g
Dietary Exchanges: 2 Starch, 1 Vegetable, 1 Lean Meat, 1 Fat

Paella

1 pound raw littleneck clams
8 ounces raw sea scallops
6 ounces raw medium shrimp
1 tablespoon plus 1 teaspoon olive oil, divided
3¼ cups fat-free reduced-sodium chicken broth, divided
1 medium onion, finely chopped
3 cloves garlic, chopped
2 cups uncooked long-grain white rice
1 teaspoon dried thyme leaves, crushed
½ teaspoon saffron threads, crushed
1 pint (about 12 ounces) cherry tomatoes, halved
1 cup frozen petite peas, thawed
1 tablespoon chopped fresh parsley

1. Scrub clams with stiff brush under cold running water. Discard any that remain open when tapped. Soak clams in mixture of ⅓ cup salt to 1 gallon of water 20 minutes. Drain; repeat 2 more times. Slice sea scallops in half crosswise. Peel shrimp, leaving tails on if desired; devein.

2. Heat 1 teaspoon oil over medium-high heat in large saucepan. Add shrimp; cook, stirring occasionally, 3 minutes or until shrimp turn pink. Transfer to bowl; cover. Add scallops to saucepan; cook 2 minutes or until scallops are opaque. Transfer to bowl with shrimp. Add clams and ¼ cup broth to pan. Cover; boil 2 to 8 minutes or until clams open. Transfer clams and broth to bowl with shrimp and scallops; discard any unopened clams.

3. Heat remaining 1 tablespoon oil in same saucepan. Add onion and garlic; cook and stir 4 minutes or until tender. Add rice; cook and stir 2 minutes. Add remaining 3 cups broth, thyme and saffron; reduce heat to medium-low. Cover; simmer 15 minutes or until rice is tender. Stir in tomatoes, peas and parsley. Stir in seafood and accumulated juices. Cover; remove from heat. Let stand 3 to 5 minutes or until seafood is hot.

Makes 6 servings

Nutrients per Serving: ⅙ of total recipe

Calories: 435, Calories from Fat: 13%, Total Fat: 6g, Saturated Fat: 1g, Cholesterol: 95mg, Sodium: 310mg, Carbohydrate: 60g, Dietary Fiber: 3g, Protein: 32g

Dietary Exchanges: 3 Starch, 2 Vegetable, 3 Lean Meat

Paella

Baked Crab-Stuffed Trout

2 small whole trout (about 6 ounces each), cleaned and boned
3 teaspoons reduced-sodium soy sauce, divided
3 ounces frozen cooked crabmeat or imitation crabmeat, thawed, shredded
½ cup fresh bread crumbs
½ cup shredded carrot
¼ cup thinly sliced celery
¼ cup thinly sliced green onions
1 egg white, lightly beaten
2 tablespoons dry white wine
1 tablespoon grated lemon peel
1 teaspoon garlic powder
½ teaspoon black pepper
    Lemon wedges

1. Preheat oven to 375°F. Wash trout; pat dry with paper towels. Place on foil-lined baking sheet. Brush inside cavities lightly with 1½ teaspoons soy sauce.

2. Combine remaining 1½ teaspoons soy sauce, crabmeat, bread crumbs, carrot, celery, onions, egg white, wine, lemon peel, garlic powder and pepper in small bowl; blend well. Divide stuffing in half; place half of stuffing inside cavity of each trout.

3. Bake 30 minutes or until trout flakes easily when tested with fork. Serve with lemon wedges. Garnish, if desired.

Makes 4 servings

Nutrients per Serving: ½ of 1 Stuffed Trout fillet (without garnish)

Calories: 217, Calories from Fat: 24%, Total Fat: 6g, Saturated Fat: 2g, Cholesterol: 61mg, Sodium: 527mg, Carbohydrate: 14g, Dietary Fiber: 1g, Protein: 25g

Dietary Exchanges: 1 Starch, 3 Lean Meat

Peppered Shrimp Skewers

16 (12-inch) wooden skewers
⅓ cup teriyaki sauce
⅓ cup ketchup
2 tablespoons dry sherry or water
2 tablespoons reduced-fat peanut butter
1 teaspoon hot pepper sauce
¼ teaspoon ground ginger
32 fresh large shrimp (about 1½ pounds)
2 large yellow bell peppers
32 fresh sugar snap peas, trimmed

1. To prevent burning, soak skewers in water at least 20 minutes before assembling kabobs.

2. Coat rack of broiler pan with nonstick cooking spray; set aside.

3. Combine teriyaki sauce, ketchup, sherry, peanut butter, pepper sauce and ginger in small saucepan. Bring to a boil, stirring constantly. Reduce heat to low; simmer, uncovered, 1 minute. Remove from heat; set aside.

4. Peel and devein shrimp, leaving tails intact.

5. Cut each bell pepper lengthwise into 4 quarters; remove stems and seeds. Cut each quarter crosswise into 4 equal pieces. Thread 2 shrimp, bell pepper pieces and sugar snap peas onto each skewer; place on prepared broiler pan. Brush with teriyaki sauce mixture.

6. Broil, 4 inches from heat, 3 minutes; turn over. Brush with teriyaki sauce mixture; broil 2 minutes longer or until shrimp turn pink. Discard any remaining teriyaki sauce mixture. Transfer skewers to serving plates; garnish, if desired. *Makes 8 servings*

Nutrients per Serving: 2 Skewers (without garnish)

Calories: 138, Calories from Fat: 13%, Total Fat: 2g, Saturated Fat: 1g, Cholesterol: 132mg, Sodium: 516mg, Carbohydrate: 12g, Dietary Fiber: 2g, Protein: 16g
Dietary Exchanges: 2 Vegetable, 2 Lean Meat

Honey Barbecued Halibut

PAM® No-Stick Cooking Spray
2 pounds halibut steaks
½ cup HUNT'S® Original Barbecue Sauce
2 tablespoons honey
1 tablespoon WESSON® Vegetable Oil
½ teaspoon red wine vinegar

1. Spray a 9×9×2-inch baking pan with cooking spray. Place fish in baking pan.

2. In a small bowl, combine *remaining* ingredients.

3. Pour ⅔ *marinade* over fish. Set aside *remaining* marinade. Turn fish to coat evenly. Cover and marinate in refrigerator at least 2 hours.

4. Remove fish from marinade; discard used marinade.

5. Cook over hot coals or in preheated broiler 4 minutes per side, basting occasionally with *remaining* marinade. *Makes 8 (5-ounce) servings*

Nutrients per Serving: 1 Halibut steak (⅛ of total recipe)

Calories: 176, Calories from Fat: 23%, Total Fat: 4g, Saturated Fat: 1g, Cholesterol: 36mg, Sodium: 251mg, Carbohydrate: 9g, Dietary Fiber: <1g, Protein: 24g
Dietary Exchanges: ½ Fruit, 3 Lean Meat

Grilled Fish with Roasted Jalapeño Rub

3 tablespoons chopped cilantro
2 tablespoons lime juice
1 tablespoon minced garlic
1 tablespoon minced fresh ginger
1 tablespoon minced roasted jalapeño peppers*
1½ pounds firm white fish fillets, such as orange roughy or red snapper
Lime wedges

To roast peppers, place them on uncovered grill over hot coals. Grill until skin is blistered, turning frequently. Remove from grill and place peppers in large resealable plastic food storage bag for 15 minutes. Remove skins. Seed peppers, if desired, and cut them into thin slices.

Combine cilantro, lime juice, garlic, ginger and peppers in small bowl. Lightly oil grid to prevent sticking. Grill fish on covered grill over hot KINGSFORD® Briquets 5 minutes. Turn; spread cilantro mixture on fish. Grill 3 to 5 minutes longer or until fish flakes easily when tested with fork. Serve with lime wedges. *Makes 4 servings*

Nutrients per Serving: 1 fillet (¼ of total recipe)

Calories: 124, Calories from Fat: 9%, Total Fat: 1g, Saturated Fat: <1g, Cholesterol: 34mg, Sodium: 108mg, Carbohydrate: 2g, Dietary Fiber: <1g, Protein: 25g
Dietary Exchanges: 3 Lean Meat

Easy Seafood Stir-Fry

5. Stir broth mixture and add to wok. Heat 2 minutes or until sauce boils and thickens.

6. Return seafood and any accumulated juices to wok; heat through. Serve over rice. Top with onions.

Makes 4 servings

Nutrients per Serving: ¼ of Stir-Fry mixture with ½ cup cooked rice

Calories: 304, Calories from Fat: 9%, Total Fat: 3g, Saturated Fat: <1g, Cholesterol: 74mg, Sodium: 335mg, Carbohydrate: 42g, Dietary Fiber: 3g, Protein: 25g

Dietary Exchanges: 2 Starch, 2 Vegetable, 2 Lean Meat

Cheese Tortellini with Tuna

1 tuna steak* (about 6 ounces)
1 package (9 ounces) uncooked refrigerated reduced-fat cheese tortellini
Nonstick cooking spray
1 cup finely chopped red bell pepper
1 cup finely chopped green bell pepper
¼ cup finely chopped onion
¾ teaspoon fennel seeds, crushed
½ cup evaporated skimmed milk
2 teaspoons all-purpose flour
½ teaspoon dry mustard
½ teaspoon black pepper

Or, substitute 1 can (6 ounces) tuna packed in water, drained, for tuna steak. Omit step 1.

1. Grill or broil tuna 4 inches from heat source until fish just begins to flake, about 7 to 9 minutes, turning once. Remove and discard skin. Cut tuna into chunks; set aside.

2. Cook pasta according to package directions, omitting salt. Drain; set aside.

3. Spray large nonstick skillet with cooking spray. Add bell peppers, onion and fennel seeds; cook over medium heat until crisp-tender.

4. Whisk together milk, flour, mustard and black pepper in small bowl until smooth; add to skillet. Cook until thickened, stirring constantly. Stir in tuna and pasta; reduce heat to low and simmer until heated through, about 3 minutes. Serve immediately. *Makes 4 servings*

Nutrients per Serving: ¼ of total recipe

Calories: 180, Calories from Fat: 19%, Total Fat: 4g, Saturated Fat: 2g, Cholesterol: 21mg, Sodium: 160mg, Carbohydrate: 21g, Dietary Fiber: 3g, Protein: 16g

Dietary Exchanges: ½ Starch, ½ Milk, 1 Vegetable, 1½ Lean Meat

Easy Seafood Stir-Fry

1 package (1 ounce) dried black Chinese mushrooms*
½ cup fat-free reduced-sodium chicken broth
2 tablespoons dry sherry
1 tablespoon reduced-sodium soy sauce
4½ teaspoons cornstarch
1 teaspoon vegetable oil, divided
½ pound bay scallops or halved sea scallops
¼ pound raw medium shrimp, peeled and deveined
2 cloves garlic, minced
6 ounces (2 cups) fresh snow peas, cut diagonally into halves
2 cups hot cooked white rice
¼ cup thinly sliced green onions

Or substitute 1½ cups sliced fresh mushrooms. Omit step 1.

1. Place mushrooms in small bowl; cover with warm water. Soak 20 minutes to soften. Drain; squeeze out excess water. Discard stems; slice caps.

2. Blend broth, sherry and soy sauce into cornstarch in another small bowl until smooth.

3. Heat ½ teaspoon oil in wok or large nonstick skillet over medium heat. Add scallops, shrimp and garlic; stir-fry 3 minutes or until seafood is opaque. Remove and reserve.

4. Add remaining ½ teaspoon oil to wok. Add mushrooms and snow peas; stir-fry 3 minutes or until snow peas are crisp-tender.

Grilled Scallops and Vegetables with Cilantro Sauce

1 teaspoon hot chili oil
1 teaspoon dark sesame oil
1 green onion, chopped
1 tablespoon finely chopped fresh ginger
1 cup fat-free reduced-sodium chicken broth
1 cup chopped fresh cilantro
1 pound raw or thawed frozen sea scallops
2 medium zucchini, cut into ½-inch slices
2 medium yellow squash, cut into ½-inch slices
1 medium yellow onion, cut into wedges
8 large mushrooms

1. Spray cold grid with nonstick cooking spray. Preheat grill to medium-high heat. Heat chili oil and sesame oil in small saucepan over medium-low heat. Add green onion; cook about 15 seconds or just until fragrant. Add ginger; cook 1 minute.

2. Add chicken broth; bring mixture to a boil. Cook until liquid is reduced by half. Cool slightly. Place mixture in blender or food processor with cilantro; blend until smooth. Set aside.

3. Thread scallops and vegetables onto 4 (12-inch) skewers. (If using wooden skewers, soak in water 25 to 30 minutes before using, to prevent skewers from burning.) Grill about 8 minutes per side or until scallops turn opaque. Serve hot with cilantro sauce. Garnish, if desired.

Makes 4 servings

Nutrients per Serving: 1 skewer (without garnish)

Calories: 169, Calories from Fat: 21%, Total Fat: 4g, Saturated Fat: <1g, Cholesterol: 48mg, Sodium: 258mg, Carbohydrate: 11g, Dietary Fiber: 3g, Protein: 24g
Dietary Exchanges: 1½ Vegetable, 2½ Lean Meat

Rice Pilaf with Fish Fillets

1 cup UNCLE BEN'S® ORIGINAL CONVERTED® Brand Rice
1 can (14½ ounces) fat-free reduced-sodium chicken broth
1 cup sliced green onions
2 cups sugar snap peas or snow peas
12 ounces Dover sole fillets
¼ cup reduced-fat Caesar salad dressing
2 tomatoes, cut into wedges
¼ cup chopped parsley

1. In large skillet, combine rice, chicken broth and ½ cup water. Bring to a boil. Cover; reduce heat and simmer 12 minutes.

2. Add green onions and peas to rice pilaf. Season to taste with salt and pepper, if desired. Place fish fillets on pilaf. Spoon salad dressing onto fillets. Cover and cook over low heat 8 minutes or until fish flakes when tested with a fork and rice is tender.

3. Garnish with tomatoes and parsley.

Makes 4 servings

Variation: Orange roughy fillets or swordfish steaks can be substituted for sole fillets.

Nutrients per Serving: ¼ of total recipe (using sole fillets) without salt and pepper seasoning

Calories: 323, Calories from Fat: 8%, Total Fat: 3g, Saturated Fat: <1g, Cholesterol: 50mg, Sodium: 452mg, Carbohydrate: 50g, Dietary Fiber: 4g, Protein: 28g
Dietary Exchanges: 2 Starch, 3 Vegetable, 2 Lean Meat

Sea Bass for Two in Lemon Apple Sauce

¾ cup *plus* 2 tablespoons apple juice, divided
    Grated peel and juice of ½ SUNKIST® lemon
½ pound sea bass fillets
¼ teaspoon dried dill weed
1 small unpeeled green apple, diced
1½ teaspoons 50% less fat margarine
1½ teaspoons honey
½ teaspoon Dijon mustard
1 tablespoon cornstarch
2 tablespoons sliced green onions
1 cup hot cooked rice (no salt added)

In large nonstick skillet, combine ¾ cup apple juice, lemon peel and juice. Add fish fillets and sprinkle with dill weed. Bring to a boil. Reduce heat; cover and simmer 10 to 12 minutes or until fish flakes easily with fork. Remove fish. To liquid in skillet add apple, margarine, honey and mustard, stirring until margarine melts. Combine cornstarch and remaining 2 tablespoons apple juice; add to apple mixture. Cook, stirring, until thickened. Return fish and add green onions; heat. Serve fish with rice and sauce.

Makes 2 servings

Nutrients per Serving: ½ of total recipe (with ½ cup cooked rice)

Calories: 368, Calories from Fat: 8%, Total Fat: 3g, Saturated Fat: 1g, Cholesterol: 60mg, Sodium: 153mg, Carbohydrate: 59g, Dietary Fiber: 2g, Protein: 25g
Dietary Exchanges: 2 Starch, 1½ Fruit, 2 Lean Meat

Caribbean Shrimp & Pasta

6 ounces uncooked medium bow tie pasta
1 tablespoon ground allspice
1 tablespoon frozen orange juice concentrate
1½ teaspoons vegetable oil, divided
1 teaspoon ground dried thyme leaves
¼ teaspoon minced scotch bonnet pepper*
12 ounces raw medium shrimp, peeled and
    deveined
    Nonstick cooking spray
½ cup fat-free reduced-sodium chicken broth
⅓ cup finely chopped green onions, green tops
    only
2 tablespoons lemon juice
1 tablespoon sesame oil
1 teaspoon Dijon mustard
¼ teaspoon salt
1 cup diced papaya
¾ cup diced mango

*Scotch bonnet peppers can sting and irritate the skin; wear rubber gloves when handling peppers and do not touch eyes. Wash hands after handling peppers.

1. Cook pasta according to package directions, omitting salt. Drain; set aside.

2. Combine allspice, orange juice concentrate, 1 teaspoon oil, thyme and pepper in small bowl; add shrimp and thoroughly coat. Spray large nonstick skillet with cooking spray. Heat over medium heat until hot. Add shrimp; cook and stir 3 to 5 minutes or until shrimp are opaque. Remove from heat.

3. Combine chicken broth, green onions, lemon juice, sesame oil, mustard, salt and remaining ½ teaspoon oil in large bowl. Add papaya and mango; toss to combine. Add cooked pasta; toss again. Serve immediately. Garnish, if desired. *Makes 6 (1-cup) servings*

Nutrients per Serving: 1 cup (without garnish)

Calories: 217, Calories from Fat: 19%, Total Fat: 5g, Saturated Fat: 1g, Cholesterol: 87mg, Sodium: 208mg, Carbohydrate: 30g, Dietary Fiber: 1g, Protein: 14g

Dietary Exchanges: 1½ Starch, ½ Fruit, 1½ Lean Meat

Caribbean Shrimp & Pasta

Snapper Veracruz

    Nonstick cooking spray
1 teaspoon olive oil
¼ large onion, thinly sliced
⅓ cup low sodium fish or vegetable broth,
    defatted* and divided
2 cloves garlic, minced
1 cup GUILTLESS GOURMET® Roasted Red
    Pepper Salsa
20 ounces fresh red snapper, tilapia, sea bass or
    halibut fillets

*To defat broth, simply chill the canned broth thoroughly. Open the can and use a spoon to lift out any solid fat floating on the surface of the broth.

Preheat oven to 400°F. Coat baking dish with cooking spray. (Dish needs to be large enough for fish to fit snugly together.) Heat oil in large nonstick skillet over medium heat until hot. Add onion; cook and stir until onion is translucent. Stir in 3 tablespoons broth. Add garlic; cook and stir 1 minute more. Stir in remaining broth and salsa. Bring mixture to a boil. Reduce heat to low; simmer about 2 minutes or until heated through.

Wash fish thoroughly; pat dry with paper towels. Place in prepared baking dish, overlapping thin edges to obtain an overall equal thickness. Pour and spread salsa mixture over fish.

Bake 15 minutes or until fish turns opaque and flakes easily when tested with fork. Serve hot. Garnish as desired. *Makes 4 servings*

Nutrients per Serving: ¼ of total recipe (without garnish)

Calories: 184, Calories from Fat: 16%, Total Fat: 3g, Saturated Fat: <1g, Cholesterol: 52mg, Sodium: 353mg, Carbohydrate: 6g, Dietary Fiber: 0g, Protein: 30g

Dietary Exchanges: ½ Vegetable, 4 Lean Meat

Catfish with Tropical Fruit Salsa

1 can (15.25 ounces) DOLE® Tropical Fruit Salad, drained
1 can (8 ounces) low-sodium whole kernel corn, drained
¼ cup chopped green onions
2 tablespoons diced mild green chilies
1 tablespoon chopped fresh cilantro or parsley
1 pound catfish or red snapper fillets
Vegetable cooking spray
2 tablespoons lime juice
½ teaspoon paprika

• Chop tropical fruit salad; stir together with corn, onions, chilies and cilantro in small bowl for salsa. Set aside.

• Arrange fish in single layer on broiler pan sprayed with vegetable cooking spray. Broil 4 minutes; turn fish over. Brush with lime juice; sprinkle with paprika. Broil 3 to 5 minutes more or until fish flakes easily with fork. Remove fish to serving platter. Serve with reserved tropical fruit salsa. Garnish with fresh cilantro sprigs and lime wedges, if desired. *Makes 4 servings*

Prep Time: 10 minutes
Broil Time: 10 minutes

Nutrients per Serving: ¼ of total recipe (without garnish)

Calories: 243, Calories from Fat: 13, Total Fat: 4g, Saturated Fat: 1g, Cholesterol: 65mg, Sodium: 86mg, Carbohydrate: 34g, Dietary Fiber: 3g, Protein: 20g

Dietary Exchanges: 1 Starch, 1 Fruit, 2 Lean Meat

Garlic Skewered Shrimp

1 pound raw large shrimp, peeled and deveined
2 tablespoons reduced-sodium soy sauce
1 tablespoon vegetable oil
3 cloves garlic, minced
¼ teaspoon red pepper flakes (optional)
3 green onions, cut into 1-inch pieces

1. Prepare grill or preheat broiler. Soak 4 (12-inch) wooden skewers in water 25 to 30 minutes.

2. Meanwhile, place shrimp in large plastic resealable food storage bag. Combine soy sauce, oil, garlic and red pepper, if desired, in cup; mix well. Pour over shrimp. Close bag securely; turn to coat. Marinate at room temperature 15 minutes.

3. Drain shrimp; reserve marinade. Alternately thread shrimp and onions onto skewers. Place skewers on grid or rack of broiler pan. Brush with reserved marinade; discard any remaining marinade. Grill, covered, over medium-hot coals or broil 5 to 6 inches from heat 5 minutes on each side or until shrimp are pink and opaque. Serve on lettuce-lined plate, if desired. *Makes 4 servings*

Serving Suggestion: For a more attractive presentation, leave the tails on the shrimp.

Nutrients per Serving: 1 Skewer (without lettuce)

Calories: 128, Calories from Fat: 32%, Total Fat: 4g, Saturated Fat: 1g, Cholesterol: 173mg, Sodium: 464mg, Carbohydrate: 2g, Dietary Fiber: <1g, Protein: 20g

Dietary Exchanges: 2½ Lean Meat

MEATLESS ENTRÉES

Saucy Broccoli and Spaghetti

3 ounces uncooked spaghetti
1 package (10 ounces) frozen chopped broccoli
½ cup thinly sliced leek, white part only
½ cup fat-free (skim) milk
2 teaspoons cornstarch
2 teaspoons chopped fresh oregano *or*
   ½ teaspoon dried oregano leaves, crushed
⅛ teaspoon hot pepper sauce
3 tablespoons softened reduced-fat cream cheese
1 tablespoon grated Romano or Parmesan cheese
1 tablespoon chopped fresh parsley

1. Prepare spaghetti according to package directions, omitting salt; drain and keep warm. Meanwhile, cook broccoli and leek together according to package directions for broccoli, omitting salt. Drain; reserve ¼ cup liquid. Add additional water, if needed, to make ¼ cup.

2. Combine milk, cornstarch, oregano and pepper sauce in medium saucepan. Stir in reserved ¼ cup liquid. Cook and stir over medium heat until mixture boils and thickens. Stir in cream cheese. Cook and stir until cheese melts. Stir in vegetables; heat through.

3. Serve vegetable mixture over pasta. Sprinkle with Romano cheese and parsley. Garnish as desired.

Makes 4 servings

Nutrients per Serving: ¼ of total recipe (without garnish)

Calories: 162, Calories from Fat: 16%, Total Fat: 3g, Saturated Fat: 2g, Cholesterol: 9mg, Sodium: 133mg, Carbohydrate: 26g, Dietary Fiber: 3g, Protein: 8g

Dietary Exchanges: 1½ Starch, 1 Vegetable, ½ Fat

Beans and Rice Vegetable Medley

1½ teaspoons CRISCO® Oil*
⅓ cup chopped celery
⅓ cup chopped green bell pepper
⅓ cup chopped onion
¼ cup chopped fresh tomato
1 can (15½ ounces) kidney beans, drained
3½ cups water
1 teaspoon salt
½ to 1 teaspoon black pepper
½ teaspoon dried thyme leaves
1½ cups uncooked brown rice

*Use your favorite Crisco Oil product.

1. Heat oil in large saucepan on medium heat. Add celery, green pepper and onion. Cook and stir 2 to 3 minutes or until crisp-tender. Stir in tomato. Cook and stir until tomato is softened.

2. Add beans, water, salt, black pepper and thyme. Bring to a boil. Stir in rice. Return to a boil. Reduce heat to low. Cover. Simmer 45 to 55 minutes or until rice is tender and water is absorbed, stirring in additional water as needed.

Makes 6 servings

Nutrients per Serving: ⅙ of total recipe

Calories: 252, Calories from Fat: 10%, Total Fat: 3g, Saturated Fat: <1g, Cholesterol: 0mg, Sodium: 648mg, Carbohydrate: 49g, Dietary Fiber: 7g, Protein: 8g

Dietary Exchanges: 3 Starch, 1 Vegetable

Creole Red Beans and Rice

1 cup uncooked dried red kidney beans
1 cup uncooked white rice
2 green bell peppers, diced
1 can (14½ ounces) original-style stewed tomatoes, undrained
1¾ cups fat-free reduced-sodium chicken broth
1 cup chopped onion
2 ribs celery, diced
¼ cup water
1 tablespoon reduced-sodium Worcestershire sauce
3 cloves garlic, minced
2 bay leaves
1 teaspoon Creole seasoning
⅛ teaspoon ground cinnamon
⅛ teaspoon ground cloves
⅛ teaspoon ground red pepper

1. Rinse beans thoroughly in colander under cold running water. Place in medium saucepan; cover with 4 inches water. Bring to a boil over high heat; boil 2 minutes. Remove from heat. Cover and let stand 1 hour. Drain well.

2. Preheat oven to 350°F. Cook rice according to package directions; set aside.

3. Combine remaining ingredients in Dutch oven. Bring to a boil over high heat; add beans.

4. Cover Dutch oven tightly with foil. Bake 1½ hours or until beans are tender. Remove from oven; discard bay leaves. Let stand 10 minutes before serving.

5. To serve, divide rice evenly among 4 serving dishes; top with bean mixture. Garnish, if desired.

Makes 6 servings

Hint: For even more flavor, add meatless smoked sausage (made with meat substitute) with the beans in this recipe.

Nutrients per Serving: ⅙ of Bean mixture with ⅓ cup cooked rice (without garnish)

Calories: 218, Calories from Fat: 5%, Total Fat: 1g, Saturated Fat: <1g, Cholesterol: 0mg, Sodium: 589mg, Carbohydrate: 42g, Dietary Fiber: 6g, Protein: 11g

Dietary Exchanges: 2 Starch, 2 Vegetable

Kasha and Bow Tie Noodles with Mushrooms and Broccoli

2 cups broccoli florets
2½ cups uncooked small bow tie pasta
2 teaspoons olive oil
½ pound fresh mushrooms, sliced ¼ inch thick
½ cup chopped onion
3 cloves garlic, minced
¾ cup uncooked kasha
1 egg
1½ cups fat-free reduced-sodium chicken broth*
1 teaspoon marjoram leaves, crushed
¼ teaspoon black pepper
Chopped red bell pepper for garnish (optional)

To defat chicken broth, skim fat from surface of broth with spoon. Or, place can of broth in refrigerator to chill at least 2 hours ahead of time. Before using, remove fat that has hardened on surface of broth.

1. Bring 3 quarts water to a boil in large saucepan over high heat. Add broccoli florets; return to a boil. Cook, uncovered, over medium-high heat 2 minutes or until crisp-tender. Remove broccoli to large bowl with slotted spoon, reserving water.

2. Return water to a boil. Add pasta; return to a boil. Cook, uncovered, over medium-high heat 5 minutes or until just tender. *Do not overcook.* Drain; add pasta to broccoli and mix gently. Set aside.

3. Wipe saucepan with paper towel. Add oil, mushrooms, onion and garlic to pan; cook and stir 5 minutes or until onion is soft. Stir into broccoli mixture.

4. Add kasha and egg to saucepan; stir until blended. Cook and stir over medium heat 3 minutes or until kasha is dry and grains are separated.

5. Stir in chicken broth, marjoram and black pepper. Bring to a boil over medium-high heat. Reduce heat to low. Cook, covered, 10 minutes, stirring occasionally. Remove from heat; let stand, covered, 10 minutes. Gently mix with bow tie mixture. Garnish each serving with bell pepper, if desired.

Makes 4 servings

Nutrients per Serving: ¼ of total recipe (without garnish)

Calories: 278, Calories from Fat: 18%, Total Fat: 1g, Saturated Fat: 1g, Cholesterol: 76mg, Sodium: 52mg, Carbohydrate: 48g, Dietary Fiber: 5g, Protein: 12g

Dietary Exchanges: 2½ Starch, 2 Vegetable, 1 Fat

Broccoli Lasagna

1 tablespoon CRISCO® Oil* plus additional for
    oiling
1 cup chopped onion
3 cloves garlic, minced
1 can (14½ ounces) no salt added tomatoes,
    undrained and chopped
1 can (8 ounces) no salt added tomato sauce
1 can (6 ounces) no salt added tomato paste
1 cup thinly sliced fresh mushrooms
¼ cup chopped fresh parsley
1 tablespoon red wine vinegar
1 teaspoon dried oregano leaves
1 teaspoon dried basil leaves
1 bay leaf
½ teaspoon salt
¼ teaspoon crushed red pepper
1½ cups lowfat cottage cheese
   1 cup (4 ounces) shredded low moisture part-
    skim mozzarella cheese, divided
   6 lasagna noodles, cooked (without salt or fat)
    and well drained
   3 cups chopped broccoli, cooked and well
    drained
   1 tablespoon grated Parmesan cheese

*Use your favorite Crisco Oil product.

1. Heat oven to 350°F. Oil 11³/₄×7½×2-inch baking dish
lightly.

2. Heat 1 tablespoon oil in large saucepan on medium
heat. Add onion and garlic. Cook and stir until tender. Stir
in tomatoes, tomato sauce, tomato paste, mushrooms,
parsley, vinegar, oregano, basil, bay leaf, salt and crushed
red pepper. Bring to a boil. Reduce heat to low. Cover.
Simmer 30 minutes, stirring occasionally. Remove bay leaf.

3. Combine cottage cheese and ½ cup mozzarella cheese
in small bowl. Stir well.

4. Place 2 lasagna noodles in bottom of baking dish. Layer
with one cup broccoli, one-third of the tomato sauce and
one-third of the cottage cheese mixture. Repeat layers.
Cover with foil.

5. Bake at 350°F for 25 minutes. Uncover. Sprinkle with
remaining ½ cup mozzarella cheese and Parmesan cheese.
Bake, uncovered, 10 minutes or until cheese melts. *Do not
overbake.* Let stand 10 minutes before serving.

Makes 8 servings

**Nutrients per Serving: 1 Lasagna wedge (⅛ of
total recipe)**

Calories: 201, Calories from Fat: 24%, Total Fat: 5g,
Saturated Fat: 2g, Cholesterol: 12mg, Sodium: 439mg,
Carbohydrate: 25g, Dietary Fiber: 4g, Protein: 14g

Dietary Exchanges: 1 Starch, 2 Vegetable, 1 Lean Meat, ½ Fat

Crowd-Pleasing Burritos

  1 pound (2½ cups) dried pinto beans, rinsed
  6 cups water
  2 cups chopped onions
  3 jalapeño peppers,* seeded and minced
  4 cloves garlic, minced
  2 teaspoons salt
16 (10-inch) flour tortillas
  4 cups shredded iceberg lettuce
  4 cups shredded romaine lettuce
  1 cup reduced-fat sour cream
  2 cups (8 ounces) reduced-fat Cheddar cheese
  2 cups salsa
  1 cup minced fresh cilantro

*Jalapeño peppers can sting and irritate the skin; wear rubber gloves
when handling peppers and do not touch eyes. Wash hands after
handling peppers.*

1. Place beans in Dutch oven. Cover with 2 inches of
water. Bring to a boil; reduce heat to low. Simmer
5 minutes. Remove from heat and let stand, covered,
1 hour. Drain liquid from beans.

2. Add 6 cups water, onions, peppers, garlic and salt. Bring
to a boil; reduce heat to low. Simmer, covered, 1 hour or
until beans are tender. Drain liquid from beans.

3. Preheat oven to 300°F. Stack tortillas and wrap in foil.
Bake 20 minutes or until heated through. Combine
lettuces. Top tortillas with beans, lettuces, sour cream,
cheese, salsa and cilantro. Fold in 2 sides; roll to enclose
filling.
Makes 16 servings

Nutrients per Serving: 1 Burrito

Calories: 291, Calories from Fat: 19%, Total Fat: 6g,
Saturated Fat: 2g, Cholesterol: 13mg, Sodium: 908mg,
Carbohydrate: 44g, Dietary Fiber: 9g, Protein: 14g

Dietary Exchanges: 3 Starch, 1 Lean Meat

Broccoli Lasagna

Vegetable Paella

½ cup chopped onion
1 clove garlic, minced
 Olive oil-flavored nonstick cooking spray
1 can (14½ ounces) fat-free reduced-sodium
 chicken or vegetable broth
1 cup uncooked rice
1 cup chopped plum tomatoes*
¼ cup water
½ teaspoon dried oregano
½ teaspoon chili powder
⅛ teaspoon salt
⅛ teaspoon turmeric
 Black pepper (optional)
1 medium red bell pepper, cut into short strips
1 jar (6 ounces) marinated artichoke hearts,
 drained and quartered
½ cup frozen peas
⅛ teaspoon hot pepper sauce

If plum tomatoes are unavailable, substitute 1 can (14½ ounces) undrained diced tomatoes. Omit water.

1. Place onion and garlic in 2-quart microwavable casserole. Spray lightly with cooking spray. Microwave at HIGH 30 seconds.

2. Add broth, rice, tomatoes, water, oregano, chili powder, salt, turmeric and black pepper, if desired. Cover with vented plastic wrap. Microwave at HIGH 5 minutes. Stir in bell pepper, artichokes, peas and hot sauce. Microwave at MEDIUM (50% power) 15 to 18 minutes or until broth is absorbed and rice is tender. *Makes 4 servings*

Nutrients per Serving: ¼ of total recipe

Calories: 262, Calories from Fat: 15%, Total Fat: 4g,
Saturated Fat: <1g, Cholesterol: 11mg, Sodium: 331mg,
Carbohydrate: 49g, Dietary Fiber: 5g, Protein: 8g
Dietary Exchanges: 3 Starch, 1 Vegetable, ½ Fat

Low-Fat Chimichangas

1 (16-ounce) can black beans, rinsed and
 drained
1 (8-ounce) can stewed tomatoes
2 to 3 teaspoons chili powder
1 teaspoon dried oregano
22 to 24 corn tortillas (6-inch)
1 cup finely chopped green onions including
 tops
1½ cups (6 ounces) shredded JARLSBERG LITE™
 Cheese

Mix beans, tomatoes, chili powder and oregano in medium saucepan. Cover and simmer 5 minutes. Uncover and simmer, stirring and crushing some of beans with wooden spoon, 5 minutes longer. Set aside. Warm tortillas according to package directions; keep warm. Place one tablespoon bean mixture on center of each tortilla. Sprinkle with rounded teaspoon onion, then rounded tablespoon cheese. Fold opposite sides of tortillas over mixture, forming square packets. Place folded sides down in nonstick skillet. Repeat until all ingredients are used. Cook, covered, over low heat 3 to 5 minutes until heated through and bottoms are crispy. Serve at once or keep warm on covered warming tray. *Makes 6 to 8 servings*

Nutrients per Serving: 3½ Chimichangas (⅙ of total recipe)

Calories: 371, Calories from Fat: 20%, Total Fat: 9g,
Saturated Fat: 4g, Cholesterol: 20mg, Sodium: 727mg,
Carbohydrate: 60g, Dietary Fiber: 9g, Protein: 17g
Dietary Exchanges: 4 Starch, 1 Lean Meat, 1 Fat

Cheese Ravioli with Pumpkin Sauce

 Nonstick cooking spray
⅓ cup sliced green onions
1 to 2 cloves garlic, minced
½ teaspoon fennel seeds
1 cup evaporated skimmed milk
1 tablespoon all-purpose flour
¼ teaspoon salt
⅛ teaspoon black pepper
½ cup solid-pack pumpkin
2 packages (9 ounces each) uncoooked
 refrigerated low-fat cheese ravioli
2 tablespoons grated Parmesan cheese (optional)

1. Spray medium nonstick saucepan with cooking spray; heat over medium heat. Add onions, garlic and fennel seeds; cook and stir 3 minutes or until onions are tender.

2. Combine milk, flour, salt and pepper in small bowl until smooth; stir into saucepan. Bring to a boil over high heat; boil until thickened, stirring constantly. Stir in pumpkin; reduce heat to low.

3. Meanwhile, cook pasta according to package directions, omitting salt; rinse and drain. Divide ravioli evenly among 6 plates; top each with equal amount of pumpkin sauce. Sprinkle cheese evenly over top of each serving. Serve immediately. Garnish as desired. *Makes 6 servings*

Nutrients per Serving: ⅙ of total recipe (without garnish)

Calories: 270, Calories from Fat: 7%, Total Fat: 2g,
Saturated Fat: 1g, Cholesterol: 6mg, Sodium: 556mg,
Carbohydrate: 45g, Dietary Fiber: 1g, Protein: 18g
Dietary Exchanges: 2½ Starch, ½ Milk, 1 Lean Meat

Couscous with Chick-Peas and Vegetables

1. Sort and rinse chick-peas. Cover with water and let soak overnight; drain. Place in Dutch oven with chicken broth; bring to a boil over high heat.

2. Add onion, garlic, cinnamon, red pepper flakes, paprika and saffron, if desired; reduce heat to low. Cover and simmer 1 hour or until chick-peas are tender. Stir in salt.

3. Add eggplant and sweet potato; cook 10 minutes. Add zucchini and tomatoes; cook 10 minutes or just until all vegetables are tender. Stir in parsley and cilantro; spoon mixture over hot couscous. Garnish with sweet potato slices and chives, if desired. *Makes 6 servings*

Nutrients per Serving: ⅙ of Chick-Pea mixture with about ⅔ cup cooked Couscous (without garnish)

Calories: 324, Calories from Fat: 7%, Total Fat: 2g, Saturated Fat: <1g, Cholesterol: 0mg, Sodium: 330mg, Carbohydrate: 63g, Dietary Fiber: 9g, Protein: 14g

Dietary Exchanges: 4 Starch, 1 Vegetable, ½ Fat

Couscous with Chick-Peas and Vegetables

1 cup dried chick-peas (garbanzo beans)
2 cans (14½ ounces each) fat-free reduced-
  sodium chicken broth
1 large onion, quartered and sliced
2 large cloves garlic, minced
1 teaspoon ground cinnamon
1 teaspoon red pepper flakes
½ teaspoon paprika
½ teaspoon saffron or turmeric (optional)
½ teaspoon salt
½ pound eggplant, cut into ¾-inch cubes
1 large sweet potato, peeled and cut into
  ¾-inch cubes
¾ pound zucchini, cut into ¾-inch cubes
1 can (14½ ounces) chopped tomatoes
2 tablespoons finely chopped fresh parsley
2 tablespoons finely chopped fresh cilantro
4 cups hot cooked couscous (cooked without
  added salt or fat)

Vegetable Lo Mein

8 ounces uncooked vermicelli or thin spaghetti,
  cooked and drained
¾ teaspoon dark sesame oil
½ teaspoon vegetable oil
3 cloves garlic, minced
1 teaspoon grated fresh ginger
2 cups sliced bok choy
½ cup sliced green onions
2 cups shredded carrots
6 ounces firm tofu, drained and cubed
¼ cup plus 2 tablespoons rice wine vinegar
¼ cup plum preserves
¼ cup water
1 teaspoon reduced-sodium soy sauce
½ teaspoon red pepper flakes

1. Toss vermicelli with sesame oil in large bowl until well coated; set aside. Heat vegetable oil in large nonstick skillet or wok over medium heat. Stir in garlic and ginger; stir-fry 10 seconds. Add bok choy and onions; stir-fry 3 to 4 minutes or until crisp-tender. Add carrots and tofu; stir-fry 2 to 3 minutes or until carrots are crisp-tender.

2. Combine vinegar, preserves, water, soy sauce and red pepper flakes in small saucepan. Heat over medium heat until preserves are melted, stirring constantly. Combine noodles, vegetable mixture and sauce in large bowl; mix well. *Makes 6 servings*

Nutrients per Serving: ⅙ of total recipe

Calories: 248, Calories from Fat: 13%, Total Fat: 4g, Saturated Fat: <1g, Cholesterol: <1mg, Sodium: 791mg, Carbohydrate: 45g, Dietary Fiber: 2g, Protein: 9g

Dietary Exchanges: 2 Starch, 2 Vegetable, ½ Lean Meat, ½ Fat

Cannelloni with Tomato-Eggplant Sauce

1 package (10 ounces) fresh spinach
1 cup fat-free ricotta cheese
4 egg whites, beaten
¼ cup (1 ounce) grated Parmesan cheese
2 tablespoons finely chopped fresh parsley
½ teaspoon salt (optional)
8 manicotti (about 4 ounces uncooked), cooked (without added salt) and cooled
Tomato-Eggplant Sauce (recipe follows)
1 cup (4 ounces) shredded reduced-fat mozzarella cheese

1. Preheat oven to 350°F.

2. Wash spinach; do not pat dry. Place spinach in saucepan; cook, covered, over medium-high heat 3 to 5 minutes or until spinach is wilted. Cool slightly and drain; chop finely.

3. Combine ricotta cheese, spinach, egg whites, Parmesan cheese, parsley and salt, if desired, in large bowl; mix well. Spoon mixture into manicotti shells; arrange in 13×9-inch baking pan. Spoon Tomato-Eggplant Sauce over manicotti; sprinkle evenly with mozzarella cheese.

4. Bake, uncovered, 25 to 30 minutes or until hot and bubbly. *Makes 4 servings*

Tomato-Eggplant Sauce

Olive oil-flavored nonstick cooking spray
1 small eggplant, coarsely chopped
½ cup chopped onion
2 cloves garlic, minced
½ teaspoon dried tarragon leaves
¼ teaspoon dried thyme leaves
1 can (16 ounces) no-salt-added whole tomatoes, undrained, coarsely chopped
Salt and black pepper (optional)

1. Spray large nonstick skillet with cooking spray; heat over medium heat until hot. Add eggplant, onion, garlic, tarragon and thyme; cook and stir about 5 minutes or until vegetables are tender.

2. Stir in tomatoes with juice; bring to a boil. Reduce heat and simmer, uncovered, 3 to 4 minutes. Season to taste with salt and pepper, if desired. *Makes about 2½ cups*

Nutrients per Serving: 2 filled manicotti shells with about ½ cup Sauce (without salt and pepper seasoning) and ¼ cup mozzarella cheese (2 tablespoons per shell)

Calories: 338, Calories from Fat: 19%, Total Fat: 7g, Saturated Fat: 4g, Cholesterol: 26mg, Sodium: 632mg, Carbohydrate: 40g, Dietary Fiber: 3g, Protein: 30g
Dietary Exchanges: 1½ Starch, 3 Vegetable, 3 Lean Meat

Chile, Egg & Cheese Casserole

1 tablespoon WESSON® Vegetable Oil, divided
½ cup *each:* chopped green bell pepper, red bell pepper and yellow bell pepper
1 cup chopped onion
2 jalapeño peppers, seeded and minced
3 containers (8 ounces each) fat free egg substitute (or 12 eggs)
1 teaspoon salt
10 corn tortillas, torn into bits
1 can (14.5 ounces) HUNT'S® Diced Tomatoes in Juice
1½ cups low fat shredded Cheddar cheese, divided
PAM® No-Stick Cooking Spray
1 tablespoon chopped fresh cilantro

1. Preheat oven to 400°F. In large skillet, heat ½ tablespoon of Wesson® Oil over medium-high heat. Sauté bell peppers, onion and jalapeños until tender, about 5 minutes.

2. Meanwhile, in large mixing bowl, combine egg substitute and salt; stir in tortillas. When vegetables are cooked, stir into egg mixture.

3. Pour *remaining* oil into skillet; heat over medium heat. Add egg mixture and cook about 2 minutes, or until eggs are halfway cooked; remove from heat. Stir in Hunt's® Diced Tomatoes in Juice and ¾ cup cheese.

4. Transfer egg mixture to 13×9×2-inch baking dish, lightly sprayed with PAM® Cooking Spray. Top with *remaining* cheese. Bake, uncovered, about 25 minutes, or until lightly browned. Sprinkle with cilantro.
Makes 10 (8-ounce) servings

Nutrients per Serving: 1 (8-ounce) Casserole wedge (1/10 of total recipe) made with egg substitute

Calories: 158, Calories from Fat: 20%, Total Fat: 3g, Saturated Fat: 1g, Cholesterol: 4mg, Sodium: 640mg, Carbohydrate: 18g, Dietary Fiber: 2g, Protein: 14g
Dietary Exchanges: 1 Starch, 1½ Lean Meat

Black Beans & Rice-Stuffed Chilies

Olive-oil flavored nonstick cooking spray
2 large poblano chili peppers*
½ (15½-ounce) can black beans, rinsed and drained
½ cup cooked brown rice
⅓ cup mild or medium chunky salsa
⅓ cup reduced-fat Cheddar cheese or shredded pepper Jack cheese, divided

Poblano peppers can sting and irritate the skin; wear rubber gloves when handling peppers and do not touch eyes. Wash hands after handling peppers.

1. Preheat oven to 375°F. Lightly spray shallow baking pan with cooking spray. Cut thin slice from one side of each pepper; chop 2 slices and set aside. In medium saucepan, cook peppers in boiling water 6 minutes. Drain and rinse with cold water. Remove and discard seeds and membranes.

2. Stir together beans, rice, salsa, chopped pepper and ¼ cup cheese. Spoon into peppers, mounding mixture. Place peppers in prepared pan. Cover with foil. Bake 12 to 15 minutes or until heated through. Sprinkle with remaining cheese. Bake 2 minutes more or until cheese melts. *Makes 2 servings*

Nutrients per Serving: 1 Stuffed Chili (½ of total recipe)

Calories: 236, Calories from Fat: 15%, Total Fat: 4g, Saturated Fat: 2g, Cholesterol: 7mg, Sodium: 772mg, Carbohydrate: 38g, Dietary Fiber: 5g, Protein: 14g
Dietary Exchanges: 2 Starch, 1 Vegetable, 1 Meat

Picante Pintos and Rice

2 cups dried pinto beans
Water
1 can (14½ ounces) no-salt-added stewed tomatoes
1 cup coarsely chopped onion
¾ cup coarsely chopped green bell pepper
¼ cup sliced celery
4 cloves garlic, minced
½ small jalapeño pepper,* seeded and chopped
2 teaspoons dried oregano leaves
2 teaspoons chili powder
½ teaspoon ground red pepper
2 cups chopped kale
3 cups hot cooked rice

Jalapeño peppers can sting and irritate the skin; wear rubber gloves when handling peppers and do not touch eyes. Wash hands after handling peppers.

1. Place beans in large saucepan; add water to cover beans by 2 inches. Bring to a boil over high heat; boil 2 minutes. Remove pan from heat; let stand, covered, 1 hour. Drain beans; discard water. Return beans to saucepan. Add 2 cups water, tomatoes, onion, bell pepper, celery, garlic, jalapeño pepper, oregano, chili powder and ground red pepper to saucepan; bring to a boil over high heat. Reduce heat to low. Simmer, covered, about 1½ hours or until beans are tender, stirring occasionally.

2. Gently stir in kale. Simmer, uncovered, 30 minutes. (Beans will be very tender and mixture will be consistency of thick sauce.) Serve over rice. *Makes 8 servings*

Nutrients per Serving: ⅛ of bean mixture with about ⅓ cup cooked rice

Calories: 270, Calories from Fat: 4%, Total Fat: 1g, Saturated Fat: <1g, Cholesterol: 0mg, Sodium: 35mg, Carbohydrate: 53g, Dietary Fiber: 13g, Protein: 13g
Dietary Exchanges: 3 Starch, 1½ Vegetable

Mexican Strata Olé

4 (6-inch) corn tortillas, halved, divided
1 cup chopped onion
½ cup chopped green bell pepper
1 clove garlic, crushed
1 teaspoon dried oregano leaves
½ teaspoon ground cumin
1 teaspoon FLEISCHMANN'S® Original Margarine
1 cup dried kidney beans, cooked in unsalted water according to package directions
½ cup (2 ounces) shredded reduced-fat Cheddar cheese
1½ cups fat-free (skim) milk
1 cup EGG BEATERS® Healthy Real Egg Product
1 cup thick and chunky salsa

Arrange half the tortilla pieces in bottom of greased 12×8×2-inch baking dish; set aside. In large nonstick skillet, over medium-high heat, sauté onion, bell pepper, garlic, oregano and cumin in margarine until tender; stir in beans. Spoon half the mixture over tortillas; repeat layers once. Sprinkle with cheese.

In medium bowl, combine milk and Egg Beaters®; pour evenly over cheese. Bake at 350°F for 40 minutes or until puffed and golden brown. Let stand 10 minutes before serving. Serve topped with salsa. *Makes 8 servings*

Nutrients per Serving: 1 Strata wedge with 2 tablespoons salsa (⅛ of total recipe)

Calories: 185, Calories from Fat: 13%, Total Fat: 3g, Saturated Fat: 1g, Cholesterol: 6mg, Sodium: 397mg, Carbohydrate: 27g, Dietary Fiber: 7g, Protein: 13g
Dietary Exchanges: 2 Starch, 1 Lean Meat

Bean Threads with Tofu and Vegetables

8 ounces firm tofu, drained and cubed
1 tablespoon dark sesame oil
3 teaspoons reduced-sodium soy sauce, divided
1 can (14½ ounces) fat-free reduced-sodium chicken broth
1 package (3¾ ounces) uncooked bean threads
1 package (16 ounces) frozen mixed vegetable medley such as broccoli, carrots and red pepper, thawed
¼ cup rice wine vinegar
½ teaspoon red pepper flakes

1. Place tofu on shallow plate; drizzle with oil and 1½ teaspoons soy sauce.

2. Combine broth and remaining 1½ teaspoons soy sauce in deep skillet or large saucepan. Bring to a boil over high heat; reduce heat. Add bean threads; simmer, uncovered, 7 minutes or until noodles absorb liquid, stirring occasionally to separate noodles.

3. Stir in vegetables and vinegar; heat through. Stir in tofu mixture and red pepper flakes; heat through, about 1 minute.   *Makes 4 servings*

Nutrients per Serving: ¼ of total recipe

Calories: 251, Calories from Fat: 32%, Total Fat: 9g, Saturated Fat: 2g, Cholesterol: 0mg, Sodium: 195mg, Carbohydrate: 35g, Dietary Fiber: 5g, Protein: 12g
Dietary Exchanges: 2 Starch, 1 Vegetable, ½ Lean Meat, 1 Fat

Bean Threads with Tofu and Vegetables

Ravioli with Homemade Tomato Sauce

3 cloves garlic, peeled
½ cup fresh basil leaves
3 cups seeded peeled tomatoes, cut into quarters
2 tablespoons tomato paste
2 tablespoons fat-free Italian salad dressing
1 tablespoon balsamic vinegar
¼ teaspoon black pepper
1 package (9 ounces) uncooked refrigerated reduced-fat cheese ravioli
2 cups shredded spinach leaves
1 cup (4 ounces) shredded part-skim mozzarella cheese

Microwave Directions

1. To prepare tomato sauce, process garlic in food processor until coarsely chopped. Add basil; process until coarsely chopped. Add tomatoes, tomato paste, salad dressing, vinegar and pepper; process, using on/off pulsing action, until tomatoes are chopped.

2. Spray 9-inch square microwavable dish with nonstick cooking spray. Spread 1 cup tomato sauce in dish. Layer half of ravioli and spinach over tomato sauce. Repeat layers with 1 cup tomato sauce and remaining ravioli and spinach. Top with remaining 1 cup tomato sauce. Cover with plastic wrap; refrigerate 1 to 8 hours.

3. Vent plastic wrap. Microwave at MEDIUM (50% power) 20 minutes or until pasta is tender and hot. Sprinkle with cheese. Microwave at HIGH 3 minutes or just until cheese melts. Let stand, covered, 5 minutes before serving.   *Makes 6 servings*

Nutrients per Serving: ⅙ of total recipe

Calories: 206, Calories from Fat: 26%, Total Fat: 6g, Saturated Fat: 3g, Cholesterol: 40mg, Sodium: 401mg, Carbohydrate: 26g, Dietary Fiber: 3g, Protein: 13g
Dietary Exchanges: 1 Starch, 2 Vegetable, 1 Lean Meat, ½ Fat

TIP Bean threads are also known as cellophane noodles. They are sold in dried form and can be found in the ethnic sections of supermarkets and in Asian grocery stores.

Broccoli-Tofu Stir-Fry

2 cups uncooked rice
1 can (14½ ounces) vegetable broth, divided
3 tablespoons cornstarch
1 tablespoon reduced-sodium soy sauce
½ teaspoon sugar
¼ teaspoon dark sesame oil
1 package (16 ounces) extra-firm tofu
1 teaspoon peanut oil
1 tablespoon minced fresh ginger
3 cloves garlic, minced
3 cups broccoli florets
2 cups sliced mushrooms
½ cup chopped green onions
1 large red bell pepper, seeded and cut into strips
    Prepared Szechwan sauce (optional)

1. Cook rice according to package directions. Combine ¼ cup vegetable broth, cornstarch, soy sauce, sugar and sesame oil in small bowl; set aside. Drain tofu and cut into 1-inch cubes; set aside.

2. Heat peanut oil in large nonstick wok or skillet over medium heat until hot. Add ginger and garlic. Cook and stir 5 minutes. Add remaining vegetable broth and broccoli, mushrooms, green onions and bell pepper. Cook and stir over medium-high heat 5 minutes or until vegetables are crisp-tender. Add tofu; cook 2 minutes, stirring occasionally. Stir cornstarch mixture; add to vegetable mixture. Cook and stir until sauce thickens. Serve over rice with Szechwan sauce, if desired. Garnish, if desired.   *Makes 6 servings*

Nutrients per Serving: ⅙ of Stir-Fry mixture with about ⅔ cup cooked white rice (without Szechwan sauce and garnish)

Calories: 410, Calories from Fat: 18%, Total Fat: 8g, Saturated Fat: 1g, Cholesterol: 0mg, Sodium: 316mg, Carbohydrate: 67g, Dietary Fiber: 4g, Protein: 20g
Dietary Exchanges: 4 Starch, 1 Vegetable, 1½ Lean Meat, ½ Fat

Bow Tie Pasta with Savory Lentil Sauce

1 can (13¾ ounces) chicken broth
½ cup water
½ cup dry lentils, rinsed and drained
1 jar (1 pound 10 ounces) RAGÚ® Light Pasta Sauce
1 tablespoon balsamic vinegar
1 box (16 ounces) bow tie pasta, cooked and drained

In 3-quart saucepot or Dutch oven, bring chicken broth, water and lentils to a boil over high heat. Reduce heat to low and simmer covered, stirring occasionally, 20 minutes. Stir in RAGÚ® Light Pasta Sauce and vinegar. Simmer covered, stirring occasionally, an additional 20 minutes or until lentils are tender. Serve over hot pasta.
        Makes 8 servings

Nutrients per Serving: 1 cup Pasta with ⅛ of Sauce

Calories: 293, Calories from Fat: 4%, Total Fat: 1g, Saturated Fat: <1g, Cholesterol: 0mg, Sodium: 479mg, Carbohydrate: 57g, Dietary Fiber: 6g, Protein: 13g
Dietary Exchanges: 4 Starch

Bulgur Pilaf with Tomato and Zucchini

1 cup uncooked bulgur
1 tablespoon olive oil
¾ cup chopped onion
2 cloves garlic, minced
½ pound zucchini, thinly sliced
1 can (14½ ounces) no-salt-added whole tomatoes, drained and coarsely chopped
1 cup fat-free reduced-sodium chicken broth
1 teaspoon dried basil leaves, crushed
⅛ teaspoon black pepper

1. Rinse bulgur thoroughly in colander under cold water, removing any debris. Drain well; set aside.

2. Heat oil in large saucepan over medium heat. Add onion and garlic; cook and stir 3 minutes or until onion is tender. Stir in zucchini and tomatoes; reduce heat to medium-low. Cook, covered, 15 minutes or until zucchini is almost tender, stirring occasionally.

3. Stir chicken broth, bulgur, basil and pepper into vegetable mixture. Bring to a boil over high heat. Reduce heat to low. Cook, covered, over low heat 15 minutes or until bulgur is tender and liquid is almost completely absorbed, stirring occasionally. Remove from heat; let stand, covered, 10 minutes. Stir gently before serving.
        Makes 4 servings

Nutrients per Serving: ¼ of total recipe

Calories: 196, Calories from Fat: 18%, Total Fat: 4g, Saturated Fat: 1g, Cholesterol: 0mg, Sodium: 184mg, Carbohydrate: 36g, Dietary Fiber: 10g, Protein: 6g
Dietary Exchanges: 2 Starch, 1 Vegetable, ½ Fat

Mu Shu Vegetables

Peanut Sauce (recipe follows)
3 tablespoons reduced-sodium soy sauce
2 tablespoons dry sherry
2 teaspoons cornstarch
1½ tablespoons minced fresh ginger
3 cloves garlic, minced
1½ teaspoons sesame oil
1 tablespoon peanut oil
3 leeks, washed and cut into 2-inch slivers
3 carrots, peeled and julienned
1 cup thinly sliced fresh shiitake mushrooms
1 small head napa or savoy cabbage, shredded
     (about 4 cups)
2 cups mung bean sprouts, rinsed and drained
8 ounces firm tofu, drained and cut into
     2½×¼-inch strips
12 (8-inch) fat-free flour tortillas, warmed*
¾ cup finely chopped honey-roasted peanuts

Tortillas can be softened and warmed in microwave oven just before using. Stack tortillas and wrap in plastic wrap. Microwave at HIGH 30 seconds to 1 minute, turning over and rotating a quarter turn once during heating.

1. Prepare Peanut Sauce; set aside. Combine soy sauce, sherry, cornstarch, ginger, garlic and sesame oil in small bowl until smooth; set aside.

2. Heat wok over medium-high heat 1 minute or until hot. Drizzle peanut oil into wok and heat 30 seconds. Add leeks, carrots and mushrooms; stir-fry 2 minutes. Add cabbage; stir-fry 3 minutes or until just tender. Add bean sprouts and tofu; stir-fry 1 minute or until hot. Stir soy sauce mixture; add to wok. Cook and stir 1 minute or until sauce is thickened.

3. Spread each tortilla with about 1 teaspoon Peanut Sauce. Spoon ½ cup vegetable mixture onto bottom half of each tortilla; sprinkle with 1 tablespoon peanuts. Fold bottom edge of tortilla over filling; fold in side edges. Roll up to completely enclose filling. Or, spoon ½ cup vegetable mixture onto one half of tortilla. Fold bottom edge over filling. Fold in one side edge.

4. Serve with Peanut Sauce. *Makes 12 servings*

Peanut Sauce

3 tablespoons sugar
3 tablespoons dry sherry
3 tablespoons reduced-sodium soy sauce
3 tablespoons water
2 teaspoons white wine vinegar
⅓ cup creamy reduced-fat peanut butter

Combine all ingredients except peanut butter in small saucepan. Bring to a boil over medium-high heat, stirring constantly. Boil 1 minute or until sugar melts. Stir in peanut butter until smooth; cool to room temperature.

Makes ⅔ cup

Nutrients per Serving: 1 filled tortilla with about 2 teaspoons Peanut Sauce

Calories: 238, Calories from Fat: 33%, Total Fat: 9g, Saturated Fat: 2g, Cholesterol: 0mg, Sodium: 521mg, Carbohydrate: 32g, Dietary Fiber: 9g, Protein: 9g
Dietary Exchanges: 1½ Starch, 1½ Vegetable, ½ Lean Meat, 1½ Fat

Eggplant Parmesan

2 tablespoons olive oil, divided
1 package (12 ounces) frozen soy crumbles
1 tablespoon Italian seasoning
1 jar (26 ounces) meatless pasta sauce
1 medium to large eggplant (1½ pounds),
     trimmed and cut into 16 slices
½ teaspoon salt
½ teaspoon black pepper
1 egg beaten with 1 tablespoon water
½ cup grated reduced-fat Parmesan cheese
     Hot cooked pasta (optional)

1. Preheat oven to 350°F. Heat 1 tablespoon oil in small nonstick skillet over medium heat. Mix crumbles with Italian seasoning and cook in skillet, stirring occasionally, until lightly browned, about 10 minutes; keep warm.

2. Heat pasta sauce in small saucepan; keep warm.

3. Heat remaining 1 tablespoon oil in large nonstick skillet over medium-high heat. Sprinkle eggplant slices lightly with salt and pepper. Dip slices into beaten egg mixture. Fry until brown, about 5 to 6 minutes; turn and fry other side until eggplant is cooked through but not mushy, about 5 minutes.

4. Spray 13×9-inch glass baking dish with nonstick cooking spray. Place 8 cooked eggplant slices in single layer in bottom of prepared dish. Top with soy mixture. Place remaining 8 cooked eggplant slices on top of soy mixture. Spoon pasta sauce over all. Sprinkle evenly with cheese. Bake about 10 minutes or until heated through. Serve over cooked pasta, if desired. *Makes 8 servings*

Nutrients per Serving: ⅛ of total recipe (without pasta)

Calories: 211, Calories from Fat: 38%, Total Fat: 9g, Saturated Fat: 1g, Cholesterol: 27mg, Sodium: 588mg, Carbohydrate: 20g, Dietary Fiber: 7g, Protein: 14g
Dietary Exchanges: ½ Starch, 3 Vegetable, 1 Lean Meat, 1 Fat

Pasta Primavera

Spinach Lasagna

5 uncooked lasagna noodles
  Nonstick cooking spray
2 cups sliced fresh mushrooms
1 cup chopped onion
1 cup chopped green bell pepper
2 cloves garlic, minced
2 cans (8 ounces each) no-salt-added tomato
  sauce
1 teaspoon chopped fresh basil *or* ¼ teaspoon
  dried basil leaves
1 teaspoon chopped fresh oregano *or*
  ¼ teaspoon dried oregano leaves
¼ teaspoon ground red pepper
2 egg whites
1½ cups low-fat (1%) cottage cheese or reduced-
  fat ricotta cheese
¼ cup grated Romano or Parmesan cheese
3 tablespoons fine dry bread crumbs
1 package (10 ounces) frozen chopped spinach,
  thawed and well drained
¾ cup (3 ounces) shredded part-skim mozzarella
  cheese
¼ cup chopped fresh parsley

1. Prepare noodles according to package directions, omitting salt; drain. Rinse under cold water; drain.

2. Coat large nonstick skillet with cooking spray. Add mushrooms, onion, bell pepper and garlic; cook and stir over medium heat until vegetables are tender. Stir in tomato sauce, basil, oregano and red pepper. Bring to a boil over medium-high heat. Reduce heat to medium-low. Simmer, uncovered, 10 minutes, stirring occasionally.

3. Preheat oven to 350°F. Combine egg whites, cottage cheese, Romano cheese and bread crumbs in medium bowl. Stir spinach into cottage cheese mixture. Cut noodles in half crosswise. Spread ½ cup sauce in ungreased 8- or 9-inch square baking dish. Top with half the noodles, half the spinach mixture and half the remaining sauce. Repeat layers.

4. Cover and bake 45 minutes or until hot and bubbly. Sprinkle with mozzarella cheese. Bake, uncovered, 2 to 3 minutes more or until cheese melts. Sprinkle with parsley. Let stand 10 minutes. Cut into 4 wedges before serving.
Makes 4 servings

Nutrients per Serving: 1 Lasagna wedge (¼ of total recipe)

Calories: 350, Calories from Fat: 21%, Total Fat: 8g, Saturated Fat: 4g, Cholesterol: 23mg, Sodium: 746mg, Carbohydrate: 40g, Dietary Fiber: 7g, Protein: 30g

Dietary Exchanges: 1 Starch, 5 Vegetable, 2½ Lean Meat, ½ Fat

Pasta Primavera

8 ounces uncooked linguine or medium pasta
  shells
1 tablespoon reduced-fat margarine
2 green onions, diagonally sliced
1 clove garlic, minced
1 cup fresh mushroom slices
1 cup broccoli florets
2½ cups fresh snow peas
4 to 8 asparagus spears, cut into 2-inch pieces
1 medium red bell pepper, cut into thin strips
½ cup evaporated skimmed milk
½ teaspoon dried tarragon leaves
½ teaspoon black pepper
⅓ cup grated Parmesan cheese

1. Cook pasta according to package directions, omitting salt. Drain and set aside.

2. Melt margarine in large nonstick skillet. Add green onions and garlic; cook over medium heat until softened. Add mushrooms and broccoli. Cover; cook 3 minutes or until mushrooms are tender. Add snow peas, asparagus, bell pepper, milk, tarragon and black pepper. Cook and stir until vegetables are crisp-tender and lightly coated. Add cheese; toss to coat evenly. Serve immediately.
Makes 4 servings

Nutrients per Serving: 2 cups

Calories: 282, Calories from Fat: 15%, Total Fat: 5g, Saturated Fat: 2g, Cholesterol: 6mg, Sodium: 308mg, Carbohydrate: 47g, Dietary Fiber: 6g, Protein: 15g

Dietary Exchanges: 2 Starch, 3 Vegetable, 1 Fat

Spaghetti Squash with Black Beans and Zucchini

1 spaghetti squash (about 2 pounds)
2 medium zucchini, cut lengthwise into ¼-inch-thick slices
   Nonstick cooking spray
2 cups chopped seeded tomatoes
1 can (about 15 ounces) black beans, drained and rinsed
2 tablespoons chopped fresh basil
2 tablespoons olive oil
2 tablespoons red wine vinegar
1 large clove garlic, minced
½ teaspoon salt

1. Pierce spaghetti squash in several places with fork. Wrap in large piece of heavy-duty foil, using Drugstore Wrap technique.* Grill squash on covered grill over medium coals 45 minutes to 1 hour or until easily depressed with back of long-handled spoon, turning a quarter turn every 15 minutes. Remove squash from grill and let stand in foil 10 to 15 minutes.

2. To grill zucchini, spray both sides of slices with cooking spray. Grill on uncovered grill over medium coals 4 minutes or until tender, turning once.

3. Remove spaghetti squash from foil and cut in half; scoop out seeds. With two forks, comb strands of pulp from each half and place in large salad bowl. Add tomatoes, beans, zucchini and basil.

4. Combine olive oil, vinegar, garlic and salt in small bowl; mix thoroughly. Add to vegetables and toss gently to combine. Serve with grilled French bread and garnish, if desired. *Makes 4 servings*

*Place food in the center of an oblong piece of heavy-duty foil, leaving at least a two-inch border around the food. Bring the two long sides together above the food; fold down in a series of locked folds, allowing room for heat circulation and expansion. Fold short ends up and over again. Press folds firmly to seal the foil packet.

Nutrients per Serving: ¼ of total recipe (without French bread and garnish)

Calories: 219, Calories from Fat: 30%, Total Fat: 8g, Saturated Fat: 1g, Cholesterol: 0mg, Sodium: 613mg, Carbohydrate: 34g, Dietary Fiber: 8g, Protein: 12g
Dietary Exchanges: 1½ Starch, 1½ Vegetable, 1½ Fat

Vegetable-Enchilada Casserole

1 small eggplant, peeled and quartered
1 medium zucchini
½ pound fresh mushrooms
   Nonstick cooking spray
½ cup chopped green onions, divided
2 cloves garlic, minced
1 jar (16 ounces) GUILTLESS GOURMET® Southwestern Grill Salsa
7 ounce bag GUILTLESS GOURMET® Baked Tortilla chips (yellow, red or blue corn)
1 jar (16 ounces) GUILTLESS GOURMET® Black Bean Dip (Spicy or Mild)
¾ cup low fat shredded Cheddar cheese
2½ cups shredded lettuce
1 medium tomato, chopped
3 tablespoons low fat sour cream

Slice eggplant, zucchini and mushrooms; set aside. Coat large nonstick skillet with cooking spray. Heat over medium-high heat until hot. Add reserved vegetables, ¼ cup onions and garlic; cover and cook 5 minutes or until tender, stirring occasionally. Stir in salsa. Reduce heat to low; cover and simmer 30 minutes. Preheat over to 350°F. To assemble casserole, coat 12×8-inch baking dish with cooking spray. Arrange half the tortilla chips in dish and top with vegetable mixture. Cover; bake 20 to 30 minutes or until heated through. Dollop with rounded teaspoons of black bean dip on top of vegetables. Coarsely crush remaining tortilla chips; sprinkle over vegetable mixture. Sprinkle cheese over chips. Bake, uncovered, 5 minutes or more until chips are crisp and lightly browned. To serve, divided lettuce among 8 individual serving plates or spread on serving platter. Spoon casserole over lettuce. Sprinkle with chopped tomato and remaining ¼ cup onions. Dollop with sour cream. *Makes 8 servings*

Nutrients per Serving: ⅛ of total recipe

Calories: 242, Calories from Fat: 15%, Total Fat: 4g, Saturated Fat: 1g, Cholesterol: 6mg, Sodium: 699mg, Carbohydrate: 41g, Dietary Fiber: 7g, Protein: 12g
Dietary Exchanges: 2 Starch, 2 Vegetable, 1 Fat

TIP While fiber has been shown to help prevent heart disease and several forms of cancer, very few Americans consume the recommended 21-38 grams a day. Low in fat and loaded with fiber, beans are a great way to meet your daily goal.

Spaghetti Squash with Black Beans and Zucchini

Latin-Style Pasta & Beans

8 ounces uncooked mostaccioli, penne or bow tie pasta
1 tablespoon olive oil
1 medium onion, chopped
1 medium yellow or red bell pepper, diced
4 cloves garlic, minced
1 can (15 ounces) red or black beans, rinsed and drained
¾ cup canned vegetable broth
¾ cup medium-hot salsa or picante sauce
2 teaspoons ground cumin
⅓ cup coarsely chopped fresh cilantro
Lime wedges

1. Cook pasta according to package directions, omitting salt. Drain; set aside.

2. Meanwhile, heat oil in large nonstick skillet over medium heat. Add onion; cook 5 minutes, stirring occasionally. Add bell pepper and garlic; cook 3 minutes, stirring occasionally. Add beans, vegetable broth, salsa and cumin; simmer, uncovered, 5 minutes.

3. Add cooked pasta to skillet; cook 1 minute, tossing frequently. Stir in cilantro; spoon evenly onto 4 plates. Serve with lime wedges.   *Makes 4 servings*

Nutrients per Serving: ¼ of total recipe

Calories: 390, Calories from Fat: 12%, Total Fat: 6g, Saturated Fat: 1g, Cholesterol: 0mg, Sodium: 557mg, Carbohydrate: 74g, Dietary Fiber: 8g, Protein: 18g

Dietary Exchanges: 4 Starch, 2 Vegetable, ½ Fat

Zesty Zucchini Burritos

6 (6-inch) fat-free flour tortillas
2 teaspoons olive oil
1 medium zucchini, chopped
¼ cup chopped onion
¾ cup prepared pinto bean dip
¼ cup prepared green salsa
1 tablespoon chopped fresh cilantro
2 cups shredded romaine lettuce
1 cup prepared tomato salsa

1. Preheat oven to 350°F.

2. Wrap tortillas in foil; place on center rack of oven. Heat 10 minutes or until warm.

3. Meanwhile, heat oil in large skillet over medium-high heat until hot. Add zucchini and onion. Cook and stir until zucchini is crisp-tender; stir in bean dip, green salsa and cilantro.

4. Divide lettuce evenly among 6 plates. Spoon zucchini mixture evenly onto tortillas. Roll up tortillas; place on top of lettuce. Top with tomato salsa. Garnish as desired.   *Makes 6 servings*

Nutrients per Serving: 1 Burrito with 2 tablespoons plus 2 teaspoons tomato salsa (without garnish)

Calories: 118, Calories from Fat: 13%, Total Fat: 2g, Saturated Fat: <1g, Cholesterol: 0mg, Sodium: 677mg, Carbohydrate: 22g, Dietary Fiber: 8g, Protein: 4g

Dietary Exchanges: 1 Starch, 2 Vegetable

Latin-Style Pasta & Beans

Vegetable Strata

2 slices white bread, cubed
¼ cup shredded reduced-fat Swiss cheese
½ cup sliced carrots
½ cup sliced mushrooms
¼ cup chopped onion
1 clove garlic, crushed
1 teaspoon FLEISCHMANN'S® Original Margarine
½ cup chopped tomato
½ cup snow peas
1 cup EGG BEATERS® Healthy Real Egg Product
¾ cup skim milk

Place bread cubes evenly on bottom of greased 1½-quart casserole dish. Sprinkle with cheese; set aside.

In medium nonstick skillet, over medium heat, sauté carrots, mushrooms, onion and garlic in margarine until tender. Stir in tomato and snow peas; cook 1 to 2 minutes more. Spoon over cheese. In small bowl, combine Egg Beaters® and milk; pour over vegetable mixture. Bake at 375°F for 45 to 50 minutes or until knife inserted into center comes out clean. Let stand 10 minutes before serving. *Makes 6 servings*

Prep Time: 15 minutes
Cook Time: 55 minutes

Nutrients per Serving: ⅙ of total recipe

Calories: 83, Calories from Fat: 13%, Total Fat: 1g, Saturated Fat: <1g, Cholesterol: 3mg, Sodium: 161mg, Carbohydrate: 10g, Dietary Fiber: 1g, Protein: 8g
Dietary Exchanges: 2 Vegetable, ½ Lean Meat

Spinach Ziti Casserole

1 pound uncooked ziti or other pasta
2 teaspoons vegetable oil
1 medium onion, chopped
1 (16-ounce) can tomato sauce
2 teaspoons sugar
2 tablespoons dried oregano leaves
½ teaspoon black pepper
½ teaspoon chili powder
1 (10-ounce) package frozen spinach, thawed and squeezed dry
1 (16-ounce) container fat-free cottage cheese
1 (15-ounce) can kidney beans, drained and rinsed

Cook pasta in large saucepan according to package directions, omitting salt. Drain and return to saucepan. Meanwhile, heat oil in medium saucepan over low heat. Add onion; cook and stir 5 minutes.

Add tomato sauce, sugar, oregano, pepper, chili powder and spinach. Cook over low heat 15 minutes. Add tomato sauce mixture, cottage cheese and kidney beans to pasta; mix well. Pour into 2-quart baking dish. Cover and bake in 350°F oven 20 minutes. *Makes 8 servings*

Note: If desired, recipe can be heated just on the stovetop. Do not remove pasta mixture from saucepan; heat thoroughly, over medium heat, stirring occasionally.

Favorite recipe from *The Sugar Association, Inc.*

Nutrients per Serving: ⅛ of total recipe

Calories: 353, Calories from Fat: 7%, Total Fat: 3g, Saturated Fat: 1g, Cholesterol: 4mg, Sodium: 562mg, Carbohydrate: 60g, Dietary Fiber: 7g, Protein: 22g
Dietary Exchanges: 3½ Starch, 1½ Vegetable, ½ Lean Meat

Brown Rice Black Bean Burrito

1 tablespoon vegetable oil
1 medium onion, chopped
2 cloves garlic, minced
1½ teaspoons chili powder
½ teaspoon ground cumin
3 cups cooked brown rice
1 (15- to 16-ounce) can black beans, drained and rinsed
1 (11-ounce) can corn, drained
6 (8-inch) flour tortillas
¾ cup (6 ounces) shredded reduced-fat Cheddar cheese
2 green onions, thinly sliced
¼ cup plain low-fat yogurt
¼ cup prepared salsa

Heat oil in large skillet over medium-high heat until hot. Add onion, garlic, chili powder and cumin. Sauté 3 to 5 minutes until onion is tender. Add rice, beans and corn; cook, stirring, 2 to 3 minutes until mixture is thoroughly heated. Remove from heat.

Spoon ½ cup rice mixture down center of each tortilla. Top each evenly with cheese, green onions and yogurt. Roll up and top evenly with salsa. *Makes 6 servings*

Favorite recipe from *USA Rice Federation*

Nutrients per Serving: 1 Burrito

Calories: 386, Calories from Fat: 20%, Total Fat: 9g, Saturated Fat: 3g, Cholesterol: 6mg, Sodium: 631mg, Carbohydrate: 64g, Dietary Fiber: 7g, Protein: 15g
Dietary Exchanges: 4 Starch, 1 Lean Meat, 1 Fat

Black Bean Tostadas

1 cup rinsed and drained canned black beans, mashed
2 teaspoons chili powder
   Nonstick cooking spray
4 (8-inch) corn tortillas
1 cup washed torn romaine lettuce leaves
1 cup chopped seeded tomato
½ cup chopped onion
½ cup plain nonfat yogurt
2 jalapeño peppers,* seeded and finely chopped

Jalapeño peppers can sting and irritate the skin. Wear rubber gloves when handling peppers and do not touch eyes. Wash hands after handling peppers.

1. Combine beans and chili powder in small saucepan. Cook over medium heat 5 minutes or until heated through, stirring occasionally.

2. Spray large nonstick skillet with cooking spray. Heat over medium heat until hot. Sprinkle tortillas with water; place in skillet, one at a time. Cook 20 to 30 seconds or until hot and pliable, turning once during cooking.

3. Spread bean mixture evenly over tortillas; layer with lettuce, tomato, onion, yogurt and peppers. Garnish with cilantro, sliced tomatoes and peppers, if desired. Serve immediately.   *Makes 4 servings*

Nutrients per Serving: 1 Tostada (without garnish)

Calories: 146, Calories from Fat: 9%, Total Fat: 2g, Saturated Fat: <1g, Cholesterol: 1mg, Sodium: 466mg, Carbohydrate: 29g, Dietary Fiber: 5g, Protein: 9g

Dietary Exchanges: 1½ Starch, 1½ Vegetable

Cavatelli and Vegetable Stir-Fry

¾ cup uncooked cavatelli or elbow macaroni
   Nonstick cooking spray
6 ounces fresh snow peas, cut lengthwise into halves
½ cup thinly sliced carrot
1 teaspoon minced fresh ginger
½ cup chopped yellow or green bell pepper
½ cup chopped onion
¼ cup chopped fresh parsley
1 tablespoon chopped fresh oregano *or*
      1 teaspoon dried oregano leaves, crushed
1 tablespoon reduced-fat margarine
2 tablespoons water
1 tablespoon reduced-sodium soy sauce

1. Prepare cavatelli according to package directions, omitting salt; drain and set aside.

2. Coat wok or large nonstick skillet with cooking spray. Add snow peas, carrot and ginger; stir-fry 2 minutes over medium-high heat. Add bell pepper, onion, parsley, oregano and margarine. Stir-fry 2 to 3 minutes or until vegetables are crisp-tender. Stir in water and soy sauce. Stir in pasta; heat through.   *Makes 4 servings*

Nutrients per Serving: ¼ of total recipe

Calories: 130, Calories from Fat: 14%, Total Fat: 2g, Saturated Fat: <1g, Cholesterol: 0mg, Sodium: 175mg, Carbohydrate: 23g, Dietary Fiber: 3g, Protein: 5g

Dietary Exchanges: 1 Starch, 1½ Vegetable, ½ Fat

INTERNATIONAL FARE

Turkey and Bean Tostadas

6 (8-inch) flour tortillas
1 pound 93% lean ground turkey
1 can (15 ounces) chili beans in chili sauce
½ teaspoon chili powder
3 cups washed and shredded romaine lettuce
1 large tomato, chopped
¼ cup chopped fresh cilantro
¼ cup (1 ounce) shredded reduced-fat Monterey Jack cheese
½ cup low-fat sour cream (optional)

1. Preheat oven to 350°F. Place tortillas on baking sheets. Bake 7 minutes or until crisp. Place on individual plates.

2. Heat large nonstick skillet over medium-high heat until hot. Add turkey. Cook and stir until turkey is browned; drain. Add beans and chili powder. Cook 5 minutes over medium heat. Divide turkey mixture evenly among 6 tortillas. Top evenly with remaining ingredients. *Makes 6 servings*

Prep and Cook Time: 20 minutes

Nutrients per Serving: 1 Tostada

Calories: 288, Calories from Fat: 30%, Total Fat: 10g, Saturated Fat: 2g, Cholesterol: 30mg, Sodium: 494mg, Carbohydrate: 34g, Dietary Fiber: 2g, Protein: 19g

Dietary Exchanges: 1½ Starch, 1 Vegetable, 2 Lean Meat, 1 Fat

Chicken Véronique

1 tablespoon reduced-fat margarine
1 cup sliced mushrooms
½ cup chopped onion
4 boneless skinless chicken breasts (about 1 pound)
1 cup fat-free reduced-sodium chicken broth*
⅛ teaspoon black pepper
2 tablespoons dry white wine
1 tablespoon cornstarch
2 cups red or green grapes, cut into halves

To defat chicken broth, skim fat from surface of broth with spoon. Or, place can of broth in refrigerator at least 2 hours ahead of time. Before using, remove fat that has hardened on surface of broth.

1. Melt margarine in large nonstick skillet over medium heat. Add mushrooms and onion; cook and stir about 3 minutes or until onion is softened. Add chicken; cook until browned, turning once to brown both sides. Add chicken broth and pepper; reduce heat to low. Simmer, covered, 15 minutes.

2. Combine wine and cornstarch in small cup until smooth. Add cornstarch mixture and grapes to chicken mixture in skillet; cook and stir over medium-high heat until mixture boils and thickens. Cook and stir 1 minute more. *Makes 4 servings*

Note: Serve this dish over rice or noodles, if desired.

Nutrients per Serving: ¼ of total recipe (without rice or noodles)

Calories: 229, Calories from Fat: 14%, Total Fat: 4g, Saturated Fat: 1g, Cholesterol: 72mg, Sodium: 159mg, Carbohydrate: 19g, Dietary Fiber: 1g, Protein: 29g

Dietary Exchanges: 1 Fruit, 1 Vegetable, 3 Lean Meat

Szechwan Shrimp Stir-Fry

6 ounces uncooked spaghetti or Chinese noodles
¾ pound raw large shrimp, peeled and deveined
¼ cup reduced-sodium soy sauce
½ teaspoon red pepper flakes
2 teaspoons dark sesame oil
1 cup snow peas
1 medium red or yellow bell pepper, cut lengthwise in half, then crosswise into thin strips
½ cup shredded carrots
2 teaspoons fresh or bottled minced ginger
1½ teaspoons fresh or bottled minced garlic
3 tablespoons water
2 teaspoons cornstarch
¼ cup thinly sliced green onions or chopped fresh cilantro

1. Cook spaghetti according to package directions, omitting salt. Drain; keep warm.

2. Combine shrimp, soy sauce and red pepper flakes in small bowl; toss to coat. Set aside.

3. Heat oil in large nonstick skillet or wok over medium-high heat until hot. Add snow peas, bell pepper, carrots, ginger and garlic; stir-fry 3 minutes.

4. Remove shrimp from bowl, reserving soy sauce mixture. Add shrimp to skillet; stir-fry 2 minutes.

5. Combine water and cornstarch in small bowl; mix well. Add to skillet with reserved soy sauce mixture; stir-fry 2 minutes or until shrimp are pink and opaque and sauce thickens.

6. Serve shrimp mixture with spaghetti; garnish with green onions.

Makes 4 servings

Nutrients per Serving: ¼ of shrimp mixture with ¾ cup cooked spaghetti

Calories: 326, Calories from Fat: 11%, Total Fat: 4g, Saturated Fat: 1g, Cholesterol: 130mg, Sodium: 692mg, Carbohydrate: 48g, Dietary Fiber: 5g, Protein: 23g

Dietary Exchanges: 2½ Starch, 2 Vegetable, 1½ Lean Meat

Eggplant & Orzo Soup with Roasted Red Pepper Salsa

2 medium eggplants (1 pound each)
1½ cups finely chopped onions
2 cloves garlic, minced
2 cans (14.5 ounces each) low sodium chicken broth, defatted
1 jar (16 ounces) GUILTLESS GOURMET® Roasted Red Pepper Salsa
1 teaspoon coarsely ground black pepper
¾ cup uncooked orzo, cooked according to package directions
6 sprigs fresh thyme (optional)

Preheat oven to 425°F. Coat baking sheet with nonstick cooking spray. Halve eggplants lengthwise and place cut sides down on baking sheet. Bake about 15 to 20 minutes or until skins are wrinkled and slightly charred. Allow eggplants to cool until safe enough to handle. Peel eggplants; carefully remove and discard seeds. Finely chop eggplants; set aside.

Combine onions and garlic in 2-quart microwave-safe casserole. Cover with vented plastic wrap or lid; microwave on HIGH (100% power) 5 to 6 minutes or until onions are tender. Add eggplants, broth, salsa and pepper; cover. Microwave on HIGH 6 to 8 minutes more or until soup bubbles. To serve, place ⅓ cup orzo into each of 6 individual soup bowls. Ladle 1 cup soup over orzo in each bowl. Garnish with thyme, if desired.

Makes 6 servings

Stove Top Directions: Prepare eggplants as directed. Bring ¼ cup broth to a boil in 2-quart saucepan over medium-high heat. Add onions and garlic; cook and stir until onions are tender. Add eggplants, remaining broth, salsa and pepper. Return to a boil. Serve as directed.

Nutrients per Serving: 1 cup Soup with ⅓ cup cooked Orzo (without garnish)

Calories: 206, Calories from Fat: 4%, Total Fat: 1g, Saturated Fat: <1g, Cholesterol: 0mg, Sodium: 405mg, Carbohydrate: 40g, Dietary Fiber: 5g, Protein: 9g

Dietary Exchanges: 2 Starch, 2 Vegetable

Sausage and Mushroom Pizza

New York-Style Pizza Crust (recipe follows)
1 large red bell pepper or ½ cup roasted red bell peppers, drained
3 cloves garlic, minced
1 teaspoon dried oregano leaves
2 teaspoons olive oil
4 ounces fat-free or reduced-fat sausage, cut into ⅛-inch-thick slices
5 medium mushrooms, thinly sliced
¼ cup chopped onion
½ cup (2 ounces) shredded part-skim mozzarella cheese or reduced-fat Monterey Jack cheese
Red pepper flakes

1. Prepare New York-Style Pizza Crust. Preheat broiler. Cut bell pepper in half lengthwise. Discard stem and seeds. Place bell pepper halves, cut sides down, on baking sheet. Broil 1 to 2 inches from heat source 15 minutes or until skin turns black. Transfer bell pepper halves to plate and cover with plastic wrap. Let stand until cool enough to handle. Move oven rack to lowest position in oven and preheat oven to 500°F.

2. Peel skin from bell pepper halves and discard; coarsely chop bell pepper. Combine bell pepper, garlic and oregano in food processor; process until smooth. Set aside. Brush prepared crust with oil. Bake 3 to 4 minutes or until surface is dry and crisp. Spread bell pepper mixture over crust, leaving 1-inch border. Top with sausage, mushrooms, onion and cheese. Bake about 6 minutes or until crust is golden brown. Sprinkle with red pepper flakes, and cut into 8 wedges. Garnish as desired.   *Makes 4 servings*

New York-Style Pizza Crust

⅔ cup warm water (110° to 115°F)
1 teaspoon sugar
½ (¼-ounce) package rapid-rise or active dry yeast
1¾ cups all-purpose or bread flour
½ teaspoon salt
1 tablespoon cornmeal (optional)

1. Combine water and sugar in small bowl; stir to dissolve sugar. Sprinkle yeast on top; stir to combine. Let stand 5 to 10 minutes or until foamy.

2. Combine flour and salt in medium bowl. Stir in yeast mixture. Mix until mixture forms soft dough. Remove dough to lightly floured surface. Knead 5 minutes or until dough is smooth and elastic, adding additional flour, 1 tablespoon at a time, as needed. Place dough in medium bowl coated with nonstick cooking spray. Turn dough in bowl so top is coated with cooking spray; cover with towel or plastic wrap. Let rise in warm place 30 minutes or until doubled in bulk.

3. Punch dough down; place on lightly floured surface and knead about 2 minutes or until smooth. Pat dough into flat disc about 7 inches in diameter. Let rest 2 to 3 minutes. Pat and gently stretch dough from edges until dough seems to not stretch anymore. Let rest 2 to 3 minutes. Continue patting and stretching until dough is 12 inches in diameter. Spray 12-inch pizza pan with cooking spray; sprinkle with cornmeal, if desired. Press dough into pan.
Makes 1 medium-thin 12-inch crust

Nutrients per Serving: 2 Pizza wedges (made with fat-free sausage) without garnish

Calories: 339, Calories from Fat: 20%, Total Fat: 7g, Saturated Fat: 2g, Cholesterol: 26mg, Sodium: 573mg, Carbohydrate: 52g, Dietary Fiber: 3g, Protein: 16g
Dietary Exchanges: 3 Starch, 1 Vegetable, ½ Lean Meat, 1 Fat

Lentil Stew over Couscous

1 large onion, chopped
1 medium green bell pepper, chopped
4 ribs celery, chopped
1 medium carrot, cut lengthwise in half, then cut into 1-inch pieces
2 cloves garlic, chopped
3 cups dried lentils (1 pound), rinsed
1 can (14½ ounces) diced tomatoes, undrained
1 can (14½ ounces) fat-free reduced-sodium chicken broth
3 cups water
¼ teaspoon black pepper
1 teaspoon dried marjoram leaves
1 tablespoon cider vinegar
1 tablespoon olive oil
4½ cups hot cooked couscous

Slow Cooker Directions
Combine onion, green bell pepper, celery, carrot, garlic, lentils, tomatoes, broth, water, black pepper and marjoram in slow cooker. Stir; cover and cook on LOW 8 to 9 hours. Stir in vinegar and olive oil. Serve over couscous.
Makes 12 servings

Nutrients per Serving: 1/12 of Lentil Stew with about ⅓ cup cooked couscous

Calories: 203, Calories from Fat: 9%, Total Fat: 2g, Saturated Fat: <1g, Cholesterol: 0mg, Sodium: 128mg, Carbohydrate: 37g, Dietary Fiber: 4g, Protein: 11g
Dietary Exchanges: 2 Starch, 1 Vegetable, ½ Lean Meat

Moo Shu Pork

Pad Thai

8 ounces uncooked rice noodles, ⅛ inch wide
1½ tablespoons fish sauce*
1 to 2 tablespoons fresh lemon juice
2 tablespoons rice wine vinegar
1 tablespoon ketchup
2 teaspoons sugar
¼ teaspoon red pepper flakes
1 tablespoon vegetable oil
1 boneless skinless chicken breast (about 4 ounces), finely chopped
2 green onions, thinly sliced
2 cloves garlic, minced
3 ounces raw small shrimp, peeled and deveined
2 cups fresh bean sprouts
1 medium carrot, shredded
3 tablespoons minced fresh cilantro
2 tablespoons chopped unsalted dry-roasted peanuts

Fish sauce is available at most larger supermarkets and Asian markets.

1. Place noodles in medium bowl. Cover with lukewarm water; let stand 30 minutes or until soft. Drain and set aside. Whisk fish sauce, lemon juice, rice wine vinegar, ketchup, sugar and red pepper flakes in small bowl; set aside.

2. Heat oil in wok or large nonstick skillet over medium-high heat. Add chicken, green onions and garlic. Cook and stir until chicken is no longer pink. Stir in noodles; cook 1 minute. Add shrimp and bean sprouts; cook just until shrimp turn pink and opaque, about 3 minutes. Stir in fish sauce mixture; toss to coat evenly. Cook until heated through, about 2 minutes.

3. Arrange noodle mixture on platter; sprinkle with carrot, cilantro and peanuts. Serve with shredded carrot, shredded red cabbage, fresh bean sprouts, chopped fresh cilantro and lime wedges, if desired. *Makes 5 servings*

Moo Shu Pork

1 cup DOLE® Pineapple Juice
1 tablespoon low-sodium soy sauce
2 teaspoons sesame seed oil
2 teaspoons cornstarch
8 ounces pork tenderloin, cut into thin strips
1½ cups Oriental-style mixed vegetables
¼ cup hoisin sauce (optional)
8 (8-inch) flour tortillas, warmed
2 green onions, cut into thin strips

• Stir juice, soy sauce, sesame seed oil and cornstarch in shallow, nonmetallic dish until blended; remove ½ cup mixture for sauce.

• Add pork to remaining juice mixture in shallow dish. Cover and marinate 15 minutes in refrigerator. Drain pork; discard marinade.

• Cook and stir pork in large, nonstick skillet over medium-high heat 2 minutes or until pork is lightly browned. Add vegetables; cook and stir 3 to 4 minutes or until vegetables are tender-crisp. Stir in reserved ½ cup juice mixture; cook 1 minute or until sauce thickens.

• Spread hoisin sauce onto center of each tortilla, if desired; top with moo shu pork. Sprinkle with green onions. Fold opposite sides of tortilla over filling; fold remaining sides of tortilla over filling. Garnish with slivered green onions, kumquats and fresh herbs, if desired.

Makes 4 servings

Chicken & Chile Chimichangas

2 boneless skinless chicken breasts (about 10 ounces)
½ teaspoon ground cumin
1 cup (4 ounces) shredded reduced-fat Monterey Jack cheese
1 can (4 ounces) diced mild green chilies, drained
6 (7-inch) flour tortillas
    Green Onion-Cilantro Sauce (recipe follows)
    Shredded romaine lettuce (optional)
    Fresh red and yellow tomato slices (optional)

1. Preheat oven to 400°F. Bring 4 cups water to a boil in large saucepan over high heat. Add chicken; cover and remove from heat. Let stand 15 minutes or until chicken is no longer pink in center. Drain; let cool slightly. Tear chicken into small pieces. Place in medium bowl and sprinkle with cumin. Add cheese and chilies; stir to combine.

2. Spoon about ½ cup chicken mixture down center of each tortilla. Fold bottom of tortilla up over filling, then fold sides over filling. Brush each chimichanga lightly with water, coating all around. Place chimichangas on baking sheet, about 1 inch apart. Bake 12 to 15 minutes or until tortillas are crisp and just barely golden. Serve with Green Onion-Cilantro Sauce and lettuce and tomato slices, if desired.
Makes 6 servings

Green Onion-Cilantro Sauce

¼ cup plain nonfat yogurt
¼ cup reduced-fat sour cream
⅓ cup chopped green onions
⅓ cup lightly packed fresh cilantro

Combine all ingredients in food processor or blender; process until smooth.
Makes about 1 cup sauce

Nutrients per Serving: 1 Chimichanga with about 2½ tablespoons Green Onion-Cilantro Sauce (without lettuce and tomato slices)

Calories: 248, Calories from Fat: 29%, Total Fat: 8g, Saturated Fat: 3g, Cholesterol: 43mg, Sodium: 578mg, Carbohydrate: 23g, Dietary Fiber: <1g, Protein: 20g
Dietary Exchanges: 1½ Starch, ½ Vegetable, 2 Lean Meat, ½ Fat

Moroccan Stir-Fry

4 to 6 cloves garlic, minced
2 teaspoons ground ginger
1 teaspoon ground cumin
½ teaspoon ground cinnamon
    Nonstick cooking spray
1 medium onion, chopped
12 ounces boneless skinless chicken thighs, cut into 1-inch pieces
1¼ pounds butternut squash, peeled and cut into 1-inch pieces
1 can (14½ ounces) fat-free reduced-sodium chicken broth
½ cup raisins
1 medium zucchini, cut in half lengthwise and sliced crosswise
2 tablespoons chopped fresh cilantro
1 cup water
⅔ cup uncooked quick-cooking couscous

1. Combine garlic, ginger, cumin and cinnamon in small bowl; set aside.

2. Spray large nonstick skillet with cooking spray; heat over high heat. Add onion; cook and stir until crisp-tender and golden. Add chicken; cook, without stirring, 1 minute or until golden. Turn chicken; cook 1 minute more.

3. Add spice mixture to skillet; stir 30 seconds or until fragrant. Stir in butternut squash, chicken broth and raisins; bring to a boil. Reduce heat to low; simmer, covered, 15 to 20 minutes or until butternut squash is tender when pierced.

4. Add zucchini to skillet. Simmer, uncovered, 5 to 7 minutes or until zucchini is tender. Stir in cilantro.

5. Meanwhile, place water in small saucepan over high heat; bring to a boil. Stir in couscous; cover and remove from heat. Let stand 5 minutes. Fluff couscous with fork; spoon onto serving platter. Arrange chicken mixture over couscous.
Makes 4 servings

Nutrients per Serving: ¼ of total recipe

Calories: 388, Calories from Fat: 10%, Total Fat: 5g, Saturated Fat: 1g, Cholesterol: 81mg, Sodium: 177mg, Carbohydrate: 63g, Dietary Fiber: 4g, Protein: 27g
Dietary Exchanges: 4 Starch, 2 Lean Meat

Chicken Chop Suey

1 package (1 ounce) dried black Chinese mushrooms
3 tablespoons reduced-sodium soy sauce
1 tablespoon cornstarch
1 pound boneless skinless chicken breasts or thighs
2 cloves garlic, minced
1 tablespoon peanut or vegetable oil
½ cup *each* thinly sliced celery, sliced water chestnuts and bamboo shoots
1 cup fat-free reduced-sodium chicken broth
2 cups hot cooked white rice or chow mein noodles
    Thinly sliced green onions (optional)

1. Place mushrooms in small bowl; cover with warm water. Soak 20 minutes to soften. Drain; squeeze out excess water. Discard stems; cut caps into quarters. Blend soy sauce with cornstarch in cup until smooth.

2. Cut chicken into 1-inch pieces; toss with garlic in small bowl. Heat wok or large skillet over medium-high heat; add oil. Add chicken mixture and celery; stir-fry 2 minutes. Add water chestnuts and bamboo shoots; stir-fry 1 minute. Add broth and mushrooms; cook and stir 3 minutes or until chicken is no longer pink.

3. Stir soy sauce mixture; add to wok. Cook and stir 1 to 2 minutes or until sauce boils and thickens. Serve over rice. Garnish with green onions. *Makes 4 servings*

Nutrients per Serving: ¼ Chicken mixture with ½ cup cooked rice (without garnish)

Calories: 208, Calories from Fat: 28%, Total Fat: 6g, Saturated Fat: 1g, Cholesterol: 58mg, Sodium: 657mg, Carbohydrate: 11g, Dietary Fiber: 1g, Protein: 25g
Dietary Exchanges: 2 Vegetable, 3 Lean Meat

Pizza Margherita

1 recipe Wheaty Pizza Dough (recipe follows)
1½ pounds ripe Roma tomatoes (about 10 medium)*
2 tablespoons balsamic vinegar
¼ teaspoon salt (optional)
2 cups (8 ounces) shredded reduced-fat Swiss cheese *or* 8 (1-ounce) slices
6 fresh basil leaves**

Roma tomatoes are best because they are meatier, less juicy and have fewer seeds than other varieties. If not available, substitute a 28-ounce can of drained, no-salt-added diced tomatoes, and proceed with step 2 of recipe.

**Substitute for fresh basil by mincing ¼ cup fresh Italian flat-leaf parsley with 1 teaspoon dried basil leaves; sprinkle herb mixture over cheese.*

1. While dough rises, core tomatoes, slice in half and squeeze out seeds and excess juice. Slice halves into ¼-inch slices. Place tomato slices in non-reactive bowl. Add vinegar and salt, if desired; toss to mix. Let marinate 20 minutes, tossing occasionally. Place tomatoes in colander to drain.

2. On lightly floured surface, roll dough into 15-inch circle. Ease onto 15-inch pizza pan lightly sprayed with nonstick cooking spray. Sprinkle cheese evenly over dough. Distribute basil leaves. Top with sliced tomatoes. Spray edges of dough lightly with cooking spray. Bake on bottom rack of preheated 400° to 425°F oven 17 to 20 minutes or until crust is cooked through and cheese is bubbly.
Makes 8 slices

Wheaty Pizza Dough

¾ cup warm water (110°F)
1 package (¼ ounce) active dry yeast (2¼ teaspoons)
1 tablespoon extra-virgin olive oil
1 cup unbleached all-purpose flour
1 cup whole wheat flour
    Unbleached all-purpose flour, as needed

1. Place water in 4- to 6-quart bowl. Sprinkle yeast over top. Stir to dissolve yeast. Add olive oil.

2. Spoon 1 cup flour lightly into cup measure placed on sheet of waxed paper; level with straight-edge. Add to yeast-water mixture. Stir with large spoon until dough forms loose mass. Dip hands into remaining flour, if needed, to keep dough from sticking.

3. Knead dough in bowl 3 to 5 minutes or until dough comes together, all flour is absorbed and dough is smooth and elastic. Lift dough with one hand (bowl doesn't need to be washed); spray bowl lightly with nonstick cooking spray. Return dough to bowl; turn over once so coated side is up.

4. Cover bowl with plastic wrap and let dough rise in warm place (85°F) 45 minutes to one hour or until doubled and impression made with finger remains in dough.

5. When ready to roll dough, do not knead.* Turn dough out onto lightly floured surface, scraping bits of dough from bowl, and pat into circle. Roll with rolling pin, flouring lightly as needed. *Makes 8 slices*

Dough that is not kneaded after rising is more relaxed and easier to roll out. Kneading dough after it rises makes it tight and elastic. If you forget and knead the dough, let it rest 5 to 10 minutes covered with a damp cloth. It will relax.

Nutrients per Serving: 1 Pizza slice

Calories: 199, Calories from Fat: 17%, Total Fat: 4g, Saturated Fat: 1g, Cholesterol: 10mg, Sodium: 84mg, Carbohydrate: 29g, Dietary Fiber: 3g, Protein: 13g
Dietary Exchanges: 2 Starch, 1 Lean Meat

Chicken Cordon Bleu

6 boneless skinless chicken breasts (about
    1¼ pounds)
1 tablespoon Dijon mustard
3 slices (1 ounce each) lean ham, cut into
    halves
3 slices (1 ounce each) reduced-fat Swiss
    cheese, cut into halves
   Nonstick cooking spray
¼ cup unseasoned dry bread crumbs
2 tablespoons minced fresh parsley
3 cups hot cooked white rice

1. Preheat oven to 350°F. Pound chicken breasts between 2 pieces of plastic wrap to ¼-inch thickness using flat side of meat mallet or rolling pin. Brush mustard on 1 side of each chicken breast; layer 1 slice each of ham and cheese over mustard. Roll up each chicken breast from short end; secure with wooden picks. Spray tops of chicken rolls with cooking spray; sprinkle with bread crumbs.

2. Arrange chicken rolls in 11×7-inch baking pan. Cover; bake 10 minutes. Uncover; bake about 20 minutes or until chicken is no longer pink in center.

3. Stir parsley into rice; serve with chicken. Serve with vegetables, if desired.   *Makes 6 servings*

Nutrients per Serving: 1 Chicken Roll with ½ cup cooked rice (without vegetables)

Calories: 290, Calories from Fat: 17%, Total Fat: 5g, Saturated Fat: 2g, Cholesterol: 70mg, Sodium: 442mg, Carbohydrate: 27g, Dietary Fiber: <1g, Protein: 29g

Dietary Exchanges: 1½ Starch, 3 Lean Meat

Beef and Broccoli

1 pound lean beef tenderloin
2 teaspoons minced fresh ginger
2 cloves garlic, minced
½ teaspoon vegetable oil
3 cups broccoli florets
¼ cup water
2 tablespoons teriyaki sauce
2 cups hot cooked white rice
   Red bell pepper strips, for garnish (optional)

1. Cut beef across the grain into ⅛-inch slices; cut each slice into 1½-inch pieces. Toss beef with ginger and garlic in medium bowl.

2. Heat oil in wok or large nonstick skillet over medium heat. Add beef mixture; stir-fry 3 to 4 minutes or until beef is barely pink in center. Remove and reserve.

3. Add broccoli and water to wok; cover and steam 3 to 5 minutes or until broccoli is crisp-tender.

4. Return beef and any accumulated juices to wok. Add teriyaki sauce. Cook until heated through. Serve over rice. Garnish with red bell pepper strips, if desired.

Makes 6 servings

Nutrients per Serving: ⅙ of Beef and Broccoli mixture with ⅓ cup cooked rice (without garnish)

Calories: 261, Calories from Fat: 25%, Total Fat: 7g, Saturated Fat: 3g, Cholesterol: 63mg, Sodium: 262mg, Carbohydrate: 23g, Dietary Fiber: 2g, Protein: 25g

Dietary Exchanges: 1 Starch, ½ Vegetable, 3 Lean Meat

Chicken Cordon Bleu

Chicken Chow Mein

6 ounces uncooked fresh Chinese egg noodles
Nonstick cooking spray
½ cup fat-free reduced-sodium chicken broth
2 tablespoons reduced-sodium soy sauce
1½ teaspoons cornstarch
½ teaspoon black pepper
½ teaspoon dark sesame oil
⅛ teaspoon Chinese five-spice powder
6 ounces boneless skinless chicken breasts, coarsely chopped
2 green onions, sliced
2 cups thinly sliced bok choy
1½ cups frozen mixed vegetables, thawed and drained
1 can (8 ounces) sliced water chestnuts, rinsed and drained
1 cup fresh bean sprouts

1. Preheat oven to 400°F. Cook noodles according to package directions, omitting salt. Drain and rinse well under cold water until pasta is cool; drain well.

2. Lightly spray 9-inch cake pan with cooking spray. Spread noodles in pan, pressing firmly. Lightly spray top of noodles with cooking spray. Bake 10 minutes.

3. Invert noodles onto baking sheet or large plate. Carefully slide noodle cake back into cake pan. Bake 10 to 15 minutes or until top is crisp and lightly browned. Transfer to serving platter.

4. Whisk together chicken broth, soy sauce, cornstarch, sesame oil, pepper and five-spice powder in small bowl until cornstarch is dissolved; set aside.

5. Spray large nonstick skillet with cooking spray. Add chicken and green onions. Cook, stirring frequently, until chicken is no longer pink, about 5 minutes. Stir in bok choy, mixed vegetables and water chestnuts. Cook 3 minutes or until vegetables are crisp-tender. Push vegetables to one side of skillet; stir in prepared sauce. Cook and stir until thickened, about 2 minutes. Stir in bean sprouts. Spoon over noodle cake.

Makes 4 servings

Nutrients per Serving: ¼ of total recipe

Calories: 284, Calories from Fat: 6%, Total Fat: 2g, Saturated Fat: <1g, Cholesterol: 22mg, Sodium: 322mg, Carbohydrate: 52g, Dietary Fiber: 3g, Protein: 16g

Dietary Exchanges: 2 Starch, 3 Vegetable, 1 Lean Meat

Grilled Fish with Pineapple-Cilantro Sauce

1 medium pineapple (about 2 pounds), peeled, cored and cut into scant 1-inch chunks
¾ cup unsweetened pineapple juice
2 tablespoons lime juice
2 cloves garlic, minced
½ to 1 teaspoon minced jalapeño pepper
2 tablespoons minced cilantro
2 tablespoons cold water
1 tablespoon cornstarch
1 to 1½ teaspoons EQUAL® FOR RECIPES *or* 3 to 4 packets EQUAL® sweetener *or* 2 to 3 tablespoons EQUAL® SPOONFUL™
Salt and pepper (optional)
6 halibut, haddock or salmon steaks or fillets (about 4 ounces each), grilled

• Heat pineapple, pineapple juice, lime juice, garlic and jalapeño pepper to boiling in medium saucepan. Reduce heat and simmer, uncovered, 5 minutes. Stir in cilantro; heat to boiling.

• Mix cold water and cornstarch; stir into boiling mixture. Boil, stirring constantly, until thickened. Remove from heat; cool 2 to 3 minutes.

• Stir in Equal®; season to taste with salt and pepper, if desired. Serve warm sauce over fish.   *Makes 6 servings*

Nutrients per Serving: 1 halibut fillet with ⅙ of Sauce (without added salt and pepper seasoning)

Calories: 207, Calories from Fat: 13%, Total Fat: 3g, Saturated Fat: <1g, Cholesterol: 36mg, Sodium: 63mg, Carbohydrate: 20g, Dietary Fiber: 1g, Protein: 25g

Dietary Exchanges: 1 Fruit, 3 Lean Meat

TIP Pineapple-Cilantro Sauce is also excellent served with pork or lamb.

Fusilli Pizzaiola with Turkey Meatballs

3. Place onion, carrots, garlic and oil in medium saucepan. Cook and stir over high heat 5 minutes or until onion is tender. Add tomatoes, basil, tomato paste, thyme, bay leaf and remaining ⅛ teaspoon black pepper. Bring to a boil; reduce heat to low. Simmer 25 minutes; add meatballs. Cover; simmer 5 to 10 minutes or until sauce thickens slightly. Remove and discard bay leaf.

4. Cook pasta according to package directions, omitting salt. Drain well. Place in large serving bowl. Spoon meatballs and sauce over pasta. Garnish as desired.

Makes 4 servings

Nutrients per Serving: 1 cup cooked pasta with 1¼ cups meatballs and sauce (6 meatballs) without garnish

Calories: 333, Calories from Fat: 27%, Total Fat: 10g, Saturated Fat: 2g, Cholesterol: 116mg, Sodium: 111mg, Carbohydrate: 39g, Dietary Fiber: 3g, Protein: 21g

Dietary Exchanges: 2 Starch, 2 Vegetable, 2 Lean Meat, ½ Fat

Fusilli Pizzaiola with Turkey Meatballs

    1 pound ground turkey breast
    1 egg, lightly beaten
    1 tablespoon fat-free (skim) milk
    ¼ cup Italian-seasoned dry bread crumbs
    2 tablespoons chopped fresh parsley
    ¼ teaspoon black pepper, divided
    ½ cup chopped onion
    ½ cup grated carrots
    1 clove garlic, minced
    2 teaspoons olive oil
    2 cans (14½ ounces each) no-salt-added diced
        tomatoes, undrained
    2 tablespoons chopped fresh basil *or*
        2 teaspoons dried basil leaves
    1 tablespoon no-salt-added tomato paste
    ½ teaspoon dried thyme leaves
    1 bay leaf
    8 ounces uncooked fusilli or other spiral-shaped
        pasta

1. Preheat oven to 350°F. Combine turkey, egg and milk in medium bowl. Add bread crumbs, parsley and ⅛ teaspoon black pepper; mix well. With wet hands, shape turkey mixture into 24 (1-inch) meatballs.

2. Spray baking sheet with nonstick cooking spray. Arrange meatballs on baking sheet. Bake 25 minutes or until no longer pink in center.

Beef & Bean Burritos

    Nonstick cooking spray
    ½ pound beef round steak, cut into ½-inch
        pieces
    3 cloves garlic, minced
    1 can (about 15 ounces) pinto beans, rinsed
        and drained
    1 can (4 ounces) diced mild green chilies,
        drained
    ¼ cup finely chopped fresh cilantro
    6 (6-inch) flour tortillas
    ½ cup (2 ounces) shredded reduced-fat Cheddar
        cheese
    Salsa and nonfat sour cream (optional)

1. Spray nonstick skillet with cooking spray; heat over medium heat until hot. Add steak and garlic; cook and stir 5 minutes or until steak is cooked to desired doneness. Stir beans, chilies and cilantro into skillet; cook and stir 5 minutes or until heated through.

2. Spoon steak mixture evenly down center of each tortilla; sprinkle cheese evenly over each tortilla. Fold bottom end of tortilla over filling; roll to enclose. Serve with salsa and nonfat sour cream, if desired.

Makes 6 servings

Nutrients per Serving: 1 Burrito (without salsa and sour cream)

Calories: 278, Calories from Fat: 22%, Total Fat: 7g, Saturated Fat: 2g, Cholesterol: 31mg, Sodium: 956mg, Carbohydrate: 36g, Dietary Fiber: 1g, Protein: 19g

Dietary Exchanges: 2 Starch, 1 Vegetable, 1½ Lean Meat, ½ Fat

Spicy Pork Stir-Fry

1 can (14½ ounces) fat-free reduced-sodium
   chicken broth, divided
2 tablespoons cornstarch
2 tablespoons reduced-sodium soy sauce
1 tablespoon grated orange peel
1 lean pork tenderloin (about 10 ounces), well
   trimmed
2 tablespoons peanut oil, divided
1 tablespoon sesame seeds
2 cloves garlic, minced
2 cups broccoli florets
2 cups sliced carrots
1 teaspoon Szechwan seasoning
3 cups hot cooked white rice

1. Combine 1½ cups chicken broth, cornstarch, soy sauce and orange peel in medium bowl. Cut pork lengthwise, then crosswise into ¼-inch-thick slices.

2. Heat 1 tablespoon oil in wok over high heat until hot. Add pork, sesame seeds and garlic. Stir-fry 3 minutes or until pork is barely pink in center. Remove from wok.

3. Heat remaining 1 tablespoon oil in wok until hot. Add broccoli, carrots, Szechwan seasoning and remaining chicken broth. Cook and stir 5 minutes or until vegetables are crisp-tender. Add pork. Stir chicken broth mixture and add to wok. Cook and stir over medium heat until sauce thickens. Serve over rice. *Makes 6 servings*

Nutrients per Serving: ⅙ of Stir-Fry with ½ cup cooked rice

Calories: 266, Calories from Fat: 26%, Total Fat: 8g, Saturated Fat: 1g, Cholesterol: 38mg, Sodium: 325mg, Carbohydrate: 32g, Dietary Fiber: 3g, Protein: 16g

Dietary Exchanges: 2 Starch, 2 Lean Meat

Turkey Stuffed Chiles Rellenos

1 package (1½ pounds) BUTTERBALL® 99%
   Fat Free Fresh Ground Turkey Breast
1 envelope (1¼ ounces) taco seasoning mix
⅓ cup water
6 large poblano chiles, stems on, slit lengthwise
   and seeded
1 cup (4 ounces) shredded reduced fat Cheddar
   cheese
1½ cups tomato salsa

Spray large nonstick skillet with nonstick cooking spray; heat over medium heat until hot. Brown turkey in skillet over medium-high heat 6 to 8 minutes or until no longer pink, stirring to separate meat. Add taco seasoning and water. Bring to a boil. Reduce heat to low; simmer 5 minutes, stirring occasionally. In separate pan, cook chiles in boiling water 5 minutes; remove and drain. Combine turkey mixture and Cheddar cheese. Fill chiles with mixture. Pour salsa into 11×7-inch baking dish. Place stuffed chiles slit side up in baking dish. Bake, uncovered, in preheated 400°F oven 15 minutes. Serve hot with additional salsa and sour cream, if desired.

Makes 6 servings

Preparation Time: 30 minutes

Nutrients per Serving: 1 Stuffed Chile (without additional salsa and sour cream)

Calories: 244, Calories from Fat: 19%, Total Fat: 5g, Saturated Fat: 3g, Cholesterol: 75mg, Sodium: 848mg, Carbohydrate: 15g, Dietary Fiber: 1g, Protein: 35g

Dietary Exchanges: 2 Vegetable, 4 Lean Meat

Spaghetti with Marinara Sauce

1 teaspoon olive oil
¾ cup chopped onion
3 cloves garlic, finely chopped
2 cups water
1 can (16 ounces) no-salt-added tomato sauce
1 can (6 ounces) tomato paste
2 bay leaves
1 teaspoon dried oregano leaves
1 teaspoon dried basil leaves
½ teaspoon dried marjoram leaves
½ teaspoon honey
¼ teaspoon black pepper
8 ounces uncooked spaghetti, cooked, drained
   and kept hot

1. Heat oil in large saucepan. Add onion and garlic. Cook and stir 5 minutes or until onion is tender. Add water, tomato sauce, tomato paste, bay leaves, oregano, basil, marjoram, honey and pepper. Bring to a boil, stirring occasionally. Reduce heat; simmer 1 hour, stirring occasionally.

2. Remove and discard bay leaves. Serve sauce over cooked pasta. *Makes 4 servings*

Nutrients per Serving: 1 cup cooked Spaghetti with ¼ of Marinara Sauce

Calories: 289, Calories from Fat: <1%, Total Fat: 2g, Saturated Fat: <1g, Cholesterol: 0mg, Sodium: 213mg, Carbohydrate: 58g, Dietary Fiber: 3g, Protein: 10g

Dietary Exchanges: 3 Starch, 2½ Vegetable

Sesame Chicken and Vegetable Stir-Fry

1 tablespoon dark sesame oil
1 pound chicken tenders, cut into 1-inch pieces
2 cups broccoli florets
1 small red bell pepper, sliced
½ cup onion slices (about 1 small)
½ cup snow peas
1 can (8 ounces) sliced water chestnuts, drained
2 cloves garlic, minced
1 teaspoon Chinese five-spice powder
1 cup fat-free reduced-sodium chicken broth
2 teaspoons cornstarch
2 tablespoons cold water
2 cups hot cooked rice

1. Heat sesame oil in wok or large nonstick skillet over medium heat until hot. Add chicken; stir-fry about 8 minutes or until chicken is no longer pink in center. Remove chicken from wok.

2. Add broccoli, bell pepper, onion, peas, water chestnuts and garlic to wok; stir-fry 5 to 8 minutes or until vegetables are crisp-tender. Sprinkle with five-spice powder; cook and stir 1 minute.

3. Return chicken to wok. Add chicken broth; heat to a boil. Combine cornstarch and water in small bowl; stir into broth mixture. Boil 1 to 2 minutes, stirring constantly. Serve over rice.   *Makes 4 servings*

Nutrients per Serving: 2 cups Chicken mixture with ½ cup cooked rice

Calories: 304, Calories from Fat: 19%, Total Fat: 5g, Saturated Fat: 1g, Cholesterol: 48mg, Sodium: 396mg, Carbohydrate: 38g, Dietary Fiber: 4g, Protein: 28g
Dietary Exchanges: 2 Starch, 1 Vegetable, 3 Lean Meat

Thai-Style Tuna Steaks

2 tablespoons reduced-sodium soy sauce
2 teaspoons brown sugar
1 teaspoon ground cumin
1 teaspoon sesame oil or vegetable oil
¼ teaspoon crushed red pepper
1 clove garlic, minced
4 (4- to 5-ounce) tuna steaks
4 green onions, diagonally sliced
3 cups cooked white rice

Combine soy sauce, brown sugar, cumin, sesame oil, red pepper and garlic in a 11×7-inch microwave-safe baking dish. Add tuna and turn to coat both sides. Let marinate 5 to 15 minutes.

Turn tuna over and cover with lid or waxed paper. Microwave at HIGH (100% power) 1½ minutes, rotating dish ¼ turn. Sprinkle with green onions and continue to cook 1½ minutes longer or until tuna begins to flake easily when tested with a fork. Let stand, covered, 2 minutes. Serve tuna and sauce over rice.   *Makes 4 servings*

Favorite recipe from *National Fisheries Institute*

Nutrients per Serving: ¼ of total recipe (with 1 tuna steak and ¾ cup cooked rice)

Calories: 352, Calories from Fat: 19%, Total Fat: 7g, Saturated Fat: 2g, Cholesterol: 43mg, Sodium: 303mg, Carbohydrate: 38g, Dietary Fiber: 1g, Protein: 31g
Dietary Exchanges: 2½ Starch, 3 Lean Meat

Spanish Braised Chicken with Green Olives and Rice

2 pounds bone-in skinless chicken thighs
1 teaspoon paprika
  Nonstick cooking spray
¾ cup dry sherry
1 can (14½ ounces) fat-free reduced-sodium chicken broth plus water to measure 2¼ cups
¾ cup sliced pimiento-stuffed green olives
1½ teaspoons dried sage leaves
1½ cups uncooked long-grain white rice

1. Sprinkle chicken thighs with paprika. Spray large nonstick skillet with cooking spray; heat over medium-high heat. Add thighs; cook, without stirring, 3 to 4 minutes or until golden. Turn chicken; cook 3 to 4 minutes.

2. Add sherry to skillet. Slide metal spatula under chicken and scrape cooked bits from bottom of skillet. Add chicken broth, olives and sage; bring to a boil. Reduce heat to low; cover and simmer 10 minutes.

3. Pour rice into liquid around chicken; gently stir to distribute evenly in skillet. Return to a boil; cover and simmer 18 minutes or until liquid is absorbed and rice is tender.   *Makes 6 servings*

Nutrients per Serving: ⅙ of total recipe

Calories: 376, Calories from Fat: 25%, Total Fat: 10g, Saturated Fat: 2g, Cholesterol: 62mg, Sodium: 522mg, Carbohydrate: 40g, Dietary Fiber: 1g, Protein: 21g
Dietary Exchanges: 2½ Starch, 2 Lean Meat, 1 Fat

Beef Bourguignon

1 boneless beef sirloin steak, ½ inch thick, trimmed and cut into ½-inch pieces (about 3 pounds)
½ cup all-purpose flour
4 slices bacon, diced
2 medium carrots, diced
8 small new red potatoes, unpeeled, cut into quarters
8 to 10 mushrooms, sliced
20 to 24 pearl onions
3 cloves garlic, minced
1 bay leaf
1 teaspoon dried marjoram leaves
½ teaspoon dried thyme leaves
½ teaspoon salt
Black pepper
2½ cups Burgundy wine or beef broth

Slow Cooker Directions

1. Coat beef with flour, shaking off excess. Set aside.

2. Cook bacon in large nonstick skillet over medium heat until partially cooked. Add beef; cook until browned. Remove beef and bacon with slotted spoon.

3. Layer carrots, potatoes, mushrooms, onions, garlic, bay leaf, marjoram, thyme, salt, pepper to taste, beef and bacon mixture, and wine in slow cooker. Cover and cook on LOW 8 to 9 hours or until beef is tender. Remove and discard bay leaf before serving. *Makes 10 servings*

Nutrients per Serving: 1 bowl Bourguignon (¹⁄₁₀ of total recipe)

Calories: 268, Calories from Fat: 23%, Total Fat: 7g, Saturated Fat: 3g, Cholesterol: 73mg, Sodium: 287mg, Carbohydrate: 14g, Dietary Fiber: 1g, Protein: 26g

Dietary Exchanges: 1 Starch, 3 Lean Meat, ½ Fat

Beef Bourguignon

Fiesta Beef Enchiladas

8 ounces 95% lean ground beef
½ cup sliced green onions
2 teaspoons fresh minced or bottled garlic
1 cup cold cooked white or brown rice
1½ cups chopped tomato, divided
¾ cup frozen corn, thawed
1 cup (4 ounces) shredded reduced-fat Mexican cheese blend or Cheddar cheese, divided
½ cup salsa or picante sauce
12 (6- to 7-inch) corn tortillas
1 can (10 ounces) mild or hot enchilada sauce
1 cup shredded romaine lettuce

1. Preheat oven to 375°F. Spray 13×9-inch baking dish with nonstick cooking spray; set aside.

2. Cook ground beef in medium nonstick skillet over medium heat until no longer pink; drain. Add green onions and garlic; cook and stir 2 minutes.

3. Add rice, 1 cup tomato, corn, ½ cup cheese and salsa to meat mixture; mix well. Spoon mixture evenly down centers of tortillas. Roll up; place seam-side down in prepared dish. Spoon enchilada sauce evenly over top.

4. Cover with foil; bake 20 minutes or until hot. Sprinkle evenly with remaining ½ cup cheese; bake 5 minutes or until cheese melts. Top evenly with lettuce and remaining ½ cup tomato. *Makes 12 servings*

Prep Time: 15 minutes
Cook Time: 35 minutes

Nutrients per Serving: 1 Enchilada (¹⁄₁₂ of total recipe)

Calories: 171, Calories from Fat: 30%, Total Fat: 6g, Saturated Fat: 2g, Cholesterol: 19mg, Sodium: 232mg, Carbohydrate: 22g, Dietary Fiber: 2g, Protein: 9g

Dietary Exchanges: 1 Starch, 1 Vegetable, 1 Lean Meat, ½ Fat

Korean-Style Beef and Pasta

¾ pound lean beef round steak
2 tablespoons reduced-sodium soy sauce
1 tablespoon rice wine
2 teaspoons sugar
Korean-Style Dressing (recipe follows)
1 package (6¾ ounces) rice noodles
2 cups thinly sliced napa cabbage
1¾ cups thinly sliced yellow bell peppers
½ cup thinly sliced radishes
1 medium carrot, shredded
2 green onions, thinly sliced

1. Freeze beef until partially firm; cut into very thin slices.

2. Combine soy sauce, rice wine and sugar in small nonmetallic bowl. Add beef slices; toss to coat evenly. Cover and refrigerate 8 hours or overnight.

3. Drain and grill beef over medium-hot coals 2 to 3 minutes or until desired doneness.

4. Meanwhile, prepare Korean-Style Dressing; set aside.

5. Cook noodles in boiling water 1 to 2 minutes or until tender; drain and rinse under cold water. Arrange noodles on serving platter.

6. Combine cabbage, bell peppers, radishes, carrot, green onions and beef in medium bowl. Add Korean-Style Dressing; toss to coat evenly. Serve over noodles. Garnish with green onion brush and carrot ribbons, if desired.

Makes 8 servings

Korean-Style Dressing

2 teaspoons sesame seeds
⅓ cup orange juice
2 tablespoons rice wine
2 teaspoons reduced-sodium soy sauce
1 teaspoon sugar
1 teaspoon grated fresh ginger
1 teaspoon dark sesame oil
1 clove garlic, minced
⅛ teaspoon red pepper flakes

1. Place sesame seeds in small nonstick skillet. Cook and stir over medium heat until lightly browned and toasted, about 5 minutes. Cool completely.

2. Crush sesame seeds using mortar and pestle or wooden spoon; transfer to small bowl.

3. Add remaining ingredients. Blend well.

Nutrients per Serving: 1 cup (without garnish)

Calories: 194, Calories from Fat: 19%, Total Fat: 4g, Saturated Fat: 1g, Cholesterol: 29mg, Sodium: 668mg, Carbohydrate: 24g, Dietary Fiber: 1g, Protein: 13g

Dietary Exchanges: 1½ Starch, ½ Vegetable, 1 Lean Meat

Scampi Italienne

½ pound uncooked shrimp, peeled and deveined
¼ cup *plus* 1 tablespoon CRISCO® Oil,* divided
3 tablespoons dry white wine
½ teaspoon grated lemon peel
1 tablespoon lemon juice
½ teaspoon dried basil leaves
½ teaspoon dried oregano leaves
1 clove garlic, minced
¼ teaspoon salt
⅛ teaspoon pepper
2 drops hot pepper sauce
¾ cup uncooked rice
1½ cups water
2 tomatoes, cut into ½-inch pieces
¼ cup chopped fresh parsley
2 green onions with tops, sliced

*Use your favorite Crisco Oil product.

1. Place shrimp in medium glass or stainless steel bowl.

2. Combine ¼ cup oil, wine, lemon peel, lemon juice, basil, oregano, garlic, salt, pepper and hot pepper sauce in container with tight-fitting lid. Shake well. Remove 1 tablespoon oil mixture. Reserve. Pour remaining oil mixture over shrimp. Turn to coat. Refrigerate 30 minutes, turning after 15 minutes.

3. Heat reserved 1 tablespoon marinade in medium saucepan on medium-high heat. Add rice. Stir 1 minute. Pour water over rice. Stir. Bring to a boil. Reduce heat to low. Cover. Simmer 15 to 20 minutes or until tender. Remove from heat. Fluff with fork. Stir in tomatoes. Cover.

4. Heat remaining 1 tablespoon oil in large skillet on high heat. Drain shrimp. Add to skillet. Stir-fry 1 minute or until shrimp turn pink.

5. Spoon rice mixture onto serving platter. Pour shrimp mixture over rice. Sprinkle with parsley and green onions. Season with additional salt and pepper, if desired.

Makes 4 servings

Nutrients per Serving: ¼ of total recipe (without additional salt and pepper seasoning)

Calories: 250, Calories from Fat: 23%, Total Fat: 6g, Saturated Fat: 1g, Cholesterol: 85mg, Sodium: 135mg, Carbohydrate: 32g, Dietary Fiber: 2g, Protein: 15g

Dietary Exchanges: 2 Starch, ½ Vegetable, 1 Lean Meat, ½ Fat

Soft Turkey Tacos

8 (6-inch) corn tortillas
1½ teaspoons vegetable oil
1 pound ground turkey breast
1 small onion, chopped
1 teaspoon dried oregano leaves
¼ teaspoon salt
⅛ teaspoon black pepper
1 cup chopped fresh tomatoes
.1 cup shredded lettuce
½ cup salsa
  Refried beans (optional)

1. Wrap tortillas in foil. Place in cold oven; set temperature to 350°F.*

2. Heat oil in large skillet over medium heat. Add turkey and onion; cook until turkey is no longer pink, stirring occasionally. Stir in oregano, salt and pepper. Keep warm.

3. For each taco, fill warm tortilla with turkey mixture. Divide tomatoes, lettuce and salsa evenly among tacos. Serve with refried beans, if desired.   *Makes 8 servings*

To warm tortillas in microwave oven, wrap loosely in damp paper towel. Microwave at HIGH 2 minutes or until hot.

Nutrients per Serving: 1 Taco (without refried beans)

Calories: 287, Calories from Fat: 16%, Total Fat: 5g, Saturated Fat: 1g, Cholesterol: 68mg, Sodium: 358mg, Carbohydrate: 30g, Dietary Fiber: 4g, Protein: 31g
Dietary Exchanges: 2 Starch, 3 Lean Meat

Island Chicken with Pineapple

4 boneless, skinless chicken breast halves
¼ teaspoon garlic salt
1 tablespoon vegetable oil
1 can (8 ounces) pineapple slices in natural juice, drained, juice reserved
2 tablespoons honey
2 tablespoons reduced-sodium soy sauce
  Grated peel and juice of 1 lime
¼ teaspoon ground ginger
¼ teaspoon crushed red pepper flakes
1 tablespoon water
1 teaspoon cornstarch
1 tablespoon sliced green onion

Sprinkle chicken with garlic salt. In skillet, place oil and heat to medium-high temperature. Add chicken and cook, turning, about 10 minutes or until chicken is brown. In small bowl, mix together reserved pineapple juice, honey, soy sauce, lime juice, ginger and red pepper flakes. Place one pineapple slice over each chicken breast half; pour pineapple mixture over chicken. Reduce heat and cook, basting occasionally, about 10 minutes or until chicken is fork-tender. Transfer chicken to serving platter. In a small dish, mix water and cornstarch; stir into sauce remaining in skillet. Cook, stirring, about 1 minute or until sauce thickens slightly. Spoon sauce over chicken; sprinkle with grated lime peel and green onion.   *Makes 4 servings*

Favorite recipe from *Delmarva Poultry Industry, Inc.*

Nutrients per Serving: 1 (4-ounce) uncooked Chicken breast half, cooked, with ¼ of sauce

Calories: 236, Calories from Fat: 18%, Total Fat: 5g, Saturated Fat: 1g, Cholesterol: 66mg, Sodium: 373mg, Carbohydrate: 21g, Dietary Fiber: 1g, Protein: 27g
Dietary Exchanges: 1½ Fruit, 3 Lean Meat

Rosarita Refried Soup

  PAM® No-Stick Cooking Spray
1 cup diced onion
1 can (16 ounces) ROSARITA® Traditional No-Fat Refried Beans
6 cups fat free, low sodium chicken broth
1 can (14.5-ounce) HUNT'S® Diced Tomatoes in Juice
4 cups baked tortilla chips
½ cup shredded reduced fat Monterey Jack cheese
¼ cup chopped fresh cilantro

1. Spray a large saucepan with PAM® Cooking Spray. Sauté onion over low heat for 5 minutes.

2. Add Rosarita® Beans, broth and Hunt's® Tomatoes; mix well. Cook until heated through.

3. Place ½ cup tortilla chips in *each* bowl. Ladle soup into bowls. Garnish with cheese and cilantro.
          Makes 12 (1-cup) servings

Nutrients per Serving: 1 cup Soup with ⅓ cup tortilla chips, 2 teaspoons cheese and 1 teaspoon fresh cilantro

Calories: 110, Calories from Fat: 20%, Total Fat: 2g, Saturated Fat: 1g, Cholesterol: 16mg, Sodium: 471mg, Carbohydrate: 14g, Dietary Fiber: 3g, Protein: 8g
Dietary Exchanges: 1 Starch, ½ Fat

Ginger Noodles with Sesame Egg Strips

5 egg whites
6 teaspoons teriyaki sauce, divided
3 teaspoons toasted sesame seeds,* divided
1 teaspoon dark sesame oil
½ cup fat-free reduced-sodium chicken broth
1 tablespoon minced fresh ginger
6 ounces uncooked Chinese rice noodles or vermicelli, cooked and well drained
⅓ cup sliced green onions

*To toast sesame seeds, spread seeds in small skillet. Shake skillet over medium heat 2 minutes or until seeds begin to pop and turn golden.

1. Beat together egg whites, 2 teaspoons teriyaki sauce and 1 teaspoon sesame seeds.

2. Heat large nonstick skillet over medium heat. Add oil; heat until hot. Pour egg mixture into skillet; cook 1½ to 2 minutes or until bottom of omelet is set. Turn omelet over; cook 30 seconds to 1 minute. Slide out onto plate; cool and cut into ½-inch strips.

3. Add broth, ginger and remaining 4 teaspoons teriyaki sauce to skillet. Bring to a boil over high heat; reduce heat to medium. Add noodles; heat through. Add omelet strips and onions; heat through. Sprinkle with remaining 2 teaspoons sesame seeds. *Makes 4 side-dish servings*

Nutrients per Serving: ¼ of total recipe

Calories: 111, Calories from Fat: 19%, Total Fat: 2g, Saturated Fat: 1g, Cholesterol: 0mg, Sodium: 226mg, Carbohydrate: 16g, Dietary Fiber: <1g, Protein: 7g

Dietary Exchanges: 1 Starch, ½ Lean Meat, ½ Fat

Hawaiian Stir-Fry

1 can (8 ounces) pineapple chunks in juice, undrained
2 teaspoons cornstarch
1 tablespoon vegetable oil
1 medium red bell pepper, cut into strips
1 teaspoon curry powder
8 ounces (about 3 cups) snow peas, ends trimmed
⅓ cup diagonally sliced green onions
2 teaspoons reduced-sodium soy sauce

1. Drain pineapple; reserve juice. Combine juice and cornstarch in small bowl; stir to blend. Set aside.

2. Heat large nonstick skillet or wok 1 minute over medium-high heat. Add oil, bell pepper and curry powder; stir-fry 1 minute. Add pineapple chunks; stir-fry 1 minute. Add pea pods; stir-fry 1 minute. Add reserved pineapple juice mixture; bring sauce to a boil. Boil 1 minute or until sauce is thickened.

3. Stir in green onions and soy sauce. Serve with grilled chicken breasts or broiled fish, if desired.

Makes 6 servings

Nutrients per Serving: ⅙ of Stir-Fry (without chicken or fish)

Calories: 77, Calories from Fat: 28%, Total Fat: 3g, Saturated Fat: <1g, Cholesterol: <1mg, Sodium: 61mg, Carbohydrate: 13g, Dietary Fiber: 1g, Protein: 2g

Dietary Exchanges: ½ Fruit, 1 Vegetable, ½ Fat

Ginger Noodles with Sesame Egg Strips

SIDE DISHES

Mediterranean-Style Roasted Vegetables

1½ pounds red potatoes
1 tablespoon plus 1½ teaspoons olive oil, divided
1 medium red bell pepper
1 medium yellow or orange bell pepper
1 small red onion
2 cloves garlic, minced
½ teaspoon salt
¼ teaspoon black pepper
1 tablespoon balsamic vinegar
¼ cup chopped fresh basil leaves

1. Preheat oven to 425°F. Spray large shallow metal roasting pan with nonstick cooking spray. Cut potatoes into 1½-inch chunks; place in pan. Drizzle 1 tablespoon oil over potatoes; toss to coat. Bake 10 minutes.

2. Cut bell peppers into 1½-inch pieces. Cut onion through core into ½-inch wedges. Add bell peppers and onion to pan. Drizzle remaining 1½ teaspoons oil over vegetables; sprinkle with garlic, salt and black pepper. Toss well to coat. Return to oven; bake 18 to 20 minutes or until vegetables are brown and tender, stirring once.

3. Transfer to large serving bowl. Drizzle vinegar over vegetables; toss to coat. Add basil; toss again. Serve warm or at room temperature with additional black pepper, if desired.

Makes 6 servings

Nutrients per Serving: ⅙ of total recipe (without additional black pepper)

Calories: 170, Calories from Fat: 19%, Total Fat: 4g, Saturated Fat: <1g, Cholesterol: 0mg, Sodium: 185mg, Carbohydrate: 33g, Dietary Fiber: 1g, Protein: 3g

Dietary Exchanges: 2 Starch, ½ Fat

Savory Green Bean Casserole

2 teaspoons CRISCO® Oil*
1 medium onion, chopped
½ medium green bell pepper, chopped
1 package (10 ounces) frozen green beans, thawed
1 can (8 ounces) tomatoes, drained
2 tablespoons nonfat mayonnaise dressing
¼ teaspoon salt
⅛ teaspoon crushed red pepper
⅛ teaspoon garlic powder
¼ cup plain dry bread crumbs

*Use your favorite Crisco Oil product.

1. Heat oven to 375°F. Oil 1-quart casserole lightly. Place cooling rack on countertop.

2. Heat 2 teaspoons oil in large skillet on medium heat. Add onion and green pepper. Cook and stir until tender.

3. Add beans, tomatoes, mayonnaise dressing, salt, red pepper and garlic powder. Heat thoroughly, stirring occasionally.

4. Spoon into casserole. Sprinkle with bread crumbs. Bake at 375°F for 30 minutes. *Do not overbake.* Remove casserole to cooling rack. Serve warm.

Makes 8 servings

Nutrients per Serving: ⅛ of total recipe

Calories: 51, Calories from Fat: 26%, Total Fat: 1g, Saturated Fat: <1g, Cholesterol: 0mg, Sodium: 179mg, Carbohydrate: 8g, Dietary Fiber: 2g, Protein: 1g

Dietary Exchanges: 2 Vegetable

Grilled Vegetables

Variation: Cut vegetables into 1-inch cubes and thread onto skewers. Spray with cooking spray and sprinkle with herb mixture. Grill as directed above.

Nutrients per Serving: ⅙ of total recipe

Calories: 34, Calories from Fat: 6%, Total Fat: <1g, Saturated Fat: <1g, Cholesterol: 0mg, Sodium: 190mg, Carbohydrate: 8g, Dietary Fiber: 2g, Protein: 1g

Dietary Exchanges: 1½ Vegetable

Grilled Vegetables

¼ cup minced fresh herbs, such as parsley, thyme, rosemary, oregano or basil
1 small eggplant (about ¾ pound), cut into ¼-inch-thick slices
½ teaspoon salt
1 *each* medium red, green and yellow bell pepper, quartered and seeded
2 medium zucchini, cut lengthwise into ¼-inch-thick slices
1 fennel bulb, cut lengthwise into ¼-inch-thick slices
    Nonstick cooking spray

1. Combine herbs in small bowl; let stand 3 hours or overnight.

2. Place eggplant in large colander over bowl; sprinkle with salt. Drain 1 hour.

3. Heat grill until coals are glowing red. Spray vegetables with cooking spray and sprinkle with herb mixture. Grill 10 to 15 minutes or until fork-tender and lightly browned on both sides. (Cooking times vary depending on vegetable type; remove vegetables as they are done, to avoid overcooking.)
Makes 6 servings

Double-Baked Potatoes

3 large baking potatoes
4 tablespoons fat-free (skim) milk, warmed
1 cup (4 ounces) shredded reduced-fat Cheddar cheese
¾ cup corn
½ teaspoon chili powder
1 tablespoon finely chopped fresh oregano *or* 1 teaspoon dried oregano leaves
    Nonstick cooking spray
1 cup chopped onion
½ to 1 cup chopped poblano chili peppers
3 cloves garlic, minced
½ teaspoon salt
¼ teaspoon black pepper
3 tablespoons chopped fresh cilantro

1. Preheat oven to 400°F. Scrub potatoes under running water with soft vegetable brush; rinse. Pierce each potato with fork. Wrap each potato in foil. Bake about 1 hour or until fork-tender. Remove potatoes; cool slightly. *Reduce oven temperature to 350°F.*

2. Cut potatoes in half lengthwise; scoop out insides, being careful not to tear shells. Set shells aside. Beat potatoes in large bowl with electric mixer until coarsely mashed. Add milk; beat until smooth. Stir in cheese, corn, chili powder and oregano. Set aside.

3. Spray medium nonstick skillet with cooking spray. Add onion, poblano peppers and garlic; cook and stir 5 to 8 minutes or until tender. Stir in salt and black pepper.

4. Spoon potato mixture into reserved potato shells. Sprinkle evenly with onion mixture. Place stuffed potatoes in small baking pan. Bake 20 to 30 minutes or until heated through. Sprinkle with cilantro.
Makes 6 servings

Nutrients per Serving: 1 stuffed Baked Potato half

Calories: 176, Calories from Fat: 15%, Total Fat: 3g, Saturated Fat: 1g, Cholesterol: 10mg, Sodium: 451mg, Carbohydrate: 31g, Dietary Fiber: 1g, Protein: 7g

Dietary Exchanges: 1½ Starch, 1 Vegetable, ½ Lean Meat, ½ Fat

Vegetables with Spinach Fettuccine

6 solid-pack sun-dried tomatoes
3 ounces uncooked spinach florentine
    fettuccine or spinach fettuccine
1 tablespoon olive oil
¼ cup chopped onion
¼ cup sliced red bell pepper
1 clove garlic, minced
½ cup sliced mushrooms
½ cup coarsely chopped fresh spinach
¼ teaspoon salt
¼ teaspoon ground nutmeg
⅛ teaspoon black pepper

1. Place sun-dried tomatoes in small bowl; pour boiling water over tomatoes to cover. Let stand 10 to 15 minutes or until tomatoes are tender. Drain tomatoes; discard liquid. Cut tomatoes into strips.

2. Cook pasta according to package directions, omitting salt. Drain.

3. Heat oil in large nonstick skillet over medium heat. Add onion, bell pepper and garlic; cook and stir 3 minutes or until vegetables are crisp-tender. Add mushrooms and spinach; cook and stir 1 minute. Add sun-dried tomatoes, pasta, salt, nutmeg and black pepper; cook and stir 1 to 2 minutes or until heated through. Garnish as desired.

Makes 6 servings

Nutrients per Serving: ⅙ of total recipe (without garnish)

Calories: 82, Calories from Fat: 30%, Total Fat: 3g, Saturated Fat: <1g, Cholesterol: 3mg, Sodium: 101mg, Carbohydrate: 13g, Dietary Fiber: 1g, Protein: 3g

Dietary Exchanges: ½ Starch, 1 Vegetable, ½ Fat

Fresh Fruit Cocktail

3 cups unsweetened apple juice
1 cinnamon stick
1 under-ripe pear
1 Washington Rome Beauty apple
½ fresh pineapple
2 fresh apricots or peaches
1 cup seedless green grapes

1. In large pot, combine apple juice and cinnamon stick; bring to a boil. Meanwhile, core and coarsely chop pear and apple. Slice off skin of pineapple and remove "eyes" with end of vegetable peeler. Cut out and discard core of pineapple; cut remaining pineapple into bite-size chunks.

2. When juice comes to a boil, add chopped pear, apple and pineapple; simmer juice and fruit 4 minutes. Halve, pit and quarter apricots; add to simmering mixture along with grapes. Cook 2 minutes.

3. With slotted spoon, transfer all fruit from pot to large bowl. Bring juice, with cinnamon stick, to a boil; boil until reduced to 1 cup. Pour juice over fruit, stirring gently to blend. Let fruit cocktail cool to room temperature, then cover and refrigerate.

Makes 4 cups

Prep Time: 10 minutes
Cook Time: 20 minutes

Favorite recipe from *Washington Apple Commission*

Nutrients per Serving: ½ cup

Calories: 99, Calories from Fat: 5%, Total Fat: 1g, Saturated Fat: <1g, Cholesterol: 0mg, Sodium: 4mg, Carbohydrate: 25g, Dietary Fiber: 2g, Protein: 1g

Dietary Exchanges: 1½ Fruit

Bulgur-Lentil Pilaf

1 tablespoon canola oil
1 cup lentils, preferably red
1 cup uncooked coarse or medium-grain bulgur
1 small onion, finely chopped
2 cups reduced-sodium broth
¼ cup finely chopped parsley
    Chopped green onions (optional)
    Hollowed-out cherry tomatoes, endive leaves,
      mushroom caps or cucumber rounds

Heat canola oil in large saucepan over medium heat. Add lentils and bulgur and toss until well toasted, about 2 to 3 minutes. Add onion and cook until softened, about 4 to 5 minutes. Add broth. Reduce heat to medium-low. Cover and cook 15 minutes.

Remove from heat but leave covered until all liquid is absorbed. Fluff with fork. Stir in parsley and green onions. Season with salt and pepper, if desired. Refrigerate to cool. Scoop pilaf into vegetables.

Makes 4 cups

Favorite recipe from *Canada's Canola Industry*

Nutrients per Serving: 1 cup Pilaf (made with fat-free reduced-sodium chicken broth) without hollowed-out vegetables, green onions and salt and pepper seasoning

Calories: 348, Calories from Fat: 13%, Total Fat: 5g, Saturated Fat: <1, Cholesterol: 13mg, Sodium: 139mg, Carbohydrate: 57g, Dietary Fiber: 22g, Protein: 22g

Dietary Exchanges: 4 Starch, 1 Lean Meat

Creamed Spinach

3 cups water
2 bags (10 ounces each) fresh spinach, washed,
    stems removed and leaves chopped
2 teaspoons margarine
2 tablespoons all-purpose flour
1 cup fat-free (skim) milk
2 tablespoons grated Parmesan cheese
⅛ teaspoon white pepper
    Ground nutmeg

1. Bring water to a boil; add spinach. Reduce heat and simmer, covered, about 5 minutes or until spinach is wilted. Drain well. Set aside.

2. Melt margarine in small saucepan; stir in flour and cook over medium-low heat 1 minute, stirring constantly. Using wire whisk, stir in milk; bring to a boil. Cook, whisking constantly, 1 to 2 minutes or until mixture thickens. Stir in cheese and pepper.

3. Stir spinach into sauce; heat thoroughly. Spoon into serving bowl; sprinkle lightly with nutmeg. Garnish as desired.

Makes 4 servings

Nutrients per Serving: ¼ of total recipe (without garnish)

Calories: 91, Calories from Fat: 30%, Total Fat: 3g, Saturated Fat: 1g, Cholesterol: 3mg, Sodium: 188mg, Carbohydrate: 10g, Dietary Fiber: 0g, Protein: 7g

Dietary Exchanges: ½ Starch, 1 Vegetable, ½ Fat

Broccoli with Red Pepper and Shallots

2 bunches fresh broccoli (about 2¼ pounds),
    cut into florets, stalks cut into 1-inch pieces
2 teaspoons margarine or butter
1 large red bell pepper, cut into short thin strips
3 large shallots (3 ounces) *or* 1 small onion,
    thinly sliced
½ teaspoon salt
¼ teaspoon black pepper
¼ cup sliced almonds, toasted (optional)

1. Bring 2 quarts water to a boil in large saucepan over high heat Add broccoli; boil, uncovered, 3 to 5 minutes or until bright green and tender. Drain and rinse under cold water; drain well.

2. Melt margarine in 12-inch nonstick skillet over medium heat. Add bell pepper and shallots. Cook 3 minutes, stirring occasionally. Add broccoli. Cook 4 to 6 minutes, stirring occasionally. Sprinkle with salt and black pepper; mix well. Garnish with almonds, if desired.

Makes 6 servings

Nutrients per Serving: ⅙ of total recipe (without almonds)

Calories: 65, Calories from Fat: 21%, Total Fat: 2g, Saturated Fat: <1g, Cholesterol: 0mg, Sodium: 248mg, Carbohydrate: 11g, Dietary Fiber: 4g, Protein: 5g

Dietary Exchanges: 2 Vegetable

Creamed Spinach

Garden-Style Risotto

   1 can (14½ ounces) low-sodium chicken broth
1¾ cups water
   2 garlic cloves, finely chopped
   1 teaspoon dried basil leaves, crushed
  ½ teaspoon dried thyme leaves, crushed
   1 cup arborio rice
   2 cups packed DOLE® Fresh Spinach, torn
   1 cup DOLE® Shredded Carrots
   3 tablespoons grated Parmesan cheese

• Combine broth, water, garlic, basil and thyme in large saucepan. Bring to boil; meanwhile, prepare rice.

• Place rice in large, nonstick saucepan sprayed with vegetable cooking spray. Cook and stir rice over medium heat about 2 minutes or until rice is browned.

• Pour 1 cup boiling broth into saucepan with rice; cook, stirring constantly, until broth is almost absorbed (there should be some broth left).

• Add enough broth to barely cover rice; continue to cook, stirring constantly, until broth is almost absorbed. Repeat adding broth and cooking, stirring constantly, until broth is almost absorbed, about 15 minutes; add spinach and carrots with the last addition of broth.

• Cook 3 to 5 minutes more, stirring constantly, or until broth is almost absorbed and rice and vegetables are tender. Do not overcook. (Risotto will be saucy and have a creamy texture.) Stir in Parmesan cheese. Serve warm.

Makes 6 servings

Garden Pilaf: Substitute 1 cup uncooked long grain white rice for arborio rice and reduce water from 1³/₄ cups to ½ cup. Prepare broth as directed above with ½ cup water; meanwhile, brown rice as directed above. Carefully add browned rice to boiling broth. Reduce heat to low; cover and cook 15 minutes. Stir in vegetables; cover and cook 4 to 5 minutes longer or until rice and vegetables are tender. Stir in Parmesan cheese.

Prep Time: 5 minutes
Cook Time: 25 minutes

Nutrients per Serving: ⅙ of Garden-Style Risotto

Calories: 170, Calories from Fat: 10%, Total Fat: 2g,
Saturated Fat: <1g, Cholesterol: 4mg, Sodium: 155mg,
Carbohydrate: 29g, Dietary Fiber: 2g, Protein: 5g
Dietary Exchanges: 1 Starch, 3 Vegetable

Lemon Brussels Sprouts

   1 package (10 ounces) frozen Brussels sprouts
   1 tablespoon water
  ½ teaspoon lemon juice
  ¼ teaspoon grated lemon peel
    Dash black pepper
    Dash ground thyme

Microwave Directions
Combine Brussels sprouts, water, lemon juice and lemon peel in 1-quart microwavable casserole; cover. Microwave at HIGH 3 minutes. Stir to break apart; cover. Microwave at HIGH 2 to 3 minutes or until Brussels sprouts are tender. Drain; sprinkle with pepper and thyme.

Makes 4 servings

Nutrients per Serving: ¼ of total recipe

Calories: 30, Calories from Fat: 7%, Total Fat: <1g,
Saturated Fat: <1g, Cholesterol: 0mg, Sodium: 16mg,
Carbohydrate: 6g, Dietary Fiber: 2g, Protein: 3g
Dietary Exchanges: 1 Vegetable

Scalloped Potatoes

   4 small potatoes, thinly sliced
  ¼ cup chopped onion
   2 teaspoons margarine
  ½ cup low-fat buttermilk
   1 tablespoon all-purpose flour
  ¼ teaspoon dried oregano leaves

1. Preheat oven to 350°F. Combine potato slices and onion in 2-quart microwavable ovenproof baking dish; dot with margarine. Cover with plastic wrap; microwave at HIGH 5 minutes.

2. Combine buttermilk, flour and oregano in small bowl; mix well. Pour over potatoes. Bake, uncovered, 35 minutes or until top is lightly browned and potatoes are tender.

Makes 4 servings

Nutrients per Serving: ¼ of total recipe

Calories: 153, Calories from Fat: 13%, Total Fat: 2g,
Saturated Fat: 1g, Cholesterol: 1mg, Sodium: 62mg,
Carbohydrate: 30g, Dietary Fiber: <1g, Protein: 4g
Dietary Exchanges: 2 Starch

Vegetables in Garlic Cream Sauce

1 cup water
4 cups cut-up vegetables such as DOLE®
  Asparagus, Bell Peppers, Broccoli, Carrots,
  Cauliflower or Sugar Peas
1 teaspoon olive or vegetable oil
4 cloves garlic, finely chopped
⅓ cup fat free or reduced fat mayonnaise
⅓ cup nonfat or low fat milk
2 tablespoons chopped fresh parsley

• Place water in large saucepan; bring to a boil. Add vegetables; reduce heat to low. Cook, uncovered, 9 to 12 minutes or until vegetables are tender-crisp; meanwhile, prepare sauce.

• Heat oil in small saucepan over medium heat. Add garlic; cook and stir garlic until golden brown. Remove from heat; stir in mayonnaise and milk.

• Drain vegetables; place in serving bowl. Pour in garlic sauce; toss to evenly coat. Sprinkle with parsley.

Makes 4 servings

Prep Time: 10 minutes
Cook Time: 15 minutes

Nutrients per Serving: ¼ of total recipe

Calories: 72, Calories from Fat: 17%, Total Fat: 1g, Saturated Fat: <1g, Cholesterol: <1mg, Sodium: 190mg, Carbohydrate: 13g, Dietary Fiber: 3g, Protein: 3g

Dietary Exchanges: 2 Vegetable

Roasted Red Pepper & Tomato Casserole

1 jar (12 ounces) roasted red peppers, drained
1½ teaspoons red wine vinegar
1 teaspoon olive oil
1 clove garlic, minced
¼ teaspoon salt
¼ teaspoon black pepper
⅓ cup grated Parmesan cheese, divided
3 medium tomatoes (about 1½ pounds), sliced
½ cup (about 1 ounce) herb-flavored croutons, crushed

1. Combine red peppers, vinegar, oil, garlic, salt and black pepper in food processor; process, using on/off pulsing action, 1 minute or until slightly chunky. Reserve 2 tablespoons cheese for garnish. Stir remaining cheese into red pepper mixture.

2. Arrange tomato slices in 8-inch round microwavable baking dish; microwave at HIGH 1 minute. Spoon red pepper mixture on top; microwave at HIGH 2 to 3 minutes or until tomatoes are slightly soft. Sprinkle with reserved cheese and croutons. Garnish. *Makes 6 servings*

Nutrients per Serving: ⅙ of total recipe (without garnish)

Calories: 80, Calories from Fat: 30%, Total Fat: 2g, Saturated Fat: 1g, Cholesterol: 3mg, Sodium: 342mg, Carbohydrate: 9g, Dietary Fiber: 1g, Protein: 3g

Dietary Exchanges: 2 Vegetable, ½ Fat

Polenta Triangles

½ cup yellow corn grits
1½ cups fat-free reduced-sodium chicken broth, divided
2 cloves garlic, minced
½ cup (2 ounces) crumbled feta cheese
1 medium red bell pepper, roasted,* peeled and finely chopped

Place pepper on foil-lined broiler pan; broil 15 minutes or until blackened on all sides, turning every 5 minutes. Place pepper in paper bag; close bag and let stand 15 minutes before peeling.

1. Combine grits and ½ cup chicken broth in small bowl; mix well and set aside. Pour remaining 1 cup broth into large heavy saucepan; bring to a boil. Add garlic and moistened grits; mix well and return to a boil. Reduce heat to low; cover and cook 20 minutes. Remove from heat; add feta cheese. Stir until cheese is completely melted. Add roasted bell pepper; mix well.

2. Spray 8-inch square pan with nonstick cooking spray. Spoon grits mixture into prepared pan. Press grits evenly into pan with wet fingertips. Refrigerate until cold.

3. Spray grid with nonstick cooking spray. Prepare grill for direct cooking. Turn polenta out onto cutting board and cut into 2-inch squares. Cut each square diagonally into 2 triangles.

4. Place polenta triangles on grid. Grill over medium-high heat 1 minute or until bottoms are lightly browned. Turn triangles over and grill until browned and crisp. Serve warm or at room temperature.   *Makes 8 servings*

Nutrients per Serving: 4 triangles

Calories: 62, Calories from Fat: 26%, Total Fat: 2g, Saturated Fat: 1g, Cholesterol: 6mg, Sodium: 142mg, Carbohydrate: 9g, Dietary Fiber: <1g, Protein: 3g
Dietary Exchanges: 1 Starch

Garlicky Mustard Greens

2 pounds mustard greens
1 teaspoon olive oil
1 cup chopped onion
2 cloves garlic, minced
¾ cup chopped red bell pepper
½ cup fat-free reduced-sodium chicken broth*
1 tablespoon cider vinegar
1 teaspoon sugar

To defat chicken broth, skim fat from surface of broth with spoon. Or, place can of broth in refrigerator at least 2 hours ahead of time. Before using, remove fat that has hardened on surface of broth.

1. Wash greens well; remove stems and any wilted leaves. Stack several leaves; roll up jelly-roll style. Cut crosswise into 1-inch slices. Repeat with remaining greens.

2. Heat oil in Dutch oven or large saucepan over medium heat. Add onion and garlic; cook and stir 5 minutes or until onion is tender. Stir in greens, bell pepper and chicken broth. Reduce heat to low. Cook, covered, 25 minutes or until greens are tender, stirring occasionally.

3. Stir vinegar and sugar in small cup until sugar is dissolved. Stir into cooked greens; remove from heat. Serve immediately.   *Makes 4 servings*

Nutrients per Serving: ¼ of total recipe

Calories: 72, Calories from Fat: 19%, Total Fat: 2g, Saturated Fat: <1g, Cholesterol: 0mg, Sodium: 42mg, Carbohydrate: 11g, Dietary Fiber: 5g, Protein: 6g
Dietary Exchanges: 2½ Vegetable

Tabbouleh

½ cup uncooked bulgur
¾ cup boiling water
¼ teaspoon salt
5 teaspoons lemon juice
2 teaspoons olive oil
½ teaspoon dried basil leaves, crushed
¼ teaspoon black pepper
1 green onion, thinly sliced
½ cup chopped cucumber
½ cup chopped green bell pepper
½ cup chopped tomato
¼ cup chopped fresh parsley
2 teaspoons chopped mint (optional)

1. Rinse bulgur thoroughly in colander under cold water, picking out any debris; drain well. Transfer to medium heatproof bowl. Stir in boiling water and salt. Cover; let stand 30 minutes. Drain well.

2. Combine lemon juice, oil, basil and black pepper in small bowl. Pour over bulgur; mix well.

3. Layer bulgur, onion, cucumber, bell pepper and tomato in clear glass bowl; sprinkle with parsley and mint, if desired.

4. Refrigerate, covered, at least 2 hours to allow flavors to blend. Serve layered or toss before serving.
           Makes 8 servings

Nutrients per Serving: ⅛ of total recipe (without mint)

Calories: 49, Calories from Fat: 23%, Total Fat: 1g, Saturated Fat: <1g, Cholesterol: 0mg, Sodium: 71mg, Carbohydrate: 9g, Dietary Fiber: 3g, Protein: 1g
Dietary Exchanges: ½ Starch, ½ Vegetable

Cranberry Salad

2 cups cranberries
1 cup water
1 cup EQUAL® SPOONFUL*
1 small package cranberry or cherry sugar-free
    gelatin
1 cup boiling water
1 cup diced celery
1 can (7¼ ounces) crushed pineapple, in juice
½ cup chopped walnuts

*May substitute 24 packets Equal® sweetener.

• Bring cranberries and 1 cup water to a boil. Remove
from heat when cranberries have popped open. Add Equal®
and stir. Set aside to cool.

• Dissolve gelatin with 1 cup boiling water. Add cranberry
sauce; mix thoroughly. Add celery, pineapple and walnuts.
Pour into mold or bowl. Place in refrigerator until set.

Makes 8 servings

Nutrients per Serving: ⅛ of total recipe

Calories: 94, Calories from Fat: 46%, Total Fat: 5g,
Saturated Fat: <1g, Cholesterol: 0mg, Sodium: 57mg,
Carbohydrate: 11g, Dietary Fiber: 2g, Protein: 2g

Dietary Exchanges: 1 Fruit, 1 Fat

Oven-Roasted Peppers and Onions

Olive oil-flavored nonstick cooking spray
2 medium green bell peppers
2 medium red bell peppers
2 medium yellow bell peppers
4 small onions
1 teaspoon Italian herb seasoning
½ teaspoon dried basil leaves
¼ teaspoon ground cumin

1. Preheat oven to 375°F. Spray 15×10-inch jelly-roll pan
with cooking spray. Cut bell peppers into 1½-inch pieces.
Cut onions into quarters. Place vegetables on prepared pan.
Spray vegetables with cooking spray. Bake 20 minutes; stir.
Sprinkle with Italian herb blend, basil and cumin.

2. *Increase oven temperature to 425°F. Bake 20 minutes
or until edges are darkened and vegetables are crisp-tender.*

Makes 6 servings

Nutrients per Serving: ⅙ of total recipe

Calories: 84, Calories from Fat: 6%, Total Fat: 1g,
Saturated Fat: <1g, Cholesterol: 0mg, Sodium: 4mg,
Carbohydrate: 20g, Dietary Fiber: 4g, Protein: 3g

Dietary Exchanges: 3½ Vegetable

Cranberry Salad

Low-Fat Cajun Wedges

Low-Fat Cottage Fries: Follow step 1 as directed. Cut potatoes crosswise into ¼-inch-thick slices. Place in single layer on prepared baking sheet; spray and season as directed. Bake 15 to 20 minutes or until browned and fork-tender. Serve immediately.

Nutrients per Serving: 3 Wedges (¼ of total recipe)

Calories: 116, Calories from Fat: 1%, Total Fat: <1g, Saturated Fat: <1g, Cholesterol: 0mg, Sodium: 53mg, Carbohydrate: 27g, Dietary Fiber: 2g, Protein: 2g

Dietary Exchanges: 1½ Starch

Boston Baked Beans

2 cans (about 15 ounces each) navy or Great Northern beans, rinsed and drained
½ cup beer (not dark beer)
⅓ cup minced red or yellow onion
⅓ cup ketchup
3 tablespoons light molasses
2 teaspoons Worcestershire sauce
1 teaspoon dry mustard
½ teaspoon ground ginger
4 slices turkey bacon

1. Preheat oven to 350°F. Place beans in 11×7-inch glass baking dish. Combine beer, onion, ketchup, molasses, Worcestershire sauce, mustard and ginger in medium bowl. Pour over beans; toss to coat.

2. Cut bacon into 1-inch pieces; arrange in single layer over beans. Bake, uncovered, 40 to 45 minutes or until most of liquid is absorbed and bacon is browned.

Makes 8 servings

Nutrients per Serving: ⅛ of total recipe

Calories: 179, Calories from Fat: 10%, Total Fat: 2g, Saturated Fat: 1g, Cholesterol: 5mg, Sodium: 728mg, Carbohydrate: 31g, Dietary Fiber: <1g, Protein: 10g

Dietary Exchanges: 2 Starch, ½ Fat

T I P Dry mustard is ground mustard seed. You can find it in the spices aisle of your grocery store.

Low-Fat Cajun Wedges

2 medium russet potatoes
Nonstick cooking spray
2 tablespoons Cajun seasoning or other seasoning, such as paprika
Purple kale and fresh sage leaves, for garnish

1. Preheat oven to 400°F. To prepare potatoes, scrub under running water with soft vegetable brush; rinse. Dry well. (Do not peel.) Line baking sheet with aluminum foil and spray with cooking spray.

2. Cut potatoes in half lengthwise; then cut each half lengthwise into 3 wedges. Place potatoes, skin sides down, in single layer on prepared baking sheet.

3. Spray potatoes lightly with cooking spray and sprinkle evenly with seasoning.

4. Bake 25 minutes or until browned and fork-tender. Garnish, if desired. Serve immediately.

Makes 4 servings

Low-Fat Potato Chips: Follow step 1 as directed. Slice potatoes crosswise as thin as possible with chef's knife or mandoline slicer. Place in single layer on prepared baking sheet; spray and season as directed. Bake 10 to 15 minutes or until browned and crisp. Serve immediately.

Balsamic-Herb Ratatouille

4 tablespoons balsamic vinegar, divided
1 tablespoon olive oil
2 medium yellow or red Grilled Bell Peppers (recipe follows)
1 medium eggplant (about 1 pound)
1 small onion, peeled and quartered
    Balsamic-Herb Vinaigrette (recipe follows)
½ pint cherry tomatoes, grilled*
12 mushrooms
2 small yellow zucchini, halved lengthwise
⅓ cup slivered fresh basil leaves

To grill cherry tomatoes, thread tomatoes onto prepared skewers. Grill on covered grill over medium coals 5 minutes or until blistered and browned, basting and turning once.

1. Spray medium nonmetallic grillproof casserole with nonstick cooking spray; set aside. To make basting mixture, combine 2 tablespoons vinegar with oil in small bowl.

2. Prepare Grilled Bell Peppers; set aside. Remove strips of peel from eggplant, lengthwise at 1-inch intervals, and remove ends. Slice eggplant into ½-inch-thick rounds. Thread eggplant and onion quarters onto metal skewers; baste. Grill on covered grill over medium coals 20 to 30 minutes or until grill-marked and tender, basting and turning every 10 minutes.

3. Meanwhile, heat oven to 325°F. Prepare Balsamic-Herb Vinaigrette. Remove eggplant and onion from grill. Cut eggplant into ½-inch strips; place eggplant and onion in prepared casserole with Balsamic-Herb Vinaigrette. Cover loosely and place in oven to hold. Or, place casserole on upper rack of grill to hold.

4. Grill cherry tomatoes. To grill mushrooms, thread whole mushrooms onto 2 or 3 metal skewers; baste mushrooms and cut sides of zucchini. Grill mushrooms and zucchini on covered grill over medium coals 10 to 15 minutes or until browned and tender, basting and turning once. Remove from grill; cut zucchini into ½-inch-thick slices. Add zucchini and mushrooms to eggplant mixture. Dice bell peppers. Add bell peppers and tomatoes to eggplant mixture. Stir in remaining 2 tablespoons vinegar and basil. Garnish as desired.   *Makes 6 servings*

Grilled Bell Pepper

1 bell pepper (any color), stemmed, seeded and halved

Grill bell pepper halves, skin sides down, on covered grill over medium to hot coals 15 to 25 minutes or until skin is charred, without turning. Remove from grill and place in plastic bag until cool enough to handle, about 10 minutes. Remove skin with paring knife and discard.

Balsamic-Herb Vinaigrette

4 cloves garlic, minced
3 tablespoons balsamic vinegar
1 teaspoon dried oregano leaves *or* 1 tablespoon minced fresh oregano
1 teaspoon dried thyme leaves *or* 1 tablespoon minced fresh thyme
1 teaspoon Dijon mustard
1 teaspoon black pepper

Whisk together all ingredients in small bowl; set aside.

Nutrients per Serving: ⅙ of total recipe (without garnish)

Calories: 102, Calories from Fat: 24%, Total Fat: 3g, Saturated Fat: <1g, Cholesterol: 0mg, Sodium: 22mg, Carbohydrate: 19g, Dietary Fiber: 1g, Protein: 3g
Dietary Exchanges: 3 Vegetable, ½ Fat

Harvest Rice

1 cup thinly sliced carrots
1 tablespoon vegetable oil
2 medium apples, cored and chopped
1 cup sliced green onions
3 cups cooked brown rice
½ cup raisins
1 tablespoon sesame seeds, toasted
½ teaspoon salt

Cook carrots in oil in large skillet over medium-high heat until tender-crisp. Add apples and onions; cook 5 minutes. Stir in rice, raisins, sesame seeds and salt. Cook, stirring, until thoroughly heated.   *Makes 6 servings*

Microwave Directions: Combine carrots and oil in 2-quart microproof baking dish. Cook on HIGH (100% power) 2 to 3 minutes or until tender-crisp. Add apples and onions; continue cooking on HIGH 3 to 4 minutes. Stir in rice, raisins, sesame seeds and salt. Cover with waxed paper and cook on HIGH 3 to 4 minutes, stirring after 2 minutes, or until thoroughly heated.

Favorite recipe from *USA Rice Federation*

Nutrients per Serving: ⅙ of total recipe

Calories: 219, Calories from Fat: 16%, Total Fat: 4g, Saturated Fat: 1g, Cholesterol: 0mg, Sodium: 210mg, Carbohydrate: 44g, Dietary Fiber: 5g, Protein: 4g
Dietary Exchanges: 3 Starch

Balsamic-Herb Ratatouille ⌇ 303

Zucchini-Tomato Bake

1 pound eggplant, coarsely chopped
2 cups zucchini slices
2 cups mushroom slices
3 sheets (18×12 inches) heavy-duty foil, lightly sprayed with nonstick cooking spray
2 teaspoons olive oil
½ cup chopped onion
½ cup chopped fresh fennel (optional)
2 cloves garlic, minced
1 can (14½ ounces) no-salt-added whole tomatoes, undrained
1 tablespoon no-salt-added tomato paste
2 teaspoons dried basil leaves
1 teaspoon sugar

1. Preheat oven to 400°F. Divide eggplant, zucchini and mushrooms into 3 portions, each on separate foil sheet.

2. Heat oil in small nonstick skillet over medium heat. Add onion, fennel, if desired, and garlic. Cook and stir 3 to 4 minutes or until onion is tender. Add tomatoes, tomato paste, basil and sugar. Cook and stir about 4 minutes or until sauce thickens.

3. Pour sauce over eggplant mixture, dividing evenly among 3 portions. Double-fold sides and ends of foil to seal packets, leaving head space for heat circulation. Place on baking sheet.

Zucchini-Tomato Bake

4. Bake 30 minutes. Remove from oven. Carefully open one end of each packet to allow steam to escape. Open and transfer contents to serving dish. Garnish as desired.

Makes 6 servings

Nutrients per Serving: ⅙ of total recipe (without garnish)

Calories: 71, Calories from Fat: 23%, Total Fat: 2g, Saturated Fat: 0g, Cholesterol: 0mg, Sodium: 39mg, Carbohydrate: 13g, Dietary Fiber: 3g, Protein: 3g

Dietary Exchanges: 2 Vegetable, ½ Fat

Wild & Brown Rice with Exotic Mushrooms

1⅔ cups packaged unseasoned brown and wild rice blend
6 cups water
½ ounce dried porcini or morel mushrooms
¾ cup boiling water
2 tablespoons margarine
8 ounces cremini (brown) or button mushrooms, sliced
2 cloves garlic, minced
2 tablespoons chopped fresh thyme *or* 2 teaspoons dried thyme leaves
1 teaspoon salt
¼ teaspoon black pepper
½ cup sliced green onions

1. Combine rice and water in large saucepan; bring to a boil over high heat. Cover; simmer over low heat until rice is tender (check package for cooking time). Drain, but do not rinse.

2. Meanwhile, combine porcini mushrooms and boiling water in small bowl; let stand 30 minutes or until mushrooms are tender. Drain mushrooms, reserving liquid. Chop mushrooms; set aside.

3. Melt margarine in large, deep skillet over medium heat. Add cremini mushrooms and garlic; cook and stir 5 minutes. Sprinkle thyme, salt and pepper over mushrooms; cook and stir 1 minute or until mushrooms are tender.

4. Add drained rice, porcini mushrooms and reserved mushroom liquid to skillet; cook and stir over medium-low heat 5 minutes or until hot. Stir in green onions. Garnish as desired.

Makes 8 servings

Nutrients per Serving: ⅛ of total recipe (without garnish)

Calories: 175, Calories from Fat: 21%, Total Fat: 4g, Saturated Fat: 1g, Cholesterol: <1mg, Sodium: 304mg, Carbohydrate: 30g, Dietary Fiber: 2g, Protein: 5g

Dietary Exchanges: 2 Starch, 1 Fat

Sweet Potato Puffs

2 pounds sweet potatoes
⅓ cup orange juice
1 egg, beaten
1 tablespoon grated orange peel
½ teaspoon ground nutmeg
¼ cup chopped pecans

1. Peel and cut sweet potatoes into 1-inch pieces. Place potatoes in medium saucepan. Add enough water to cover; bring to a boil over medium-high heat. Cook 10 to 15 minutes or until tender. Drain potatoes and place in large bowl; mash until smooth. Add orange juice, egg, orange peel and nutmeg; mix well.

2. Preheat oven to 375°F. Spray baking sheet with nonstick cooking spray. Spoon potato mixture into 10 mounds on prepared baking sheet. Sprinkle pecans evenly over tops of mounds.

3. Bake 30 minutes or until centers are hot. Garnish, if desired. *Makes 10 servings*

Nutrients per Serving: 1 Puff

Calories: 103, Calories from Fat: 21%, Total Fat: 3g, Saturated Fat: <1g, Cholesterol: 21mg, Sodium: 14mg, Carbohydrate: 19g, Dietary Fiber: 2g, Protein: 2g

Dietary Exchanges: 1 Starch, ½ Fat

Low-Calorie Mashed Potatoes

2 pounds medium red boiling potatoes, peeled and cut into chunks
4 large cloves garlic, peeled
¾ cup low-fat buttermilk
½ teaspoon salt
¼ teaspoon black pepper
2 tablespoons chopped chives, for garnish

1. Place potatoes and garlic in large saucepan. Add enough water to cover; bring to a boil over high heat. Reduce heat and simmer, uncovered, 20 to 30 minutes or until potatoes are fork-tender. Drain.

2. Place potatoes and garlic in medium bowl. Mash with potato masher or beat with electric mixer at medium speed until smooth.* Add buttermilk, salt and pepper. Stir with fork until just combined. Garnish, if desired.

Makes 8 servings

*For a smoother texture, force potatoes through potato ricer or food mill into medium bowl. Finish as directed in step 2.

Nutrients per Serving: ⅛ of total recipe (without garnish)

Calories: 101, Calories from Fat: 3%, Total Fat: <1g, Saturated Fat: <1g, Cholesterol: 1mg, Sodium: 175mg, Carbohydrate: 22g, Dietary Fiber: 2g, Protein: 3g

Dietary Exchanges: 1½ Starch

Citrus Asparagus

Orange Sauce

> 2 teaspoons reduced-fat margarine
> 1 clove garlic, minced
> Juice of 1 large orange (about ⅓ cup)
> 1¼ teaspoons balsamic vinegar
> ¼ teaspoon Dijon mustard
> ½ teaspoon grated orange peel
> Salt (optional)

Asparagus

> Olive oil-flavored nonstick cooking spray
> 1 small onion, diced
> 1 pound fresh asparagus, lower half of stalks peeled*
> ⅔ cup diced red bell pepper
> ½ cup water

If using pencil-thin asparagus, do not peel. Reduce cooking time to 4 to 5 minutes.

1. For Orange Sauce, heat margarine in small saucepan over medium heat. Add garlic; cook and stir 2 minutes or until soft. Stir in orange juice; bring to a boil. Add vinegar and mustard; reduce heat and simmer 2 minutes. Remove from heat and add orange peel. Season to taste with salt, if desired; reserve and keep warm.

2. For Asparagus, spray medium saucepan with cooking spray; heat over medium-high heat. Add onion; cook and stir 2 minutes. Add asparagus, bell pepper and water. Reduce heat to medium-low. Cover and simmer 7 minutes or until asparagus is crisp-tender. Remove vegetables with slotted spoon to serving dish; serve with reserved Orange Sauce. *Makes 4 servings*

Nutrients per Serving: ¼ of total recipe (without added salt)

Calories: 58, Calories from Fat: 19%, Total Fat: 1g, Saturated Fat: <1g, Cholesterol: <1mg, Sodium: 37mg, Carbohydrate: 10g, Dietary Fiber: 2g, Protein: 3g

Dietary Exchanges: 2 Vegetable

Honeyed Beets

> ¼ cup unsweetened apple juice
> 2 tablespoons cider vinegar
> 1 tablespoon honey
> 2 teaspoons cornstarch
> 2 cans (8 ounces each) sliced beets, drained
> Salt and black pepper (optional)

Combine apple juice, vinegar, honey and cornstarch in large nonstick saucepan. Cook, stirring occasionally, over medium heat until simmering. Stir in beets and season to taste with salt and pepper, if desired; simmer 3 minutes. *Makes 4 servings*

Nutrients per Serving: ¼ of total recipe (without salt and pepper seasoning)

Calories: 63, Calories from Fat: 2%, Total Fat: <1g, Saturated Fat: <1g, Cholesterol: 0mg, Sodium: 312mg, Carbohydrate: 16g, Dietary Fiber: 3g, Protein: 1g

Dietary Exchanges: ½ Fruit, 1½ Vegetable

Mashed Squash

> 1 medium acorn squash, halved and seeded
> 1 tablespoon maple syrup or maple-flavored syrup
> ½ teaspoon pumpkin pie spice
> Black pepper and butter-flavored salt (optional)

Preheat oven to 400°F. Place squash halves, cut sides down, on baking sheet. Bake 30 minutes or until tender. Scoop squash pulp into mixing bowl; beat with electric mixer. Stir in syrup and pumpkin pie spice. Season to taste with pepper and salt, if desired. *Makes 4 servings*

Nutrients per Serving: ¼ of total recipe (without added pepper and salt seasoning)

Calories: 70, Calories from Fat: 2%, Total Fat: <1g, Saturated Fat: <1g, Cholesterol: 0mg, Sodium: 5mg, Carbohydrate: 18g, Dietary Fiber: 2g, Protein: 1g

Dietary Exchanges: 1 Starch

Rigatoni with Broccoli

> 8 ounces uncooked rigatoni pasta
> 1 bunch fresh broccoli, trimmed and separated into florets with 1-inch stems
> 1 tablespoon FILIPPO BERIO® Extra Virgin Olive Oil
> 1 clove garlic, minced
> Crushed red pepper
> 2 tablespoons grated Parmesan cheese

Cook pasta according to package directions until al dente (tender but still firm). Add broccoli during last 5 minutes of cooking time; cook until broccoli is tender-crisp. Drain pasta and broccoli; transfer to large bowl. Meanwhile, in small skillet, heat olive oil over medium heat until hot. Add garlic; cook and stir 1 to 2 minutes or until golden. Pour oil mixture over hot pasta mixture; toss until lightly coated. Season to taste with red pepper. Top with cheese. *Makes 4 servings*

Nutrients per Serving: ¼ of total recipe

Calories: 278, Calories from Fat: 17%, Total Fat: 5g, Saturated Fat: 1g, Cholesterol: 2mg, Sodium: 72mg, Carbohydrate: 47g, Dietary Fiber: 4g, Protein: 11g

Dietary Exchanges: 3 Starch, 1 Vegetable, ½ Fat

Green Chili Rice

1 cup uncooked white rice
1 can (14½ ounces) fat-free reduced-sodium
    chicken broth plus water to measure 2 cups
1 can (4 ounces) chopped mild green chilies
½ medium yellow onion, peeled and diced
1 teaspoon dried oregano leaves
½ teaspoon salt (optional)
½ teaspoon cumin seeds
3 green onions, thinly sliced
⅓ to ½ cup fresh cilantro leaves

Combine rice, broth, chilies, yellow onion, oregano, salt, if desired, and cumin in large saucepan. Bring to a boil, uncovered, over high heat. Reduce heat to low; cover and simmer 18 minutes or until liquid is absorbed and rice is tender. Stir in green onions and cilantro. Garnish as desired. *Makes 6 servings*

Nutrients per Serving: ⅙ of total recipe (without garnish)

Calories: 134, Calories from Fat: 7%, Total Fat: 1g,
Saturated Fat: 0g, Cholesterol: 1mg, Sodium: 99mg,
Carbohydrate: 27g, Dietary Fiber: 1g, Protein: 3g

Dietary Exchanges: 1½ Starch

Portobello Mushrooms Sesame

4 large portobello mushrooms
2 tablespoons sweet rice wine
2 tablespoons reduced-sodium soy sauce
2 cloves garlic, minced
1 teaspoon dark sesame oil

1. Remove and discard stems from mushrooms; set caps aside. Combine remaining ingredients in small bowl.

2. Brush both sides of mushroom caps with soy sauce mixture. Grill mushrooms, top sides up, on covered grill over medium coals 3 to 4 minutes. Brush tops with soy sauce mixture and turn over; grill 2 minutes more or until mushrooms are lightly browned. Turn again and grill, basting frequently, 4 to 5 minutes or until tender when pressed with back of spatula. Remove mushrooms and cut diagonally into ½-inch-thick slices. *Makes 4 servings*

Nutrients per Serving: 1 grilled Mushroom cap

Calories: 67, Calories from Fat: 21%, Total Fat: 2g,
Saturated Fat: <1g, Cholesterol: 0mg, Sodium: 268mg,
Carbohydrate: 9g, Dietary Fiber: <1g, Protein: 4g

Dietary Exchanges: 2 Vegetable, ½ Fat

Green Chili Rice

CAKES & PIES

Scrumptious Apple Cake

3 egg whites
1½ cups sugar
1 cup unsweetened applesauce
1 teaspoon vanilla
2 cups all-purpose flour
2 teaspoons ground cinnamon
1 teaspoon baking soda
¼ teaspoon salt
4 cups cored peeled tart apple slices (McIntosh or Crispin)
Yogurt Glaze (recipe follows)

Preheat oven to 350°F. Beat egg whites until slightly foamy; add sugar, applesauce and vanilla. Combine flour, cinnamon, baking soda and salt in separate bowl; add to applesauce mixture. Spread apples in 13×9-inch pan or 9-inch round springform pan sprayed with nonstick cooking spray. Spread batter over apples. Bake 35 to 40 minutes or until wooden toothpick inserted into center comes out clean; cool on wire rack. Prepare Yogurt Glaze; spread evenly over cooled cake.   *Makes 15 to 20 servings*

Favorite recipe from *New York Apple Association, Inc.*

Yogurt Glaze: Combine 1½ cups plain or vanilla nonfat yogurt, 3 tablespoons brown sugar (or to taste) and 1 teaspoon vanilla or 1 teaspoon lemon juice. Stir together until smooth.

Nutrients per Serving: 1 Cake square (¹⁄₁₅ of total recipe) without garnish

Calories: 189, Calories from Fat: 2%, Total Fat: <1g, Saturated Fat: <1g, Cholesterol: <1mg, Sodium: 155mg, Carbohydrate: 43g, Dietary Fiber: 2g, Protein: 4g

Dietary Exchanges: 1 Starch, 2 Fruit

Fresh Fruit Tart

3 cups cooked rice
¼ cup granulated sugar
1 egg, beaten
    Vegetable cooking spray
1 package (8 ounces) light cream cheese, softened
¼ cup plain nonfat yogurt
¼ cup confectioners' sugar
1 teaspoon vanilla extract
⅓ cup low-sugar apricot or peach spread
1 tablespoon water
2 to 3 cups fresh fruit (sliced strawberries, raspberries, blueberries, sliced kiwifruit, grape halves)

Combine rice, granulated sugar and egg in medium bowl. Press into 12-inch pizza pan or 10-inch pie pan coated with cooking spray. Bake at 350°F. for 10 minutes. Cool.

Beat cream cheese and yogurt in medium bowl until light and fluffy. Add confectioners' sugar and vanilla; beat until well blended. Spread over crust.

Heat apricot spread and water in small saucepan over low heat. Strain; cool. Brush half of glaze over filling. Arrange fruit attractively over crust, starting at outer edge. Brush remaining glaze evenly over fruit. Cover and chill 1 to 2 hours before serving.   *Makes 8 servings*

Favorite recipe from *USA Rice Federation*

Nutrients per Serving: ⅛ of total recipe (made with 2 cups fresh fruit)

Calories: 222, Calories from Fat: 22%, Total Fat: 5g, Saturated Fat: 3g, Cholesterol: 40mg, Sodium: 148mg, Carbohydrate: 36g, Dietary Fiber: 2g, Protein: 6g

Dietary Exchanges: 1½ Starch, 1 Fruit, 1 Fat

Mixed Berry Tart with Ginger-Raspberry Glaze

1 refrigerated pie crust, at room temperature
¾ cup no-sugar-added seedless raspberry fruit spread
½ teaspoon grated fresh ginger *or* ¼ teaspoon ground ginger
2 cups fresh or frozen blueberries, thawed
2 cups fresh or frozen blackberries, thawed
1 peach, peeled and thinly sliced

1. Preheat oven to 450°F. Coat 9-inch pie pan or tart pan with nonstick cooking spray. Carefully place pie crust on bottom of pan. Turn edge of pie crust inward to form ½-inch-thick edge. Press edge firmly against side of pan. Using fork, pierce several times over entire bottom of pan to prevent crust from puffing while baking. Bake 12 minutes or until golden brown. Cool completely on wire rack.

2. To prepare glaze, heat fruit spread in small saucepan over high heat; stir until completely melted. Immediately remove from heat; stir in ginger and set aside to cool slightly.

3. Combine blueberries, blackberries and all but 2 tablespoons glaze; set aside.

4. Brush remaining 2 tablespoons glaze evenly over bottom of cooled crust. Decoratively arrange peach slices on top of crust and mound berries on top of peach slices. Refrigerate at least 2 hours. *Makes 8 servings*

Nutrients per Serving: 1 Tart wedge (⅛ of total recipe)

Calories: 191, Calories from Fat: 33%, Total Fat: 7g, Saturated Fat: 3g, Cholesterol: 5mg, Sodium: 172mg, Carbohydrate: 32g, Dietary Fiber: 3g, Protein: 1g
Dietary Exchanges: 1 Starch, 1 Fruit, 1½ Fat

TIP Berries are packed with antioxidants, the substances in foods that may help fight cancer, heart disease, Alzheimer's and other diseases of aging. So savor every bite of a piece of this scrumptious tart. Not only will you be eating light, you'll be eating for your health!

Chocolate Angel Fruit Torte

1 package angel food cake mix
½ cup unsweetened cocoa
2 medium bananas, thinly sliced
1½ teaspoons lemon juice
1 can (12 ounces) evaporated skimmed milk, divided
⅓ cup sugar
¼ cup cornstarch
⅓ cup cholesterol-free egg substitute
3 tablespoons fat-free sour cream
3 teaspoons vanilla
3 large kiwis, peeled and thinly sliced
1 can (11 ounces) mandarin orange segments, rinsed and drained

1. Prepare cake according to package directions, mixing cocoa with dry ingredients; cool completely. Cut horizontally in half to form 2 layers; set aside.

2. Place banana slices in medium bowl. Add lemon juice; toss to coat. Set aside.

3. Combine ¼ cup milk, sugar and cornstarch in small saucepan; whisk until smooth. Whisk in remaining milk. Bring to a boil over high heat, stirring constantly. Boil 1 minute or until mixture thickens, stirring constantly. Reduce heat to medium-low.

4. Blend ⅓ cup hot milk mixture and egg substitute in small bowl. Add to saucepan. Cook 2 minutes, stirring constantly. Remove saucepan from heat. Let stand 10 minutes, stirring frequently. Add sour cream and vanilla; blend well.

5. Place bottom half of cake on serving plate. Spread with half of milk mixture. Arrange half of banana slices, kiwi slices and mandarin orange segments on milk mixture. Place remaining half of cake, cut side down, over fruit. Top with remaining milk mixture and fruit.

Makes 12 servings

Nutrients per Serving: 1 Torte slice (1/12 of total recipe

Calories: 233, Calories from Fat: 1%, Total Fat: <1g, Saturated Fat: <1g, Cholesterol: 1mg, Sodium: 306mg, Carbohydrate: 52g, Dietary Fiber: 1g, Protein: 7g
Dietary Exchanges: 2½ Starch, 1 Fruit

Tropical Fruit Coconut Tart

5. Continue boiling 1 minute, stirring constantly. Remove from heat; cool completely. Stir in sugar substitute and coconut extract, if desired. Combine pineapple, mango slices and banana slices in medium bowl. Spoon into pan; drizzle with pineapple juice mixture. Cover with plastic wrap and refrigerate 2 hours. Garnish with pineapple leaves, if desired. *Makes 8 servings*

Note: The crust may be made 24 hours in advance, if desired.

Nutrients per Serving: 1 Tart slice (⅛ of total recipe) without garnish

Calories: 139, Calories from Fat: 25%, Total Fat: 4g, Saturated Fat: 4g, Cholesterol: 0mg, Sodium: 59mg, Carbohydrate: 25g, Dietary Fiber: 2g, Protein: 2g
Dietary Exchanges: 1 Starch, ½ Fruit, 1 Fat

Lemon Pound Cake with Strawberries

2 cups all-purpose flour
1 teaspoon baking powder
1 teaspoon baking soda
½ teaspoon salt
½ cup reduced-fat sour cream
½ cup fat-free (skim) milk
⅓ cup sugar
¼ cup vegetable oil
¼ cup cholesterol-free egg substitute
2 tablespoons lemon juice
1 teaspoon grated lemon peel
3 pints strawberries
   Sugar substitute (optional)

1. Preheat oven to 350°F. Coat 8×4-inch loaf pan with nonstick cooking spray; set aside. Combine flour, baking powder, baking soda and salt in large bowl.

2. Combine sour cream, milk, sugar, oil, egg substitute, lemon juice and lemon peel in medium bowl. Stir sour cream mixture into flour mixture until well combined; pour batter into prepared pan. Bake 45 to 50 minutes or until toothpick inserted into center comes out clean.

3. Let cake cool 20 minutes before removing from pan; cool completely. Meanwhile, slice strawberries. Sprinkle to taste with sugar substitute, if desired. Slice cake and serve with strawberries. *Makes 16 servings*

Nutrients per Serving: 1 Cake slice with about 3 tablespoons strawberry slices

Calories: 180, Calories from Fat: 29%, Total Fat: 6g, Saturated Fat: 1g, Cholesterol: 4mg, Sodium: 264mg, Carbohydrate: 28g, Dietary Fiber: 2g, Protein: 4g
Dietary Exchanges: 1 Starch, 1 Fruit, 1 Fat

Tropical Fruit Coconut Tart

1 cup cornflakes, crushed
1 can (3½ ounces) sweetened flaked coconut
2 egg whites
1 can (15¼ ounces) pineapple tidbits in juice
2 teaspoons cornstarch
2 packets sugar substitute *or* equivalent of
   4 teaspoons sugar
1 teaspoon coconut extract (optional)
1 mango, peeled and thinly sliced
1 medium banana, thinly sliced

1. Preheat oven to 425°F. Coat 9-inch springform pan with nonstick cooking spray; set aside.

2. Combine cornflakes, coconut and egg whites in medium bowl; toss gently to blend. Place coconut mixture in prepared pan; press firmly to cover bottom and ½ inch up side of pan.

3. Bake 8 minutes or until edge begins to brown. Cool completely on wire rack.

4. Drain pineapple, reserving pineapple juice. Combine pineapple juice and cornstarch in small saucepan; stir until cornstarch is dissolved. Bring to a boil over high heat.

Three-Berry Kuchen

1¾ cups all-purpose flour, divided
2 teaspoons baking powder
½ teaspoon baking soda
½ teaspoon salt
⅔ cup MOTT'S® Apple Sauce
4 egg whites
¼ cup plain nonfat yogurt
2 tablespoons granulated sugar
1 teaspoon grated lemon peel
2 cups assorted fresh or thawed, frozen
    blueberries, raspberries or blackberries
¼ cup firmly packed light brown sugar
2 tablespoons margarine

1. Preheat oven to 350°F. Spray 10-inch round cake pan with nonstick cooking spray.

2. In small bowl, combine 1½ cups flour, baking powder, baking soda and salt.

3. In large bowl, whisk together apple sauce, egg whites, yogurt, granulated sugar and lemon peel.

4. Add flour mixture to apple sauce mixture; stir until well blended. Spread batter into prepared pan.

5. Sprinkle berries over batter. Combine remaining ¼ cup flour and brown sugar in small bowl. Cut in margarine with pastry blender or fork until mixture resembles coarse crumbs. Sprinkle over berries.

Three-Berry Kuchen

6. Bake 50 to 55 minutes or until lightly browned. Cool on wire rack 20 minutes. Serve warm or cool completely. Cut into 9 slices. *Makes 9 servings*

Nutrients per Serving: 1 Kuchen slice (⅑ of total recipe)

Calories: 182 Calories from Fat: 14%, Total Fat: 3g, Saturated Fat: 1g, Cholesterol: <1mg, Sodium: 372mg, Carbohydrate: 35g, Dietary Fiber: 2g, Protein: 5g

Dietary Exchanges: 1½ Starch, 1 Fruit, ½ Fat

Pumpkin-Fig Cheesecake

12 nonfat fig bar cookies
2 packages (8 ounces each) fat-free cream
    cheese, softened
1 package (8 ounces) reduced-fat cream
    cheese, softened
1 can (15 ounces) pumpkin
1 cup SPLENDA® No-Calorie Sweetener,
    granular form
1 cup cholesterol-free egg substitute
½ cup nonfat evaporated milk
1 tablespoon vanilla extract
2 teaspoons pumpkin pie spice mix
¼ teaspoon salt
½ cup chopped dried figs
2 tablespoons walnut pieces

1. Preheat oven to 325°F. Lightly coat 8- to 9-inch springform baking pan with nonstick cooking spray.

2. Break up cookies with fingers, then chop by hand with knife or process in food processor until crumbly. Lightly press cookie crumbs onto bottom and side of pan. Bake 15 minutes; cool slightly while preparing filling.

3. In large bowl, beat cream cheese with mixer at high speed until smooth. Add pumpkin, SPLENDA®, egg substitute, milk, vanilla, spice mix and salt. Beat until smooth. Spread filling evenly over crust.

4. Place springform pan on baking sheet. Bake 1 hour and 15 minutes or until top begins to crack and center moves very little when pan is jiggled. Cool on wire rack to room temperature; refrigerate 4 to 6 hours or overnight before serving. Just before serving, arrange figs and nuts around edge of cheesecake. *Makes 16 slices*

Nutrients per Serving: 1 Cheesecake slice (1/16 of total recipe)

Calories: 157, Calories from Fat: 20%, Total Fat: 3g, Saturated Fat: 2g, Cholesterol: 9mg, Sodium: 310mg, Carbohydrate: 22g, Dietary Fiber: 2g, Protein: 9g

Dietary Exchanges: 1½ Starch, 1 Lean Meat

Luscious Lime Angel Food Cake Rolls

1 package (16 ounces) angel food cake mix
2 drops green food coloring (optional)
2 containers (8 ounces each) lime-flavored nonfat sugar-free yogurt
Lime slices (optional)

1. Preheat oven to 350°F. Line two 17×11¼×1-inch jelly-roll pans with parchment or waxed paper; set aside.

2. Prepare angel food cake mix according to package directions. Divide batter evenly between prepared pans. Draw knife through batter to remove large air bubbles. Bake 12 minutes or until cakes are lightly browned and toothpick inserted into centers comes out clean.

3. Invert each cake onto separate clean towel. Starting at short end, roll up warm cake, jelly-roll fashion, with towel inside. Cool cakes completely.

4. Place 1 to 2 drops green food coloring in each container of yogurt, if desired; stir well. Unroll cakes; remove towels. Spread each cake with 1 container yogurt, leaving 1-inch border. Roll up cakes; place seam-side down. Slice each cake roll evenly into 8 pieces. Garnish with lime slices, if desired. Serve immediately or refrigerate.

Makes 16 servings

Nutrients per Serving: 1 Cake slice (⅛ of 1 Roll) without garnish

Calories: 136, Calories from Fat: 1%, Total Fat: <1g, Saturated Fat: <1g, Cholesterol: 0mg, Sodium: 252mg, Carbohydrate: 30g, Dietary Fiber: <1g, Protein: 4g

Dietary Exchanges: 2 Starch

Cherry Cocoa Cake

1 cup water
½ cup cocoa
½ cup margarine
2 cups all-purpose flour
1¾ cups sugar
½ cup low-fat cherry yogurt
1 egg, slightly beaten
1 teaspoon baking soda
1 teaspoon vanilla
½ teaspoon salt
1 tablespoon powdered sugar

In a large saucepan, combine water, cocoa and margarine. Cook over medium heat, stirring frequently, until mixture comes to a full boil. Remove from heat; stir in flour and sugar. Add yogurt, egg, baking soda, vanilla and salt; mix thoroughly.

Pour batter into a 15½×10-inch baking pan coated with nonstick cooking spray. Bake at 375°F for 20 to 25 minutes or until wooden pick inserted into center comes out clean. Cool in pan on wire rack. Sprinkle powdered sugar over top. Cut into 32 squares. *Makes 32 servings*

Favorite recipe from *North Dakota Wheat Commission*

Nutrients per Serving: 1 Cake square (¹⁄₃₂ of total recipe)

Calories: 105, Calories from Fat: 27%, Total Fat: 3g, Saturated Fat: 1g, Cholesterol: 7mg, Sodium: 113mg, Carbohydrate: 18g, Dietary Fiber: <1g, Protein: 1g

Dietary Exchanges: 1 Starch, ½ Fat

Banana Pistachio Pie

¾ cup cinnamon graham cracker crumbs
2 tablespoons reduced-fat margarine, melted
2 packages (4-serving-size each) fat-free sugar-free pistachio instant pudding and pie filling mix
2½ cups fat-free (skim) milk
1 large ripe banana, sliced
¼ teaspoon ground cinnamon
1 cup thawed frozen reduced-fat nondairy whipped topping
Additional thawed frozen reduced-fat nondairy whipped topping (optional)

1. Combine graham cracker crumbs and margarine in small bowl, stirring with fork until crumbly. Press onto bottom of 9-inch pie plate.

2. Prepare pudding mix according to manufacturer's pie directions, using 2½ cups milk. Gently stir in banana and cinnamon; fold in 1 cup whipped topping. Pour into prepared crust. Refrigerate at least 1 hour. Top with additional whipped topping before serving, if desired.

Makes 8 servings

Nutrients per Serving: 1 Pie slice (⅛ of total recipe) without additional whipped topping

Calories: 117, Calories from Fat: 27%, Total Fat: 4g, Saturated Fat: 2g, Cholesterol: 1mg, Sodium: 119mg, Carbohydrate: 18g, Dietary Fiber: 1g, Protein: 3g

Dietary Exchanges: 1 Starch, ½ Fat

Mocha Marble Pound Cake

Mocha Marble Pound Cake

2 cups all-purpose flour
2 teaspoons baking powder
1 teaspoon baking soda
½ teaspoon salt
1 cup sugar
¼ cup FLEISCHMANN'S® Original Margarine, softened
1 teaspoon vanilla extract
½ cup EGG BEATERS® Healthy Real Egg Product
1 (8-ounce) container low-fat coffee yogurt
¼ cup unsweetened cocoa
Mocha Yogurt Glaze (recipe follows)

In small bowl, combine flour, baking powder, baking soda and salt; set aside.

In large bowl, with electric mixer at medium speed, beat sugar, margarine and vanilla until creamy. Add Egg Beaters®; beat until smooth. With mixer at low speed, add yogurt alternately with flour mixture, beating well after each addition. Remove half of batter to medium bowl. Add cocoa to batter remaining in large bowl; beat until blended. Alternately spoon coffee and chocolate batters into greased 9×5×3-inch loaf pan. With knife, cut through batters to create marbled effect.

Bake at 325°F for 60 to 65 minutes or until toothpick inserted into center comes out clean. Cool in pan on wire rack for 10 minutes. Remove from pan; cool completely on wire rack. Frost with Mocha Yogurt Glaze.

Makes 16 servings

Mocha Yogurt Glaze: In small bowl, combine ½ cup powdered sugar, 1 tablespoon unsweetened cocoa and 1 tablespoon low-fat coffee yogurt until smooth; add more yogurt, if necessary, to make spreading consistency.

Prep Time: 20 minutes
Bake Time: 65 minutes

Nutrients per Serving: 1 Cake slice (¹⁄₁₆ of total recipe)

Calories: 167, Calories from Fat: 18%, Total Fat: 4g, Saturated Fat: 1g, Cholesterol: 1mg, Sodium: 275mg, Carbohydrate: 31g, Dietary Fiber: 1g, Protein: 3g

Dietary Exchanges: 2 Starch, ½ Fat

Blueberry Lemon Pudding Cake

¼ cup sugar
¼ cup all-purpose flour
1 cup fat-free (skim) milk
1 egg yolk
3 tablespoons fresh lemon juice
2 tablespoons margarine
2 teaspoons finely grated lemon peel
3 egg whites
1 cup sugar-free strawberry fruit spread
2 cups fresh or frozen (not thawed) blueberries

1. Preheat oven to 350°F. Lightly spray 8-inch square glass or ceramic baking dish with nonstick cooking spray.

2. Combine sugar and flour in small bowl.

3. Combine milk, egg yolk, lemon juice, margarine and lemon peel in large bowl. Add sugar mixture to milk mixture; stir until just blended.

4. Beat egg whites in medium bowl until stiff, but not dry. Gently fold beaten egg whites into milk mixture; spread into bottom of prepared baking dish. Place dish in 13×9-inch baking pan; pour 1 inch hot water into outer pan. Bake 15 minutes.

5. Meanwhile, melt fruit spread. Drop blueberries evenly over top of cake; carefully brush with fruit spread. Bake about 35 minutes or until set and lightly golden.

6. Let cool slightly; serve warm or chilled.

Makes 6 servings

Nutrients per Serving: 1 Cake square (⅙ of total recipe)

Calories: 200, Calories from Fat: 22%, Total Fat: 5g, Saturated Fat: 1g, Cholesterol: 36mg, Sodium: 150mg, Carbohydrate: 35g, Dietary Fiber: 2g, Protein: 5g

Dietary Exchanges: 1 Starch, 1½ Fruit, 1 Fat

Angel Food Cake with Pineapple Sauce

1 can (20 ounces) DOLE® Crushed Pineapple,
   undrained
2 tablespoons sugar
1 tablespoon cornstarch
1 tablespoon orange marmalade, peach or
   apricot fruit spread
1 prepared angel food cake

• Combine crushed pineapple with juice, sugar, cornstarch and orange marmalade in small saucepan. Bring to a boil. Reduce heat to low; cook, stirring constantly, 2 minutes or until sauce thickens. Cool slightly. Sauce can be served warm or chilled.

• Cut angel food cake into 12 slices. To serve, spoon sauce over each slice.   *Makes 12 servings*

Prep Time: 10 minutes
Cook Time: 5 minutes

Nutrients per Serving: 1 Cake slice with about 3 tablespoons Sauce (¹⁄₁₂ of total recipe)

Calories: 116, Calories from Fat: 2%, Total Fat: <1g, Saturated Fat: <1g, Cholesterol: 0mg, Sodium: 214mg, Carbohydrate: 28g, Dietary Fiber: 1g, Protein: 2g

Dietary Exchanges: 1 Starch, 1 Fruit

Light Banana Cream Pie

1 package (1.9 ounces) sugar-free vanilla
   instant pudding and pie filling (4 servings)
2¾ cups low fat milk
4 ripe, medium DOLE® Bananas, sliced
1 (9-inch) ready-made graham cracker pie crust
1 firm, medium DOLE® Banana (optional)
   Light frozen non-dairy whipped topping,
   thawed (optional)

• **Prepare** pudding as directed, using 2¾ cups low fat milk. Stir in 4 sliced ripe bananas.

• **Spoon** banana mixture into pie crust. Place plastic wrap over pie, lightly pressing plastic to completely cover filling. Chill 1 hour or until filling is set. Remove plastic wrap.

• **Cut** firm banana into ½-inch slices. Garnish pie with whipped topping and banana slices.   *Makes 8 servings*

Nutrients per Serving: 1 Pie slice (⅛ of total recipe) without garnish

Calories: 227, Calories from Fat: 27%, Total Fat: 8g, Saturated Fat: 2g, Cholesterol: 7mg, Sodium: 455mg, Carbohydrate: 37g, Dietary Fiber: 2g, Protein: 4g

Dietary Exchanges: 2 Starch, ½ Fruit, 1 Fat

Lemon Poppy Seed Cake

6 tablespoons margarine, softened
½ cup packed light brown sugar
½ cup plain low-fat yogurt
1 whole egg
2 egg whites
1 tablespoon fresh lemon juice
1¾ cups all-purpose flour
1 teaspoon baking powder
½ teaspoon baking soda
¼ teaspoon salt
⅓ cup fat-free (skim) milk
2 tablespoons poppy seeds
1 tablespoon grated lemon peel

Lemon Glaze

1 cup powdered sugar
2 tablespoons plus 1½ teaspoons fresh lemon juice
½ teaspoon poppy seeds

1. Preheat oven to 350°F. Grease and flour 6-cup Bundt pan. Beat margarine in large bowl with electric mixer until fluffy. Beat in brown sugar, yogurt, whole egg, egg whites and 1 tablespoon lemon juice. Set aside.

2. Combine flour, baking powder, baking soda and salt in medium bowl. Add flour mixture to margarine mixture alternately with milk, beginning and ending with flour mixture. Mix in 2 tablespoons poppy seeds and lemon peel. Pour batter into prepared pan. Bake about 40 minutes or until cake is golden brown and wooden pick inserted into center comes out clean. Cool in pan on wire rack 10 minutes; remove cake from pan and cool on wire rack.

3. For Lemon Glaze, mix powdered sugar with lemon juice until desired consistency. Spoon glaze evenly over cake and sprinkle with ½ teaspoon poppy seeds.

Makes 12 servings

Nutrients per Serving: 1 Cake slice (¹⁄₁₂ of total recipe)

Calories: 217, Calories from Fat: 29%, Total Fat: 7g, Saturated Fat: 1g, Cholesterol: 18mg, Sodium: 219mg, Carbohydrate: 34g, Dietary Fiber: 1g, Protein: 4g

Dietary Exchanges: 2½ Starch, 1 Fat

Cherry-Pineapple Cheesecake Gems

1 jar (10 ounces) maraschino cherries, drained, stems removed, halved
1¼ cups graham cracker crumbs
⅛ cup canola oil
2 packages (8 ounces each) fat-free cream cheese, softened
1 package (8 ounces) reduced-fat cream cheese, softened
1 cup SPLENDA® No-Calorie Sweetener, granular form
1 cup cholesterol-free egg substitute
½ cup nonfat evaporated milk
2 teaspoons almond extract
¼ teaspoon salt
1 can (8 ounces) crushed pineapple in its own juice, drained

1. Preheat oven to 325°F. Line mini muffin baking pans with cupcake liners. Place cherry half in bottom of each cup.

2. Place crumbs in medium bowl. While briskly stirring crumbs with fork, drizzle in oil a little at a time, stirring until mixture resembles coarse crumbs.

3. In large bowl, beat cream cheese with mixer at high speed until smooth. Add SPLENDA®, egg substitute, milk, almond extract and salt. Beat until smooth. Chop remaining cherries; stir into filling with pineapple. Spoon filling into each muffin cup, covering cherries. Sprinkle each cup with crust mixture. Press crust lightly into filling.

4. Place pan on baking sheet. Bake 15 to 20 minutes or until filling puffs and begins to crack. Cool on wire rack. Refrigerate 4 to 6 hours or overnight before serving. To serve, peel away cupcake liners and invert gems cherry-side up onto serving plate.

Makes 16 servings (about 48 bite-sized gems)

Nutrients per Serving: 3 Gems

Calories: 160, Calories from Fat: 30%, Total Fat: 5g, Saturated Fat: 2g, Cholesterol: 9mg, Sodium: 364mg, Carbohydrate: 19g, Dietary Fiber: <1g, Protein: 8g

Dietary Exchanges: 1 Starch

Lemon Poppy Seed Cake

Berry Bundt Cake

2 cups all-purpose flour
1 tablespoon baking powder
1 teaspoon baking soda
¼ teaspoon salt
1 cup sugar
¾ cup buttermilk
½ cup cholesterol-free egg substitute
¼ cup vegetable oil
2 cups frozen unsweetened raspberries
2 cups frozen unsweetened blueberries

1. Preheat oven to 350°F. Spray 6-cup Bundt pan with nonstick cooking spray; set aside.

2. Combine flour, baking powder, baking soda and salt in large bowl. Combine sugar, buttermilk, egg substitute and oil in medium bowl. Add sugar mixture to flour mixture; stir just until moistened.

3. Fold in raspberries and blueberries. Pour batter into prepared pan. Bake 1 hour or until toothpick inserted into center comes out clean. Cool in pan on wire rack. Serve with fresh berries, if desired.   *Makes 12 servings*

Nutrients per Serving: 1 Cake slice (¹⁄₁₂ of total recipe) without additional fresh berries

Calories: 215, Calories from Fat: 21%, Total Fat: 5g, Saturated Fat: 1g, Cholesterol: 1mg, Sodium: 262mg, Carbohydrate: 39g, Dietary Fiber: 2g, Protein: 4g
Dietary Exchanges: 2 Starch, ½ Fruit, 1 Fat

Berry Bundt Cake

Farmhouse Lemon Meringue Pie

1 frozen reduced-fat pie crust
4 eggs, at room temperature
3 tablespoons lemon juice
2 tablespoons reduced-fat margarine
2 teaspoons grated lemon peel
3 drops yellow food coloring (optional)
1 cup cold water
⅔ cup sugar, divided
¼ cup cornstarch
⅛ teaspoon salt
¼ teaspoon vanilla

1. Preheat oven to 425°F. Bake pie crust according to package directions. Cool on wire rack.

2. Separate eggs, discarding 2 egg yolks; set aside. Mix lemon juice, margarine, lemon peel and food coloring, if desired, in small bowl; set aside.

3. Combine water, all but 2 tablespoons sugar, cornstarch and salt in medium saucepan; whisk until smooth. Heat over medium-high heat, whisking constantly, until mixture begins to boil. Reduce heat to medium. Continue to boil 1 minute, stirring constantly; remove from heat.

4. Stir ¼ cup boiling sugar mixture into egg yolks; whisk constantly until completely blended. Slowly whisk egg yolk mixture back into boiling sugar mixture. Cook over medium heat 3 minutes, whisking constantly. Remove from heat; stir in lemon juice mixture until well blended. Pour into baked pie crust.

5. Beat egg whites in large bowl with electric mixer at high speed until soft peaks form. Gradually beat in remaining 2 tablespoons sugar and vanilla; beat until stiff peaks form. Spread meringue over pie filling with rubber spatula, making sure meringue completely covers filling and touches edge of pie crust.

6. Bake 15 minutes. Remove from oven; cool completely on wire rack. Cover with plastic wrap; refrigerate 8 hours or overnight until setting is firm and pie is chilled thoroughly. Garnish as desired.   *Makes 10 servings*

Nutrients per Serving: 1 Pie slice (¹⁄₁₀ of total recipe) without garnish

Calories: 209, Calories from Fat: 41%, Total Fat: 10g, Saturated Fat: 2g, Cholesterol: 88mg, Sodium: 182mg, Carbohydrate: 27g, Dietary Fiber: 1g, Protein: 4g
Dietary Exchanges: 2 Starch, 2 Fat

Mixed Berry Cheesecake

Crust

1½ cups fruit-juice-sweetened breakfast cereal flakes*

15 sugar-free low-fat butter-flavored cookies*

1 tablespoon vegetable oil

Cheesecake

2 packages (8 ounces each) fat-free cream cheese, softened

2 cartons (8 ounces each) raspberry nonfat yogurt

1 package (8 ounces) Neufchâtel cream cheese, softened

½ cup no-sugar-added seedless blackberry preserves

½ cup no-sugar-added blueberry preserves

6 packages sugar substitute *or* equivalent of ¼ cup sugar

1 tablespoon vanilla

¼ cup water

1 package (4-serving-size) sugar-free strawberry-flavored gelatin

Topping

3 cups fresh or frozen unsweetened mixed berries, thawed

*Available in the health food section of supermarkets.

1. Preheat oven to 400°F. Spray 10-inch springform pan with nonstick cooking spray.

2. To prepare crust, combine cereal, cookies and oil in food processor; process with on/off pulses until finely crushed. Press firmly onto bottom and ½ inch up side of pan. Bake 5 to 8 minutes or until crust is golden brown.

3. To prepare cheesecake, combine cream cheese, yogurt, Neufchâtel cheese, preserves, sugar substitute and vanilla in large bowl. Beat with electric mixer at high speed until smooth.

4. Combine water and gelatin in small microwavable bowl; microwave at HIGH 30 seconds to 1 minute or until water is boiling and gelatin is dissolved. Cool slightly. Add to cheese mixture; beat an additional 2 to 3 minutes or until well blended. Pour into prepared pan; cover and refrigerate at least 24 hours. Top cheesecake with berries before serving. *Makes 16 servings*

Nutrients per Serving: 1 Cheesecake slice with 3 tablespoons berries for topping (1/16 of total recipe)

Calories: 186, Calories from Fat: 24%, Total Fat: 5g, Saturated Fat: 2g, Cholesterol: 11mg, Sodium: 290mg, Carbohydrate: 26g, Dietary Fiber: 2g, Protein: 8g

Dietary Exchanges: ½ Starch, 1½ Fruit, 1 Lean Meat, ½ Fat

Blackberry Custard Pie

Pie Crust (recipe follows)

½ cup sugar

3 tablespoons cornstarch

1¼ cups low-fat (1%) milk

1 tablespoon lemon juice

2 teaspoons grated lemon peel

2 eggs, lightly beaten

1 pint blackberries

1. Preheat oven to 425°F. Prepare Pie Crust. Pierce crust with fork at ¼-inch intervals, about 40 times. Cut square of foil about 4 inches larger than pie plate. Line crust with foil; fill with dried beans, uncooked rice or ceramic pie weights. Bake 10 minutes or until set. Remove crust from oven; gently remove foil lining and beans. Return crust to oven; bake 5 minutes more or until crust is light brown. Cool completely on wire rack.

2. Combine sugar and cornstarch in small saucepan. Stir in milk, lemon juice and lemon peel; cook and stir over medium heat until mixture boils and thickens. Boil 1 minute, stirring constantly.

3. Stir about ½ cup hot milk mixture into eggs; stir egg mixture back into saucepan. Cook over low heat until thickened; stir constantly. Spoon hot custard into crust. Cool to room temperature; refrigerate 3 hours or until set. Arrange berries evenly over top. *Makes 8 servings*

Pie Crust

1¼ cups all-purpose flour

¼ teaspoon baking powder

Dash salt

¼ cup canola or vegetable oil

3 tablespoons fat-free (skim) milk, divided

1. Combine flour, baking powder and salt in medium bowl. Add oil and 2 tablespoons milk; mix well. Add enough remaining milk to hold mixture together. Shape dough into a ball.

2. Flatten dough to 1-inch thickness on 12-inch square of waxed paper; cover with second square of waxed paper. Roll out gently to form 12-inch round crust. Mend any tears or ragged edges by pressing together with fingers. *Do not moisten.* Remove 1 layer of waxed paper from crust. Place dough, paper side up, in 9-inch pie pan. Carefully peel off remaining paper. Press pastry gently into pan and flute edge.

Nutrients per Serving: 1 Pie slice (1/8 of total recipe)

Calories: 245, Calories from Fat: 32%, Total Fat: 9g, Saturated Fat: 1g, Cholesterol: 55mg, Sodium: 54mg, Carbohydrate: 37g, Dietary Fiber: 3g, Protein: 5g

Dietary Exchanges: 2 Starch, ½ Fruit, 1½ Fat

Cranberry Apple Pie with Soft Gingersnap Crust

20 gingersnaps
1½ tablespoons margarine
2 McIntosh apples
1 cup fresh cranberries
5 tablespoons packed dark brown sugar
¼ teaspoon ground cinnamon
¼ teaspoon vanilla
1 teaspoon granulated sugar

Preheat oven to 375°F. Combine gingersnaps and margarine in food processor; process until well combined. Press gingersnap mixture into 8-inch pie plate. Press on crust with slightly smaller pie plate to make crust even. Bake 5 to 8 minutes; remove crust from oven and let cool. Slice apples in food processor. Add cranberries, brown sugar, cinnamon and vanilla; stir just until mixed. Spoon mixture into separate pie plate or casserole dish; sprinkle with granulated sugar. Bake 35 minutes or until tender. Spoon over gingersnap crust and serve immediately.

Makes 8 servings

Favorite recipe from *The Sugar Association, Inc.*

Nutrients per Serving: 1 Pie slice (⅛ of total recipe)

Calories: 154, Calories from Fat: 23%, Total Fat: 4g, Saturated Fat: 1g, Cholesterol: 0mg, Sodium: 143mg, Carbohydrate: 29g, Dietary Fiber: 2g, Protein: 1g
Dietary Exchanges: 1 Starch, 1 Fruit, ½ Fat

Marbled Angel Cake

1 package (16 ounces) angel food cake mix
¼ cup HERSHEY'S Cocoa
Chocolate Glaze (recipe follows)

1. Place oven rack in lowest position. Heat oven to 375°F. Prepare cake batter as directed on package. Transfer 4 cups batter to medium bowl; gradually fold in cocoa until well blended, being careful not to deflate batter. Alternately pour vanilla and chocolate batters into ungreased 10-inch tube pan. With knife or metal spatula, cut through batters for marble effect.

2. Bake 30 to 35 minutes or until top crust is firm and looks very dry. *Do not underbake.* Invert pan on heatproof funnel or bottle; cool completely, at least 1½ hours. Carefully run knife along side of pan to loosen cake; remove from pan. Place on serving plate; drizzle with Chocolate Glaze. Let stand until set. Store, covered, at room temperature.

Makes 16 servings

Chocolate Glaze: Combine ⅓ cup sugar and ¼ cup water in small saucepan. Cook over medium heat, stirring constantly, until mixture comes to a boil. Stir until sugar dissolves; remove from heat. Immediately add 1 cup HERSHEY'S MINI CHIPS® Semi-Sweet Chocolate Chips; stir until chips are melted and mixture is smooth. Cool to desired consistency; use immediately.

About ⅔ cup glaze

Nutrients per Serving: 1 Cake slice (1/16 of total recipe)

Calories: 180, Calories from Fat: 19%, Total Fat: 4g, Saturated Fat: 3g, Cholesterol: 0mg, Sodium: 214mg, Carbohydrate: 33g, Dietary Fiber: <1g, Protein: 3g
Dietary Exchanges: 2 Starch, 1 Fat

Cranberry Apple Pie with Soft Gingersnap Crust

Boston Babies

1 package (18¼ ounces) yellow cake mix
3 eggs *or* ¾ cup cholesterol-free egg substitute
⅓ cup unsweetened applesauce
1 package (4-serving-size) sugar-free vanilla
    pudding and pie filling mix
2 cups low-fat (1%) milk *or* fat-free (skim) milk
⅓ cup sugar
⅓ cup unsweetened cocoa powder
1 tablespoon cornstarch
1½ cups water
1½ teaspoons vanilla

1. Line 24 (2½-inch) muffin cups with paper liners; set aside.

2. Prepare cake mix according to lower fat package directions, using 3 eggs and applesauce. Pour batter into prepared muffin cups. Bake according to package directions; cool completely. Freeze 12 cupcakes for another use.

3. Prepare pudding according to package directions, using 2 cups milk; cover and refrigerate.

4. Combine sugar, cocoa, cornstarch and water in large microwavable bowl; whisk until smooth. Microwave at HIGH 4 to 6 minutes, stirring every 2 minutes, until slightly thickened. Stir in vanilla.

5. To serve, drizzle 2 tablespoons chocolate glaze over each dessert plate. Cut cupcakes in half; place 2 halves on top of chocolate on each dessert plate. Top each with about 2 heaping tablespoonfuls pudding. Garnish, if desired. Serve immediately. *Makes 12 servings*
(1 cupcake each)

Nutrients per Serving: 1 Boston Baby with about 2 tablespoons pudding (without garnish)

Calories: 158, Calories from Fat: 22%, Total Fat: 4g,
Saturated Fat: 1g, Cholesterol: 29mg, Sodium: 175mg,
Carbohydrate: 28g, Dietary Fiber: <1g, Protein: 3g

Dietary Exchanges: 2 Starch, ½ Fat

Boston Baby

Key Lime Tarts

¾ cup fat-free (skim) milk
6 tablespoons fresh lime juice
2 tablespoons cornstarch
½ cup cholesterol-free egg substitute
½ cup reduced-fat sour cream
12 packages sugar substitute *or* equivalent of
    ½ cup sugar
4 sheets phyllo dough*
    Butter-flavored nonstick cooking spray
¾ cup thawed frozen fat-free nondairy whipped
    topping

Cover with damp kitchen towel to prevent dough from drying out.

1. Combine milk, lime juice and cornstarch in medium saucepan. Cook over medium heat 2 to 3 minutes, stirring constantly until thickened. Remove from heat.

2. Add egg substitute; whisk constantly for 30 seconds to allow egg substitute to cook. Stir in sour cream and sugar substitute; cover and refrigerate until cool.

3. Preheat oven to 350°F. Spray 8 (2½-inch) muffin cups with cooking spray; set aside.

4. Place 1 sheet of phyllo dough on cutting board; lightly spray with cooking spray. Top with 3 more sheets of phyllo dough, lightly spraying each sheet with cooking spray.

5. Cut stack of phyllo dough into 8 squares. Gently fit each stacked square into prepared muffin cup; press firmly against bottom and side. Bake 8 to 10 minutes or until golden brown. Carefully remove from muffin cups; cool on wire rack.

6. Divide lime mixture evenly among phyllo cups; top with whipped topping. Garnish, if desired.

Makes 8 servings

Nutrients per Serving: 1 Tart (without garnish)

Calories: 82, Calories from Fat: 17%, Total Fat: 1g,
Saturated Fat: <1g, Cholesterol: 5mg, Sodium: 88mg,
Carbohydrate: 13g, Dietary Fiber: <1g, Protein: 3g

Dietary Exchanges: 1 Starch

Pineapple Upside-Down Cake

6. Bake 35 to 40 minutes or until lightly browned. Cool on wire rack 10 minutes. Invert cake onto serving plate. Serve warm or cool completely. Cut into 12 pieces.

Makes 12 servings

Nutrients per Serving: 1 Cake piece (¹⁄₁₂ of total recipe)

Calories: 200, Calories from Fat: 11%, Total Fat: 2g, Saturated Fat: 1g, Cholesterol: 18mg, Sodium: 339mg, Carbohydrate: 42g, Dietary Fiber: 1g, Protein: 3g

Dietary Exchanges: 2½ Starch, ½ Fat

Pear-Ginger Upside-Down Cake

2 unpeeled Bosc or Anjou pears, cored and
   sliced ¼-inch thick
3 tablespoons fresh lemon juice
1 to 2 tablespoons melted butter
1 to 2 tablespoons packed brown sugar
1 cup all-purpose flour
1 teaspoon baking powder
1 teaspoon ground cinnamon
¼ teaspoon baking soda
⅛ teaspoon salt
⅓ cup fat-free (skim) milk
3 tablespoons no-sugar-added apricot spread
1 egg
1 tablespoon vegetable oil
1 tablespoon minced fresh ginger

1. Preheat oven to 375°F. Spray 10-inch deep-dish pie pan with nonstick cooking spray; set aside.

2. Toss pears in lemon juice; drain. Brush butter evenly onto bottom of prepared pan; sprinkle sugar over butter. Arrange pears in dish; bake 10 minutes.

3. Meanwhile, combine flour, baking powder, cinnamon, baking soda and salt in small bowl; set aside. Combine milk, apricot spread, egg, oil and ginger in medium bowl; mix well. Add flour mixture; stir until well mixed (batter is very thick). Carefully spread batter evenly over pears to edge of pan. Bake 20 to 25 minutes or until golden brown and toothpick inserted into center comes out clean.

4. Cool 5 minutes; use knife to loosen cake from side of pan. Place 10-inch plate over top of pan; quickly turn over to transfer cake to plate. Place any pears left in pan on top of cake. Serve warm. *Makes 8 servings*

Nutrients per Serving: 1 Cake slice (⅛ of total recipe)

Calories: 139, Calories from Fat: 27%, Total Fat: 4g, Saturated Fat: 1g, Cholesterol: 31mg, Sodium: 174mg, Carbohydrate: 23g, Dietary Fiber: 2g, Protein: 3g

Dietary Exchanges: 1½ Starch, ½ Fat

Pineapple Upside-Down Cake

1 (8-ounce) can crushed pineapple in juice,
   undrained
2 tablespoons margarine, melted, divided
½ cup firmly packed light brown sugar
6 whole maraschino cherries
1½ cups all-purpose flour
2 tablespoons baking powder
¼ teaspoon salt
1 cup granulated sugar
½ cup MOTT'S® Natural Apple Sauce
1 whole egg
3 egg whites, beaten until stiff

1. Preheat oven to 375°F. Drain pineapple; reserve juice. Spray sides of 8-inch square baking pan with nonstick cooking spray.

2. Spread 1 tablespoon melted margarine evenly in bottom of prepared pan. Sprinkle with brown sugar; top with pineapple. Slice cherries in half. Arrange cherries, cut sides up, so that when cake is cut, each piece will have cherry half in center.

3. In small bowl, combine flour, baking powder and salt.

4. In large bowl, combine granulated sugar, apple sauce, whole egg, remaining 1 tablespoon melted margarine and reserved pineapple juice.

5. Add flour mixture to apple sauce mixture; stir until well blended. Fold in egg whites. Gently pour batter over fruit, spreading evenly.

Luscious Chocolate Cheesecake

    2 cups (1 pound) nonfat cottage cheese
    ¾ cup liquid egg substitute
    ⅔ cup sugar
    4 ounces (½ of 8-ounce package) Neufchâtel
        cheese (⅓ less fat cream cheese), softened
    ⅓ cup HERSHEY'S Cocoa or HERSHEY'S Dutch
        Processed Cocoa
    ½ teaspoon vanilla extract
        Yogurt Topping (recipe follows)
        Sliced strawberries or mandarin orange
        segments (optional)

1. Heat oven to 300°F. Spray 9-inch springform pan with vegetable cooking spray.

2. Place cottage cheese, egg substitute, sugar, Neufchâtel cheese, cocoa and vanilla in food processor; process until smooth. Pour into prepared pan.

3. Bake 35 minutes or until edges are set.

4. Meanwhile, prepare Yogurt Topping. Carefully spread topping over cheesecake. Continue baking 5 minutes. Remove from oven to wire rack. With knife, loosen cheesecake from side of pan. Cool completely.

5. Cover; refrigerate until chilled. Remove side of pan. Serve with strawberries or mandarin orange segments, if desired. Refrigerate leftover cheesecake.

Makes 12 servings

Luscious Chocolate Cheesecake

Yogurt Topping

    ⅔ cup plain nonfat yogurt
    2 tablespoons sugar

1. Stir together yogurt and sugar in small bowl until well blended.

Nutrients per Serving: 1 Cheesecake slice (¹⁄₁₂ of total recipe) without strawberries and mandarin orange segments

Calories: 84, Calories from Fat: 27%, Total Fat: 2g, Saturated Fat: 1g, Cholesterol: 7mg, Sodium: 199mg, Carbohydrate: 6g, Dietary Fiber: <1g, Protein: 8g
Dietary Exchanges: ½ Starch, 1 Lean Meat

Reduced Fat Double Layered Chocolate Pie

    1½ cups plus 1 tablespoon cold skim milk,
        divided
    2 (4-serving-size) packages chocolate flavor
        instant pudding & pie filling
    1 (6-ounce) READY CRUST® Graham Cracker
        Pie Crust
    4 ounces reduced-fat cream cheese, softened
    1 tablespoon sugar
    1½ cups thawed frozen light whipped topping
    2 teaspoons grated semi-sweet or milk
        chocolate candy bar (optional)

1. Pour 1½ cups milk into medium bowl; add pudding mixes. Beat with electric mixer at medium speed 1 minute. (Mixture will be very thick.) Spread mixture evenly into crust.

2. Beat cream cheese, sugar and remaining 1 tablespoon milk on medium speed until smooth. Fold in whipped topping. Spread cream cheese mixture over chocolate mixture. Sprinkle with chocolate, if desired.

3. Chill at least 3 hours before serving. Refrigerate leftovers.   *Makes 8 servings*

Preparation Time: 15 minutes
Chilling Time: 3 hours

Nutrients per Serving: 1 Pie slice (⅛ of total recipe) without sprinkled chocolate

Calories: 284, Calories from Fat: 30%, Total Fat: 9g, Saturated Fat: 4g, Cholesterol: 8mg, Sodium: 315mg, Carbohydrate: 44g, Dietary Fiber: 1g, Protein: 5g
Dietary Exchanges: 3 Starch, 1½ Fat

Chocolate Roulade with Creamy Yogurt Filling

- 1 container (8 ounces) plain lowfat yogurt, no gelatin added
- 3 egg whites
- ½ cup granulated sugar, divided
- 1 container (8 ounces) liquid egg substitute
- ½ cup cake flour
- ¼ cup HERSHEY'S Cocoa
- 1 teaspoon baking powder
- ⅛ teaspoon salt
- 2 tablespoons water
- 1 teaspoon vanilla extract
- 2 teaspoons powdered sugar
  Creamy Yogurt Filling (recipe follows)
  Peach Sauce (recipe follows)

1. Prepare yogurt cheese about 24 hours before needed for use in Creamy Yogurt Filling. Line non-rusting colander or sieve with large piece of double thickness cheesecloth or large coffee filter; place colander over deep bowl. Spoon yogurt into prepared colander; cover with plastic wrap. Refrigerate until liquid no longer drains from yogurt, about 24 hours. Remove yogurt cheese from cheesecloth; discard liquid.

2. Heat oven to 375°F. Line 15½×10½×1-inch jelly-roll pan with foil; spray with vegetable cooking spray.

3. Beat egg whites in large bowl on medium speed of mixer until foamy; gradually add ¼ cup granulated sugar, beating on high speed until stiff peaks form. Beat egg substitute in small bowl on medium speed until foamy; gradually add remaining ¼ cup granulated sugar, beating until mixture is thick. Fold egg substitute mixture into egg white mixture.

4. Stir together flour, cocoa, baking powder and salt; gently fold into egg mixture alternately with water and vanilla. Spread batter evenly into prepared pan.

5. Bake 10 to 12 minutes or until top springs back when touched lightly in center. Immediately invert onto clean, lint-free dishtowel sprinkled with powdered sugar; peel off foil. Starting at narrow end, roll up cake and towel together. Cool completely on wire rack.

6. Prepare Creamy Yogurt Filling. Unroll cake; remove towel. Spread with Creamy Yogurt Filling to within ½ inch of edges of cake. Reroll cake; place, seam-side down, on serving plate. Cover; refrigerate 2 to 3 hours or until chilled. Prepare Peach Sauce. Garnish as desired.

Makes 10 servings

Creamy Yogurt Filling

- 1 envelope (1.3 ounces) dry whipped topping mix
- ⅓ cup cold nonfat milk
- 1 teaspoon vanilla extract
- ⅛ to ¼ teaspoon almond extract
  Yogurt cheese

1. Place topping mix in small, deep bowl with narrow bottom. Add milk, vanilla and almond extract; beat on high speed of mixer until stiff peaks form. Fold yogurt cheese into whipped topping.

Makes about 1⅓ cups filling

Peach Sauce

- 1½ cups fresh peach slices
- 1 tablespoon sugar
- ¼ cup water
- 1½ teaspoon cornstarch

1. Place peach slices and sugar in blender container. Cover; blend until smooth.

2. Combine water and cornstarch in medium microwave-safe bowl, stirring until smooth. Add peach mixture; stir. Microwave at HIGH (100%) 2½ minutes or until mixture boils and thickens, stirring after each minute. Cool completely.

Makes 1½ cups

Nutrients per Serving: 1 Cake slice with about 2½ tablespoons Peach Sauce (without garnish)

Calories: 155, Calories from Fat: 10%, Total Fat: 2g, Saturated Fat: 1g, Cholesterol: 3mg, Sodium: 167mg, Carbohydrate: 29g, Dietary Fiber: 2g, Protein: 7g

Dietary Exchanges: 2 Starch

T I P This cake is best when eaten the same day it is prepared.

MORE SWEETS

Brownies

½ cup boiling water
½ cup unsweetened cocoa powder
1¼ cups all-purpose flour
¾ cup granulated sugar
¾ cup packed light brown sugar
4 egg whites, lightly beaten
⅓ cup vegetable oil
1½ teaspoons vanilla
1 teaspoon baking powder
¼ teaspoon salt
½ cup chopped unsalted mixed nuts (optional)

1. Preheat oven to 350°F.

2. Spray 13×9-inch baking pan with nonstick cooking spray. Combine boiling water and cocoa in large bowl. Mix until completely dissolved. Add flour, granulated sugar, brown sugar, egg whites, oil, vanilla, baking powder and salt; mix well. Fold in chopped nuts, if desired.

3. Pour mixture into prepared pan. Bake 25 minutes or until brownies spring back when lightly touched. Do not overbake. Cool in pan on wire rack; cut into 32 squares.

Makes 32 brownies

Nutrients per Serving: 1 Brownie

Calories: 81, Calories from Fat: 26%, Total Fat: 2g, Saturated Fat: <1g, Cholesterol: 0mg, Sodium: 37mg, Carbohydrate: 14g, Dietary Fiber: 0g, Protein: 1g

Dietary Exchanges: 1 Starch, ½ Fat

Oatmeal-Molasses Cookies

1 cup whole wheat flour
1 cup all-purpose flour
1 teaspoon baking soda
1 teaspoon ground cinnamon
½ teaspoon salt
½ teaspoon ground ginger
½ cup cholesterol-free egg substitute
½ cup granulated sugar
¼ cup packed light brown sugar
¼ cup (½ stick) margarine or butter
¼ cup mild-flavored molasses
1 cup uncooked quick oats
½ cup raisins

1. Preheat oven to 350°F. Lightly coat cookie sheet with nonstick cooking spray; set aside.

2. Combine whole wheat flour, all-purpose flour, baking soda, cinnamon, salt and ginger in medium bowl; set aside.

3. Combine egg substitute, sugars, margarine and molasses in large bowl with electric mixer at high speed until well blended. Add flour mixture. Stir in oats and raisins. Drop dough by teaspoonfuls onto prepared cookie sheet.

4. Bake 10 minutes or until firm to touch. Remove to wire rack and cool completely. *Makes 3 dozen cookies*

Nutrients per Serving: 1 Cookie

Calories: 71, Calories from Fat: 18%, Total Fat: 2g, Saturated Fat: <1g, Cholesterol: 0mg, Sodium: 90mg, Carbohydrate: 13g, Dietary Fiber: 1g, Protein: 2g

Dietary Exchanges: 1 Starch

Cranberry Biscotti

2¼ cups GOLD MEDAL® all-purpose flour
¾ cup sugar
1 teaspoon baking powder
1 teaspoon ground cinnamon
½ teaspoon baking soda
2 eggs
2 egg whites
1½ teaspoons almond extract
1 cup FIBER ONE® cereal
½ cup dried cranberries

1. Heat oven to 350°F. Spray cookie sheet with nonstick cooking spray.

2. Stir together flour, sugar, baking powder, cinnamon and baking soda in large bowl. Beat eggs, egg whites and almond extract with wire whisk until foamy. Stir egg mixture into flour mixture until well blended. Work in cereal and cranberries with hands. Place dough on floured surface. Knead lightly 8 to 10 times. Shape into 1 (16-inch roll) or 2 (8-inch rolls). Place on cookie sheet. Flatten to about 1 inch thick.

3. Bake 30 minutes. Remove from cookie sheet; cool on wire rack 10 minutes. Cut into ½-inch-thick slices. *Reduce oven temperature to 300°F.* Stand slices upright on cookie sheet; bake about 20 minutes longer or until crisp and light brown. Cool completely on wire rack.

Makes 32 cookies

Prep Time: 20 minutes
Bake Time: 50 minutes

Nutrients per Serving: 1 Cookie

Calories: 67, Calories from Fat: 5%, Total Fat: <1g, Saturated Fat: <1g, Cholesterol: 13mg, Sodium: 51mg, Carbohydrate: 15g, Dietary Fiber: 1g, Protein: 2g

Dietary Exchanges: 1 Starch

Custard Brûlée

3 cups fat-free (skim) milk
3 eggs
4 egg whites
½ cup granulated sugar
1 teaspoon vanilla
1 teaspoon ground cinnamon
Ground nutmeg (optional)
¼ cup packed light brown sugar

1. Preheat oven to 350°F. Heat milk in 1-quart saucepan over low heat until hot; do not boil.

2. Beat eggs, egg whites and sugar in medium bowl with electric mixer at medium speed 5 minutes or until slightly thickened. Gradually beat in milk and vanilla. Pour milk mixture into 1½-quart soufflé dish or casserole; sprinkle lightly with cinnamon and nutmeg, if desired. Place soufflé dish in roasting pan and place on oven rack; pour 2 inches hot water into roasting pan.

3. Bake, covered, 40 to 50 minutes or until knife inserted halfway between center and edge of custard comes out clean. Cool to room temperature on wire rack. Cover; refrigerate 3 to 4 hours or until chilled.

4. When ready to serve, press brown sugar through a sieve over custard. Broil 4 inches from heat 2 to 3 minutes or until sugar is melted and caramelized. Serve immediately.

Makes 8 servings

Nutrients per Serving: ⅛ of total recipe

Calories: 146, Calories from Fat: 13%, Total Fat: 2g, Saturated Fat: 1g, Cholesterol: 81mg, Sodium: 101mg, Carbohydrate: 24g, Dietary Fiber: 0g, Protein: 7g

Dietary Exchanges: 1½ Starch, ½ Lean Meat

Cranberry Biscotti

Berries with Orange Scones

1¼ cups all-purpose flour
2 teaspoons sugar
1½ teaspoons baking powder
¼ teaspoon salt
1 ounce cold reduced-fat cream cheese, cut into 6 pieces
1 tablespoon cold butter, cut into 6 pieces
1 egg
¼ cup low-fat (1%) milk
1 tablespoon plus 1 teaspoon finely grated orange peel
1½ cups fresh strawberries, sliced, divided
1⅓ cups fresh blueberries, divided
2 packets sugar substitute or equivalent of 4 teaspoons sugar
1 tablespoon orange liqueur (optional)
1½ cups sugar-free vanilla ice cream (optional)

1. Preheat oven to 425°F. Spray medium baking sheet with nonstick cooking spray.

2. Combine flour, sugar, baking powder and salt in medium bowl; mix well. Using pastry blender or two knives, cut cream cheese and butter into flour mixture until mixture resembles coarse crumbs. Set aside.

3. Beat egg, milk and orange peel in small bowl. Pour all at once into flour mixture; stir until just moistened. Gather dough into a ball; place on lightly floured board.

4. If dough is sticky, sprinkle with a little additional flour; knead 13 times. Press dough into 8×3-inch rectangle, about ½ inch thick. Cut into 3 squares; cut squares in half to make 6 triangles. Place 1 inch apart on prepared baking sheet. Bake about 12 to 14 minutes or until lightly browned and set.

5. Meanwhile, purée ½ cup strawberries and ⅓ cup blueberries. Add remaining berries, sugar substitute and liqueur, if desired; toss to coat. Let stand 15 minutes.

6. Slice scones in half horizontally. Place 2 scone halves on each plate; top with about ⅓ cup berry sauce and ¼ cup ice cream, if desired. Serve immediately.

Makes 6 servings

Nutrients per Serving: 2 Scones with about ⅓ cup Berry sauce (without ice cream)

Calories: 177, Calories from Fat: 21%, Total Fat: 4g,
Saturated Fat: 2g, Cholesterol: 43mg, Sodium: 280mg,
Carbohydrate: 30g, Dietary Fiber: 3g, Protein: 5g

Dietary Exchanges: 1 Starch, 1 Fruit, 1 Fat

Fruitful Frozen Yogurt

1 envelope unflavored gelatin
¼ cup cold water
1½ cups puréed fresh fruit
1 carton (16 ounces) vanilla low-fat yogurt
¼ to ½ cup sugar

1. Sprinkle gelatin over cold water in small saucepan; let stand 5 minutes to soften. Stir over low heat until gelatin dissolves. Remove from heat. Stir in fruit purée, yogurt and sugar to taste. Pour into 9-inch square pan; freeze until almost firm.

2. Coarsely chop mixture; spoon into chilled bowl. Beat with electric mixer until smooth. Cover; store in freezer.

Makes 5 servings

Favorite recipe from *Wisconsin Milk Marketing Board*

Nutrients per Serving: ⅕ of total recipe (made with ¼ cup sugar)

Calories: 185, Calories from Fat: 8%, Total Fat: 2g,
Saturated Fat: 1g, Cholesterol: 5mg, Sodium: 71mg,
Carbohydrate: 38g, Dietary Fiber: 2g, Protein: 6g

Dietary Exchanges: 1½ Fruit, 1 Milk

TIP Dark fruits such as strawberries, raspberries and cherries make this Fruitful Frozen Yogurt as pleasing to the eye as it is to the palate.

Chocolate Mousse

½ cup plus 2 tablespoons sugar, divided
¼ cup unsweetened cocoa powder
1 envelope unflavored gelatin
2 tablespoons coffee-flavored liqueur
2 cups fat-free (skim) milk
¼ cup cholesterol-free egg substitute
2 egg whites
⅛ teaspoon cream of tartar
½ cup thawed frozen reduced-fat nondairy
   whipped topping

1. Combine ½ cup sugar, cocoa and gelatin in medium saucepan. Add coffee-flavored liqueur; let stand 2 minutes. Add milk; heat over medium heat. Stir until sugar and gelatin are dissolved. Stir in egg substitute. Set aside.

2. Beat egg whites in medium bowl with electric mixer until foamy; add cream of tartar. Beat until soft peaks form. Gradually beat in remaining 2 tablespoons sugar; continue beating until stiff peaks form.

3. Gently fold egg whites into cocoa mixture. Fold in whipped topping. Divide evenly between 8 dessert dishes. Refrigerate until thickened. Garnish as desired.

Makes 8 servings

Chocolate Mousse

Nutrients per Serving: 1 dessert dish of Mousse (⅛ of total recipe) without garnish

Calories: 125, Calories from Fat: 6%, Total Fat: 1g, Saturated Fat: 1g, Cholesterol: 1mg, Sodium: 60mg, Carbohydrate: 23g, Dietary Fiber: <1g, Protein: 5g

Dietary Exchanges: 1½ Starch

Lemon Mousse Squares

1 cup graham cracker crumbs
2 tablespoons reduced-fat margarine, melted
1 packet sugar substitute *or* equivalent of
   2 teaspoons sugar
⅓ cup cold water
1 packet unflavored gelatin
2 eggs, well beaten
½ cup lemon juice
¼ cup sugar
2 teaspoon grated lemon peel
2 cups thawed frozen fat-free nondairy whipped
   topping
1 container (8 ounces) lemon-flavored nonfat
   yogurt with aspartame sweetener

1. Spray 9-inch square baking pan with nonstick cooking spray. Stir together graham cracker crumbs, margarine and sugar substitute in small bowl. Press into bottom of pan with fork; set aside.

2. Combine cold water and gelatin in small microwavable bowl; let stand 2 minutes. Microwave at HIGH 40 seconds to dissolve gelatin; set aside.

3. Combine eggs, lemon juice, sugar and lemon peel in top of double boiler. Cook, stirring constantly, over boiling water, about 4 minutes or until thickened. Remove from heat; stir in gelatin mixture. Refrigerate about 25 minutes or until mixture is thoroughly cooled and begins to set.

4. Gently combine lemon-gelatin mixture, whipped topping and lemon yogurt. Pour into prepared crust. Refrigerate 1 hour or until firm. Cut into 9 squares before serving.

Makes 9 servings

Nutrients per Serving: 1 Square (⅑ of total recipe)

Calories: 154, Calories from Fat: 29%, Total Fat: 5g, Saturated Fat: 1g, Cholesterol: 47mg, Sodium: 124mg, Carbohydrate: 24g, Dietary Fiber: 1g, Protein: 3g

Dietary Exchanges: 1½ Starch, 1 Fat

Tiramisu

3 cups water
3 tablespoons honey
1 cup nonfat dry milk powder
2 tablespoons cornstarch
¼ teaspoon ground cinnamon
⅛ teaspoon salt
⅛ teaspoon ground cloves
½ cup cholesterol-free egg substitute
½ cup brewed espresso coffee
2 tablespoons orange extract
12 ladyfingers, cut in half lengthwise
¼ cup grated semisweet chocolate
Powdered sugar (optional)

1. Bring water and honey to a boil in medium saucepan over high heat. Reduce heat; simmer, uncovered, 20 minutes. Remove from heat.

2. Combine dry milk, cornstarch, cinnamon, salt and cloves in medium bowl. Slowly add milk mixture to honey mixture, stirring until smooth. Bring to a boil, stirring constantly, over medium heat. Remove from heat.

3. Pour egg substitute into small bowl. Add ½ cup hot milk mixture to egg substitute; blend well. Stir egg mixture back into remaining milk mixture in saucepan. Cook over low heat 2 minutes or until thickened. Cool 15 minutes.

4. Combine coffee with orange extract in another small bowl.

5. Arrange 6 ladyfingers in 1-quart serving bowl. Drizzle half the coffee mixture over ladyfingers. Spread half the custard over ladyfingers. Sprinkle with half the grated chocolate. Repeat layers.

6. Cover and refrigerate 2 hours. Spoon evenly into 6 individual bowls. Garnish with powdered sugar before serving, if desired. *Makes 6 servings*

Nutrients per Serving: 1 bowl Tiramisu (⅙ of total recipe) without garnish

Calories: 223, Calories from Fat: 19%, Total Fat: 5g, Saturated Fat: 2g, Cholesterol: 82mg, Sodium: 167mg, Carbohydrate: 36g, Dietary Fiber: 0g, Protein: 8g
Dietary Exchanges: 2 Starch, ½ Milk, 1 Fat

Gingerbread Muffins

1½ cups all-purpose flour
2 cups Kellogg's® Special K® cereal, crushed to 1 cup
¾ cup EQUAL® SPOONFUL *or* 18 packets Equal® Sweetener
½ cup raisins
1 tablespoon baking powder
1 teaspoon ground cinnamon
½ teaspoon ground ginger
¼ teaspoon ground cloves
¼ teaspoon baking soda
¼ teaspoon salt
1 cup low-fat buttermilk
2 egg whites
2 tablespoons vegetable oil
3 tablespoons light molasses

• Combine flour, crushed cereal, Equal®, raisins, baking powder, cinnamon, ginger, cloves, baking soda and salt in large mixing bowl.

• Stir in buttermilk, egg whites, vegetable oil and molasses just until all ingredients are moistened. Fill paper-lined 2½-inch muffin cups ⅔ full.

• Bake in preheated 400°F oven 18 to 20 minutes or until wooden pick inserted into centers comes out clean.

• Cool in pan on wire rack 2 to 3 minutes. Remove muffins from pan and serve warm or at room temperature.
Makes 12 muffins

Nutrients per Serving: 1 Muffin

Calories: 146, Calories from Fat: 16%, Total Fat: 3g, Saturated Fat: <1g, Cholesterol: 1mg, Sodium: 271mg, Carbohydrate: 27g, Dietary Fiber: 1g, Protein: 4g
Dietary Exchanges: 2 Starch, ½ Fat

Strawberry-Banana Granité

Nutrients per Serving: ⅕ of total recipe (without garnish)

Calories: 87, Calories from Fat: 3%, Total Fat: <1g, Saturated Fat: <1g, Cholesterol: 0mg, Sodium: 2mg, Carbohydrate: 22g, Dietary Fiber: 2g, Protein: 1g

Dietary Exchanges: 1½ Fruit

Raspberry Shortcakes

1½ cups frozen whole raspberries, divided
6 tablespoons sugar, divided
1 cup all-purpose flour
1 teaspoon baking powder
¼ teaspoon baking soda
1 tablespoon margarine
1 egg white
⅓ cup evaporated skim milk
¼ teaspoon almond extract
¾ cup low-fat cottage cheese
1 teaspoon lemon juice

Preheat oven to 450°F. Spray baking sheet with nonstick cooking spray.

Toss 1¼ cups raspberries with 2½ tablespoons sugar; set aside in refrigerator. Combine flour, 2 tablespoons sugar, baking powder and baking soda in medium bowl. Cut in margarine with pastry blender or 2 knives; set aside. Beat egg white, milk and almond extract in small bowl; add to flour mixture and mix lightly. Knead slightly on lightly floured board. Roll out to ½-inch thickness. Cut out 8 biscuits with 2½-inch biscuit cutter. Place biscuits on prepared baking sheet. Bake 10 minutes or until lightly browned on top.

Meanwhile, place cottage cheese, remaining 1½ tablespoons sugar and lemon juice in food processor or blender; process until smooth. Fold in remaining ¼ cup raspberries. To serve, split biscuits in half and place each bottom half on individual serving dish. Top each with 2 tablespoons reserved raspberries and 1 tablespoon cheese mixture. Cover with biscuit top. Spoon remaining reserved raspberries and cheese mixture over tops.

Makes 8 servings

Favorite recipe from *The Sugar Association, Inc.*

Strawberry-Banana Granité

2 ripe medium bananas, peeled and sliced (about 2 cups)
2 cups unsweetened frozen strawberries *(do not thaw)*
¼ cup no-sugar-added strawberry pourable fruit*
Whole fresh strawberries (optional)
Fresh mint leaves (optional)

*3 tablespoons no-sugar-added strawberry fruit spread combined with 1 tablespoon warm water may be substituted.

1. Place banana slices in plastic bag; freeze until firm.

2. Place frozen banana slices and frozen strawberries in food processor container. Let stand 10 minutes for fruit to soften slightly. Add pourable fruit. Remove plunger from top of food processor to allow air to be incorporated. Process until smooth, scraping down sides of container frequently. Serve immediately. Garnish with fresh strawberries and mint leaves, if desired. Freeze leftovers.

Makes 5 servings

Note: Granité may be transferred to airtight container and frozen up to 1 month. Let stand at room temperature 10 minutes to soften slightly before serving.

Nutrients per Serving: 1 Shortcake

Calories: 142, Calories from Fat: 12%, Total Fat: 2g, Saturated Fat: <1g, Cholesterol: 1mg, Sodium: 222mg, Carbohydrate: 26g, Dietary Fiber: 2g, Protein: 6g

Dietary Exchanges: 1½ Starch, ½ Fruit

Choco-Lowfat Strawberry Shortbread Bars

¼ cup (½ stick) vegetable oil spread (60% oil)
½ cup sugar
1 egg white
1¼ cups all-purpose flour
¼ cup HERSHEY'S Cocoa or HERSHEY'S Dutch Processed Cocoa
¾ teaspoon cream of tartar
½ teaspoon baking soda
Dash salt
½ cup strawberry all-fruit spread
White Chip Drizzle (recipe follows)

1. Heat oven to 375°F. Lightly spray 13×9×2-inch baking pan with vegetable cooking spray.

2. Combine corn oil spread and sugar in medium bowl; beat on medium speed of mixer until well blended. Add egg white; beat until well blended. Stir together flour, cocoa, cream of tartar, baking soda and salt; gradually add to sugar mixture, beating well. Gently press mixture onto bottom of prepared pan.

3. Bake 10 to 12 minutes or just until set. Cool completely in pan on wire rack. Spread fruit spread evenly over crust. Cut into bars or other desired shapes with cookie cutters. Prepare White Chip Drizzle; drizzle over tops of bars. Let stand until set. *Makes 3 dozen bars*

White Chip Drizzle

⅓ cup HERSHEY'S Premier White Chips
½ teaspoon shortening (do *not* use butter, margarine, spread or oil)

1. Place white chips and shortening in small microwave-safe bowl. Microwave at HIGH (100% power) 30 seconds; stir. If necessary, microwave at HIGH an additional 15 seconds at a time, stirring after each heating, just until chips are melted when stirred. Use immediately.

Nutrients per Serving: 1 Bar

Calories: 56, Calories from Fat: 25%, Total Fat: 2g, Saturated Fat: 1g, Cholesterol: <1mg, Sodium: 29mg, Carbohydrate: 9g, Dietary Fiber: <1g, Protein: 1g
Dietary Exchanges: ½ Starch, ½ Fat

Apple Clafouti

2 jars (23 ounces each) MOTT'S® Chunky Apple Sauce
⅔ cup raisins
1 teaspoon ground cinnamon
1 cup all-purpose flour
1 teaspoon baking powder
½ teaspoon salt
3 egg whites
¼ cup low fat buttermilk
¼ cup honey
Powdered sugar (optional)

1. Preheat oven to 400°F. Spray two 9-inch glass pie plates with nonstick cooking spray.

2. In large bowl, combine apple sauce, raisins and cinnamon.

3. In small bowl, combine flour, baking powder and salt.

4. In medium bowl, whisk together egg whites, buttermilk and honey until slightly frothy.

5. Add flour mixture to egg white mixture; whisk until well blended. Pour ½ cup batter into each prepared pie plate.

6. Bake 4 to 5 minutes or until lightly browned. Pour half of apple sauce mixture over each baked layer. Spoon remaining batter over apple sauce mixture; spread evenly.

7. Reduce oven temperature to 350°F. Bake 15 to 20 minutes or until tops are puffy and lightly browned.

8. Cool completely on wire racks; sprinkle tops with powdered sugar. Slice each dessert into 6 wedges. Refrigerate leftovers. *Makes 12 servings*

Nutrients per Serving: 1 wedge (¹⁄₁₂ of total recipe) without powdered sugar garnish

Calories: 140, Calories from Fat: 2%, Total Fat: <1g, Saturated Fat: <1g, Cholesterol: <1mg, Sodium: 160mg, Carbohydrate: 34g, Dietary Fiber: 2g, Protein: 3g
Dietary Exchanges: 1 Starch, 1 Fruit

TIP Fresh low-fat (1%) milk can be soured and used as a substitute for buttermilk. If a recipe calls for ¼ cup of low-fat buttermilk, place ¾ teaspoon lemon juice or distilled white vinegar in a measuring cup and add enough low-fat milk to measure ¼ cup. Stir and let the mixture stand at room temperature for 5 minutes.

Summertime Fruit Medley

2 large ripe peaches, peeled and sliced
2 large ripe nectarines, sliced
1 large mango, peeled and cut into 1-inch
    chunks
1 cup blueberries
2 cups orange juice
¼ cup amaretto *or* ½ teaspoon almond extract
2 tablespoons sugar

1. Combine peaches, nectarines, mango and blueberries in large bowl.

2. Whisk orange juice, amaretto and sugar in small bowl until sugar is dissolved. Pour over fruit mixture; toss. Marinate 1 hour at room temperature, gently stirring occasionally. Garnish with fresh mint, if desired.

Makes 8 servings

Nutrients per Serving: ⅛ of total recipe (without garnish)

Calories: 126, Calories from Fat: 3%, Total Fat: <1g,
Saturated Fat: <1g, Cholesterol: 0mg, Sodium: 2mg,
Carbohydrate: 28g, Dietary Fiber: 3g, Protein: 1g

Dietary Exchanges: 2 Fruit

Banana Cream Parfaits

1 package (4-serving-size) sugar-free vanilla
    pudding and pie filling mix
2 cups low-fat (1%) milk
1 cup coarsely crushed sugar-free cookies
2 large ripe bananas, peeled and sliced
    Mint sprigs (optional)

1. Prepare pudding according to package directions, using low-fat milk; cool 10 minutes, stirring occasionally.

2. In each of 4 parfait or wine glasses, layer 2 tablespoons cookie crumbs, ¼ cup banana slices and ¼ cup pudding. Repeat layering. Cover; chill at least 1 hour or up to 6 hours before serving. Garnish with mint sprigs, if desired.

Makes 4 servings

Variation: Sugar-free chocolate pudding and pie filling mix may be substituted for vanilla pudding.

Prep Time: 20 minutes
Cook Time: 5 minutes
Chill Time: at least 1 hour

Nutrients per Serving: 1 Parfait (without garnish)

Calories: 222, Calories from Fat: 16%, Total Fat: 4g,
Saturated Fat: 2g, Cholesterol: 5mg, Sodium: 416mg,
Carbohydrate: 40g, Dietary Fiber: 3g, Protein: 6g

Dietary Exchanges: 2½ Starch, 1 Fat

Strawberry Crêpes Suzette

12 Crêpes (recipe follows)
1 cup fresh orange juice
2 teaspoons cornstarch
2 tablespoons sugar
2 teaspoons grated orange peel
3 cups fresh strawberry slices
¼ cup orange-flavored liqueur
1 teaspoon margarine

1. Prepare crêpes. Set aside.

2. Combine orange juice and cornstarch in large saucepan. Stir until cornstarch is dissolved. Add sugar, grated orange peel and strawberries; mix well. Bring to a boil over medium heat. Reduce heat to low and simmer, stirring until slightly thickened. Remove from heat; stir in liqueur and margarine.

3. Arrange crêpes, folded in quarters, on serving dish. Spoon sauce evenly over top. Garnish as desired. Serve immediately. *Makes 12 servings*

Crêpes

1 cup fat-free (skim) milk
2 egg whites
½ cup whole wheat flour
¼ cup all-purpose flour
1 tablespoon sugar
⅛ teaspoon salt
½ tablespoon margarine

1. Combine milk, egg whites, both flours, sugar and salt in food processor or blender; process until well blended. Pour mixture into large bowl.

2. Melt margarine in nonstick crêpe or omelet pan over medium heat. Pour melted margarine into crêpe batter; mix well. Wipe pan with paper towel; save towel for later use. Heat pan over medium heat.

3. Spoon 2 tablespoons batter into hot pan; roll from side to side to cover entire pan surface. When edges of batter curl away from sides of pan, turn crêpe. Brown. Repeat with remaining batter; wipe pan with reserved paper towel between each crêpe. Keep crêpes warm in covered container until ready to use. *Makes 12 crêpes*

Nutrients per Serving: 1 Crêpe with ¹⁄₁₂ of Strawberry sauce (without garnish)

Calories: 94, Calories from Fat: 10%, Total Fat: 1g, Saturated Fat: 0g, Cholesterol: 0mg, Sodium: 52mg, Carbohydrate: 17g, Dietary Fiber: 1g, Protein: 2g
Dietary Exchanges: ½ Starch, ½ Fruit, ½ Fat

Nutty Spice Cookies

½ cup light molasses
⅓ cup sugar
¼ cup cholesterol-free egg substitute
¼ cup water
2 tablespoons canola or vegetable oil
2¼ cups all-purpose flour
1 teaspoon baking soda
1 teaspoon ground ginger
½ teaspoon ground nutmeg
½ teaspoon ground cinnamon
¼ teaspoon ground cloves
⅓ cup chopped walnuts

1. Spray cookie sheets lightly with nonstick cooking spray; set aside.

2. Stir molasses, sugar, egg substitute, water and oil in medium bowl until sugar is dissolved.

3. Sift flour, baking soda, ginger, nutmeg, cinnamon and cloves into large bowl; stir to combine. Add molasses mixture; stir with wooden spoon until smooth. (Dough will be stiff.) Refrigerate, covered, at least 2 hours or up to 2 days.

4. Preheat oven to 375°F. Roll out dough into 12-inch square on floured surface. If dough cracks, press together. Sprinkle walnuts evenly over dough, pressing nuts into dough with fingers. Cut square into 8 lengthwise strips, and then 8 crosswise strips to form 64 squares.

5. Place cookies 1 inch apart on prepared cookie sheets. Bake, 1 sheet at a time, 8 minutes or until edges begin to brown. Remove cookies to wire racks; cool completely. Store in airtight container.
Makes about 5 dozen cookies

Nutrients per Serving: 1 Cookie

Calories: 34, Calories from Fat: 20%, Total Fat: 1g, Saturated Fat: <1g, Cholesterol: 0mg, Sodium: 15mg, Carbohydrate: 6g, Dietary Fiber: <1g, Protein: 1g
Dietary Exchanges: ½ Starch

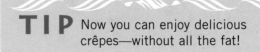

TIP Now you can enjoy delicious crêpes—without all the fat!

Peach and Blueberry Crisp

3 cups fresh or thawed frozen sliced peeled
    peaches, undrained
1 cup fresh or thawed frozen blueberries,
    undrained
2 tablespoons granulated sugar
¼ teaspoon ground nutmeg
2 tablespoons uncooked old-fashioned oats
2 tablespoons crisp rice cereal
2 tablespoons all-purpose flour
1 tablespoon packed brown sugar
1 tablespoon reduced-fat margarine, melted
⅛ teaspoon ground cinnamon

1. Preheat oven to 375°F. Combine peaches and
blueberries in ungreased 8-inch round baking pan.
Combine granulated sugar and nutmeg in small bowl.
Sprinkle over fruit; toss gently to combine.

2. Combine oats, rice cereal, flour, brown sugar, margarine
and cinnamon in small bowl. Sprinkle over fruit. Bake,
uncovered, 35 to 40 minutes or until peaches are tender
and topping is golden brown. *Makes 4 servings*

Nutrients per Serving: ¼ of total recipe

Calories: 153, Calories from Fat: 11%, Total Fat: 2g,
Saturated Fat: <1g, Cholesterol: 0mg, Sodium: 46mg,
Carbohydrate: 34g, Dietary Fiber: 3g, Protein: 2g

Dietary Exchanges: 1 Starch, 1½ Fruit

Caffè en Forchetta

2 cups reduced-fat (2%) milk
1 cup cholesterol-free egg substitute
½ cup sugar
2 tablespoons no-sugar-added mocha-flavored
    instant coffee
  Grated chocolate *or* 6 chocolate-covered
    coffee beans (optional)

1. Preheat oven to 325°F. Combine all ingredients except
grated chocolate in medium bowl. Whisk until instant
coffee has dissolved and mixture is foamy. Pour into
6 individual custard cups. Place cups in 13×9-inch baking
pan. Fill pan with hot water halfway up sides of cups.

2. Bake 55 to 60 minutes or until knife inserted halfway
between centers and edges comes out clean. Serve warm or
at room temperature. Garnish with grated chocolate or
chocolate-covered coffee bean, if desired.
Makes 6 servings

**Nutrients per Serving: 1 custard cup Caffè en
Forchetta (⅙ of total recipe)**

Calories: 111, Calories from Fat: 16%, Total Fat: 2g,
Saturated Fat: 1g, Cholesterol: 6mg, Sodium: 136mg,
Carbohydrate: 17g, Dietary Fiber: 0g, Protein: 7g

Dietary Exchanges: 1 Starch, 1 Lean Meat

Peach and Blueberry Crisp

Mocha Cookies

2 tablespoons plus 1½ teaspoons instant coffee granules
1½ tablespoons skim milk
⅓ cup packed light brown sugar
¼ cup granulated sugar
¼ cup margarine
1 egg
½ teaspoon almond extract
2 cups all-purpose flour, sifted
¼ cup wheat flakes
½ teaspoon ground cinnamon
¼ teaspoon baking powder

Preheat oven to 350°F. Spray cookie sheets with nonstick cooking spray. Dissolve coffee granules in milk. In large bowl, beat brown sugar, granulated sugar and margarine until smooth and creamy. Beat in egg, almond extract and coffee mixture. Combine flour, wheat flakes, cinnamon and baking powder; gradually beat flour mixture into sugar mixture. Drop by teaspoonfuls onto prepared cookie sheets; flatten with back of fork. Bake 8 to 10 minutes.

Makes about 40 cookies

Favorite recipe from *The Sugar Association, Inc.*

Nutrients per Serving: 1 Cookie

Calories: 47, Calories from Fat: 23%, Total Fat: 1g, Saturated Fat: <1g, Cholesterol: <1mg, Sodium: 21mg, Carbohydrate: 8g, Dietary Fiber: <1g, Protein: 1g
Dietary Exchanges: ½ Starch

Chocolate Orange Meringues

3 egg whites
½ teaspoon vanilla extract
⅛ teaspoon orange extract
¾ cup sugar
¼ cup HERSHEY'S Cocoa
½ teaspoon freshly grated orange peel

1. Heat oven to 300°F. Cover cookie sheet with parchment paper or foil.

2. Beat egg whites, vanilla and orange extract in large bowl on high speed of mixer until soft peaks form. Gradually add sugar, beating well after each addition until stiff peaks hold their shape, sugar is dissolved and mixture is glossy. Sprinkle half of cocoa and all of orange peel over egg white mixture; gently fold in just until combined. Repeat with remaining cocoa.

3. Spoon mixture into pastry bag fitted with large star tip; pipe 1½-inch-diameter stars onto prepared cookie sheet.

4. Bake 35 to 40 minutes or until dry. Cool slightly; peel paper from cookies. Cool completely on wire rack. Store, covered, at room temperature. *Makes 5 dozen cookies*

Nutrients per Serving: 3 Cookies

Calories: 35, Calories from Fat: 3%, Total Fat: <1g, Saturated Fat: 0g, Cholesterol: 0mg, Sodium: 8mg, Carbohydrate: 8g, Dietary Fiber: <1g, Protein: 1g
Dietary Exchanges: ½ Starch

Citrus Sorbet

1 can (12 ounces) DOLE® Orange Peach Mango or Tropical Fruit Frozen Juice Concentrate
1 can (8 ounces) DOLE® Crushed Pineapple or Pineapple Tidbits, drained
½ cup plain nonfat or low fat yogurt
2½ cups cold water

• Combine frozen juice concentrate, crushed pineapple and yogurt in blender or food processor container; blend until smooth. Stir in water.

• Pour mixture into container of ice cream maker.* Freeze according to manufacturer's directions.

• Serve sorbet in dessert dishes. *Makes 10 servings*

Or, pour sorbet mixture into 8-inch square metal pan; cover. Freeze 1½ to 2 hours or until slightly firm. Place in large bowl; beat with electric mixer on medium speed 1 minute or until slushy. Return mixture to metal pan; repeat freezing and beating steps. Freeze until firm, about 6 hours or overnight.

Passion-Banana Sorbet: Substitute DOLE® Pine-Orange-Banana Frozen Juice Concentrate for frozen juice concentrate. Prepare sorbet as directed above except reduce water to 2 cups and omit canned pineapple.

Prep Time: 20 minutes
Freeze Time: 20 minutes

Nutrients per Serving: ⅒ of Citrus Sorbet

Calories: 86, Calories from Fat: <1%, Total Fat: <1g, Saturated Fat: <1g, Cholesterol: <1mg, Sodium: 22mg, Carbohydrate: 21g, Dietary Fiber: <1g, Protein: 1g
Dietary Exchanges: 1½ Fruit

Speedy Pineapple-Lime Sorbet

1 ripe pineapple, cut into cubes (about 4 cups)
⅓ cup frozen limeade concentrate, thawed
1 to 2 tablespoons fresh lime juice
1 teaspoon grated lime peel

1. Arrange pineapple in single layer on large sheet pan; freeze at least 1 hour or until very firm. Use metal spatula to transfer pineapple to resealable plastic freezer food storage bags; freeze up to 1 month.

2. Combine pineapple, limeade, lime juice and lime peel in food processor; process until smooth and fluffy. If pineapple doesn't become smooth and fluffy, let stand 30 minutes to soften slightly; repeat processing. Garnish as desired. Serve immediately.   *Makes 8 servings*

Note: This dessert is best if served immediately; but it may be made ahead, stored in the freezer, then softened several minutes before being served.

Nutrients per Serving: ½ cup Sorbet (without garnish)

Calories: 56, Calories from Fat: 5%, Total Fat: <1g, Saturated Fat: <1g, Cholesterol: 0mg, Sodium: 1mg, Carbohydrate: 15g, Dietary Fiber: 1g, Protein: <1g

Dietary Exchanges: 1 Fruit

Speedy Pineapple-Lime Sorbet

Strawberry Trifle

1½ cups fat-free half-and-half
¼ cup sugar
3 tablespoons cornstarch
⅓ cup cholesterol-free egg substitute
2 tablespoons low-fat sour cream
2 teaspoons vanilla
2¾ cups sliced fresh strawberries, divided
1 tablespoon Marsala wine or orange juice
1 can (15 ounces) mandarin orange segments, well drained
1 can (11 ounces) mandarin orange segments, well drained
1 large banana, thinly sliced
1½ teaspoons lemon juice
1 prepared (10 ounces) angel food cake, cut into 1-inch cubes

1. Blend half-and-half, sugar and cornstarch together in small saucepan. Bring to a boil over medium heat, stirring constantly. Boil 1 minute or until mixture thickens, stirring constantly. Reduce heat to medium-low.

2. Blend ⅓ cup hot half-and-half mixture into egg substitute in small bowl. Stir into remaining half-and-half mixture. Cook 2 minutes, stirring constantly. Remove from heat. Let stand 10 minutes, stirring frequently. Stir in sour cream and vanilla.

3. Place ¾ cup strawberries and wine in blender or food processor; purée until smooth. Reserve 15 orange segments and ¼ cup strawberries in small bowl; set aside. Combine banana, remaining 1¾ cups strawberries, remaining orange segments and lemon juice in medium bowl.

4. Place half the cake cubes in bottom of 2- to 3-quart trifle dish or straight-sided glass serving bowl. Drizzle half of strawberry purée over cake. Top with half of fruit mixture and half of custard. Repeat layers with remaining cake, purée and fruit mixture. Spoon remaining custard over fruit mixture.

5. Arrange reserved orange segments and reserved strawberries decoratively over custard.
Makes 12 servings

Nutrients per Serving: ¹⁄₁₂ of total recipe

Calories: 160, Calories from Fat: 3%, Total Fat: 1g, Saturated Fat: <1g, Cholesterol: 1mg, Sodium: 222mg, Carbohydrate: 34g, Dietary Fiber: 1g, Protein: 4g

Dietary Exchanges: 1½ Starch, 1 Fruit

Baked Apple Crisp

8 cups thinly sliced unpeeled apples (about 8 medium)
2 tablespoons granulated sugar
4½ teaspoons lemon juice
4 teaspoons ground cinnamon, divided
1½ cups MOTT'S® Natural Apple Sauce
1 cup uncooked rolled oats
½ cup firmly packed light brown sugar
⅓ cup all-purpose flour
⅓ cup evaporated skimmed milk
¼ cup nonfat dry milk powder
1 cup vanilla nonfat yogurt

1. Preheat oven to 350°F. Spray 2-quart casserole dish with nonstick cooking spray.

2. In large bowl, toss apple slices with granulated sugar, lemon juice and 2 teaspoons cinnamon. Spoon into prepared dish. Spread apple sauce evenly over apple mixture.

3. In medium bowl, combine oats, brown sugar, flour, evaporated milk, dry milk powder and remaining 2 teaspoons cinnamon. Spread over apple sauce.

4. Bake 35 to 40 minutes or until lightly browned and bubbly. Cool slightly; serve warm. Top each serving with dollop of yogurt.   *Makes 12 servings*

Nutrients per Serving: 1/12 **of total recipe**

Calories: 163, Calories from Fat: 5%, Total Fat: 1g, Saturated Fat: <1g, Cholesterol: 1mg, Sodium: 33mg, Carbohydrate: 37g, Dietary Fiber: 4g, Protein: 3g
Dietary Exchanges: 1½ Starch, 1 Fruit

All-American Tapioca with Quick Apricot Sauce

2¾ cups low-fat (1%) milk
3 tablespoons sugar
3 tablespoons uncooked tapioca
1 egg, beaten
1 teaspoon vanilla
3 packets sugar substitute *or* equivalent of 2 tablespoons sugar
¼ cup no-sugar-added apricot spread
1 tablespoon water

1. Combine milk, sugar and tapioca in large microwavable bowl. Mix and let stand 5 minutes.

2. Microwave milk mixture at HIGH 10 minutes, stirring every 2 minutes. Pour small amount hot milk mixture into beaten egg in small bowl; beat well. Pour egg mixture back into hot milk mixture; microwave at HIGH an additional 2 minutes; stir in vanilla. Let cool, stirring occasionally, about 10 minutes. Stir in sugar substitute.

3. Combine spread and 1 tablespoon water in small microwavable bowl. Microwave at HIGH 30 seconds or just until warm. Distribute tapioca evenly among 6 dessert dishes; top evenly with apricot sauce. Serve warm or cold.
Makes 6 servings

Nutrients per Serving: 1 **dessert dish Tapioca with** 1/6 **of Sauce**

Calories: 121, Calories from Fat: 15%, Total Fat: 2g, Saturated Fat: 1g, Cholesterol: 40mg, Sodium: 80mg, Carbohydrate: 20g, Dietary Fiber: 0g, Protein: 5g
Dietary Exchanges: 1 Starch, ½ Milk, ½ Fat

Chocolate Crackles

⅓ cup CRISCO® Oil*
1½ cups granulated sugar
1½ teaspoons vanilla
1 egg
2 egg whites
1⅔ cups all-purpose flour
½ cup unsweetened cocoa powder
1½ teaspoons baking powder
½ teaspoon salt
½ cup confectioners' sugar

*Use your favorite Crisco Oil product.

1. Heat oven to 350°F. Place sheets of foil on countertop for cooling cookies.

2. Combine oil, granulated sugar and vanilla in large bowl. Beat at medium speed of electric mixer until blended. Add egg and egg whites. Beat until well blended. Stir in flour, cocoa, baking powder and salt with spoon.

3. Place confectioners' sugar in shallow dish or large plastic food storage bag.

4. Shape dough into 1-inch balls. Roll or shake in confectioners' sugar until coated. Place about 2 inches apart on ungreased baking sheet.

5. Bake at 350°F for 7 to 8 minutes or until almost no indentation remains when touched lightly. (Do not overbake.) Cool on baking sheet 2 minutes. Remove cookies to foil to cool completely.
Makes 4 dozen cookies

Nutrients per Serving: 1 **cookie**

Calories: 63, Calories from Fat: 25%, Total Fat: 2g, Saturated Fat: <1g, Cholesterol: 4mg, Sodium: 43mg, Carbohydrate: 11g, Dietary Fiber: <1g, Protein: 1g
Dietary Exchanges: ½ Starch, ½ Fat

Cinnamon Dessert Taco with Fruit Salsa

Cinnamon Dessert Tacos with Fruit Salsa

1 cup sliced fresh strawberries
1 cup cubed fresh pineapple
1 cup cubed peeled kiwi
½ teaspoon minced jalapeño pepper* (optional)
2 packets sugar substitute *or* equivalent of
    4 teaspoons sugar (optional)
3 tablespoons sugar
1 tablespoon ground cinnamon
6 (8-inch) flour tortillas
   Nonstick cooking spray

Jalapeño peppers can sting and irritate the skin; wear rubber gloves when handling peppers and do not touch eyes. Wash hands after handling peppers.

1. Stir together strawberries, pineapple, kiwi, jalapeño pepper and sugar substitute in large bowl; set aside. Combine sugar and cinnamon in small bowl; set aside.

2. Spray tortilla lightly on both sides with cooking spray. Heat over medium heat in nonstick skillet until slightly puffed and golden brown. Remove from heat; immediately dust both sides with cinnamon-sugar mixture. Shake excess cinnamon-sugar back into small bowl. Repeat cooking and dusting process until all tortillas are warmed.

3. Fold tortillas in half and fill with fruit mixture. Serve immediately. *Makes 6 servings*

Nutrients per Serving: 1 Dessert Taco with ⅙ of Fruit Salsa

Calories: 183, Calories from Fat: 14%, Total Fat: 3g, Saturated Fat: <1g, Cholesterol: 0mg, Sodium: 169mg, Carbohydrate: 36g, Dietary Fiber: 4g, Protein: 4g

Dietary Exchanges: 1½ Starch, 1 Fruit, ½ Fat

Chocolate Cherry Cookies

1 package (8 ounces) low-fat sugar-free
   chocolate cake mix
3 tablespoons fat-free (skim) milk
½ teaspoon almond extract
10 maraschino cherries, rinsed, drained and cut
   into halves
2 tablespoons white chocolate chips
½ teaspoon vegetable oil

1. Preheat oven to 350°F. Spray baking sheets with nonstick cooking spray; set aside.

2. Beat cake mix, milk and almond extract in medium bowl with electric mixer at low speed. Increase speed to medium when mixture looks crumbly; beat 2 minutes or until smooth dough forms. (Dough will be very sticky.)

3. Coat hands with cooking spray. Shape dough into 1-inch balls. Place balls 2½ inches apart on prepared baking sheets. Flatten each ball slightly. Place cherry half in center of each cookie.

4. Bake 8 to 9 minutes or until cookies lose their shininess and tops begin to crack. *Do not overbake.* Remove to wire racks; cool completely.

5. Heat white chocolate chips and oil in small saucepan over very low heat until chips melt. Drizzle cookies with melted chips. Allow drizzle to set before serving.
Makes 20 cookies

Nutrients per Serving: 1 Cookie

Calories: 54, Calories from Fat: 18%, Total Fat: 1g, Saturated Fat: <1g, Cholesterol: 0mg, Sodium: 9mg, Carbohydrate: 12g, Dietary Fiber: 0g, Protein: 1g

Dietary Exchanges: 1 Starch

Spun Sugar Berries with Yogurt Crème

2 cups fresh raspberries*
1 container (8 ounces) lemon-flavored nonfat yogurt with aspartame sweetener
1 cup thawed frozen fat-free nondairy whipped topping
3 tablespoons sugar

*You may substitute your favorite fresh berries for the fresh raspberries.

1. Arrange berries in 4 glass dessert dishes.

2. Combine yogurt and whipped topping in medium bowl. (If not using immediately, cover and refrigerate.) Top berries with yogurt mixture.

3. To prepare spun sugar, pour sugar into heavy medium saucepan. Cook over medium-high heat until sugar melts, shaking pan occasionally. *Do not stir.* As sugar begins to melt, reduce heat to low and cook about 10 minutes or until sugar is completely melted and has turned light golden brown.

4. Remove from heat; let stand 1 minute. Coat metal fork with sugar mixture. Drizzle sugar over berries with circular or back and forth motion. Ropes of spun sugar will harden quickly. Garnish as desired. Serve immediately.

Makes 4 servings

Nutrients per Serving: 1 dessert dish (¼ of total recipe) made with fresh raspberries

Calories: 119, Calories from Fat: 2%, Total Fat: <1g, Saturated Fat: <1g, Cholesterol: 0mg, Sodium: 45mg, Carbohydrate: 26g, Dietary Fiber: 4g, Protein: 3g
Dietary Exchanges: 2 Fruit

Cranberry-Orange Bread Pudding

2 cups cubed cinnamon bread
¼ cup dried cranberries
2 cups low-fat (1%) milk
1 package (4-serving-size) sugar-free vanilla pudding and pie filling mix*
½ cup cholesterol-free egg substitute
1 teaspoon vanilla
1 teaspoon grated orange peel
½ teaspoon ground cinnamon
    Low-fat no-sugar-added vanilla ice cream (optional)

Do not use instant pudding and pie filling.

1. Preheat oven to 325°F. Spray 9 custard cups with nonstick cooking spray. Place bread cubes in custard cups. Bake 10 minutes; add cranberries.

2. Combine remaining ingredients except ice cream in medium bowl. Carefully pour over mixture in custard cups. Let stand 5 to 10 minutes.

3. Place cups on baking sheet; bake 25 to 30 minutes or until centers are almost set. Let stand 10 minutes. Serve with ice cream, if desired.
Makes 9 servings

Nutrients per Serving: 1 custard cup (⅑ of total recipe) without ice cream

Calories: 67, Calories from Fat: 13%, Total Fat: 1g, Saturated Fat: <1g, Cholesterol: 2mg, Sodium: 190mg, Carbohydrate: 11g, Dietary Fiber: <1g, Protein: 4g
Dietary Exchanges: 1 Starch

Fat-Free Cappuccino Flan

1 cup EGG BEATERS® Healthy Real Egg Product
½ cup sugar
1 tablespoon instant espresso or coffee powder
½ teaspoon vanilla extract
⅛ teaspoon ground cinnamon
2⅓ cups fat-free (skim) milk, scalded and cooled 10 minutes
    Light nondairy whipped topping and cocoa powder or additional ground cinnamon, optional

In medium bowl, combine Egg Beaters®, sugar, espresso powder, vanilla and cinnamon. Gradually stir in milk. Pour into 6 lightly greased (6-ounce) custard cups or ramekins. Set cups in pan filled with 1-inch depth hot water.

Bake at 350°F for 35 to 40 minutes or until knife inserted into centers comes out clean. Remove cups from pan; cool to room temperature. Chill until firm, about 2 hours. To serve, loosen edges with knife; invert onto individual plates. Top with whipped topping and cocoa or cinnamon, if desired.
Makes 6 servings

Prep Time: 20 minutes
Cook Time: 40 minutes

Nutrients per Serving: 1 custard cup of Flan (⅙ of total recipe) without topping and cocoa powder

Calories: 120, Calories from Fat: 1%, Total Fat: 0g, Saturated Fat: 0g, Cholesterol: 2mg, Sodium: 116mg, Carbohydrate: 22g, Dietary Fiber: 0g, Protein: 7g
Dietary Exchanges: 1 Starch, ½ Milk

ACKNOWLEDGMENTS

The publisher would like to thank
the companies and organizations listed below
for the use of their recipes and photographs in this publication.

American Lamb Council

Butterball® Turkey Company

California Tree Fruit Agreement

Canada's Canola Industry

ConAgra Foods®

Delmarva Poultry Industry, Inc.

Del Monte Corporation

Dole Food Company, Inc.

Egg Beaters®

Equal® sweetener

Filippo Berio® Olive Oil

Florida Tomato Committee

General Mills, Inc.

Grey Poupon® Dijon Mustard

Guiltless Gourmet®

Hershey Foods Corporation

Keebler® Company

The Kingsford Products Company

Lawry's® Foods

McIlhenny Company (TABASCO® brand Pepper Sauce)

Mott's® is a registered trademark of Mott's, Inc.

National Fisheries Institute

National Honey Board

National Pork Board

National Turkey Federation

Nestlé USA

New York Apple Association, Inc.

Norseland, Inc. / Lucini Italia Co.

North Dakota Wheat Commission

Perdue Farms Incorporated

The Quaker® Oatmeal Kitchens

Reckitt Benckiser Inc.

Riviana Foods Inc.

The J.M. Smucker Company

Splenda® is a registered trademark of McNeil Nutritionals

The Sugar Association, Inc.

Property of © 2003 Sunkist Growers, Inc.
All rights reserved

Texas Peanut Producers Board

Uncle Ben's Inc.

Unilever Bestfoods North America

USA Rice Federation

Washington Apple Commission

Wisconsin Milk Marketing Board

A

All-American Tapioca with Quick Apricot
    Sauce, 366
Almonds: Grilled Honey Mustard Chicken
    with Toasted Almonds, 182
Angel Food Cake with Pineapple Sauce,
    324
Angel Hair Noodles with Peanut Sauce,
    164

Apple
Apple Burgers, 102
Apple-Cherry Chutney, 10
Apple Clafouti, 354
Baked Apple Crisp, 366
Cranberry Apple Pie with Soft
    Gingersnap Crust, 332
Dreamy Orange Cheesecake Dip, 42
Fresh Fruit Cocktail, 288
Ginger Snap Sandwiches, 66
Harvest Rice, 302
Pineapple Boats with Citrus Creme,
    96
Potato Pancakes with Apple-Cherry
    Chutney, 10
Roast Turkey Breast with Apple-Corn
    Bread Stuffing, 180
Scrumptious Apple Cake, 312
Sea Bass for Two in Lemon Apple Sauce,
    218
Turkey Fruited Bow Tie Salad, 72
Apple-Cherry Chutney, 10

Apple Juice
Banana-Walnut Bread, 12
Fresh Fruit Cocktail, 288
Sweet Potato Bisque, 94

Applesauce
Apple Burgers, 102
Apple Clafouti, 354
Baked Apple Crisp, 366
Pineapple Upside-Down Cake, 336
Scrumptious Apple Cake, 312
Three-Berry Kuchen, 318

Apricot
All-American Tapioca with Quick
    Apricot Sauce, 366
Apricot-Chicken Pot Stickers, 57
Apricot Oatmeal Muffins, 23
Fresh Fruit Cocktail, 288
Asian Wraps, 104

Asparagus
Citrus Asparagus, 308
Garden Potato Salad with Basil-Yogurt
    Dressing, 68
Pasta Primavera, 244
Turkey Sausage & Pasta Toss, 164

B

Bacon: Beef Bourguignon, 276
Bacon & Cheese Dip, 52
Baked Apple Crisp, 366
Baked Crab-Stuffed Trout, 212
Baked Fish with Mediterranean Salsa,
    210
Baked Oatmeal, 12
Baked Pasta Casserole, 162
Balsamic-Herb Ratatouille, 302
Balsamic-Herb Vinaigrette, 302

Bamboo Shoots
Chicken Chop Suey, 264
Chinese Noodles and Soy Beef, 160

Banana
Banana Cream Parfaits, 356
Banana Pistachio Pie, 320
Banana-Walnut Bread, 12
Banana Yogurt Shake, 20
French Toast, 28
Fruit Antipasto Platter, 46
Fruit Smoothies, 10
Light Banana Cream Pie, 324
Orange Banana Nog, 12
Pineapple Boats with Citrus Creme,
    96
Strawberry-Banana Granité, 352
Strawberry Trifle, 364
Tropical Fruit Coconut Tart, 316
Banana Cream Parfaits, 356
Banana Pistachio Pie, 320
Banana-Walnut Bread, 12
Banana Yogurt Shake, 20
Barley Turkey Breast with Barley-Cranberry
    Stuffing, 182

Bars
Breakfast Blondies, 28
Brownies, 342
Choco-Lowfat Strawberry Shortbread
    Bars, 354
Lemon Mousse Squares, 348

Beans (see also **Chick-Peas**)
Beans and Rice Vegetable Medley, 224
Beef & Bean Burritos, 270
Beef- and Bean-Stuffed Peppers, 142
Black Bean & Rice Burritos, 108
Black Bean Cakes with Salsa Cruda, 48
Black Bean Dip, 40
Black Beans & Rice Stuffed Chilies, 236
Black Bean Tostadas, 252
Boston Baked Beans, 300
Brown Rice Black Bean Burrito, 250
Creole Red Beans and Rice, 226
Crowd-Pleasing Burritos, 228
Fish Burritos, 194
Hearty White Bean Soup, 88
Hot Black Bean Dip, 64
Latin-Style Pasta & Beans, 248
Low-Fat Chimichangas, 230
Marinated Bean and Vegetable Salad,
    86
Meatless Sloppy Joes, 110
Mexican Strata Olé, 236
Picante Pintos and Rice, 236
Quick Tuscan Bean, Tomato and Spinach
    Soup, 97
Rosarita Refried Soup, 280
Shrimp and Black Bean Wraps, 114
Shrimp with Spicy Black Bean Sauce,
    204
Southwest Bean Chili, 78
Southwestern Beef and Bean Lasagna,
    136
Spaghetti Squash with Black Beans and
    Zucchini, 246
Spicy Snapper & Black Beans, 200
Spinach Ziti Casserole, 250
Turkey and Bean Tostadas, 254
Turkey and Black Bean Soup, 78
Tuscan Chicken with White Beans, 170
Tuscan Pasta, 168
Vegetable-Enchilada Casserole, 246
Zesty Zucchini Burritos, 248
Beans and Rice Vegetable Medley, 224
Bean Threads with Tofu and Vegetables, 238

Beef
Beef & Bean Burritos, 270
Beef and Broccoli, 266
Beef and Parsnip Stroganoff, 146
Beef & Vegetable Stir-Fry, 148
Beef Bourguignon, 276
Beef Burgundy and Mushrooms, 148
Beef Tenderloin with Roasted Vegetables,
    150
Chili Beef & Red Pepper Fajitas with
    Chipotle Salsa, 139
Chinese Noodles and Soy Beef, 160
Fajita-Stuffed Shells, 140
Fruited Beef Kabobs, 134
Grilled Caribbean Steak with Tropical
    Fruit Rice, 160
Hearty Hungarian Goulash, 154
Italian-Style Brisket, 144
Korean-Style Beef and Pasta, 278
Pasta Bourguignonne, 156
Pasta Paprikash, 158
Thai Beef Salad, 97
Vietnamese Beef Soup, 96

Beef, Ground
Baked Pasta Casserole, 162
Beef- and Bean-Stuffed Peppers, 142
Bolognese Sauce & Penne Pasta, 162
Chunky Joes, 122
Fiesta Beef Enchiladas, 276
Italian Meatball Subs, 102
Mafalda and Meatballs, 142
Meatballs in Creamy Mustard Sauce, 154
Pasta Picadillo, 152
Southwestern Beef and Bean Lasagna, 136
Beef- and Bean-Stuffed Peppers, 142
Beets: Honeyed Beets, 308

Bell Pepper
Balsamic-Herb Ratatouille, 302
Beef- and Bean-Stuffed Peppers, 142
Beef & Vegetable Stir-Fry, 148
Bell Pepper Nachos, 50
Broccoli-Tofu Stir-Fry, 240
Broccoli with Red Pepper and Shallots,
    290
Brunch Rice, 26
Caponata Stir-Fry, 186
Caribbean Chutney Kabobs, 64
Cavatelli and Vegetable Stir-Fry, 252
Cheese Tortellini with Tuna, 216
Chicken Fajita Wraps, 131
Chicken Pot Pie, 166
Chile, Egg & Cheese Casserole, 234
Chili Beef & Red Pepper Fajitas with
    Chipotle Salsa, 139
Chinese Noodles and Soy Beef, 160
Chunky Joes, 122
Citrus Asparagus, 308
Creole Red Beans and Rice, 226
Eggs Primavera, 32
Fajita-Stuffed Shells, 140
Fruited Beef Kabobs, 134
Garden Gazpacho, 72
Garden Potato Salad with Basil-Yogurt
    Dressing, 68
Garlicky Mustard Greens, 296
Glazed Pork and Pepper Kabobs, 136
Grilled Bell Pepper, 82, 302
Grilled Chicken Breast and Peperonata
    Sandwiches, 122
Grilled Mozzarella & Roasted Red
    Pepper Sandwich, 108